FAMOUS IN AMERICA

Jane Fonda • George Wallace
Phyllis Schlafly • John Glenn

FAMOUS IN AMERICA

The Passion to Succeed

Peter N. Carroll

A William Abrahams Book

E. P. DUTTON • NEW YORK

Published in the United States by
E. P. Dutton, a division of New American Library,
2 Park Avenue, New York, N.Y. 10016.

Library of Congress Cataloging in Publication Data

Carroll, Peter N.
Famous in America.
"A William Abrahams book."
Includes bibliographical references and index.
1. United States—Biography. 2. Fonda, Jane,
1937–   . 3. Wallace, George C. (George Corley),
1919–   . 4. Schlafly, Phyllis. 5. Glenn, John,
1921–   . I. Title.

CT220.C38 1985   920'.073 [B]   85-10348

ISBN 0-525-24363-1

Published simultaneously in Canada by
Fitzhenry & Whiteside Limited, Toronto

10 9 8 7 6 5 4 3 2 1

COBE

First Edition

For Jeannette
"we had lunch together"

Contents

*Sixteen pages of photographs
follow page 212.*

Acknowledgments

I'd like to thank the many people who assisted me in planning and completing this project.

Michael Batinski helped me locate material about Phyllis Schlafly. Sue Ann Wood of the *St. Louis Globe-Democrat* and Julie Stuckey of the *Alton Telegraph* allowed me to use valuable newspaper files. Mrs. Schlafly herself gave me copies of her personal records as well as a detailed interview. My neighbor, Phil Muhilly, and my mother, Bessie Carroll, proved to be masters of the Xerox.

Several friends—Michael Kazin, Edward Kleinschmidt, Frances Mayes, and James Sheehan—read different drafts of the manuscript and offered suggestions for its improvement. Matthew Carroll was the expert at the Okidata printer. Natasha Carroll-Ferrary took care of the leftover holes.

Through it all, my agent, Fred Hill, remained unrelentingly friendly. My editor, William Abrahams, truly nurtured the book to completion.

Jeannette Ferrary did everything else.

FAMOUS
IN
AMERICA

Introduction

This book examines the lives of four famous and successful Americans: Jane Fonda, George Wallace, Phyllis Schlafly, and John Glenn. Treated as individuals, their stories tell of a passion to succeed that has been fulfilled. Taken collectively, they reflect—and even, in a sense, constitute—a history of our times.

In the quarter century between 1958 and 1983, each emerged and endured as a person of fame and historical significance. Many others did so too, of course, though considerably fewer remained so continuously in the public eye throughout the period. There are some figures (the presidents, for example) who played roles of such central importance that they require minutely detailed biographies. Others reveal stories not dissimilar in scale to those presented here.

By contrast to most famous Americans, however, Jane Fonda, George Wallace, Phyllis Schlafly, and John Glenn have demonstrated an unusual ability to respond to the changing times in which they have lived: hence the remarkable longevity of their fame. Yet there is a paradox that is essential to an understanding of their very different careers. Fame came to them, but it was never a prime objective—to be famous for the sake of being famous—nor did a desire for fame inspire their powerful ambitions. What drove them, rather, was a sense of personal destiny—a self-confident mission to succeed in their careers.

The temptation is to treat successful people as "personalities" and to search for underlying motives. What did it mean that Jane Fonda involved herself so intensely in the movement (or craze) for physical fitness? Why did Phyllis Schlafly abhor the Equal Rights Amendment? Why did John Glenn succeed as an astronaut? Why did George Wallace choose *not* to run for the United States Senate? In each case there is ample documentary material for psychological interpretation, which we will examine in due course.

But having admitted the importance of personality, we run the risk of psychological determinism—the assumption that people who are successful were destined all along to succeed. The reasoning is circular. Besides, psychology neglects the larger social context. Indeed, these four Americans, whose careers depended so much on public approval, have remained creatures of history.

Each has flourished in a distinct sphere. Their careers—from show business to technology to politics—illustrate various avenues of ambition and fame in America. John Glenn and Jane Fonda managed to build multiple careers, while Phyllis Schlafly and George Wallace could redefine their essential interests and enlarge their constituencies. Their ideological commitments—from the conservative right of Schlafly through the middle right and middle left of Glenn and Wallace to the radical left of Fonda—have stretched across the political landscape. Their separate lives have revealed the convergence of personality and history, the inner self meshed with the historical moment. Taken together, they represented a broad spectrum of contemporary America.

Whether measured by votes, box office receipts, or back room influence, their achievement required them to speak to and for large public followings. Fonda, the star as activist; Wallace, the populist; Schlafly, "the sweetheart of the silent majority"; Glenn, the hero-as-senator—all attained success because they could define themselves as leaders, could embody the ambitions, needs, and dreams of millions of other Americans. Their stories transcend their individual lives and add up to more than the sum of the parts.

For all of them, moreover, popularity and fame were never sufficient. Not only did they want a place in history, they also wanted to move history. They yearned to wield power. Whether they succeeded or not at a given moment, however, depended on the circumstances that surrounded them. Their changing fortunes mirrored a larger historical development.

Each embodied a different facet of society: Fonda, Hollywood's child; Wallace, the southerner; Schlafly, upwardly mobile and Catholic; Glenn, a professional soldier. Their lives have moved in parallel lines; their paths have crossed rarely and inadvertently. (Never have the four been together.) This distance from each other produced different perspectives; they saw the events of history differently.

Their careers, consequently, dramatize the immense changes of the past twenty-five years. Coming from different directions, their lives nonetheless touch many of the same fundamental issues: civil rights and racial justice, poverty and prosperity, the cold war and détente, the sexual revolution and the crisis of the family. How they reacted to these questions reflected their place in society. Their differences demonstrated the complexity of any single event: Their careers, considered as a whole, proved the complexity of the entire period.

These four lives, then, offer four versions of the same history. To emphasize the simultaneity of events, the stories are told in four chronological stages; the lives emerge in layers, as in a musical fugue, each building on an earlier layer to create a textured whole. Our perspective comes through the eye of the participants; we see their careers unfold as they themselves did. The words are always their own; all quotes are exact and taken in context.* (The curious reader may consult the sources that appear at the end of this volume.)

Fonda, Wallace, Schlafly, and Glenn provide a living history that remains unfinished. However their individual careers may yet evolve, they have embodied fully twenty-five years of our past. To gain understanding of their lives sheds light on our own. For whatever their own ambitions and expectations, we as a people have made them just who they turned out to be.

---

*Except when, for reasons of clarity, I have altered some of Wallace's reported "southernisms."

Jane
Seymour
Fonda
(I)

On an October morning in 1958 Jane Fonda stepped from a taxicab near Broadway and Fiftieth Street and followed her girlfriend into the old Capitol Theater building in New York City. She was wearing a beige suit and matching four-inch heels. Her hair was blond and set high. In the small studio the other actors awaited her arrival. As one of them later recalled: "You could feel the tension . . . swell up like an overblown balloon." Through the sudden hush she moved with determination. She was not yet twenty-one.

Jane Fonda was more nervous that day than ever before. In the Dramatic Workshop classes run by Lee Strasberg, she intended to put an end, one way or another, to the nightmares that had haunted her for the past eight years. This, she believed, was her best chance, perhaps her last. Suicide or success: For Jane Fonda it was no adolescent torment soon to be outgrown. For her there was no middle ground; there had been none since a spring day in 1950—her mother's forty-second birthday—when Jane's life slipped out of control. As Strasberg told her, "The only thing that made me take you was your eyes. There was such a panic in the eyes."

The tension had not always been there. Once, Jane had been simply the child of money and of fame—the daughter of the elegant Frances Brokaw and the movie star Henry Fonda. Growing up in southern California, she had taken her pleasant world for granted: the sunshine, the open hills, the swimming pool, a staff of household servants.

Her father was a self-made midwesterner who had become famous as Tom Joad in the movie version of Steinbeck's *The Grapes of Wrath*. In the 1930s, Hollywood movies glamorized the possibilities of escape, fantasies of opportunity that impelled desperate men like Tom Joad to see paradise in the Far West. But for Henry Fonda success and fame never seemed quite real. He never forgot the plain life that had accompanied his youth in Omaha, Nebraska, just after the turn of the century. He had struggled in Depression theaters, and he responded to his later success with considerable humility. He appreciated the ever larger salary that buffered him and his family forever from material want, and he relished the solitude that his money could buy. Yet he hated the studio system that tied actors to long-term contracts and reduced their independence to rubber-stamp agreements or oblivion. And he hated the notoriety that went with being a star.

After a brief marriage to Margaret Sullavan, Fonda chose never again to look for love in Hollywood. But in the mid-1930s he was so eligible and so vulnerable that he succumbed easily to a worldly and attractive young widow from New York, Frances Brokaw, who met him on a production stage outside London, where she was visiting and he was shooting his first technicolor film, *Wings of the Morning*, in 1936. Mrs. Brokaw pursued him, wooed him, led him on a romantic journey through Nazi Berlin, to Budapest, Paris, and New York.

Frances Seymour Brokaw had been born with the best East Coast credentials—except money. That difficulty she had solved by marriage to a wealthy former New York congressman named George Brokaw, who had tended toward alcoholism and died in a sanitorium not long after they had married. For her marriage to Fonda, Frances took charge. On Wednesday afternoon, September 16, 1936, her daughter Pan cast a carpet of petals in front of Frances and Henry as they walked down the aisle of Christ Church on Park Avenue in New York City.

Fonda felt dazzled by the pomp, but he and his bride looked like a perfect Hollywood couple—young, beautiful, and very rich. During the day Henry made movies, such as *Jezebel,* with Bette Davis, while Frances drove her Buick around Pacific Palisades in search of a proper house. At night they danced and went to parties, dined by candlelight —she blew out a match one spring evening in 1937 to announce a coming child.

Frances very much wanted a son but on December 21, 1937, she gave birth to Jane Seymour Fonda. The ordeal left Frances with a second Caesarean scar—and a second daughter. Henry was too happy to care and took lots of pictures with his Leica. But Frances felt that she had failed him, and herself too. She would try to make up for it. When Henry went back to making movies, she hired a nurse and vowed to raise their "Lady Jane," as they called her, to be perfect. They put her on a strict schedule and drew up a list of don'ts and tried to protect her from any outside contamination. All visitors, a category that included the baby's father, were ordered to wear masks in the nursery; they were allowed no kisses, unruly hugging, or fondling.

Because she was so disciplined, Frances could accomplish tremendous tasks in a mother's busy day. Besides supervising the maids, cooks, gardeners, and nurses, she managed the family's business investments and still made time to find a new house, in the Brentwood section of Los Angeles. It required considerable remodeling and redecoration, but she handled those arrangements too.

She was also prepared to take another gamble with her health. In 1940 three Caesareans were considered the medical limit, and Frances anguished about having yet another daughter. But to her delight, she delivered a son, Peter. Jane was less than elated. Seeing movies of Frances feeding the infant in the hospital, the two-year-old burst into tears and ran away.

The arrival of Peter Fonda required additional family discipline. Frances became bogged down, first in her burgeoning portfolio of stocks, and then in the design and construction of a dream house to be built on nine acres of real estate up Tigertail Road in Brentwood. She became so involved in the details that she lost track of the dreams that inspired them. She also lost weight, grew tired, and suffered physical ailments that baffled her doctors. But a three-week rest cure in La Jolla restored her vitality. In 1941 the Fondas moved to the house on Tigertail.

Jane remembered the place as "a sort of New England setup transplanted to California." Actually it was based on a hundred-year-old Pennsylvania Dutch farmhouse, surrounded by vines and flower beds and flagstone walks and arable fields (on which Henry grew vegetables and hay for the children's ponies) and a circular pool disguised to resemble a kid's secret swimming hole. The grounds also included a separate playhouse that was filled with toys and games and had an enormous mantel and fireplace at one end and a barbecue pit for grown-ups at night. Nearby were chicken coops, rabbit hutches, and a small stable. Frances decorated the rooms with Early American antiques transported from back East, which included for Jane a four-poster maple bed and patchwork quilts. It seemed they might have room enough there—were it not for the omnipresent Frances, who supervised them all with what her daughter called "an eagle eye that . . . could see through walls."

In her fifth year Jane's feelings of confinement suddenly intensified: One night in 1942 her father packed his gear and moved out, not after some family quarrel, but to serve in the United States Navy. For Jane (as for many children her age) the departure of her father proved traumatic, and it helped, perhaps in a subliminal way, to shape her later attitude toward men at war and the anxiety of broken homes. "It's not natural for a father to be away from his family as long as I have had to be," Henry wrote from a ship somewhere in the Pacific, "but we are unlucky, because a war had to come along." Its impact on Jane emerged vividly in a picture she drew for her father, showing, as Henry saw it, "a woman standing beside a fireplace and crying because her husband was away to the wars."

This dread of abandonment hovered in Jane's imagination, blurring the lines that separated illusion and reality. She was old enough to know that her father had gone to war. But one afternoon inside a movie theater she saw him come alive as a besieged warrior in John Ford's *Drums Along the Mohawk.* "I was scared to death," recalled Jane. "For two days, in the movie, my father ran from one fort to another . . . and then there was a big life-and-death battle, with the Indians massacring the whites. . . . It was the longest movie of my life." Whether her father would survive the real war seemed equally uncertain to Jane. It was surely no coincidence that she frequently reenacted the movie's plot in her childhood games with Peter and that she always insisted on playing Henry's role as hero and survivor. Nor, perhaps, was it insignificant (especially in light of Jane's later commitment to the cause of American Indians) that her "survival" depended upon killing her father's Indian enemies.

Whatever its psychological impulse, Jane's enthusiasm for cowboys and Indians well suited the sprawling landscape of the Tigertail homestead. By the age of five she was already a skilled rider and had begun to accumulate the many blue ribbons that decorated her bedroom. Living nearby were the three children of Henry's first wife, Margaret Sullavan, and his agent Leland Hayward. The Hayward children—Brooke, Bridget, and Bill—would arrive frequently by station wagon and, as Brooke recalled, "we'd all pour out and the five of us would go absolutely crazy."

In the absence of her husband, however, Frances's passion for discipline increased even more. "Whenever Jane, and later Peter, exhibited a normal childhood outburst of emotion or passion," one family friend explained, "they were quickly and soundly reprimanded." Frances insisted on a rigid routine, including daily afternoon naps. Yet Jane remained bold enough to defy the rules, accepting her mother's prompt spankings as a reasonable price for her independence. The penalty for smoking was the forced chain-smoking of a pack of Pall Malls until the children retched (though Jane, already a precocious actress, feigned illness first). And when Frances chose a private school for her children, she picked the Brentwood Town and Country School because of its reputation for traditional education and strict discipline.

This rigid family structure, a domestic equivalent, virtually, of the nation's mobilization for war, was abruptly interrupted by Henry's return from the navy in 1945. As in hundreds of thousands of other American families, the homecoming brought wonderful exhilaration— Jane picked fresh flowers for the dinner table centerpiece and chattered away endlessly for attention—but Henry's long absence had altered forever the feeling of family solidarity. In 1946 the nation's divorce rate leaped upward as many marriages of the prewar era and wartime collapsed under the strains of departure and return. The Fondas would not add to those statistics, at least not immediately, but neither did they recover their domestic tranquility.

After the war, Frances developed a series of odd and elaborate clinical symptoms that provided a convenient excuse for avoiding sexual relations. She visited doctors, took pills, and once when Henry was away shooting on location traveled secretly to Baltimore to have a hysterectomy. As Frances passed her thirty-fifth birthday, she became preoccupied with her beauty—and its disappearance. "From as early as

I can remember," Jane later wrote, "my mother, her friends, my grandmother, governesses, my sister—all the women who surrounded me—talked anxiously about the pros and cons of their physiques. . . . None of them seemed happy the way they were."

While Frances anguished about the loss of beauty, Henry plunged into his work. In three years he made seven pictures, most notably two directed by John Ford, *My Darling Clementine* and *Fort Apache.* In his own life, as in the cowboy roles he played, he preferred to stay away from his family and its troubles. After the war, according to a friend, Fonda "found that his kids were much more like their mother than himself." Disenchanted with Frances, he "extended his anger to Jane and Peter, since they were miniature models of her." Jane long remembered his terrifying rages.

She responded to these pressures by building defenses of her own. Rejecting Frances as a role model, she developed into a tomboy, and a self-destructive one at that, breaking her arm in one fight and a wrist while roller skating, and suffering numerous bruises falling off horses. "I don't remember owning a dress until I was about eight," Jane recalled. "I was always in blue jeans, day in and day out, and my hair was cut short." She was delighted when strangers asked if she were a boy or a girl; "I've spent [my childhood] wanting to be a boy, because I wanted to be like my father."

Wealth was not central to this family drama, though it facilitated the playing of its roles. With greater frequency Frances took to her bed, leaving domestic problems to the servants. Jane could indulge her equestrian fantasies at the Riviera Riding Club, where she excelled at jumping hurdles. Henry, silent, moody, edgy, disappeared onto some studio backlot to shoot yet another picture. Unhappy in Hollywood, he seized an opportunity to return to Broadway in 1948 to star in a new play about life in the wartime navy: *Mister Roberts.* In the title role, Fonda established his reputation as a major stage actor, but his tremendous success now rocked the entire Fonda family to its shaky foundations.

The great popularity of *Mister Roberts* assured Fonda a long run on Broadway, and he decided to transplant his family to the East Coast. All were reluctant to move. Yet with the added responsibility of packing, moving, and finding a new house in Greenwich, Connecticut, Frances sprang back to life. Accompanied by two Japanese servants, she supervised the migration in the summer of 1948, dazzling the children with their first glimpse of New York City at night. She lightened her hair, changed its style, and thrived on shopping sprees in Manhattan for antiques and Early American art. Frances began to plan a new dream house in Connecticut.

For Jane the move brought tangible freedoms—she could roam around the large estate or ride horses at the nearby stable—but increasingly she inhabited a world of fear. Typical of her emotional life that summer were the consequences of a bruising fight with a stable boy, which injured her arm. Despite the pain, she suffered in silence, fearing that her father would notice she was still biting her nails. At dinner Henry asked if she had washed her hands. When Jane admitted she hadn't, he flew into a rage and grabbed her arm. She felt agonizing pain. A rushed visit to the hospital revealed a broken arm that had to be placed in a cast. Throughout her life Jane would prove to be remarkably accident-prone. But her stubborn refusal to communicate pain was itself a clue to her vulnerability.

When the autumn colors spread across the New England countryside, Jane enrolled at the staid Greenwich Academy, on Maple Avenue. The daughter of a celebrity, she enjoyed instant attention, enough to make Frances warn her against getting a swelled head. But Jane felt alone that year. At school she encountered open racism for the first time, heard the word "nigger," and innocently repeated it in front of her father. "He got furious," she remembered, and he slapped her. At midterm, to Jane's great joy, the Hayward clan moved to Greenwich. She and Brooke Hayward quickly reestablished their friendship, a tight, insulated bond that separated them from their families and classmates. Alone, they created elaborate sexual fantasies about their coming adulthood when they would be co-madames of a luxury brothel.

While Jane fantasized about future triumphs, her family life steadily deteriorated. Henry commuted daily to Broadway, leaving Frances to torment herself in isolation. She felt she was ugly and worried obsessively about becoming poor and fat. Without consulting Henry, she entered a sanitorium in 1948 and stayed for eight weeks. A few months later she underwent surgery to correct a floating kidney. It required a five-week hospitalization and left her with another large scar. "They just cut me in half," she said. While recuperating, Frances attended the wedding of her oldest daughter, Pan (Jane was the flower girl), and then, oddly, decided to accompany the newlyweds on their honeymoon to Europe. She fell ill again in Paris, but she looked forward to a happy reunion with her family.

Frances's frequent absences, however, had pushed Henry beyond the possibility of reconciliation. By the summer of 1949 he had fallen in love with Susan Blanchard, twenty-one, a stepdaughter of Oscar Hammerstein. From her friends at Greenwich Academy, Jane learned that her father was seeing a young "tomato." Soon the news came to Frances; Henry confessed his affair and asked for a divorce. Jane recalled the next bleak morning: As she left for school, her mother said, "If anybody mentions that your father and I are getting a divorce, tell them you already know it." With that news, Jane went off to school.

From Brooke Hayward, Jane learned "the delicate intricacies of shuttling between divorced parents" and hoped that her father-in-exile would prove as generous as Brooke's. Henry certainly fulfilled the obvious obligations, taking his children to the circus or on fishing trips. But his own limitations kept him from understanding their problems. Jane remembered long journeys when not a word passed between them. The silence terrified her.

For Frances, public revelation of the divorce proved a great humiliation and aggravated her depression. Jane later reconstructed an evening after Henry moved out: "We were all eating in silence, and I could see that she was crying. She was crying into her food, and I was so filled with tension and anxiety that I couldn't even ask . . . what was the matter." To her intimate friends Frances bemoaned her loss of youth and beauty. "Just look at me!" she sobbed. "No one will ever have me again." Without Henry her life lost its meaning; without beauty, she thought, there was no way to recover it.

Frances returned to a sanitorium in the winter of 1950. On her forty-second birthday, April 14, 1950, she wrote special letters to each of her children and to her mother and to the doctor who was treating her. "Very sorry," she said. "This is the best way out." Then with a two-inch razor she slit her throat from ear to ear and bled to death on the bathroom floor.

When Jane arrived home from school that day, her grandmother told her not to go out because her mother was sick. But since her mother was always sick, Jane ignored the advice and went horseback riding. When she returned, Henry sat in the solemn living room. He announced that her mother had died of a heart attack. Jane went immediately to her room and closed the door. "I sat on the edge of the bed, and wondered why I couldn't cry. And I thought, 'How weird. I'm never going to see her again, and I can't cry.' I never cried." She returned to the living room.

In that brief interval, Jane had constructed an effective barrier against her own vulnerability. Resentful of her mother's long absences, she realized now the futility of any anger, indeed felt great sorrow for ever possessing it. She learned, too, as do most young bereaved children, the fragility of survival, that the idea of "never going to see her again" was literal and absolute. "If you lose your mother before you're old enough to get close to her," Jane admitted, "you almost never understand her as an individual in her own right, and that's what happened to me." In the short run she was much more worried about also losing her father.

In creating the myth of Frances's heart attack, Henry went to great lengths to shelter his children from the truth, canceling all newspaper and magazine subscriptions and persuading school authorities to order all the better-informed pupils to become accomplices. Remarkably the secret held. After Frances's death Jane lived with her mother's family in Greenwich. Some people noticed that she had become more sober, more secretive, more self-contained.

With Brooke Hayward, however, Jane continued to defy school authorities, once sneaking a movie magazine into an art class. Together they devoured the Hollywood gossip, which sometimes included morsels about Henry Fonda. One piece, Brooke discovered to her surprise, revealed the details of Frances's death and she quickly flipped the page. But Jane turned it back and silently read the full story. "Is it true?" was the only response she made, and Brooke did not answer. "I was just stunned," Jane later explained. "It was dramatic. I mean it was a combination . . . of horror and fascination. How much more interesting than a heart attack." That afternoon a visiting nurse confirmed the story. But Jane swore the nurse to secrecy, lest her father find out that she knew what he knew and, most important, that she knew he had lied to her. "I was brought up where people didn't express what they really felt," Jane said. "You hid everything. You hid your fears and your sorrows and your pain and your joys and your physical desires."

Frances's suicide became for her daughter an object lesson in the perils of womanhood. Whatever the depths of her personal grief, her fears of rejection and abandonment, Jane learned one indelible lesson in that art classroom in the fall of 1950: She could never again afford to identify with her mother without also undertaking an enormous risk to her own survival. To imitate Frances was to imitate a victim.

Jane's skill at concealing her emotions greatly accentuated her psychological troubles as she entered her teens. Like other relatives of suicides, she suffered from survivor guilt and imagined herself a cause

of Frances's death. (A few months later, when her brother Peter accidentally shot himself, Jane expressed such feelings explicitly as she
prayed for his recovery: "If you let him live, I'll never be mean to
him again." She later said it was her first memory of praying.)
Though superficially calm, her mental life became a caldron of fear.
At summer camp in New Hampshire in 1950, according to Brooke
Hayward, "Jane would wake up in the middle of the night screaming
about her mother. I mean screaming so that the entire staff had to
appear to calm her down." These nightmares persisted for years—yet
her father knew nothing of their existence, nor of the knowledge that
drew them forth.

In this repressed atmosphere Jane's need for security, for symbols
of love, could only be expressed obliquely. She became a compulsive
eater. She experienced recurring dreams about being surrounded by
roomfuls of food, all of it placed just beyond her reach. "As a young
girl," she later said, trying to interpret this fixation, "most of my dreams
evolved from the basic need of being loved and being frustrated in
fulfilling that need."

Central to Jane's dilemma was an understandable hostility to her
father for contributing to Frances's breakdown. In one of her first
amateur stage appearances, Jane adopted a curious strategy to create
a mood of sadness—she conjured up not the death of Frances but that
of Henry! Yet she dared not express her anger, lest she too arouse his
displeasure and trigger a sequence of rejection, abandonment, victimi-
zation. "By the time I was fifteen," said Jane, "I thought I was dread-
fully grown up, which meant I was already learning to suppress my
natural feelings."

The very sources of her frustration ironically provided a resolution.
Visiting her father in the hospital after he had undergone minor surgery, she unexpectedly encountered Henry's lover. To her surprise—
and delight—she found Susan to be remarkably warm, and willing to
be friends. Jane had discovered a link back to her father. Eight months
after Frances's death Henry married Susan Blanchard, and she tried
earnestly to be a mother to Jane. She took her shopping, taught her
about clothes and hairstyles, and introduced her to the theater world
she inhabited.

Jane easily identified with her stepmother and so completed the
transition from her preteen tomboy phase into adolescence. But in a
predictable way this changing image of herself accentuated Jane's feelings of inadequacy. Unlike the beautiful Susan Blanchard, she per-

ceived herself as awkward and plump. "I felt that a different, more interesting me had been imprisoned in the wrong body."

In the fall of 1951 she was sent to the Emma Willard boarding school in Troy, New York. There she found numerous classmates with whom she shared her fixation: "Eating binges . . . coffee ice cream by the gallon . . . pound cake by the pound . . . bagfuls of brownies . . . peanut butter and bacon sandwiches." They followed their orgies with binges of remorse—and vomiting. Then the cycle began again. "The more we vomited ourselves into emptiness," explained Jane, "the more we needed to eat."

These extreme efforts at controlling weight—a preoccupation not uncommon to young girls worried about their changing bodies—reflected a deeper concern about becoming a woman, a sexual person. Unlike her friends, moreover, Jane did not menstruate until she was sixteen, though she regularly purchased tampons and flushed away what she considered an appropriate number each month. Her physiological "tardiness," a source of great embarrassment to her, reinforced the fear of repeating the mistakes of her mother. At seventeen she told her father she wasn't capable of loving. "It's a phase you're going through," he replied. But, said Jane, "I knew it wasn't."

She began to cultivate her aesthetic interests. She studied ballet and enjoyed its demands for discipline and self-control. She tried painting. She made her theatrical debut—in a male role—in Christopher Fry's *The Boy with a Cart.* "It was a bit of a romp," she said. "It had nothing to do with acting." As a senior she performed in Sheridan's *The Rivals* and gained enough confidence to agree to play summer stock with her father in Omaha, Nebraska, in 1955. "I had no technique or experience in those days," Jane said, in explaining her efforts to project real feelings. "I asked one of the stagehands to whack me around . . . and that plus the petrifying fear and trembling I had of acting on the same stage with my father turned the trick."

In the fall of 1955 Jane entered her freshman year at Vassar College in Poughkeepsie, New York, where she remained detached and unmotivated. "I never went to dances, because I considered it square to go to school dances," she said. "And I never had dates. I considered myself ugly." Compounding Jane's problems was the collapse of Henry's third marriage, the departure of Susan Blanchard and her replacement by yet another young woman, Afdera Franchetti, purportedly an Italian countess.

Jane's emotions, well concealed beneath a patina of good manners, suddenly erupted in a new direction: She felt pulled, driven, toward sexual adventure. "When I discovered that boys liked me," she said of her sophomore year, "I went wild. I went out all the time. I never studied." In the words of Brooke Hayward, she acquired "a reputation for being easy. It was almost a joke." One boyfriend said that Jane "suddenly turned into a sex pistol. . . . There was something frantic about it, about her." She also began to experiment with Dexedrine—"pep pills"—which not only boosted her physical energy but also had the salutary effect, for her, of reducing weight.

The satisfactions of popularity renewed Jane's interest in the theater. In the summer of 1956 she followed one of her boyfriends to Cape Cod's Dennis Playhouse and obtained a no-dialogue part in a Restoration comedy. Standing in the back of the theater, Henry Fonda thrilled at Jane's impact on the audience. "They sat up, they sucked in their breath, they straightened up in their seats," he said of her appearance. "She had presence." But he gave her not one word of encouragement. In these early performances, Jane later admitted that she "knew almost nothing about the motivations of the characters. . . . I was self-conscious enough to look for things in the character, but I didn't know how. There was nothing behind the emotions I showed. . . . I really hadn't decided to become an actress at that point. I even thought I didn't *want* to be an actress." What she did want, she said, "was to get out of Vassar."

When blatant violations of college rules failed to get her expelled and her father refused to let her quit, Jane embarked on an escape plan common to her class and her sex in the 1950s. Despite the uncertainties of her emotional life—or, more precisely, because of them—Jane contemplated an early marriage. "Everyone was in such a hurry to get married," she recalled. "If you didn't have a ring on your finger by your junior year, forget it." But since Vassar did not permit married students to enroll, Jane realized she could achieve both objectives—a wedding ring and termination of her college career—at the same time. Involved with a Yale student, she urged him to elope with her. He prudently declined.

Jane's unlikely proposition revealed less about her acceptance of conventional values than it did about the depths of her confusion. Better than anyone, she knew all the reasons *not* to get married. Unlike most young women, moreover, she could afford to remain single; at twenty-one she expected to inherit a sizable trust fund from Frances's estate. Yet, in rejecting marriage, Jane increased her psychological burden. Earlier than most women of her generation, she understood she would have to achieve a career and an identity of her own.

Her despair deepened: "I was eighteen, an age when you know you are not happy but you don't know why and you think a geographical change will change your life." After much pleading by Jane, Henry let her take her junior year off to study painting in Paris in 1957. But she lacked fluency in French and became even more isolated. She spent her time in the cafés and bars. "After a month," she admitted, "I was sleeping more and studying less." Her father ordered her home.

The junior year abroad, designed as an interlude for self-discovery, became a nightmare of possibilities. In New York she started piano lessons at the Mannes College of Music, studied painting at the Art Students League, and attended French and Italian classes at the Berlitz School. But her ambitions were thwarted by her despair, her lack of energy and zeal. "I wanted to jump in and start playing concertos instead of studying scales," she explained. "I thought people who looked at what I painted expected something of me that I couldn't live up to." Asked by family friends about her interest in acting, Jane replied, "It's the last thing in the world I'll ever do."

She gained different satisfactions by her success as a model. In the spring of 1958 *Vogue* magazine portrayed her as "a beauty with the dazzle of a baby *femme du monde.* Miss Fonda has a rush of toast-coloured hair, sea-blue eyes, and a fair skin." A less lyrical friend described her simply as "an uptown beatnik" who specialized in knowing about good parties. One afternoon she visited a sound studio in Harlem where her father was filming *Stage Struck* with Susan Strasberg, daughter of the director, Lee. The two young women soon became friendly, and Susan introduced Jane to her circle. But the theatrical obsessions of the young actresses annoyed Jane. She thought it unhealthy for them to sacrifice a family life for a career on the stage.

When Henry went to Hollywood in the summer of 1958, Jane went along, glad to discover that she lived just down the beach from the Strasbergs, who had gone to California to coach their most famous student, Marilyn Monroe. Joining the entourage of young actors and actresses who crowded around the Strasbergs, Jane flirted with the idea of making a professional commitment. "I was feeling sort of desperate," she said. "I was almost twenty-one. I knew that at the end of the summer I'd have to come back to New York with my father. I still didn't have anything definite to do. None of the things I'd tried to do really satisfied me."

Susan Strasberg arranged for Jane to meet her father, famous for his tutelage not only of Marilyn Monroe but also of Marlon Brando, James Dean, Geraldine Page, Shelley Winters, Paul Newman, and the numerous other stars who had studied at the Actors Studio and swore by his techniques. Henry Fonda, however, was not among them— indeed, he loathed the celebrated "Method" and distrusted the man. But Strasberg, unlike Fonda, was an older man willing to listen to Jane. In his rented house in Malibu he took her aside and asked some questions. It was a new experience for her: "For the first time in my life, I felt I was talking with someone who didn't feel he *had* to be nice to me because of my father. . . . I told him I had exhausted all the things I'd *thought* I'd wanted to be. He didn't ask me to read for him. He just asked me questions. Why was I interested in the theatre? What did I expect from the theatre? Who was my favorite actress?" Then, because of the "panic in the eyes," Lee Strasberg invited Jane Fonda to enroll in his private classes at the Dramatic Workshop.

All during the month of October 1958, Jane had watched the students perform their exercises. These activities took two forms, both catalysts for self-exposure: a physical action designed to break down inhibitions; and the reenactment of an emotional memory to reveal buried feelings. In the small dark theater the young actors would move nervously to the low stage, trying to transcend the probing scrutiny of their mentor in the first row. Strasberg's principles were quite simple. "Are you a human being? Then just get up and act like a human being, don't complicate things." Jane was understandably reluctant to come for- ward: "I didn't believe in myself. I couldn't stand the thought of exposing myself, of being attacked and torn to pieces."

In November, after a month's delay, she determined to end the evasion. The theater was packed; many, herself included, predicted disaster. Strasberg was particularly attentive. "The first impression she gave was her nervousness," an older student remembered. "Then you could see her start to relax and get caught up in it. Pretty soon she was letting it all hang out." As she finished, Jane heard Strasberg's voice cut through the silence. "You are sensitive," he was saying. Jane could not absorb the words; she was sure only that he was praising her, that, as she later put it, "he saw a tremendous amount of talent."

Jane's life changed overnight: "Before, I'd been scared and ex- tremely self-conscious—I was one person. And after that exercise I was somebody else." From Strasberg Jane acquired a sense of self-worth and confidence—and energy. Lethargic for months, she now worked like a woman possessed. Whereas most students spent two hours a week in acting class, Jane was there for six, and she took lessons in singing and dancing as well. "The light bulb came on," she said. "I was a different person. I went to bed and got up loving what I was doing."

Jane's conversion resolved her uncertainties about her life's work. "Now I know that nothing that happened to me before last fall really counts," she said, conveniently erasing her first twenty years. As she sloughed off her old life, she was ecstatic about self-discovery: "It's a wonderful feeling when you finally find out where you're going. You're happier. You're more productive. You're *nicer.* Whether I'll make it is something else again, but at least I'm finally *channeled.*"

As Henry Fonda's daughter, Jane was soon taken seriously by the theatrical establishment, considered an "inevitable discovery" who had a good chance to succeed. In the Strasberg Method, Jane would find not only a career but a philosophy of life. Instead of suppressing her feelings, she tried to capture them, directing her entire psyche into theatrical illusion. Years later she explained the attraction: "The reason I loved it so much was that it offered me a way of getting behind a mask and revealing things that I, as an uptight middle-class woman, had always been told I should not show." Brooke Hayward, struck by the transformation in Jane, noticed something else: "Acting gave her the kind of applause she never got as a human being. I've never seen ambition as naked as Jane's."

"Acting is holy hell," Jane said, still in the aspiring stage of her career. "You spend your life trying to achieve what they put people into insane asylums for: making things that aren't true seem truer than truth." She was preoccupied not with particular roles but with finding the technique to play them. "Control is what I'm after," she admitted. "Control is the whole kookie secret."

Meanwhile, as a fashion model, she sped around Manhattan in taxicabs from one assignment to the next. In one year she achieved a grand slam by appearing on the covers of *Vogue, Glamour, Esquire,* and *Parade.* But she worried more than ever about her face and figure. She adopted a diet of coffee, saccharin, cigarettes, strawberry yoghurt, and Dexedrine and slimmed down to 120 pounds. But the natural puffiness of her cheeks alarmed her, and she took to a more drastic remedy—daily diuretics to eliminate excess water. She also enrolled at the June Taylor dance school to study ballet, thriving on its physical demands. The discipline of dance facilitated the self-discipline of other aspects of her life.

Despite these efforts, she agonized over her physical appearance —and its implications for her success and survival. She was still hounded by nightmares, which not only jolted her awake but drove her to rearrange furniture in the middle of the night. Sometimes she sleepwalked out the door. She felt as if her true self inhabited some other body; she feared that her own might betray her. "It's scary what's going to happen now," she told an interviewer. "Hollywood can do funny things to people. Once you start playing the game as though it's for real, you're done for."

Her aspirations precluded emotional entanglements. Terrified of being vulnerable, she vowed she would not get married unless someone gave her a good reason to do so. Her candor titillated the gossip columnists, who reported her pronouncements. Jane Fonda to Louella Parsons: "I have grown up with divorce, and I want to feel sure before I marry." Jane Fonda to Hedda Hopper: "I think marriage is going to go out, become obsolete." She acquired a reputation for outspokenness, which increased her notoriety. "The thing I object to," she said, "is that everyone seems to expect a woman to get married. Why should the burden be placed on women?"

Her demand for independence was greatly complicated by the ubiquitous Henry Fonda. Wherever she went, he had preceded her. She was her father's daughter—a familiar face on a woman's body— and she felt obliged to fulfill more than ordinary expectations. But the problem with being Henry's daughter was not merely the comparisons that would be made. For Jane there were inescapable tensions between them. She wondered aloud if her father's four marriages "had any bad effects" on her development. "I was brought up in such a restricted way; one never shows what one feels," she observed. "Now this is a great impediment to acting."

Still, the Fonda name remained useful in opening doors. "I wouldn't be anywhere if I weren't his daughter," Jane admitted. Her father's longtime friend, producer Joshua Logan, offered her a screen test for the role of a cheerleader in his film *Tall Story*. After seeing the results, Jane thought she looked "like a squirrel with nuts packed into its cheeks." But she got the part anyway. She was terrified of failure: Her nightmares increased, her skin erupted in boils, she took more sedatives.

At the Warner Brothers studio in Hollywood experts studied her body, consulted privately, proposed repairs. Some suggested breast enlargement; others recommended altering her face by breaking the jawbones and extracting a few back teeth. But they settled for false eyelashes and bright pink lips, winged eyebrows, a sprayed hairdo, and a pair of falsies.

In *Tall Story* she was to be an ingenue who goes to college to find a husband. Jane enjoyed neither the role in the film nor the ambience of the studio. Filmmaking frightened her, she regarded the camera as an enemy. It was not an auspicious debut. "Nothing could possibly save this picture," wrote a charitable reviewer in *Time* magazine, "not even a second-generation Fonda with a smile like her father's and legs like a chorus girl."

Preferring a stage career, Jane returned to New York. In December 1959 Joshua Logan sent her the script of a new play, *There Was a Little Girl*—about a girl who was gang raped and then accused of provoking the attack—and he invited her to play the lead. Henry Fonda was furious that Logan would even imagine her—his daughter —in such a seamy role. But she refused to pass up the opportunity: "I enjoyed making myself fit the part, making myself frail as a woman, and vulnerable, and weak. I had always thought of myself as strong and independent, a self-sufficient type in blue jeans, and I enjoyed playing a dependent-girl role." Even so, the play received critical scorn and soon closed. But Jane won the praise of the New York Drama Critics, who named her the most promising young actress of the year.

In the theater, she found a sense of community. "I began to see for the first time that when a group [works] together with real love, art happens," she declared. "It was like belonging to a family." And she appreciated the value of self-discipline: "I loved the routine of acting in a play every night. . . . I loved having demands made on me—to be someplace at a definite hour, with something definite to do. . . . I had a sense of belonging." She also fell in love with another Strasberg protégé, Andreas Voutsinas, who was more experienced in the theater. It was he who urged her to seek admission into Strasberg's more prestigious Actors Studio, and he directed her audition there in January 1961. Director Elia Kazan, one of the judges, praised her performance: "She could be a major talent."

Voutsinas, ambitious for his own career, welcomed the chance to promote Jane's. They became lovers. With his support she resolved to take more chances professionally. But first, determined to overcome her existing "stereotype" as a naïve ingenue looking for Mister Right, she returned to Hollywood in April 1961 to play a prostitute in the film *Walk on the Wild Side.* "I never would have thought anyone would offer me this kind of part," she said. Remembering the disaster of *Tall Story,* however, she brought along her private drama coach, Andreas Voutsinas. They whispered intently between shootings, hugged and smooched in public; and, for reasons that no one on the set could understand, he inspired her performance. "Jane Fonda cops the show," said *Variety.*

Despite the praise, Jane knew she had barely scratched the surface. Beyond the lurid world of Kitty Twist lay deeper passions, and she was eager to explore them. At a considerable price, she bought her contract back from Joshua Logan in order to take a part in George Cukor's sexy film *The Chapman Report.* She wanted to play the nymphomaniac—but instead he cast her as a frigid woman, a widow. "To do it, I don't have to be like that woman," Jane insisted. "Instead I call on what every woman has felt at some time in her life—doubts about herself. This feeling is enough to give me insight into the way the woman feels." Cukor, delighted with her work, called her "an American original." The *Harvard Lampoon* rated her "Worst Actress of the Year." But this distinction was offset by the Department of Defense, which chose her as "Miss Army Recruiting" of 1962.

She thrived on hard work. She took on a variety of roles, most notably as the nervous newlywed in the movie of Tennessee Williams's *Period of Adjustment.* But it was still the theater that attracted her, and she was eager to play the lead in Voutsinas's directorial debut on Broadway, *The Fun Couple.* It proved to be another disaster. Back she went to the movies. "A stage career is what I wanted. But somehow making movies gets to you."

Jane's private life was further shaken by personal disaster. On New Year's Day, in 1960, she learned that Henry's first wife, Margaret Sullavan, Brooke Hayward's mother, had died of an overdose of pills. Nine months later came the news of the suicide of Brooke Hayward's kid sister, Bridget. "Here were two women . . . who had infinite spirit," Jane later wrote, ". . . a certain kind of brilliance, a crazy brilliance, erratic, difficult, neurotic, but still unique. I don't think society offers solutions to people like that, especially women."

On November 5, 1961, a scorching Santa Ana wind carried a wall of flame through the canyons of Bel Air, California, destroying the old Fonda home on Tigertail Road, including some of the personal possessions left behind. Gone were the trees planted by Henry; in ashes, too, the farewell letters of Frances. "My whole childhood went up in smoke," said Jane. She visited the blackened landscape and mourned her loss. But when she left she felt freshly unburdened. As Voutsinas reported, "It's like her life started from twelve years old on."

Voutsinas remained her constant companion. In the summer of 1962 they were together in Paris. One evening, coming out of a movie theater, they saw a news headline: Marilyn Monroe was dead, another name to be added to Jane's list of suicides. She was startled at how deeply she felt about Marilyn. A few months later Bosley Crowther, writing in *The New York Times*, noticed that Jane's acting was "strangely familiar" and asked if it was "the late Marilyn Monroe that Miss Fonda seems to resemble." To Jane it was the psychological resemblance that mattered. Her interpretation of Marilyn's death was surely a projection of her own lifelong dilemmas: ". . . the enormous thing that went on around her . . . and then she may have felt ugly, and she felt scared." When an interviewer asked about her own thoughts on suicide, she replied candidly: "Yeah, yeah, I always think about it, but I would never do it. I'm telling you I value my life too much. I think I'm too important."

—Now a new talent is rising—Jane Fonda. . . .

Not conventionally pretty, she has the kind of blunt startling features and generous mouth that can be charged with passion, or the cartoon of passion as she chooses. Her slim, tall figure has thoroughbred gawky grace. Her voice is attractive and versatile. Her ear for inflections is secure. . . .

—*The New Republic,* November 24, 1962

Four years after her arrival at Strasberg's studio, she was willing to admit that there were other actors with superior talent. But she insisted that she possessed something else: "I have star quality, I have a personality, I have a presence on the stage, which makes me more important." Confident of her potential, Jane determined to broaden her experience. From Strasberg's lessons and the revelations of psychoanalysis, she had learned the importance of emotional honesty. "Now," she said, "all I want to do is live a life of truth."

But her aspirations hardly suited the mood of commercial Hollywood in the early 1960s. She headed toward another center of cinematic creativity, the French New Wave, admiring its achievements with film realism and recognizing, in addition, its growing popularity in the United States. And so she did not hesitate to sign a contract with MGM to co-star with Alain Delon in the film *Joy House.*

In the fall of 1963 she and Voutsinas flew to Paris. There her reputation had preceded her. French journalists and photographers greeted her as the next American sex goddess. "The girl's look—soft wheaten-blond hair, a dazzling smile, lovely long legs—is emphatically American," *Life* magazine declared, "and it is a look that knocks Frenchmen down." Jane loved the attention.

Her popularity eased the shedding of old skin, the layers of self-protection. First to leave was Andreas Voutsinas, and with his departure Jane realized that she had been freed of other lingering ghosts. "My rebellion against my father really ended when I went to Europe," she later remarked. "It was then that I became my own person. Maybe that's even why I went." She claimed to prefer Europe; it was easier there to prove herself on her own. Far from Hollywood and Henry Fonda, she could explore a different culture—and learn to distinguish her values from theirs.

On a Friday night in November 1963, she approached, all unwittingly, a turning point. She had planned to meet that night with the editors of the influential French film magazine *Cahiers du Cinéma,* who proposed to place her on the cover of a special issue about the *"cinéma Américain."* As they called her name in the hotel lobby, their voices were suddenly drowned in a sharp wail. At that moment Jane learned about the assassination of President Kennedy. She burst into tears and fled to her room. The editors sat stunned at the bar.

An hour later Jane invited them to her room. She was still shaken, but gradually as they talked she relaxed. Her French, tutored by Berlitz, was impeccable, and she spoke with obvious sincerity, describing the problems of Hollywood and of American film. She explained the power of the big studios. Without them she herself would be nothing, she admitted, but they were interested only in making money. "One can't make films like that," she said. She was ready for something else, eager to work with French actors and directors who could improve her performance.

She was, at this moment, the quintessential actress. Her emotions, expressed earlier in the privacy of her room, receded from view. Whatever sorrow she felt for the dead president vanished beneath professional cordiality, the obligations of the interview. "Right now," she said, on what many considered one of the saddest days in American history, "I do not wish to return to the United States."

George
Corley
Wallace
(I)

February 1958. For most of his thirty-eight years, the ex-bantamweight Golden Gloves champion, air corps veteran of World War II, former state legislator, and incumbent one-term judge of the Third Judicial District of the sovereign state of Alabama, the Honorable George Corley Wallace, had rehearsed for this next moment of his life: the opening of his campaign to become governor of Alabama.

Miss Minnie Pearl and Webb Pierce of the Grand Ole Opry Company, backed by the Jack Turner string band, stood at the microphone in the back of a flatbed truck parked at the courthouse square in the town of Ozark and tried to warm up the crowd that bent against the February gusts and forty-degree chill. "I'm as happy as a dead pig in the sunshine," chuckled Miss Minnie, despite the long johns she wore beneath her ballroom gown, "to introduce your next governor."

The Barbour County Bantam, "the handshakingest candidate," stepped to the rear of the flatbed, nodding to the local leaders who had come to see him launched. An experienced politician, he decided to shorten the misery of the thinned-out crowd still waiting in the cold to hear him speak and rushed through the issues that traditionally stirred Alabama voters. More money for public schools. Trade schools to spread industry. The enticement of new business into the forty-seventh-richest state. Higher pensions so that the elderly could "get a living rather than a mere existence." More highways. Reapportionment. Economy in government. Honesty. He knew the litany, and the cheering crowd, which had heard these lines so many times before, urged him on. Fourteen times in twenty-one minutes they interrupted the rush of campaign oratory with applause.

But in the heart of the Alabama Black Belt—so named more for the color of the soil than the complexion of its inhabitants—these country-bred folk were primarily interested in what the candidate would say about the most sensitive, frightening issue in their lives. It was not six months since President Eisenhower had sent paratroopers to integrate Central High School in Little Rock, Arkansas. South Alabamians were worried sick about the future of what Wallace called "our way of life." "You have enough good and honest people right here in Ozark to decide on matters such as that," he assured them now, "and you sure don't have to rely on any imported federal and district judges."

"We shall continue to maintain segregation in Alabama completely and absolutely," he declared, but also "without violence or ill-will—that will only compound our problems." In this climate of rising hysteria, Wallace offered a voice of reason. "I advocate hatred of no man," he swore. "We have outsmarted our enemies in the past, and we can outsmart them again."

Thus he juggled the fears and the hopes of the voters. Prosperity and progress on the one hand; stability, tradition, custom on the other. "Patience and tolerance . . . maximum value . . . fairness, dignity, and firmness." For the past four years, he had ridden around the state making speeches, shaking hands, reaching for the pulse of popular opinion. Better than any other candidate in a fourteen-man field, George Wallace knew the rituals of political success. But in this year, 1958, all the rituals had been changed.

For the purpose of the campaign, Judge Wallace produced a comic book autobiography depicting his rise from hardworking plowboy to the dapper candidate for the state mansion. Its veracity—at least as a testament of one man's fantasy—can hardly be doubted. The facts are slightly otherwise. He was born on August 25, 1919, in a small wood-frame house just outside the village of Clio (it rhymes with Oh*io*), population 900, in Barbour County, an "area of this country," he said, that "was typical of the rural Southland during the 1920s and early 1930s." The house had no electricity or indoor plumbing; there was little money, and Wallace recalled how he pined for a Sears Roebuck cowboy suit that he could not afford, at one dollar and fifteen cents. Still, he remembered it as "a sort of Tom Sawyer–Huck Finn type of life"—wearing stiff overalls to pick blackberries, shelling pecans, riding the wagons to the cotton gin. He spent the summers poling for catfish, killing snakes, and swimming in the natural spring water at Blue Springs. In a later summing-up, he remarked, "I think we were happier with our simple, improvised games than some of today's children are with their motorbikes and pocket computers."

His father, George Wallace, Sr., was a sickly man who passed through most of his life with only one lung and suffered severe sinus swellings that eventually required drastic surgery and left his skull with a permanent indentation. Too frail to farm successfully, George, Sr., leased his holdings to sharecroppers, whose payments were enough to enable him to avoid steady work. Most days he hung around the wood-burning stove at the local store, talking politics and crops, a habit he passed on to his firstborn and namesake. In the thick of the Great Depression, he had the good fortune to survive a rich uncle who drowned and left him $5,000, which he used to build a new house with a flush toilet and a telephone in the front room.

Despite his weak frame and physical miseries, George, Sr., had sufficient character and charm to attract Miss Mozelle Smith, a prim, small-built Birmingham girl who had attended boarding school in Mobile. They met while she was changing trains at the Montgomery railroad station. After a proper courtship they married, and she followed him back to his hometown. Mozelle Wallace installed herself as the music teacher at Clio Elementary School and drilled her students for the annual concerts she produced. Her oldest son, George, showed something less than enthusiasm for these efforts—"I must have been born with a tin ear"—but she made him perform at the recitals anyway, until one day he forgot the music in the middle and stormed out in a rage. She also expected her children—three boys and a girl—to accompany her to the Methodist church where she played the piano and

where they heard the Reverend Daniel Langingham's hellfire and brim-
stone sermons, which stressed the importance of individual responsibility for one's fate.

If, as in many families, there was a continuing cultural combat
between the scrappy bourbon-drinking style of George, Sr., and the
steady Christian fortitude of Mozelle, George, Jr., fortunately discovered a dependable ally who could offer him the best of both worlds.
This was Dr. George Wallace, his paternal grandfather, a respected,
affluent country physician who had once served a term as probate judge
and was noted in the community for his antipathy to alcohol. Dr.
Wallace and young George enjoyed a friendship that was stitched
inextricably when the boy was only two. They were together at the
grandfather's house the day Mozelle gave birth to her second child,
Gerald, and upon learning the news George refused to go home. "Dr.
Wallace tried to take him back," reported George's grandmother, "and
then an hour or so later returned, driving up the street with George
still sitting there beside him. It sort of stayed like that ever after."
George relished their conversations and Bible lessons as the doctor
drove around in a Model T making house calls.

Among the values young George absorbed was a respect for decency, common sense, and traditional institutions. In a society that
encouraged boys to be aggressive, he would have no part of "girlish"
piano recitals. But he would neither participate in nor condone the
ever-present violence. Bombings, burnings, murders, stabbings
(George, Sr., once slashed a youth over a girl and chased another
cracker-barrel debater with a knife)—these were common enough. But
George's aggression remained safely limited within the rules of athlet-
ics. Despite his 120 pounds, he played quarterback on the high school
football team, served as team captain in his senior year, and later
boasted, "I made up in aggressiveness what I lacked in brawn." Once,
in a baseball game, he gave his brother a six-inch spike wound. Boxing
unleashed his meanest streak. After his father bought him a pair of
gloves, George set up a ring in the living room and enticed credulous
boys of both races to come inside and take their lickings. Merciless to
opponents, he never lost; by his mid-teens he was good enough to win
the Alabama Golden Gloves twice. "I was wiry and agile, and probably
too aggressive for my own good," he later admitted. "But I thrived on
the raw, face-to-face competition." At the University of Alabama he
earned an enviable 25-4-1 record. His favorite trophy was a photograph
of himself standing triumphantly above a sprawled victim whose blood

spewed from nose and mouth. For years afterward, he kept this picture propped on his bureau.

The pleasure of manly competition took a milder turn in his early enthusiasm for the Alabama sport that most interested his father—politics. "I wasn't but about ten years old, but I was fascinated," he wrote, remembering how he had stayed up late on election night. "Watching him count those votes was like watching somebody water-ski for the first time." By the age of thirteen he was following his father through the streets of Clio, knocking on doors on behalf of local candidates. After rural electrification came to the town, the two would listen to national politics on the radio. And it was this mutual enthusiasm that carried George, for the first time, beyond the lines of Barbour County.

One day in 1935 father and son piled into the car and drove to the state capitol, in Montgomery. At sixteen George had already decided to seek public office—as a page in the state senate—and he demonstrated the political instincts that would become his trademark. Moving around the unfamiliar capitol lobby, he found every single senator, offered a handshake, and asked for a vote. He won the job 21-5. "Winning that page's election was probably the key to much of my later interest in politics," Wallace would maintain. "I enjoyed myself immensely . . . and I got an insight into political maneuvering."

Running for senate page also played a large role in coloring his political identity. When his father dropped him off in front of the state capitol, he "stood on that bottom step and looked up at that dome. It seemed so huge," he recalled. "I wasn't sure I'd be able to walk in the shoes of some of those people who had been here before." Mounting the long flight of steps, he approached the bronze star planted in marble to commemorate the spot where Jefferson Davis had taken the oath as president of the Confederacy. "I felt chill bumps all over my body," George said. "In my mind I could see myself in the future. I knew I would return to that spot. I knew I would be governor of the people of this great state."

Such adolescent fantasies, characteristically ambitious, self-confident, and narcissistic, also reflected his strong identification with the underdog, with the Lost Cause. In the 1930s the strains of the Civil War still comprised a basic theme in the American identity; a veritable cult of Lincoln flourished on Broadway, in Hollywood, in the writings of Carl Sandburg and Robert Sherwood. But for young men of the South the lessons—of defeat—were obviously very different. George's interest in books, admittedly quite limited, focused on that war and, as he put it, "people dying for a cause, brave men, North and South." He learned that the poverty of his boyhood "was a holdover from the discriminatory treatment meted to the South at the end of the War Between the States." The idea of white people being treated as second-class citizens seemed oppressive and repugnant. Such attitudes had little to do with the more delicate issue of race, about which the Wallace record in these years is virtually blank.

His grandiose dreams were nearly thwarted before they commenced. Known as a clever, if undisciplined, student, he enrolled at the University of Alabama and arrived in Tuscaloosa in the fall of 1937 with one pair of baggy pants, a baggy sports coat, two white shirts, and a fat cigar clamped in the corner of his mouth. His scholastic career began poorly. There were the traumas of finding inexpensive lodging, a series of part-time jobs (cabdriver, waiter, boardinghouse manager), borrowing books, and trying to keep up with classes. Two months into the semester he was abruptly summoned back to Clio by the death of his father. He considered quitting his studies to take over the family farm. But the tough-minded Mozelle, persistent in her own expectations, sent him back. (She held on to the family house, too, and got a job as supervisor of the local National Youth Administration sewing room. "I did it just to keep myself busy," she later told a reporter. "I could have done without it—oh, yes.")

In Tuscaloosa Wallace spread himself thin—working part-time jobs, winning a place on the university boxing team, politicking for campus offices (he lost often enough for the student newspaper to name him "best sport on campus"), and struggling through his courses. "I hung on by my fingernails," he claimed. Thanks to some adventurous summer jobs—traveling salesman, dog inoculator—he moved through college and law school by the summer of 1942, but he never did raise the money to buy his official diploma.

By then his ambitions had been diverted by the outbreak of World War II. Though eligible for a commission, he enlisted as an army air corps recruit ("I preferred to start at the bottom," he later claimed) and spent the summer of 1942 awaiting induction. To make ends meet he sold bunches of wire coat hangers and other scrap, drove a dump truck for the state highway department, and then found work as a tool checker. He ate on meal tickets at the local Kress, where he noticed a "pert" sixteen-year-old clerk named Lurleen Burns. He thought she gave "the appearance of a somewhat overmature child of twelve." They saw each other all summer, though often George interrupted their dates by knocking on some stranger's door to solicit votes for one of the gubernatorial candidates, Barbour County's Chauncey Sparks. Lurleen remembered that their main topic of conversation was politics. Already George was talking about being the governor. The only thing that troubled him was people asking him why he wasn't in uniform. After he got his marching orders, he asked Lurleen to marry him.

In military service, as in college, he struggled to make the grade, compensating for his lack of weight by swallowing gallons of water to trick the army scales, and he thrived on barracks camaraderie. He especially enjoyed playing the role of hillbilly moonshiner to the Yankee soldiers who thought themselves superior to any red-neck cracker. "This practical demonstration of the art of confounding helped to convince me that I had not been amiss in selecting a law career," he concluded. Wallace performed well in pilot-training school and was looking forward to winning his wings. Then an outbreak of spinal meningitis put him in a hospital bed, near death. "I wasn't really awake, conscious of the fact that I was dying," he said of the six-day coma, "but it left me with a profound feeling that I had lived through something very near to moving on into another life." Years later he still remembered seeing the corpses of some other victims of meningitis in the hospital. He considered himself lucky to be alive.

Returning to Alabama for recuperation, he hastened to marry Lurleen, who still needed written permission from her mother. After the civil ceremony, the threesome celebrated with chicken salad sandwiches at a Tuscaloosa lunch counter before George and Lurleen caught a slow train to Montgomery to visit Mozelle, then working for the state Bureau of Preventable Diseases. Their honeymoon night passed in a boardinghouse, and then they traveled to Clio for a brief vacation. They managed to impress George's Aunt Hadley, who died soon after and left them a $1,000 nest egg.

Still shaky from his illness and closer than ever to Lurleen, George returned to the army with a growing anxiety. "I tried to maintain my composure," he later wrote of his farewell, "but as I walked down the steps with my flight bag a feeling came over me that I might never see her again. I broke down and cried for the first time as a man." This sense of vulnerability persisted in the ensuing months. Lurleen followed him to various army bases in the South and West, both of them working off-base to pay the bills. She returned to Alabama to give birth to their first child, Bobbi Jo, and then journeyed to Alamogordo, New

Mexico, for a family reunion. There, they made their home in a re-vamped chicken house.

In June 1945 George completed his training at flight-engineering school and was shipped to the Mariana Islands aboard a B-29 named *The Sentimental Journey* to serve under General Curtis LeMay. Then, in a series of bombing runs over the coast of Japan, he confronted new and unexpected terrors. "You'd see all them other planes gettin' shot down all around you, you'd get nicked, and gas'd spew out on them hot engines, flak all over the place. . . . Man, it liked to scare me to death. My hands'd be all sweaty, my heart just athumpin' and all."

After six weeks and seven or eight missions, Sergeant Wallace was grounded in the Pacific for "flight fatigue, anxiety state." The next day the *Enola Gay* dropped an atomic bomb on Hiroshima. He was en route to Mobile, Alabama, when a second bomb exploded on Nagasaki. By August 14, 1945, V-J Day, he was safely at home, avoiding the pandemonium that swept the country. "Hell, I was too glad to be back. I wasn't about to get run over by a car downtown celebrating the victory."

The arrival of new military orders disrupted Wallace's rest. "Call it fear, call it anxiety coming to the surface, call it what you will," he said, "I decided I was through flying." Since the war was over, he rationalized, "It seemed to me pointless to embark on a training program that would have no useful purpose and could in fact be the cause of senseless accidents." Army psychiatrists decided that he was suffering from "severe anxiety state, chronic, manifested by tension states, anxiety attacks, anorexia, and loss of weight." Ten months later he received a service-connected 10 percent–disability discharge for "psychoneurosis."

Coming home in the autumn of 1945, Wallace made a firm resolve: "Never again would Lurleen have to live in a chicken house." And, presumably, neither would he. His political instincts enabled him to avoid the long unemployment lines that were already crowded with returning veterans. A call on Governor Sparks, for whom he had campaigned while courting Lurleen, resulted in his appointment as assistant attorney general at a salary of $175 a month. With this patronage reward, Wallace began a carefully calculated climb up the ladder of state government. He was twenty-six years old.

In 1946, the first year of the big veteran vote, he announced his intention to represent Barbour County in the state legislature. Handicapped by a shortage of funds, he began an eighteen-hour-day, seven-days-a-week, stump-stomping, door-knocking, handshaking campaign. "I had seen enough of politics to be wary of overconfidence," he explained. "I prefer the underdog role to that of the front-runner, who is too likely to trip over his own complacency." He was careless about his comfort or his physical appearance. To solicit votes he hitchhiked across the county, visited farmers in the fields and barnyards, stopped at crossroads stores, even went up telephone poles where men were working. Stressing that he had served as an enlisted man in the army, he appealed to the common denominator. In this first campaign, Wallace won more votes than did all his opponents combined.

He brought his zeal for politics into the legislature. George and Lurleen moved into the Montgomery boardinghouse where they had spent their wedding night. They had to share a bathroom down the hall with the blue-collar clientele. But in George's estimation the accommodations were desirable because they were close to the lobby of the Jefferson Davis Hotel, where he spent time wheeling and dealing obsessively with other politicians. "Energetic, ambitious, liberal, smart," was Governor Gordon Persons's description of the young legislator. Wallace's politics were indeed liberal. He sponsored a wide array of measures that included scholarships for disabled veterans, higher old-age pensions, an anti-lottery bill, cancer detection units, and free hog-cholera treatments. His legislative committee interests—crippled children, tuberculosis, and mental health—revealed the diversity of his social-welfare concerns. Most important to him was the passage of what became known as the Wallace Act, which provided for new vocational and trade schools and encouraged new industries to move to Alabama.

Wallace's liberal agenda reflected a long tradition of southern populism. He wished sincerely to improve the lot of the common people. But, like most politicians, he remained primarily a creature of his constituents. His commitment to reform stopped far short of any substantial change. He expressed no desire to alter the fundamental arrangements of southern society. Nor did he ever challenge the existing pattern of political leadership. He only wanted his fair share.

In 1948 Wallace entered national politics for the first time, running as an alternate delegate from Alabama to the Democratic National Convention in Philadelphia. His personal platform was unambiguous. He opposed the nomination of Harry Truman as well as the president's civil rights platform. At the convention Wallace listened angrily to the speech of another young politician, Hubert Horatio Humphrey, mayor of Minneapolis, who dared the Democrats "to get out of the shadow of states' rights and walk forthrightly into the bright sunshine of human rights." When the convention proceeded to adopt the liberal civil rights plank, a large proportion of southern delegates stormed from the meeting to form the Dixiecrat party.

Wallace was not among them. He chose instead to fight civil rights inside the hall. Paragraph by paragraph, he challenged the wording of the platform—to no avail—and, when it came to picking the party's candidate, he yielded Alabama's alphabetical first place to allow the nomination of Senator Richard Russell of Georgia, which he vociferously seconded. Not because of any "racial prejudice," he later insisted, "but my personal opposition was based on strong fears that unconstitutional methods employed for so-called good ends could later be employed for bad ends." On the floor, he cast his ballot for Russell and later supported South Carolina's Strom Thurmond, who ran for president on the Dixiecrat ticket.

Wallace left the legislature in 1952 to run for circuit judge of his native Barbour County. As in his earlier campaigns, he traveled through the entire district in his battered automobile, oblivious to hardship and inconvenience, interested only in shaking hands, giving speeches, and belittling the gentility of his wealthy opponent. He won the election by a three-to-one margin. With that modicum of security, the Wallaces bought their first home, for $8,500. He was thirty-three years old.

Wallace strove to keep politics out of his courtroom not only in the interest of judicial fairness but also because he worried about offending some possible future constituent. Disguising his own sentiments, he demonstrated considerable skill at courtroom arbitration. In more controversial cases his guiding principle was to suggest a jury trial and then abide by the verdict. In these proceedings, Wallace established an impartial record, even in cases involving whites against blacks, and he tended to be liberal in offering probation.

Wallace's willingness to support political reform led him to back Big Jim Folsom, a genuine Alabama populist who ran for governor in 1954. He served as campaign manager in the southern counties and purportedly wrote 90 percent of the candidate's speeches, which promised better highways, more schools, higher teachers' salaries, and increased aid to the aged—positions that Wallace gladly endorsed.

For his loyalty to the victorious Folsom, Wallace extracted one symbolic repayment: an appointment to the board of trustees of Tuskegee Institute, the most famous all-black educational institution in the country. "You've got to have the Negro vote from now on if you expect to run for anything," Wallace said at a time when the number of non-white voters was extremely small, "and I'm going to lay my groundwork right now." He boasted to fellow politicians about his association with the Negro community, and he began to think about following Folsom—who by law could not succeed himself—into the governor's mansion four years later. After Folsom's inauguration in January 1955, therefore, Wallace remained on the campaign trail, building alliances for the most difficult undertaking of his life.

The hectic pace of politics shaped the patterns of his private life. "I was away a lot," Wallace later admitted. "But the life of a fellow who finally runs for the Governor's office necessitates a long-term expenditure of time: You travel 150 miles to speak to a club with 15 people in it, drive 100 miles to speak to one with 20 in it, then drive to the other end of the state to make an appearance. And I did that over a period of, you might say, fifteen years." At Lurleen's insistence he would occasionally devote a weekend day to their three children, but at picnics or football games or swimming pools he usually wandered away to talk politics with the adults.

The entire family paid for his ambition. For Lurleen the world shrank into an endless muddle of domestic concerns. In public she appeared untroubled, but she resented deeply the burden of George's long absences. And the children often felt fatherless. "I remember," wrote George, Jr., his only son, years later and with no small trace of bitterness, "that he was very *busy* all the time when I was a child— always on the go. . . . His mind was on his career." Wallace's own symptoms, according to a medical report made for the Veterans Administration when he was thirty-seven, were quite obvious. "He was tense, restless, and ill at ease," said the doctor who renewed his 10 percent–disability claim, "frequently drummed the desk with his fingers, changed position frequently, sighed occasionally, and showed a tendency to stammer, resulting in the diagnosis of anxiety reaction." Such appraisals in no way altered his behavior.

Apart from any residual battle fatigue, his insecurities reflected a realistic appraisal of his political circumstances. The close identification with Big Jim Folsom, while boosting his hopes for the future, paradoxically offended other entrenched interests that might thwart his plans. To compound his difficulties, the governor refused to assist him. When Folsom rejected one of his patronage requests, Wallace realized the importance of establishing his independence. But the issue that provoked the final breach was as old as Dixie. When Wallace heard public attacks on Folsom for having served drinks at the governor's mansion to Harlem Congressman Adam Clayton Powell, he began to fear for his own future. He did not wish to be overly associated with the governor's liberalism nor his reputation for drinking. His support of Folsom, Wallace made clear, could not exceed its initial intention— the success of George Corley Wallace.

Central to the split between Wallace and Folsom was the dramatic reappearance of the issue of racial segregation. In May 1954, the very month of Folsom's victory in the Democratic primary, the United States Supreme Court ruled in *Brown v. The Board of Education* that segregated public schools were inherently unequal and so unconstitutional. The decision reverberated through the South like an earthquake. Not only did it jolt longstanding assumptions about racial inequality and second-class citizenship for blacks, but more fundamentally it challenged the legitimacy of the white-controlled state governments that had created and upheld the system of segregation. To most white southerners the Supreme Court and, indeed, the federal government now appeared as a threat to the principle of government by the consent of the governed.

Wallace articulated the prevailing opinion. "The dual school systems that existed prior to the Supreme Court decision . . . were not considered discriminatory," he said. "We felt that type of school system was in the best interests of both races." As circuit court judge, Wallace never wavered from his support of Jim Crow. In 1953 he had been the first southern judge to issue an injunction forbidding the removal of segregation signs in railroad terminals, and he had traveled to Washington, D.C., to testify against pending civil rights legislation. Three years later, in the new spirit of "massive resistance" in the South, the otherwise obscure judge took loud exception to a federal investigation of grand jury procedures in Georgia, comparing the inquiry to "Gestapo methods," and he announced that he would order the arrest of "every member of the FBI" who attempted to inspect the jury records of his jurisdiction. Since no such investigation had been planned, the statement served primarily to clarify Wallace's personal position.

Precisely because he shared the views of his colleagues and constituents, Wallace seldom needed to use racial arguments in public. His opposition to desegregation remained scrupulously within a legalistic framework. In 1956 he represented Alabama on the platform committee of the Democratic National Convention in Chicago and helped to draft a weak civil rights plank. (In the subsequent floor contest for the vice-presidency, Wallace supported the more conservative John F. Kennedy over Estes Kefauver, for which the Massachusetts senator soon afterward sent him a copy of *Profiles in Courage*, inscribed "To my good friend, Judge George C. Wallace.") A few months later Wallace journeyed to Washington to reiterate the importance of state sovereignty before a House Judiciary Subcommittee.

The intrusion of federal paratroopers to uphold civil order in Little Rock in the fall of 1957 offended Wallace's sense of fair play. "Mr. Eisenhower, who was raised with a bayonet in his hand and a pistol on his hip, has now substituted military dictatorship for the Constitution," he said. "His beliefs evidently are the same as Hitler's and the communists'—that 'might makes right.'" Yet Wallace realized, too, that Eisenhower's intervention in Little Rock provided a powerful precedent for similar actions elsewhere. He understood that constitutional arguments could not resist the force of federal arms. It was imperative, therefore, to fight the battle for segregation not in the streets of southern cities, where violence and civil disorder easily justified military solutions. The South, he believed, must stand behind the rule of law and use the power of the state governments to defend constitutional principles.

Four months after Little Rock, in January 1958, Wallace threw his hat into the ring. He intended to run for governor as a "constitutional" candidate, and he vowed to uphold the traditional separation of power "which has made it possible for all citizens, regardless of race, creed, or color, to enjoy freedom and peace." At a meeting of the white Citizens Council in the town of Calera, Wallace enunciated three principles that became the centerpiece of the current campaign, if not of his entire career. First, "Never succumb to the idea that schools and our constitutional government are doomed." Second, "Fashion legal remedies and do not resort to malicious, illegal methods to fight segregation." Third, "Don't let minority groups"—"Negroes," added the editor of the *Montgomery Advertiser*, lest the euphemism confound the subject—"forget that we're still the best friends they have." Instead of terror and violence, said Wallace, "we must continue to extend the hand of compassion to all people."

To spread the gospel of reason, he stumped the entire state, interrupting only once, on Lincoln's birthday, to address the legislature of Georgia on the importance of "total resistance to the efforts of those in other sections who would destroy constitutional government." In the small towns of the Tennessee Valley he preached the virtues of industrialization—"more jobs, higher living standards, and overall economic improvement." At Huntsville, bastion of Wernher Von Braun and the rocket program, he lamented "the shameful educational standards in Alabama" and promised better schools. To seventy-five hundred listeners at Troy State College, he repeated his commitment to "absolute and complete" segregation. "We can maintain what we want . . . in the South, and we can do it within the law," he assured the students. "Nobody is smart enough to outsmart us."

KEEP ALABAMA SOUTHERN

GEORGE C. WALLACE

FOR GOVERNOR

He appeared on the platform without a jacket, in wash-and-wear slacks—"more worn than washed," one reporter observed. His pockets bulged with a wadded handkerchief and scraps of paper from which he quoted in his speech. The formula he offered was simple: "Out-litigate 'em and out-legislate 'em." He warned especially against giving the federal government an excuse to intervene in local affairs. His campaign motto became "Fair play for all." "We will give everyone what's coming to them in health, education, and government services," he said, defending the doctrine of separate but equal, "but that crowd above the Potomac isn't going to tell us how to go about it."

By early spring the Wallace campaign had caught fire. The crowds enjoyed his amiable style, and he even won the backing of the major newspapers in Birmingham and Montgomery. By law a candidate had to win a majority of all ballots in the primary to be nominated and, in this one-party state, nomination as a Democrat was tantamount to victory. "Sure, I'm sorta tense on the inside," he admitted on the eve of the first primary in May 1958. "It's kinda like the feeling I had the first time I flew a combat mission in World War II." When the vote came, Wallace defeated all the party regulars—except for one other dark-horse candidate, Attorney General John Patterson, who led the Barbour Bantam by forty thousand votes. They had to meet again in a special runoff.

Patterson enjoyed special advantages in 1958. Four years earlier his father had been elected state attorney general on a promise to eliminate crime in notorious Phenix City, Alabama. But, before he could take office, he had been assassinated. Then the younger Patterson stepped into his father's shoes, won a special election as attorney general, and built a reputation as a valiant fighter of crime. A lingering sympathy clung to the Patterson name like a halo.

Patterson held another advantage, fresh and unexpected in Alabama politics. In his devotion to law and order, he admitted frankly that there are some foreign laws, call them federal laws, that he would not uphold, and he vowed to prevent the desegregation of the races. So obvious was the contrast between the candidates on this issue that Patterson won the backing of the Ku Klux Klan, while George Wallace, who merely promised that "neither my children, nor your children, will go to mixed schools," ran as the candidate of the Jewish community and the NAACP!

Comfortable in his lead, Patterson refused to campaign. Wallace became desperate. He bought a huge Hollywood-style four-poster bed with patchwork quilt, which he placed in the back of his campaign truck. It sat there obtrusively while Wallace presented his finest political oratory until, at last, he paused to ask, "Where is John Patterson?" The crowd twisted around, strained for a view. "Where is John Patterson?" he repeated.

"You know what they say?" he replied. "They say politics makes strange bedfellows." Keeping a straight face, he peeked under the patchwork quilt. "Is that you down there, John Patterson? Why don't you come out and face the people? What do you have to hide? Who's down there between the sheets with you, John?" said Wallace with a wink. "Are you in bed with the Ku Klux Klan?"

"Why doesn't John Patterson show himself and debate the issues?" The humor had departed. "He's afraid," answered Wallace. "He's afraid of the issues because he knows nothing about the issues. He has given no one a possible program. What will he do for you? Nothing! He's a do-nothing, know-nothing, invisible candidate."

In 1958, however, that apparently was just what the voters wanted. John Patterson, running on his reputation, trimmed Wallace by nearly sixty-five thousand votes. On election night Wallace moved sadly through the lobby of the Jefferson Davis Hotel before finally making his way upstairs into a smoky-blue room. His appeal to moderation—what appeared to represent his true position on matters of race —had failed at the polls. But Wallace continued to respect the dynamics of southern politics. Among his friends he was blunt. "John Patterson out-niggahed me," he explained. "And, boys, I'm not going to be out-niggahed again."

For the next four years he brooded on one idea. "I had set my heart on being governor," he said. "All else . . . [was] secondary." Supported by gifts from his friends, meager earnings from a moribund law practice, and the monthly disability checks, Wallace lived exclusively for the next election. He traveled constantly, visited civic groups, marched in parades, glad-handed his way down remote main streets and around courthouse squares. "You'd see him go into the Elite Cafe at least a dozen times every day," one government official recalled. "He was wearin' those little Buster Brown suits then and was shakin' hands every wakin' hour." For Wallace the rigors of campaigning served not only to muster political support but also to ease the humiliation of defeat, to restore his battered pride.

Whatever the therapeutic effects, Wallace's inexhaustible ambition brought despair and frustration to the wife and children he left behind. "The days were long," Lurleen later complained. "There was nothing to do. I didn't know when he was coming home and when he'd be stuck with people." She heard rumors of extramarital liaisons and finally gathered the children and moved into her parents' home to file for divorce. Through trusted intermediaries, Wallace managed to dissuade her. But their family life did not settle down until Lurleen became pregnant for the fourth time. The birth of Janie Lee—named after Robert E., said George, "my favorite hero"—by Caesarean section in April 1961 proved a mixed blessing. Lurleen's doctors discovered abnormal cell tissue, but they could reach no firm diagnosis.

At the start of the 1962 campaign, Wallace began to worry about his popularity. He dreaded another humiliating defeat. As his anxiety mounted he checked into a hospital, on the verge of collapse. He contemplated an early withdrawal from the race. Only when his supporters produced a substantial war chest—ample security for a good fight—did his spirits revive. But even then his efforts seemed to founder. Running against his former mentor, Big Jim Folsom, Wallace offered a familiar platform: more money for schools ("to keep pace with the space age"), better highways, higher pensions, and honesty in government. It was a practical agenda, cautious and dull.

It took something else to arouse the voters. "I couldn't make them listen," he said. "Then I began talking about niggers—and they stomped the floor." In defending segregation Wallace contrasted the benevolent paternalism of the South with the hypocrisy of the North. While "those lily-livered liberals" created black ghettos in the cities, he said, "we've got Negroes living in our backyards. We take care of 'em. We clothe 'em. We feed 'em. We don't let our people go hungry, starve on the streets, beg for their bread. . . . Southern people have soft hearts. They don't like to see their fellow man get stomped on. . . . That's our kind of civil rights."

For Wallace, opposition to the civil rights movement reflected not southern racism but constitutional principles—the traditional separation of powers. In the campaign, he used Federal District Judge Frank Johnson, a former classmate of his at the University of Alabama, as a whipping boy. Calling him "a low-down carpetbaggin', scalawaggin', race-mixin' liar," Wallace delighted audiences from Scottsboro to Mobile as he denounced "a judicial dictatorship and judicial tyranny unlike anything the nation has ever seen." The people of Alabama, he vowed, "will firmly resist . . . control by federal agencies in areas which traditionally and constitutionally are matters for state and local control. Our way of life can and must be preserved."

Cloaking himself in the tradition of states' rights, popular sovereignty, and white supremacy, Wallace sought to embody the struggle: the people—the raw democracy—against the forces of tyranny. "As your governor," he promised in words that would echo throughout his career, "I shall resist any illegal federal court order even to the point of standing at the schoolhouse door in person, if necessary." Such a personal defense, even if it resulted in the arrest of the governor, would serve to unmask "the ultimate purpose" of the civil rights movement, which, he said, aimed "to destroy every state capital, every county courthouse, and every city hall in America." It was all legal doctrine —not a word about race, creed, or color. "I pledge to stand between you and the efforts of a 'force cult' to impose . . . doctrines foreign to our way of life," he asserted. "I will face our enemies face to face, hip to hip, and toe to toe, and never surrender."

These were fighting words, touchstones of southern honor and pride, a language the voters readily understood. On election day some 340,000—the largest number in Alabama history—voted for Wallace. "How can you be too strong on what you believe in?" asked the victor. "There isn't any middle road." But the runner-up candidate, Ryan deGraffenreid, offered one final warning: "It's been the same pattern in every state where you have a loudmouth, rabble-rousing governor," he observed. "They have brought the walls of segregation tumbling down on their heads."

Instead of slaking his ambition, Wallace's victory confirmed a sense of destiny: his mission to save the republic from its enemies in Washington. "Those federal courts are not sacred, and those judges are not holy men," he told a roaring crowd in Americus, Georgia. "The time has come when we've either got to put up or shut up about a return to constitutional government." In October 1962 Wallace's attention shifted to Oxford, Mississippi, where Governor Ross Barnett encouraged an angry crowd to block the enrollment of black student James Meredith at the University of Mississippi. "Millions of Americans are grateful that at least one governor . . . has the guts to stand fast," said Wallace, promising to take a similar position in Alabama. "They'll have to arrest me. And when they put their filthy hands on the governor of a sovereign state, it'll wake this country up. We're going to create headlines here. We Anglo-Saxon folks don't like to be pushed around."

Alarmed by the violence in Mississippi, however, the "Big Mules" of Birmingham business let the governor-elect know they wanted peace and quiet in Alabama. Wallace scorned their advice. "Those people who want to destroy our educational and social order," he replied to the state chamber of commerce, "are the same people who want to destroy the free enterprise system in America. . . . I am going to resist, and my resistance will gain respect." Meanwhile Wallace and Barnett made plans to challenge President Kennedy's reelection. "I'm gonna make race the basis of politics in this state," Wallace declared on the eve of his inauguration in 1963, "and I'm gonna make it the basis of politics in this country."

Despite the cold, gray January day, Wallace savored the inaugural festivities. Too happy to sit still, he bounced around the reviewing stand in a formal cutaway coat, striped pants, and silk top hat, saluting the hundred-odd floats, marching units, and brass bands that paraded in his honor. "I'm so glad you never gave up," whispered Lurleen, who finally had moved from her modest home into a veritable mansion. Proudly she held the family Bible while brother Jack Wallace, George's successor in the Third Circuit Court, administered the oath of office.

Wallace now articulated the principles of his administration: "Today I have stood where Jefferson Davis stood, and took an oath to my people. It is very appropriate then that from this Cradle of the Confederacy, this very heartland of the great Anglo-Saxon Southland, that today we sound the drum for freedom. . . . In the name of the greatest people that have ever trod the earth, I draw the line in the dust and toss the gauntlet before the feet of tyranny. And I say"—he paused for a split second—"segregation now! Segregation tomorrow! Segregation forever!"

Wallace's language, in tone if not in content, stood in striking contrast to the sober moderation of his first gubernatorial campaign, in 1958. Not that his own opinions had really changed. His bombastic oratory reflected less the passion of his convictions than it did the moment of history. The transformation of his rhetoric testified to a larger social upheaval—the awakening of black consciousness throughout the South, the growing enthusiasm of northern liberals for the cause of civil rights, and the fear among southern whites that their society would again be conquered and overthrown. Thus Wallace defined himself as a conservative, upholding tradition. Conspicuous in its absence was any overt racial attack. Wallace, as he saw it, was merely fighting for the preservation of popular democracy, which in the state of Alabama existed for whites only. He felt no obligation to fight against history.

As governor, Wallace continued to speak in the name of the plain people. With proper press coverage, he sold one of John Patterson's state yachts and turned the other one into a patrol boat, reduced the automobile fleet by 4,000, and ordered the state police to buy regular gasoline. "I never had money to waste," he explained, "and I'm certainly not going to waste someone else's money." He expressed embarrassment upon learning he was now an honorary member of an exclusive country club. "I don't know how to order from those hifalutin' French menus," he said. "I like simple southern cooking—turnip greens, pole beans, corn bread, iced tea, everything southern. I'm a professional southerner."

But Wallace was no country bumpkin. With measured control of state patronage and state contracts, he created a solid base of friends in the business community. Then he used these allies to gain support for his legislative program. In the first year, he began a huge school-construction program, boosted teacher salaries, obtained a $100-million bond issue for asphalt highways, and attracted $250-million worth of new industry to Alabama. To Wallace, such measures proved his willingness to accommodate social change.

But there were certain changes he would not consider. "Almost instantly," Lurleen recalled, "George started talking about what was happening in Washington with the Kennedy clan. It was almost as though he sensed a destiny which he had to fulfill." One day, in April 1963, Wallace received a visit from United States Attorney General Robert F. Kennedy. "This is a fine city," said Wallace, snapping on the tape recorder for posterity. "Hope y'all enjoy your visit here." When the president's brother attempted to mix business with pleasure, Wallace breezed on about how once in 1957 he personally drove Jack Kennedy to the airport and also contributed $250 to the 1960 campaign. "Both national parties are beginning to consider the attitude of people in our section of the country," he remarked, looking toward 1964. "I feel that we've been kicked around by both parties, and especially by our own national Democratic party."

Pussyfooting aside, Wallace bluntly rebuffed Kennedy's plea for peaceful integration. "I think it's horrifying for the federal courts and the central government to rewrite all the law and force upon the people that which they don't want. . . . I will never myself submit voluntarily to any integration of any school system in Alabama." Besides, he explained, "we have more peace and law and order in Alabama in one minute than you have in an entire year up in Washington, D.C." The best thing, Wallace told Kennedy, was to back off, "let things evolve," wait maybe ten years, maybe a generation. "Listen," he insisted, "I have nothing against people of opposite color. I just don't believe in social and educational mixin'. . . . In fact, you don't have it in Washington," he said, pointing to the master of Hickory Hill. "Everybody's fled to Virginia."

The eruption of civil rights protests in Birmingham in April 1963 and the ensuing police brutality against the demonstrators provided the background for renewed conflict between the governor and the White House. To Wallace, who saw Martin Luther King, Jr., not as a spiritual leader but as "a phony and a fraud," the strategy of civil disobedience represented a fundamental assault on government authority, the stuff of revolution. When President Kennedy, shocked by the use of fire hoses and police dogs against nonviolent marchers, advocated peaceful negotiations, the Alabama governor accused the president of supporting the "pro-communists" who instigated the crisis. "This military dictatorship must be nipped in the bud," warned Wallace, "if free government is to continue."

Aware of the governor's growing popularity throughout the South, Kennedy attempted to shift the tides of public opinion. In May 1963, at the very time Wallace was challenging the president in the courts,

Kennedy flew to Alabama to celebrate the thirtieth anniversary of one of the great symbols of federal power, the Tennessee Valley Authority. The goodwill trip provided an opportunity for the two politicians to meet. "Mr. President," Wallace quipped as they entered Kennedy's helicopter, "you can sit on the left, and I'll sit on the right," and in that order they chatted about civil rights on the brief flight from Muscle Shoals to Huntsville. Neither man offered concessions. "I have no objection to the businessmen hiring who they want to," the governor assured Kennedy. "But I do object to the . . . government telling businessmen what they can and cannot do." Then, to lighten the atmosphere, Wallace regaled the president with stories about black leaders competing to see "who could go to bed with the most nigger women, and white and red women, too." Later, at a press conference, Wallace hedged about whether he would support Kennedy in 1964: "Your guess is as good as mine."

Three days later the impasse reached crisis proportions when a federal judge ordered the admission of qualified black students to the University of Alabama. "I embody the sovereignty of this state," Wallace declared, affirming his campaign promises, "and I will be present to bar the entrance of any Negro who attempts to enroll." To justify his defiance, Wallace happily cited the precedent of his arch-enemy: "If Martin Luther King, in order to test the trespass laws of a state, can break the law when he is only an individual, why can't the governor . . . test the laws?"

As national attention focused on the coming showdown at Wallace's alma mater, the governor became an overnight celebrity. He was invited to appear on NBC's "Meet the Press" (six months earlier the same network had blocked his appearance on a football halftime show), and he was forced to travel incognito; the program itself was moved from Washington to New York for reasons of security. "Down South," he told Gay Talese, then a reporter for *The New York Times*, "at least we shoot straight across the board, we tell you how we feel. Here you practice subterfuge and hypocrisy."

As Wallace waited for the cameras, he fiddled nervously with his fingers, but once the red light flashed he became cool and assured. He insisted that there was only one "basic inherent question" to be discussed: "Can the state of Alabama run its school system? . . ." He denied any desire for martyrdom; his personal disobedience, he explained, provided "a dramatic way to impress upon the American people this omnipotent march of centralized government that is going to destroy the rights and freedom and liberty of the people of this country." He also vowed to prevent violence; he would give the Kennedys no excuse to intervene. "We don't have any utopia in Alabama," he admitted. "Neither do you have it in New York City, where you can't even walk . . . at night without fear of being raped or mugged or shot." When he returned to Montgomery, Wallace bragged about his performance. "All they wanted to know about was niggers," he told a friend, "and I'm the expert."

As the day of confrontation approached, Wallace played hide-and-seek with federal marshals trying to serve a subpoena. But when a federal court issued an injunction, prohibiting Wallace's interference at the state university, he refused to retreat. "I intend to be present personally to bar the entrance of Negro students to the University of Alabama," he announced in a telegram to the press. But he also notified President Kennedy that he intended to maintain law and order, and he made several statewide television speeches urging Alabamians to stay away from Tuscaloosa. "I have kept the faith," he said; "you keep the peace."

In the 95° heat Wallace appeared quite natty in a light gray suit, blue shirt, and striped tie as he awaited the arrival of James Hood and Vivian Malone, two black students accompanied by a small army of federal agents. From the doorway of Foster Auditorium, he watched Assistant Attorney General Nicholas Katzenbach approach through the blistering heat to present a "cease and desist" order from President Kennedy. Wallace raised his hand. "The unwelcomed, unwanted, unwarranted, and force-induced intrusion . . . today of the might of the central government offers a frightful example of the oppression of the rights, privileges, and sovereignty of this state," he read from a prepared statement. "There can be no submission to the theory that the central government is anything but a servant of the people."

Wallace held his ground, while Katzenbach returned to the safety of his car and placed a call to Washington. Then he came back with orders to federalize the Alabama National Guard. Brigadier General Henry Graham, who just a few moments before had taken orders from the governor, now asked Wallace to step aside. "This is a bitter pill to swallow," Wallace replied. Chin erect, he tossed a few rhetorical thrusts that claimed victory for constitutional government. Then the governor stepped aside, and the crisis of Tuscaloosa evaporated into the heat.

Despite his defeat Wallace worked diligently to reverse the decision. When he learned that black student James Hood had apparently disparaged the University of Alabama, the governor ordered the board of trustees to levy charges, exerting enough pressure that the nervous young student, facing expulsion, withdrew voluntarily. Wallace also summoned the state board of education and persuaded it to establish mandatory classes in Bible studies to circumvent the recent Supreme Court ruling against prayers in the schools. "I want the Supreme Court to know," he said defiantly, "we are not going to conform to any such decision."

On September 2, 1963, barely a week after Martin Luther King, Jr., led a March on Washington, the Alabama governor ordered the closing of all public schools facing integration. "We will win regardless of how long the fight is," Wallace promised. "The American people are going to rise up and strike down those who have destroyed the rights of the individual and the states." After one week, however, pressure from the white community forced Wallace to open the schools, at least for whites only. But, with that wedge, the Kennedy administration obtained an injunction against segregation, federalized the National Guard, and again forced the Barbour Bantam to eat crow. "The society is coming apart at the seams," Wallace said in frustration. "What good is it doing to force these situations when white people nowhere in the South want integration? What this country needs," he remarked candidly, "is a few first-class funerals, and some political funerals, too."

Throughout the tumultuous summer, Wallace kept a close eye on his own political future. A proposal to allow the governor to succeed himself in 1966—an important clue to Wallace's limited horizons at that time—failed to win approval from the legislature. But, in the weeks after the Tuscaloosa standoff, the governor received an enormous outpouring of sympathetic letters, and his political ambition, never far from the surface, steadily grew. "It would do the nation good to have a southerner for president," Wallace assured a rally of the Citizens Council of Shreveport, Louisiana, as he launched an embryonic campaign in Dixie. "I believe millions of people throughout the country feel the same way. There is a grass roots rebellion forming." Throughout the South, he reinforced popular prejudices. He denied, for example, that segregation would hurt the American image abroad: "They go to Africa and they tell you that that fellow leaning on his spear is concerned about civil rights. The average native of Uganda doesn't know where he is, much less where Georgia is."

By November 1963 Wallace was prepared to test his popularity in the North—in the heart of Kennedy country, Harvard University. There he appealed to the conservative instincts of the Ivy League elite. With the thoroughness of a corporation lawyer, he defended segregation on the basis of the sanctity of contracts, private property, and the independence of the judiciary. He distinguished carefully between the refined Negroes of the North and "the real African" of the South, whom he depicted as a latter-day Sambo—"easygoing, basically happy, unambitious." Southern whites had borne this special burden for generations. "It is our problem, not yours," he said simply. When he was done, the packed auditorium erupted into a standing ovation. The presence of some noisy pickets outside, however, forced the governor to exit through the steam-pipe-cluttered basement of Sanders Theater.

Three weeks later Wallace was just completing the dedication ceremonies at a new high school in Haleyville, Alabama, when he learned that President Kennedy had been killed in Dallas. "We may disagree with people in public office because of philosophy and attitude," he said with genuine remorse, "but this attack on the chief executive is an attack upon the American system, and I'm sure that whoever did it had the universal malice for all people of this country." Declaring an official month of mourning in Alabama, Wallace flew to Washington to attend the ¿funeral. As he moved through the airport, a reporter approached him to ask a question, one that would haunt his conscience: "Are you glad now you have a southern president?" "This transcends any political question," Wallace replied. But for days afterward he greeted visitors with an embarrassing question of his own: "Do you think I helped kill Kennedy?"

Phyllis
Stewart
Schlafly
(I)

Phyllis MacAlpin Stewart was born on August 15, 1924, in St. Louis, Missouri. She was the first child of a modest, moderately pious Roman Catholic family that traced its lineage through three of her grandparents back to the American Revolution. She cherished her descent: "I think you're a product of your family, sure," she said in an interview long after she had become famous as Phyllis Schlafly.

Her father, John Bruce Stewart, seventeen years older than his wife, had worked as a salesman of engineering equipment for the Westinghouse Corporation since 1905. It was a good white-collar job. He loved the routine and the regular paychecks that provided his family with middle-class comforts in a rented house in the suburbs. Bruce Stewart was an engineer at heart, though not by training; he tinkered in his spare hours, hoping to achieve by sheer gimmickry the kind of success that had turned Ford and Edison and Westinghouse into household names. Phyllis's mother, Odile Dodge, a strong, determined woman from an old St. Louis family, took care of the domestic affairs, which centered primarily on Phyllis. For nearly six years she was an only child, her parents' delight, winsome, sweet-tempered, precocious. Her father called her baby and continued to do so even after she had grown up. She began public school at the age of four, a year earlier than most children, and she excelled. "We had a happy home life," she has recalled. "It was modest."

Phyllis's childhood, idyllic as any family romance, abruptly cracked apart in 1930 when the Depression struck and Westinghouse dismissed her father. His efforts to find another job were unsuccessful. Answering help-wanted ads, draining his limited savings, scrimping, always scrimping, Bruce Stewart remained optimistic about full recovery, but his prolonged unemployment inevitably affected his family. "I grew up in a poor home where a dollar meant a whole lot," Mrs. Schlafly says. Unable to provide for his wife and daughters, Bruce sent them off to live with his wife's uncle in Los Angeles, where Phyllis spent the fourth grade and where the separation from her father intensified the sense of crisis. "There were hard years," she remembers; "then he was in his 50's and too old."

Bruce Stewart, true to his Republican convictions, never accepted defeat, even after the prospects of finding work shriveled with his age. He hated FDR and the New Deal, refused to blame the American economic system for his troubles, and, to prove his faith in free enterprise, he embarked on a bold engineering project—the invention of a rotary engine—that would, he hoped, restore his standing, his fortune, and his self-esteem. After seventeen years Bruce Stewart finally obtained a patent, though he could never sell the design for production. For his eldest daughter it was not the result, however, but the effort that became the touchstone of genius. "The true stories of American inventors," she later wrote, "teach the virtues of hard work, determination in the face of tremendous odds, and personal discipline, which are the requisites of success."

While Bruce Stewart struggled for vindication, the burdens of survival slipped onto the sturdy shoulders of his wife, "a very strong woman in the face of adversity." Rejecting her exile in California, she returned with her daughters to St. Louis and took a job selling cloth and draperies in a department store, at $12 a week. She moved her family from the suburbs into an apartment they could share with her parents. She found, as a step upward, a one-year teaching job in the public schools and then, as another step, became librarian at the St. Louis Art Museum, although according to Phyllis Schlafly her mother "would much rather have been a full-time homemaker. You do what you have to do in the face of necessity." Despite Mrs. Stewart's resourcefulness, she could support only the simplest of circumstances. "We had less money than anybody I knew," her daughter would remember. "I never had a store-bought dress till I worked for one myself." One year the choice between a winter coat and a bicycle underscored the utter absence of luxury: "I never had a bicycle. . . . Never had a bicycle. Never had a bicycle."

Having witnessed the collapse of her mother's expectations, Phyllis adopted her own strategies against insecurity. She treated her young life as a job, placing emphasis on such values as obedience, self-discipline, and punctuality. As a Girl Scout she won five gold medals for perfect attendance. "I felt a compulsion," she admitted to her biographer, "to get myself trained to support myself, which my mother had done before me and very fortunately." Odile Stewart made considerable sacrifices for her daughters. She even took a second job so that they could attend the prestigious City House school, run by the Sisters of the Sacred Heart. In this disciplined atmosphere the girl thrived on the classical curriculum. She demonstrated an academic proficiency that teachers and classmates alike considered "extraordinary," "brilliant," and "serious." She finished first in her class each quarter, except for the term when she had the measles. In June 1941 she graduated as class valedictorian at age sixteen. "I've been very lucky in being in such a class at such a school," she wrote at the time. "The girls were not only versatile . . . but also came from the good, long-standing St. Louis families whose homes I was always proud to visit."

Phyllis's studies were reinforced by a deliberate pursuit of cultural elegance. Unable to afford tickets to the St. Louis Symphony, Odile had her daughter write for complimentary seats, which Phyllis received for ten consecutive seasons. Dancing lessons at the Junior League, a matinee at the ballet or the theater, or an evening ball in St. Louis society—all supplemented the academic lessons and suggest a certain worldliness. But her religious education emphasized the dangers of social intercourse and warned that physical pleasure might lead to sin. She showed no interest in sports or physical education; to be athletic, she thought, would appear unfeminine. She also distrusted her bodily instincts. "The sexual desire of men is much stronger than that of women," she would write. "The other side of the coin is that it is easier for women to control their sexual appetites."

Her great passion was for education. After high school she won a scholarship to Maryville College, another Sacred Heart institution, in south St. Louis, where again she received all A's, except in "health." But her success there merely whetted her intelligence, and she decided, against the advice of her Catholic instructors, to transfer after the first year to the more stimulating (and coeducational) Washington University, in St. Louis. "The best thing my parents gave me," she later said with pride, "was the desire for a college education—and not a dime to pay for it." Benefiting from the boom in wartime work, Phyllis took a job as a test gunner at the St. Louis Ordnance Plant, firing ammunition on swing shift and at night. She started at $105 a week, which to her dismay was $20 less than the men were paid. She worked a forty-eight-hour week. She was seventeen years old.

By day Phyllis carried a full load of coursework: "I didn't belong to a sorority, didn't go to any parties. It was a strictly budgeted, time-managed life." Nor did she envy her less industrious classmates: "I thought what I was doing was better. Better. Better." This sense of superiority paid off in her academic performance. A political science major (the quirky result of class scheduling), she crammed four years' work into three and still graduated Phi Beta Kappa, qualified for the political science honors society, and received an invitation to enroll in the Ph.D. program. Her only grades below A were in physical education and, because of her fear of the water and a loathing for public showers, she also managed to avoid the mandatory test in swimming.

Attracted to graduate school, she accepted a Whitney Fellowship to study political science at Radcliffe (Columbia had offered her more money, but she felt that Harvard would be more valuable in the future). In the autumn of 1944 the twenty-year-old graduate headed for Cambridge, Massachusetts, where she settled into another academic routine. For the first time, though, she enjoyed something of a social life, sightseeing around New England and accompanying Harvard men to concerts and the theater. "Take advantage of the wonderful opportunity," her father advised. "It is unique and so are you." Within nine months Phyllis earned her master's degree as well as some earnest solicitations to enter the Harvard doctoral program in political science. One professor urged her to enroll in the law school, which would have broken the ancient male-only tradition. But Phyllis was by now ready to leave the academic nest: "I read all the novels when I was in high school and college. . . . You go through a period of life when you have vicarious pleasure and you want to escape into the world of fiction and entertainment. And then you get down to the real world."

For an ambitious political scientist, the real world was in government. In September 1945, just after V-J Day, Phyllis went to Washington, D.C., but arrived in the very month when the federal government began to trim the war-swollen bureaucracy. Undaunted by the shrinking opportunity, she looked for work in the burgeoning industry known as government consulting, where her talents for research and writing might help the politicians formulate public policies. Like her father, Phyllis had always believed that individual initiative was much better than any "socialistic" programs. Like him, she detested the New Deal, with its alphabets and government regulations. At the American Enterprise Association, which for the previous two years had been lobbying congressmen about the virtues of the free enterprise system, they liked this levelheaded approach and gave her a job. She learned to type, took a public-speaking course (won first prize), and launched her career writing research reports and speeches from the pro-business point of view.

The Republican campaign slogan of 1946—"Had enough?"— mirrored Phyllis's feelings. After a year, she had had enough of Washington, too. She collected her excellent references and returned to St. Louis. She soon learned that a young lawyer named Claude Bakewell was running for Congress against the New Deal incumbent, and she offered to help him. As the only regular campaign worker, Phyllis wrote press releases, arranged speaking engagements, and answered the phones. She enjoyed writing speeches that denounced the Democrats for passing high taxes, creating food and housing shortages, and allowing communists to infiltrate the government. In November Bakewell's upset victory renewed her faith in the voters.

While running the congressional campaign, Phyllis also started a full-time job with a pair of St. Louis banks. She had been hired as a combination librarian, speechwriter, and editor of a four-page monthly newsletter called *The St. Louis Union Trust Company Letter.* "We believe that the people we serve are basically anti–New Deal," she wrote. "The continued success of the St. Louis Union Trust Company is obviously dependent on the continued prosperity of its customers. We believe that the continued prosperity of our customers is dependent on the preservation of a society which exalts personal integrity and freedom, rather than a society which idealizes the all-powerful state."

As the local "blond banking expert," she began to develop a career
as volunteer speaker to civic groups and luncheon clubs. Usually her
talks stressed the availability of financial opportunity. "You don't have
to be a millionaire to be concerned about trusts," she lectured the
Zonta Club of St. Louis. "When women have been able to get ade-
quate information and experience in investing, they have done as well
as men, but most women never get enough of either." In her monthly
newsletter she also extolled free enterprise. "Before the meaning of
freedom was debased by neo-liberals, freedom and responsibility went
hand in hand," she said, echoing the sentiments of her father. "The
man of modest means who sends his children to college chooses to
scrimp and save and sacrifice to do so. The left wing rejects responsibility. . . . Freedom under this definition is the freedom to gratify one's
desires without making the slightest sacrifice or suffering the slightest
inconvenience."

One happy reader, a corporation lawyer with clients such as Shell
Oil, rushed downtown to congratulate the editor, took a long look at
her fair hair and slender frame, and decided to find out more. At
thirty-nine Mr. J. (for John) Fred Schlafly, Jr., was already a prosperous
attorney in Alton, Illinois, fifteen years her senior, and a confirmed
bachelor, but, as Phyllis expressed it, "It was love at first sight." Theirs
was a cautious courtship—once-a-week dates in such places as the
nearby law library during which they indulged in endless conversation,
sometimes in verse and rhyme, about love, politics, and the cold war.
This was how Fred wrote to her of marriage:

> Cover girl with executive know-how,
> You don't desire a home now.
> For Küche, Kirche, and Kinder,
> Will sure a career hinder.

Phyllis never paused. Whatever her professional aspirations, she
remained first the daughter of a poverty-stricken family, and the offer
of marriage meant one thing she could not resist: "Fred," she liked to
say, "rescued me from the life of a working girl." Never again would
Phyllis or her family feel the strain of economic insecurity, and she
came to regard her own escape as a model for other women to imitate.

The Schlaflys' wedding in October 1949, amid "a profusion of
white chrysanthemums and snapdragons, combined with greencry and
lighted tapers" at St. Louis Cathedral did indeed knit together a mutual

passion for kitchen, church, and children. "A family cannot be run by committee," Mrs. Schlafly later stated. "If marriage is to be a successful institution, it must . . . have an ultimate decision maker, and that is the husband." Her notion of a good marriage reflected her Catholic upbringing. She believed that even good men like Fred, with their naturally strong sexual appetites, forever needed the moral restraint of women. Fred was an avid wrestler and a physical-fitness buff long before it became popular, but Phyllis claimed a superior strength· "A Positive Woman can not defeat a man in a wrestling or a boxing match, but she can motivate him, inspire him, encourage him, teach him, restrain him, reward him, and have power over him that he can never achieve over her with all his muscle." Using psychological warfare in the battle between the sexes, Mrs. Schlafly could appear more passive than she really was. "Whereas a woman's chief emotional need is active (i.e., to love)," she admitted, in a curious inversion of roles, "a man's prime emotional need is passive (i.e., to be appreciated or admired)." She had, after all, learned the same reversal in her own family.

With Fred thinking he made the decisions, Phyllis followed him across the Mississippi River to Alton, a hilly, tree-lined factory town whose chief historical significance was as the place where the abolitionist editor Elijah Lovejoy had been lynched by his pro-slavery neighbors in 1837. While Fred immersed himself in his law practice and solidified his fortune, Phyllis kept a neat house, pursued her interests in current affairs, and began to enter Alton society—the YWCA, the DAR, and various charitable organizations. A conservative Catholic, Fred imparted a more dogmatic perspective to his wife's world view. She came to share his feelings and his fears that Christian civilization was indeed imperiled by the spread of atheistic communism. The fall of China in 1949, the explosion of a Soviet A-bomb, Senator Joseph McCarthy waving lists of names, the outbreak of the Korean War—all kindled a continuing conversation between Fred and Phyllis about the precarious state of American freedom. She allowed Fred, encouraged him, to become her mentor. They named their first child, a son born in 1950, John, after his father. Yet Mrs. Schlafly clearly controlled the home front. Asked once if Fred had ever changed the diapers, she replied, "No. I did it better," and then she added, with a happy laugh, "but if he had, we'd still be living in that *little house.*"

The extent of Mrs. Schlafly's ambition emerged unexpectedly early in 1952. One evening a few of the leading Republicans in town came to call upon Fred with the suggestion that he run for Congress.

He quickly assured them that he had no interest in leaving his law practice to seek public office in the traditionally Democratic district; the three-term incumbent, Melvin Price, seemed unbeatable. But if Fred Schlafly exercised a modicum of caution, his wife felt no such restraint. No sooner had he rejected the proposal than she volunteered to run in his place. Whatever her commitments to motherhood and housewifery, she preferred the public arena. Here was an opportunity to put the lessons of political science into practice. "There are thousands of people terribly disturbed about the present situation, but most of them are doing nothing but sitting around and criticizing," she said. "I was one of these critics, too; then I decided to do something about it. To seek political office has been my goal since I started studying public affairs and government."

The "powder-puff candidate," as she was called, was off and running. She announced her candidacy in January 1952: "As a housewife, I am greatly concerned about the fact that we have the highest prices and the highest taxes in our country's history—caused by wasteful government spending, graft, and a policy of betraying our friends and arming our enemies." Adopting the national Republican formula, "C_2K_1"—Corruption, Communism, Korea—she "flapped around the district," as she put it, delivering a different speech on a different topic almost every day: "I never ran out of ammunition."

After her victory in the April primary, party leaders invited Mrs. Schlafly—"as a tribute," one of them explained, "to the important role women have in public affairs today"—to present the keynote speech at the state party convention in Springfield, Illinois. "A woman's place is in the home," the twenty-eight-year-old candidate told the delegates. "It is also true that a woman's place is to defend her home." Under Roosevelt and Truman, she said, the government exceeded its limits "and has invaded the American home," forcing "American women [to] go into politics this year [to] fight for a complete housecleaning." Cheers and applause interrupted her speech as she attacked the Democrats for "betraying our friends in Poland . . . betraying our own boys in Korea," and betraying the Constitution. The speech immediately built her reputation throughout the state.

In the summer of 1952 she accompanied Fred to the Republican National Convention in Chicago. There she watched in disgust as the Eisenhower delegates outmaneuvered conservative Robert Taft for the nomination. That Eisenhower would be the more popular candidate— perhaps with coattails long enough to help congressional candidates like herself—seemed less important to her than a loyalty to conservative principles. She would neither forgive nor forget the moderate Republicans for their ruthless tactics against Taft; indeed, the manipulation of party conventions would become a major theme in her writings. Yet she loved the sheer excitement of the experience and resolved to attend as many future conventions as she could.

Despite her energy and verve Mrs. Schlafly proved no match against her Democratic opponent, who in a landslide won the fourth of his twenty-plus consecutive terms in Congress. "I never had a chance," she recalled. Asked by a reporter if she had lost because her name was Phyllis and not Philip, she insisted that "sex had nothing to do with it." Not for a moment did the defeat lead her to reevaluate her politics or to question the conservative ideology she espoused. Instead she offered a strictly partisan explanation of the outcome: "I lost because I ran in the 24th District and I'm a Republican, not a Democrat. It's as simple as that." Although she took pride in having waged a campaign that focused on the issues, it did not occur to her that it was her ideas and arguments—not just her party affiliation—that the voters found unsatisfactory.

After her loss Mrs. Schlafly resumed her career as housewife and community worker. She held office in such civic groups as the Junior League and worked on fund raising and charity campaigns for organizations like the Community Chest. But her special pleasure, her hobby, came from political speech making. With the fervor of a missionary, she carried the conservative message through the towns and suburbs of southern Illinois and St. Louis. She always endorsed Republican candidates. Yet she preferred to speak about issues and ideas, which is to say, anti-communist themes, and she tried more to persuade her listeners to her point of view than to support a politician. During the fever of the Army-McCarthy hearings in 1954, for example, she said less about the senator's tactics than she did about the necessity of congressional investigations. Her support of McCarthy, however, was undisguised. That year she also published a bibliography titled *A Reading List for Americans,* which offered ammunition for the war against communism. The birth of a second son in 1955 and a third in 1957 cut back her activities only slightly. "My career rose and fell depending on how many diapers I had to change that year," she has explained. But she also learned to budget her time with the precision of an efficiency expert, and she continued to work actively in Republican politics on the local and state levels.

Mrs. Schlafly went to Washington in 1956 as a board member of the National Federation of Republican Women, met the Eisenhowers at the White House, and agreed to serve as "secretary of the treasury" in the president's "Kitchen Kabinet," along with such celebrities as Hedda Hopper, sharing "GOP recipes on GOP accomplishments" in a monthly newsletter called *What's Cooking in Washington.* More seriously, she directed a regional seminar, "Techniques of Communism," and developed study guides that became models for anti-communist instruction throughout the country. Based on little-known government reports, these programs provided, Mrs. Schlafly said, "one of the very best methods of combating false propaganda and of educating women to be missionaries for republican principles."

Elected as a delegate to the Republican National Convention in 1956, she backed Eisenhower and Nixon. In the general elections she campaigned actively, delighting audiences with elaborate parodies of Democratic candidate Adlai Stevenson. In a rich soprano voice, she sang:

> The eggheads like my stuff,
> The ADA is for me;
> But voters still ignore me,
> And Illinois has had enough,
> Illinois has had enough!

She also introduced a quiz game for Republicans, Information Please, which raised indelicate questions about the Democrats:

"Which New Deal millionaire, who inherited $40 million and a 150-room mansion, said . . . in 1952, 'We can stand higher taxes'?" [Averell Harriman]

"What prominent New Dealer, noted for his bitter attacks on private property, married two millionaire heiresses and made the taxpayers pay the cost of his honeymoon to Alaska?" [Harold Ickes]

Cheered by the Republican victory in November, Mrs. Schlafly still complained about the president's failure to support the anti-communist revolution in Hungary. "Had Americans understood the communist dialectic," she said, "they would have known that we could have intervened to aid the Hungarian freedom fighters . . . without running any risk of World War III." She found inspiration in Hungarian Cardinal Mindszenty, who during the uprising had found sanctuary inside the American Embassy in Budapest: "Most great leaders," she later wrote in a biography of Mindszenty, "are ordinary, uninspired people who have made the decision within themselves (1) to accept the responsibilities of leadership, and (2) to pay the painful price that leadership demands. For most people, the responsibility is too heavy a burden and the price of discipline and perseverance is too high."

Division Leaders Named for Red Cross

Mrs. Phyllis Schlafly is chairman for local organizations which she has held for the last three years. She is a member of the Community Chest budget committee, has served two terms as chairman of the Young Women's Christian Association finance committee, and is active in the St. Louis Symphony maintenance drive.

Mrs. Schlafly is Regent of Alton Chapter of the D.A.R. and state chairman of national defense.

After attending high school in St. Louis, she attended Washington University in St. Louis, and Radcliffe College in Cambridge, Mass., where she received an advanced degree.

Mrs. Schlafly is the wife of J.F. Schlafly Jr., of 1212 Callahan Dr. They are the parents of three children.

—*Alton Evening Telegraph*, March 4, 1958

On March 10, 1958, Mrs. Schlafly went to Chicago to conduct a seminar on national defense at the annual meeting of the Illinois Daughters of the American Revolution. There she described the "battle of ideas" as an endless daily struggle against propaganda and subversion. "Not outer space," said the thirty-three-year-old housewife from Alton, "but Hometown, U.S.A., is the battle line for national defense." She introduced a new quiz about communism:

"What prominent Fair Deal politician said nine times that Congressional investigations of Communism were a 'red herring'?"

"Which New Deal President told Congressman Martin Dies, 'There is nothing wrong with the Communists; some of the best friends I have got are Communists'?"

"What famous Communist document published in 1848 originated the idea (which the New Deal put into practice) of 'A heavy progressive, or graduated, income tax'?"

To her delight the answers came invariably from the other side of the aisle—Truman, Roosevelt, the Communist Manifesto. She

viewed them as statements of treason that proved the correctness of
her politics and the peril of the moment.

"What Communist spy wrote the United Nations charter and was
its first Secretary-General?"

"What former New Deal Ambassador to Soviet Russia said this:
'The word of honor of the Soviet Government is as safe as the
Bible. . . .'?"

She showed the motion picture *Communism Is a Disease.*

"Do you support organizations working to repeal the Declaration
of Independence?" she asked.

Mrs. Schlafly offered straightforward remedies. "If you have a
good, patriotic, anti-Communist, economy-minded congressman, give
him the support he needs to be reelected." Patronize companies that
advertise in pro-America publications. Insist that "discipline, hard
work, self-reliance, competition, and pride of accomplishment be restored as standards for [our] schools."

Mrs. Schlafly was a popular figure in DAR circles. In 1958 she
served as regent of the Ninian Edwards chapter of Alton, as state
chairman in charge of national defense, and as delegate to the "Continental Congress," which met in Washington, D.C., at cherry blossom
time. Between sessions she attended a concert by the United States
Army Band, visited the White House for tea, and returned to Alton,
restored in her faith. In May 1958 she was reelected regent of her
chapter. Like her hero, Cardinal Mindszenty, Mrs. Schlafly welcomed
the responsibility of leadership.

Surrounded by her children, sometimes as many as three in diapers at a time, she persevered in the crusade against atheism, communism, and liberalism. With her new baby, Phyllis, she attended the
1958 state Republican convention in Galesburg, the annual meeting of
the Illinois Federation of Republican Women in Springfield, and
joined a special reception at the governor's mansion. She was named
first-vice-president of the federation and endorsed "operation coffee
cup," a ladies' program to introduce candidates to the voters. With
these duties, her time became precious; she learned to discipline not
only her own schedule but the activities of her children as well.

Her family, she insisted, would always come first. "No woman
would ever, as Karl Marx did, spend years reading political philosophy
in the British Museum," she asserted, "while her child starved to
death." Indeed, she kept her children out of school until they were
seven so that she could supervise their education. ("When I started to

teach my children to read at home, the unanimous view of everybody of my entire acquaintance . . . was that I was somewhere between foolish and wicked.") Conscientious about homemaking, as about everything else, she established a regimen of healthy nutrition, rejecting processed foods in favor of unpasteurized milk, wheat germ, brown sugar, and bottled water. "We particularly agree on national defense, anti-communism, opposition to détente, exercise, and good nutrition," her husband later told a reporter. "We avoid many of the things that often hurt a marriage, such as alcohol and cigarettes, and we stick to foods that are not overrefined."

Inside their shuttered white-brick house on Callahan Drive, behind the maples and green pines and white picket fence, the Schlaflys would gather at the dinner table and lament the ignorance of American citizens. It was the fall of 1958. Phyllis said that "too few people understand what communism is, or recognize it under numerous disguises." Fred agreed; so did his sister Eleanor Schlafly. They decided, therefore, to start an organization "to combat communism with knowledge and facts." They named it the Cardinal Mindszenty Foundation, after their spiritual hero. Its intellectual basis, Mrs. Schlafly explained, was "the great Encyclical *Atheistic Communism,*" and its "unique pitch" would be a council of advisers consisting of Catholic leaders who had personally survived the torments of communist dictatorship. Mrs. Schlafly's tasks involved research, writing, and the development of group-study programs that provided "a realistic description of communist objectives and tactics."

She soon compiled an updated reading list for patriots, titled *Inside the Communist Conspiracy,* "designed to combat what Pope Pius XI called 'the conspiracy of silence.' " Recommending such books as *A World Gone Crazy* by Robert Welch and Senator Joseph McCarthy's *Retreat from Victory* and *The Fight for America,* the 116-title bibliography attempted to overcome "world ignorance of Communist tactics" and the "American failure to grasp the fact that we are already engaged in total war with the Communists." (The Mindszenty Foundation also distributed the magnum opus of J. Fred Schlafly, Jr.: the 1957 *Report of the American Bar Association on Communist Tactics, Strategy, and Objectives,* a condemnation of Supreme Court decisions that "threaten the right of the United States to protect itself against Communist subversion." Its original publication provoked Chief Justice Earl Warren to resign from the ABA.)

Besides the book lists, Mrs. Schlafly prepared a basic ten-lesson course in communism "that any teacher can put . . . into immediate and effective use." Within months the Mindszenty Foundation sponsored some five hundred seminars and study groups on the evils of communism, in Catholic high schools, colleges, and seminaries around the country.

To spread the alarm, Mrs. Schlafly addressed a wide variety of community groups—the county medical society, a Good Citizens luncheon, the Rotary Club, Americans for Freedom—drafted formal reports for the DAR on such topics as "Communism in the Movie Industry," participated in panel discussions and seminars, and regularly wrote "letters to the editor." "I was approaching things strictly on an intellectual basis in those days," she recalls. "I had the idea that an intellectual argument would persuade." Robert Welch, head of the John Birch Society, would describe Mrs. Schlafly as "one of our most loyal members," but she herself emphatically denied any such affiliation.

In the continuing cold war, Mrs. Schlafly claimed a special expertise. After "fifteen years of sustained study and patient research," she wrote in 1960, she had discovered the secret pattern of the communist conspiracy: "Just as the movement of the planets are predictable by astronomers, so are Communist movements predictable by those who have studied the dialectic. . . . Their future actions are plotted with all the precision of our guided missiles." She described the strategy of "semantic sabotage," the switch of ordinary words to mean the very opposite of what they seemed. "When the communists say they want peace," she said, "they really mean they want to conquer the world one piece at a time," and she warned about "the clever Communist tactics to destroy patriotism by smear words, such as super-patriot and flag-waver."

In 1960 Mrs. Schlafly served as an alternate delegate to the Republican National Convention, pledged to Vice-President Nixon. To her surprise she also received eight write-in votes in the Republican congressional primary; in the absence of any other candidate, she became the official Republican nominee for Congress. "You can't stop people from writing in," she said. But, in contrast to her position in 1952, she refused the bait. "While I believe in the two-party system and appreciate the vote I received," she declared, "I will not be a candidate." And she meant it. She waged no campaign, neither received money nor spent it, and she used her own visibility to promote the campaigns of other Republicans. "It was a hopeless situation," she said of Melvin Price's landslide in November 1960. On the brighter side, Mrs. Schlafly was elected president of the Illinois Federation of Republican Women, an organization that claimed twenty-seven thousand members, and she exerted her influence for Nixon.

At the Republican National Convention in Chicago, however, she felt betrayed by his willingness to negotiate with Governor Nelson Rockefeller, whom she considered too liberal. "I believe this to be immoral politics," she said later, quoting Barry Goldwater on the subject. For Mrs. Schlafly the seduction of Nixon by the "New York kingmakers" proved the importance of political vigilance, even among friends. She preferred forthright conservatives. As president of the host-state Republican women, she organized an elaborate "Hukilau" luncheon at the Palmer House in Chicago to honor the fiftieth state, and she invited Senator Goldwater as the main speaker. Mrs. Schlafly gleamed at the head table, wearing "a pink dress with white lace top, which looked particularly pretty with the pink orchid lei sent from Hawaii." She was excited by Goldwater's remarks, agreeing with him that Republicans "all believe in the freedom of the individual, and that's what makes us different [from the Democrats]." "Goldwater was exciting at that convention," she recalls. "I gave Goldwater his first national Republican platform."

After the convention, Mrs. Schlafly worked for Nixon and Lodge: "I made speeches; I went to meetings; I encouraged the activities of our organization on behalf of the Republican ticket." She introduced candidates at public meetings, and, in an imitation of the celebrated Nixon-Kennedy debates, she confronted Representative Melvin Price on television and derided the Democrats for "downgrading" America. Kennedy's claim that the United States had lost international prestige, she said, played into the hands of the Russians by perpetuating the myth of communist invincibility. As a poll watcher, she was appalled by Kennedy's narrow victory in Illinois. "We had the firsthand evidence of how that election was stolen in the city of Chicago," she later claimed. "There was no question of the crookedness of it." Yet, for reasons that she never understood, Nixon declined to ask for a recount.

After the election Mrs. Schlafly continued her activities as conservative polemicist and Republican leader, although the birth of her fifth child, a son, briefly interrupted her schedule. She served as recording secretary of the Illinois DAR—"the most terrible job I ever did in my whole life was to edit a lot of . . . illiterate things written by other people"—but her major concern remained the threat of international communism. In a lecture, "The Cold War Inside America," which she presented at every opportunity to women's clubs and service organizations, she reported that there were over two hundred communist-front organizations operating in the United States. "They have infiltrated every conceivable sphere of activity: youth groups, radio, television and motion picture industries; church, school, educational and cultural groups; the press, nationality and minority groups, and civil and political units."

Mrs. Schlafly despised the Kennedy administration's response to the communist menace. She condemned the president's failure to support the Bay of Pigs invasion; she attacked Secretary of Defense Robert McNamara's decision, made in the interest of cost-accounting, to dismantle the vaunted St. Louis Ordnance Plant (where once she had worked to pay her way through college) and then have the entire operation crated in boxes and shipped to India."Disarmament in the face of an enemy whose purpose is to destroy Western civilization is morally wrong," Mrs. Schlafly asserted, "a betrayal of our children's right to live in a free and independent country, and a betrayal of our persecuted brethren behind the iron curtain who pray for liberation."

Reelected as president of the Illinois Federation of Republican Women in 1962, she attended the national women's convention, at which Senator Barry Goldwater affirmed the conservative cause. "Our opposition is committed to change our way of life," he said, "and let's wake up to it." She liked that phrase. During the Cuban Missile Crisis in October 1962, Mrs. Schlafly inaugurated a weekly fifteen-minute radio show, "America, Wake Up!" Sponsored by the DAR, her commentary reiterated the communist peril and demanded "victory over this godless menace." She also supported the campaign of Senator Everett Dirksen. After the elections of November 1962, the Schlaflys moved from their modest brick house into a Tudor mansion that overlooked the bluffs of the Mississippi River. It had carved wood ceilings, polished floors, and vast spaces; also, in the basement, a partial bomb shelter stocked with food for a month, although Mrs. Schlafly later assured a reporter "you only need it for two weeks, the time it takes to get rid of the fallout."

At a time when the liberals in the Kennedy administration were saying that the complexity of governmental problems demanded sophisticated and technological solutions, Mrs. Schlafly inhabited a world that honored old-fashioned simplicity. "Civilization progresses, freedom is won, and problems are solved," she observed, "because we have wonderful people who think up simple solutions! It is not the complicated, round-about Rube Goldberg approach that accomplishes anything, but the direct approach that goes to the heart of the problem." The same simplicity, she insisted, could solve the problems that plagued President Kennedy. Take Cuba: "The Monroe Doctrine would bring peace today if we only had a government with courage enough to use it. . . . We should not submit to the international blackmail of the false claim that using the Monroe Doctrine will start World War III." As for the Berlin problem, she offered "a very simple solution"—threaten to close down the Russian Embassy in Washington. In Africa, "a very simple solution to what to do about the Congo: let the Congolese solve it!"

When President Kennedy, in a speech at American University in June 1963, called for a nuclear test ban treaty with the Soviet Union, Mrs. Schlafly protested this "official confirmation of the . . . master plan . . . that we must not seek victory of the U.S. over the Soviet Union or of capitalism over Communism." Using her connections with Senator Dirksen, she arranged to testify against the treaty before the Senate Foreign Relations Committee in August 1963: "I appear here as a mother who is eager that her five small children have the opportunity to grow up in a free and independent America, and because I do not want my children to suffer the fate of children in Cuba, China, and the 20 captive nations."

Her reasoning was simple: "All Americans want to maintain peace and prevent World War III." The nation, therefore, faced only two alternatives: "(1) To rely on American military strength, or (2) to rely on Communist promises." Citing an aphorism she attributed to Lenin —"promises are like piecrusts, made to be broken"—she scoffed at the idea of trusting the Russians: "The Communists believe in sneak attacks. . . . If the Senate approves this Moscow treaty, then America, the last, best hope of mankind, may be at the mercy of the dictators who already control a third of the world." But her testimony failed to change the mind even of Senator Dirksen.

Despite the ratification of the Nuclear Test Ban Treaty, Mrs. Schlafly expressed confidence in conservative prospects. At the twenty-fifth anniversary banquet of the Illinois Federation of Republican Women in the fall of 1963, she had arranged once more for a speech by anti-treaty Senator Barry Goldwater and felt vindicated by the enthusiastic response of his audience. "I insisted on Barry Goldwater, and I got him," she boasted. "It ranks as one of the most exciting days of my life."

Goldwater's growing popularity reflected some subtle political shifts. Within the Republican party the defeat of Nixon had weakened the position of the eastern "liberal" faction that had dominated the GOP through the 1940s and 1950s. (It was this group that had blocked Taft in 1952 and had forced Nixon to compromise on the party platform in 1960.) Yet the very narrowness of Kennedy's victory suggested that the Democrats would be vulnerable in 1964. The president's support of civil rights threatened his party's control of the once-solid South, and his muting of the cold war might weaken his appeal among liberal anti-communists. Like Goldwater, therefore, Mrs. Schlafly argued that the next election would depend upon a clear distinction of party lines, a forthright expression of the issues and ideology that separated Republicans from Democrats, conservatives from liberals. In Goldwater she recognized a candidate who might appeal not only to party labels but to a conservative revival. But first he would have to carry the national convention.

Mrs. Schlafly was attending a Republican meeting at the Jefferson Hotel in St. Louis to discuss the presidential contest when she heard the news that Kennedy had been shot in Dallas. "No one who lived through the trauma of tragedy and outrage . . . will ever forget it," she said. Her shock was blunted, however, by a certainty of how it all had happened. "It had to be some silly little Communist," she would say, quoting a statement attributed to Kennedy's widow.

But, although the assassination of President Kennedy seemed to confirm her warnings of subversion, the experience altered her career in a dramatic and fundamental way. She had been scheduled to address a "Goldwater for president" organization at Southwestern Illinois University, but she decided that in the post-assassination atmosphere "it was inappropriate to be lambasting the Democrats for all their sins, grievous as they were." Instead, she spoke about a subject that had been on her mind for years: "How Political Conventions Are Stolen." When published the next year, it firmly established her national reputation.

John Herschel Glenn (I)

The National Aeronautics and Space Administration commenced operations on October 1, 1958. In its first week it approved Project Mercury, the program to place a man in space. In December President Eisenhower ordered NASA to select its candidates from among qualified military test pilots. In another month the Committee on Life Sciences produced a psychological profile of the ideal astronaut: "There should be . . . sufficient drive and creativity . . . relative freedom from conflict and anxiety . . . [he should] not be over-dependent on others . . . able to tolerate either close associations or extreme isolation . . . able to function when out of familiar surroundings . . . [and] must show . . . ability to respond predictably. . . . There should be no evidence of impulsiveness. . . . He must be able to tolerate stress situations passively, without requiring motor activity to dissipate anxiety."

The characteristics most desired of America's first astronaut—independence, self-discipline, and predictability—closely resembled the values of small-town America in the 1920s. For John Herschel Glenn, Jr., born on July 18, 1921, in a white clapboard house in Cambridge, Ohio, these qualities reflected the expectations of his childhood and youth. "It's the kind of place," he later said of his hometown, "where there were certain things everyone was *absolutely* expected to do, like saluting the flag and showing up at the graveyard with flowers on Memorial Day." His parents were rooted people. The senior John Herschel Glenn, a farm boy descended from Ohio pioneers, kept his eyes fixed on the comfortable horizons of his ancestors, leaving home only to serve in the American Expeditionary Forces during World War I. Stationed briefly in Montgomery, Alabama, he married there his hometown sweetheart, Clara Sproat, a college graduate, who interrupted teaching school in rural Ohio to join him and then returned to Cambridge when he was shipped overseas. Their plans after the war were as modest as their circumstances. When their son, John, was born, Glenn, Sr., worked for a plumber in Cambridge. But, in the optimism of Coolidge prosperity, he moved the family nine miles to New Concord so that he could start the Glenn Plumbing Company. Later, in a flush of entrepreneurial spirit, he added a Chevy dealership but found he couldn't keep it.

Modest in worldly achievement, the Glenns placed great emphasis on their religious beliefs. "We're a Christian family," the elder Glenn said with a certain Presbyterian pride. Their faith was simple and absolute. Years later the younger John Glenn liked to repeat his mother's homilies: "She feels that our relationship to God is a fifty-fifty proposition. God placed us on earth, she believes, with certain abilities and talents. How well we use them is completely up to us. . . . I share these beliefs." It was a religion not of mystery or surprise but of dedication and perseverance: "I do not happen to believe in a fire-engine kind of religion which encourages a man to call on his Maker only when he needs help."

The Glenns socialized with a few close friends, which included the dentist's family down the street. Young John grew up with their daughter, Annie Castor, and from puppy love and pairing at parties to hayrides and ice-cream sodas, dances and dates, their friendship blossomed into love and marriage. As John Glenn later said, "having a family was something that I looked forward to long before I was married."

Family, church, neighborhood—within the tidy confines of New Concord they inspired in Glenn not the comforts of familiarity but an ambition for leadership and the self-confidence to succeed. In high school he demonstrated modest success in sports. "[He] wasn't what you would call a great athlete," said one teammate, "but he sure was a fine team player. You could always count on him to boost the team's morale when the going got a little rough." He played trumpet in the school band, sang in the glee club, and performed the male lead in his senior class drama, *Fanny and the Servant Problem*. Most indicative of his priorities was the theme he chose as president of the junior class for the annual banquet and yearbook: aviation. "NCHS Senior Airways, Inc.," read Glenn's inscription. "Dependable Safe Service."

This seemingly uncomplicated life was tempered by his family's precarious financial condition. "One of the most disturbing conversations I ever heard was during the Depression," Glenn has recalled. "It was between my parents, and they didn't know I was listening. They were worried that the house was going to be foreclosed." Glenn always worked at odd jobs: washed cars for fifty cents "Kwickly and Kompletely," served as a YMCA lifeguard in the summers, sold rhubarb from the family garden. "I was the chief tender," he said. "I hated it." Whatever his later nostalgia for New Concord, he welcomed opportunities beyond the town limits.

After high school, however, he followed Annie Castor just a few blocks away to Muskingum College, New Concord's Presbyterian liberal arts school, where he enrolled in 1939. His major was chemical engineering. He also played varsity football there, but he found greater satisfaction in a government-sponsored pilot-training program. "Both his mother and I were sick when John took up aviation," remembered the elder Glenn. "It was just like taking him out and burying him. Flying wasn't a very safe business in those days, you know." The enthusiastic son brought his physics professor home to persuade his parents that "aviation had a wonderful future and that in a few years it would probably be one of the largest and most important industries in the country." Appreciating the business ethic and the language of opportunity, the Glenns reluctantly allowed their nineteen-year-old to take flying lessons at the airport in New Philadelphia. "I was sold on flying as soon as I had a taste for it," said Glenn. "I think I would have tried to get into some branch of flying along about this time even if the war had not come along."

The attack on Pearl Harbor expanded his field of opportunity.

Glenn and his friends marched into an army air corps recruiting office, passed their physical examinations, signed up, and were sworn into military service. Then they went home to await their orders: "But none came." Rather than complete the academic year, the impatient flyers took back their oath to the army, trooped to the navy recruiter, took another physical, signed up, and were sworn in. "This time the orders came right away and we left."

World War II evoked his feelings of obligation and duty, patriotism and commitment. He was anxious to fight, and to get closer to combat he volunteered for the marines. By March 1943 he had won his airman's wings as well as a commission as a second lieutenant. Yet he paused now for another ritual shared by many men on the edge of battle. In April 1943 he returned to New Concord to marry Annie Castor in the United Presbyterian Church. Their honeymoon was as brief as a pilot's leave, and then Glenn returned to training missions that stretched from Cherry Point, North Carolina, to El Centro, California. In February 1944 his orders took him into the Pacific theater. "Well, I'm going down to the corner store and buy some chewing gum," he quipped to Annie. "Well," she replied, "don't take too long."

Lieutenant Glenn flew his first combat mission in an F4U Corsair fighter over the Marshall Islands in the summer of 1944. Almost immediately he was logging more flight hours than anyone in the squadron and accepting the most perilous and difficult assignments. Assuming leadership among the other pilots, Glenn earned their respect as a daring but disciplined commander. He helped perfect the group's dive-bombing tactics, using the risky but more accurate wheels-down approach. "Despite intense heavy antiaircraft fire," read the citation for his first Air Medal, "he successfully attacked and destroyed the buildings comprising the communications center of the island. His great courage, excellent airmanship, and steadfast devotion to duty were in keeping with the highest traditions of the United States Naval Service." After fifty-seven missions Glenn returned stateside in February 1945 to train other pilots and to test new aircraft, and he had just earned a promotion to captain when the Japanese surrendered.

With the war over and Annie pregnant, Glenn confronted his first career choices at the age of twenty-four. His father wanted him to return to New Concord to join the plumbing business. He might also have chosen an early discharge to get a head start in civilian aviation. But by 1945 he had come to love the camaraderie of the corps and the thrill of flying fast planes. He chose to stay in the military.

New Concord remained his legal residence, but only in the most nominal sense would he ever again be able to call it his home. The duties of a professional fighter pilot imposed continuing upheaval and migration. Glenn served overseas again, flying patrol duty off the China coast and in Guam, then returned to a series of assignments in every corner of the country. When the Korean War began in 1950, he was eager to return to combat. By then he had become expert in the art of "sniveling". "It means going around and getting what you want to, even if you're not slated to get it," Glenn later explained. "There's nothing wrong with it—and I was superb at it."

Gaining a promotion to major, he won the coveted assignment to Korea. "You do all kinds of things in wartime that you would not normally do," he said about his tour of duty. "You go out into an unknown every time you fly in combat, and you often face stress situations that are far more exacting than the mere physical strains." Yet Glenn was exhilarated by the risk, flying sixty-three missions in fewer than four months. His plane was hit by antiaircraft fire seven times—once getting over 200 holes, another time a gaping wound in the tail—and he proudly bore the nickname Old Magnet Tail.

Glenn's narrow escapes—for others, such as George Wallace, the stuff of nightmares—merely increased his appetite for action. Arranging an exchange assignment with the air force, he volunteered to patrol "MIG alley" along the Yalu River. Nine days before the end of the war, he fulfilled another personal goal: "Today, I finally got a MIG cold as can be. Of course, I'm not excited at this point. Not much!" In the closing days of battle he earned two additional kills, but he ran out of war before he could get the five victims necessary to qualify as an ace.

For Glenn the triumphs of combat reinforced his sense of destiny. Three decades after Korea he still exhibited on his desktop the steel shrapnel that testified to his survival. "Now, you may think it's silly for a sixty-one-year-old man to have all this war crap around," he would admit. "But it's something to look at when I'm down-in-the-mouth, something to remind me how lucky I am to still be here."

After Korea Glenn attempted to prolong the sense of adventure by volunteering as a military test pilot. Above Chesapeake Bay he flew a variety of fighter planes, whipping the craft through climbs, spins, and flameouts while testing guns and ammunition. The arrival of the Chance Vought F8U-1 Crusader in 1957 offered him an opportunity to prove the versatility of American technology—and his own skill as well. Transferred to the navy's Fighter Design Branch, he began a one-man lobbying effort to get authorization for a test flight to break the cross-country speed record set by the air force in 1956. He had to send the plan through channels four times before he got his chance.

Glenn called it Operation Bullet because he intended to fly his plane at a speed faster than a bullet fired from a .45-caliber gun; he also hoped to exceed the speed of sound in the air. But the project depended on a meticulously calculated flight plan and three midair refuelings with high-flying tankers. On the morning of July 16, 1957, Glenn raced down the east runway at Los Alamitos Naval Air Station in California and within minutes was cruising at one thousand miles per hour at an altitude of fifty thousand feet. His success would require perfect navigation. Besides monitoring communications from the ground, he had to check on his status and fuel every three and a half minutes: "Just about the time I got it done, it was time to start over again." As he passed over New Concord, he managed to drop a sonic boom by way of greeting to his parents and smashed windows in Pittsburgh, before landing at Floyd Bennett Field on Long Island with forty gallons of gasoline to spare, "maybe enough," he said with a grin, "to circle the field once and come in for a dry run."

The band from the Brooklyn Navy Yard played "Anchors Aweigh" and then "The Marines Hymn" as Glenn snapped back the plexiglass cockpit cover, pushed up his gold crash helmet, and climbed down the steps of the fuselage. "I didn't have time to think up any fine patriotic statements," he said, while hugging Annie and his daughter, Lyn, and giving his son, David, a "hearty rub" on the crew cut. "This was a real team job. The airplane worked real fine. . . . There were a million details. But they were all worked out in advance."

Supersonic Champion

At 36, Major Glenn is reaching the practical age limit for piloting complicated pieces of machinery through the air at speeds that can only be compared with those of sound and of the earth's turning on its axis.
—*The New York Times*, July 17, 1957

Having established the transcontinental speed-flying record of three hours twenty-three minutes eight and four-tenths seconds, Glenn earned a brief moment in the headlines. *The New York Times* featured him as the "man in the news"; Admiral Thurston Clark awarded him a fourth Distinguished Flying Cross; he appeared on television quiz shows, winning $15,000 on "Name That Tune." But soon the cheering stopped. "The flight was real fine. No strain at all," he said. "But now I've got to go back to work." The fastest pilot in America returned to his desk in Washington, D.C.

Three months later the launching of the Soviet Sputnik reopened his horizons. With the creation of NASA and the announcement of Project Mercury, Glenn allowed himself to dream about a new career: "I [knew] that space travel was at the frontier of my profession." Already he had begun his preparations. When NASA asked for volunteers to test prototypes of space equipment, he arranged to ride the space simulators as well as a giant centrifuge designed to produce huge gravitational forces against the human body. "I enjoyed this stint very much," he said. He also represented the navy on the service review board that would evaluate the proposed space capsule. "I felt that many of my experiences had added up to prepare me for the kind of challenge that Project Mercury presented," Glenn said about his qualifications, "and that I would be remiss if I did not volunteer to put some of this background to good use."

In January 1959 he was one of 508 potential astronauts—chosen on the basis of physical size, education, and pilot experience. A review of the files soon reduced the group to 110. In February he journeyed to the Lovelace Clinic in Albuquerque, New Mexico, for a battery of medical tests to determine his physical fitness. "I didn't know the human body had so many openings to explore," Glenn said of the seven-day ordeal, which included seventeen separate eye examinations, twenty-seven laboratory tests, multiple urine specimens, brain wave measurements, blood counts, sperm counts, barium enemas, electrical stimulations, gastric analyses by way of swallowed tubes, tilt table tests, treadmill exercises, specific gravity body dives, hearing and speech tests, water-in-the-ear nystagmus balance tests, and a trip to Los Alamos for a body radiation count.

NASA then shuttled the candidates to Wright-Patterson Air Force Base at Dayton, Ohio, for elaborate personality tests. To measure aptitude they ticked through the boxes of the Wechsler Adult Intelligence Scale, Miller Analogies Test, Raven Progressive Matrices, Doppelt Mathematical Reasoning Test, Engineering Analogies, Mechanical Comprehension, Air Force Qualification Test, Aviation Qualification Test, Space Memory Test, Spacial Orientation, Gottschildt Hidden Figures, and Guildford-Zimmerman Spacial Visualization Test. They were baked in ovens, frozen in ice cubes, and left to thaw in black-box isolation cells. They passed through multiple interviews with psychologists, which were interspersed with the classics of American behavioral psychology, specifically, the Rorschach inkblots, Thematic Apperception Tests, Draw-A-Person, Sentence Completion Test, Minnesota Multiphasic Personality Inventory, Who Am I?, Gordon Personal Profile, Edwards Personal Preference Schedule, Shipley Personal Inventory, Outer-Inner Preferences, Pensacola Z-Scale, Officer Effectiveness Inventory, and Peer Ratings.

"From some of the strange questions the doctors asked us," said Glenn, "it was hard to imagine what they were really looking for. We joked later . . . that perhaps the doctors picked us and let the 'good' ones go." He was particularly intrigued by the Who Am I? test, a measurement of personal identity based on the spontaneous listing of what he thought were his most essential characteristics. Glenn's own list pointed in one direction: "I am a man; I am a marine; I am a flyer; I am an officer; I am a father." None were ambiguous. Glenn, as he perceived himself, avoided categories of feeling or emotion. He selected clearly defined roles, all intrinsically male. "When you got down near the end," he admitted, "it was not so easy to figure out much further just *who* you were."

It was precisely this lack of ambivalence that appealed to the psychologists. When NASA unveiled the seven chosen astronauts at a press conference on April 9, 1959, the oldest volunteer, John Glenn, stole the show. First he made jokes: He said his wife "thinks I'm just about out of this world anyway. I might as well go all the way" and that "I'm probably doing this because it is the nearest to heaven I'll ever get." Then he justified the space program as an expression of traditional American values. "I don't think any of us could really go on with something like this if we didn't have pretty good backing at home, really," he said, paying homage to the American family. "I am a Presbyterian, a Protestant Presbyterian, and I take my religion very seriously as a matter of fact." He described a latter-day Manifest Destiny to expand across new frontiers: "We are placed here with certain talents and capabilities. It is up to each of us to use these talents and capabilities as best [we] can. If [we] do that I think there is a power greater than any of us that will place the opportunities in our way." In the space program the will of God blended with obligations to the flag: "I think we would be most remiss in our duty if we didn't make the fullest use of our talents in volunteering for something that is as important as this is to our country and to the world in general right now. This can mean an awful lot to this country, of course."

Glenn's performance fit the predictions of the NASA psychiatrists. "Although relationships with their families are warm and stable," Marine Corps psychiatrist George Ruff reported, "they do not become overinvolved with others." For all the invocation of his family, Glenn could readily leave it behind, as he had throughout his career, to embark on a national crusade. Unlike the other astronaut families, the Glenns decided to maintain their household in Arlington while John moved into bachelor quarters at Langley Field in Virginia. His asceticism was made easier by weekend visits to the family. "On Sunday nights we always eat in the living room in front of the fireplace," explained Annie, "and afterward we sing everything from Broadway musicals to Presbyterian hymns while I play the organ."

Glenn exuded self-confidence. Asked at the press conference about their expectations of returning to Earth safely, each astronaut happily raised a hand; John Glenn raised two. "I have had a lot of experience in clutch situations," he said; "there's no question that I'll need—and will have—all of my confidence." He was also untroubled by emotional inhibitions; he took pride in his steadfast self-control. He was the kind of man who spanked his children not on impulse but as an expression of disciplined anger. A friend said of him: "John tries to behave as if every impressionable youngster in the country were watching him every moment of the day."

After reporting for duty on April 27, 1959, Glenn began the unavoidable rivalry with the other astronauts about which of them would be the first in space, even as they agreed to share equally in the profits of fame. At a time when Glenn's basic salary was about $1000 a month, the astronauts negotiated a $500,000 contract with *Life* magazine for their personal stories—a one-for-all, all-for-one package that translated into $70,000 per man. "I did not deny the old argument that a soldier going into combat might share an equal danger with astronauts," Glenn said in defending the windfall, "but I felt that if there was enough interest in that soldier's home life, background, or childhood, then he, too, should have the right to receive compensation for opening his home, his family, and his innermost thoughts to public scrutiny." Besides providing economic security, the *Life* contract also sealed off the astronauts from "public scrutiny." With its exclusive rights, *Life* gladly joined NASA in presenting the All-American Boys in only the most correct light.

Determined to win his place on the first flight, Glenn plunged into the regimen of training—running mile after mile each morning before breakfast to force his 185-pound body down to 170; putting in the weekly three hours of loops, spins, and dives; and, for him the toughest part, assimilating vast amounts of information about biology, spacecraft design, and celestial mechanics. The astronauts went to the McDonnell factory in St. Louis to examine the space capsule, to B. F. Goodrich in Akron to measure their spacesuits and then to Dayton to try them on, to Cape Canaveral to observe missile launchings, and to San Diego to watch the Atlas rocket move through the Convair assembly line. In four months they logged 200,000 miles, nearly ten times the circumference of the earth. To share their expertise, they divided their assignments. Glenn drew responsibility for capsule design. "You don't climb into the Mercury spacecraft, you put it on," he said. "You squeeze past all the gear that is mounted inside, like a man sliding under a bed. Once inside, you almost feel like just one more piece of equipment." From this perspective, he detected flaws in the cockpit design, challenged the engineers about the body harness, and questioned the proposed scheme of capsule recovery.

For his acuity and sheer doggedness, he won the respect of his colleagues. But this triumph also bolstered his pride. When a San Diego newspaper prepared to print a story about the peccadillos of one of the astronauts, Glenn pleaded with the editor to kill it, stressing the risk to the space program and the continuing competition against godless communism. Then, having saved the program from public humiliation, he privately denounced any irresponsible behavior by an astronaut during off-hours. As symbols of American virtue, he said, they could not afford to offend public opinion: "What [are] we to do with a responsibility like that?" he asked. "See how many bars we [can] hit?" Some of his colleagues did not like his advice. The mask of friendly competition remained firmly in place, but Glenn would pay dearly for his moral exertions.

> This past eight or nine months has really been a hectic program, to say the least, and by far the most interesting thing in which I have ever taken part, outside of combat.
> —John Glenn, December 17, 1959

The physical exertions continued into 1960. As a passenger in rapidly descending aircraft, Glenn luxuriated in the freedom of weightlessness: "Contrary to this being a problem, I think I have finally found the element in which I belong. . . . That was a real ball." Amid eight-foot swells in the Gulf of Mexico, he and Scott Carpenter played games, transforming an emergency raft exercise into a surfboarding excursion through the high seas. And in a survival-training session in the 110° heat of the Nevada desert, Glenn, Alan Shepard, and a few others deliberately avoided water for several hours just to experience the shock of extreme dehydration. Asked about his readiness, Glenn remained optimistic: "We're anxious to get the tin can off the ground," he said in the same month that presidential candidate John F. Kennedy complained that "if a man orbits earth this year his name will be Ivan."

Glenn appeared unperturbed by a series of technological failures that delayed the program. Instead he emphasized the importance of careful planning: "If you don't know what to expect, you would be like the Ubangis in mid-Africa, suspicious of everything, jumping at every leaf that moves. When you get educated you are no longer fearful." To remove even a potential anxiety, he forced his imagination to anticipate the excitement of a flight into space. "When the time comes . . . I want to feel as if I've been through the whole thing many, many times before. . . . As much as I am able . . . I consciously try to prelive the experience that lies ahead. I try to visualize the whole day . . . and I notice more anxiety in the people around me than I feel in myself." Not some ecstatic vision but the drone of experience would determine Glenn's response to the unknown—"if," as he prudently added, "I am chosen."

"Anyone who doesn't *want* to be first doesn't belong in this program," he said. Confident that his skill, discipline, and moral virtue would catapult him ahead of the others, he was only slightly cautious when, in December 1960, NASA director Robert Gilruth asked the astronauts to take a peer vote—to choose, in secrecy, whom each astronaut would pick to go first, assuming, of course, that he himself was out of the running. Then, a month later, one day before the inauguration of President Kennedy, Gilruth abruptly proclaimed a change in policy. To take the pressure off the primary astronaut, he designated *three* front-runners, one of whom would go on the first flight. They were presented to the public in alphabetical order: John Glenn, Gus Grissom, Alan Shepard. In the secrecy of the astronaut conclave, however, Gilruth made an additional announcement: The first astronaut would be Shepard.

"It's an understatement to say that I'm happy," Glenn assured the press. But beneath his smiling face there was pain. "He was real, real shook," reported one of his old friends. "It was the only thing Johnny ever lost in his life." But Glenn refused to accept defeat. Taking advantage of the change in presidential administrations, he attempted to persuade the NASA bureaucracy to reverse the decision, to ignore the peer vote. But the new administration was reluctant to intervene. "This really hit John with a blow," said a close friend and neighbor. "When he came home weekends, he wouldn't go anywhere. He didn't want to see any of his friends, because he actually felt that he had failed, personally." Given his sense of duty, obligation, call, Glenn lacked any other explanation. "Those were pretty rough days for me," he admitted later. "I guess I am a fairly dogged competitor, and getting left behind . . . was a little like always being a bridesmaid but never a bride."

As backup pilot for Shepard and Grissom, Glenn pretended to prepare for the first flight. To the press he remained the fair-haired boy and, because of the alphabet, he always ranked first. As the launch date approached, he worked feverishly on the final checkouts, refresher tests, medical examinations, and countdowns. Always in his mind lurked the thought that something might yet happen to Shepard. But even that uncomfortable fantasy diminished in importance when on April 11, 1961, the Soviet Union announced the launching of "cosmo-naut" Yuri Gagarin. "I am, naturally, disappointed that we did not make the first flight to open this new era," said Glenn in what the press interpreted as a magnanimous gesture.

Three weeks later, on May 5, 1961, Glenn tucked Shepard into the Mercury capsule for the first American suborbital flight. In July he did the same for Gus Grissom. By then Glenn had passed his fortieth birthday—the upper age limit for Project Mercury astronauts—and he worried about his future with NASA.

Not until Thanksgiving Day in 1961 did he learn that he had been picked to fly the first orbital flight: "It seems incredible to me now that in just a few weeks' time I will be the first American to fly across the country—from San Diego to Savannah . . .—in just eight minutes." Despite his excitement—indeed, because of it—Glenn struggled to minimize the sense of novelty, to blunt the possibility of surprise: "Actually there's nothing spooky or supernatural about space flight. Like any flying, it is simply a product of human skill and technical proficiency." Nor would he admit any fear: "I suppose the thing that sustains me most is that I have complete confidence in the mission and in the hardware . . . [and] in myself."

He was untroubled when bad weather and technical malfunctions forced additional delays: "I learned very early in the flight-test business that you have to control your emotions—you can't let these things throw you or affect your ability to perform the mission." During one long postponement Glenn returned to Arlington for a family reunion and then, at the invitation of President Kennedy, visited the White House. The two men talked, in Glenn's words, "as one guy to another." He told Kennedy that there was too much "personal publicity but not enough emphasis on the scientific aspects of Mercury." Kennedy reminded him of the importance of humanizing the technical project. "It was just a very cordial get-together," said Glenn.

With a target date of February 20, 1962, he spent the preceding evening reading the flight controller's handbook on automatic stabilization and systems control before drifting into what his physician described as "dozing, light sleep." He was awakened at 1:30 A.M.; showered, shaved, ate a high-protein breakfast, and was glued to a set of biomedical sensors that recorded his vital signs (pulse 68; pressure 118 over 80; 14 breaths per minute; temperature 98.2° F.; nude weight 171 pounds, 7 ounces). "I was aware of some apprehension," he admitted. But the stress was subsumed by the rush of detail. Then the hatch was bolted shut: "Quite a moment—and a good one." He received a final phone call from Annie.

"Well, I'm going down to the corner store and buy some chewing gum," he said.

"Well, don't take too long."

At T minus eighteen seconds, Scott Carpenter signaled the final sequence: "Godspeed, John Glenn." At precisely 9:47:39 Eastern Standard Time America's third astronaut felt the Atlas rocket lift off the pad:

oo oo 03	Roger. The clock is operating. We're under way.
oo oo 08	Roger. We're programming in roll okay.
oo oo 13	Little bumpy along about here.
oo oo 19	Roger.
oo oo 23	Roger. Backup clock is started.
oo oo 43	Roger. Checks okay. . . .
oo oo 48	Have some vibration area coming up here now.
oo oo 55	Roger. Coming into high Q a little bit; and a little contrail went by the window or something there.
oo 01 03	. . . Still okay

oo o1 12	We're smoothing out now, getting out of the vibration area.
oo o1 19	Roger. Feels good, through max. Q and smoothing out real fine.
oo o1 26	Cabin pressure coming down . . . ; flight very smooth now.
oo o1 31	Sky looking very dark outside.

Aiming toward a preprogrammed position that would put the craft into orbit, Glenn kept his left hand on the abort handle while he monitored the dials and gauges that registered oxygen levels, fuel capacity, electrical circuits, and cabin pressure.

| oo o5 12 | Zero-g and I feel fine. Capsule is turning around. |

In a state of weightlessness, Glenn raced through space facing backward, just as flight engineers rode B-29s in World War II.

oo o5 18	Oh, that view is tremendous!
oo o5 23	. . . It was beautiful.
oo o5 44	This is Friendship Seven. Can see clear back; a big cloud pattern all the way back across toward the Cape. Beautiful sight.

With no additional comment—with literally no word of description, much less of analysis—Glenn passed beyond radio range. In a wink he sailed over Bermuda, preoccupied inside the capsule with his itinerary. First he checked the retrorockets that were indispensable for a safe reentry: "A little like riding a commuter train on a very bad night. . . . You would want to make sure before you settled down that you were ready to get off at your station." Then, in a complicated two-handed procedure, he tested the control stick for roll, pitch, and yaw: "Working just like clockwork." Soon he was flying over the Canary Islands. (The designated orbit, Shepard later explained, "would take the capsule over friendly land masses all the way—which was a political factor of some importance. . . .") Here Glenn presented a long status report, his senses tuned more to the dials in the cockpit than the Earth spinning below. In the same breath he discussed the retrosequence and the darkening horizon—"A brilliant . . ." he groped for the right word, "a brilliant blue," he said before reverting to the more comfortable "beautiful." By then he was over Kano, then Zanzibar; then he was talking to a NASA ship on the Indian Ocean: "The sunset was beautiful . . . brilliant blue . . . redness . . . absolutely black, completely black." He squeezed a tube of applesauce into his mouth: "Having no trouble at all eating, very good. . . . In the periscope, I can see the brilliant blue horizon. . . . Man, this is beautiful."

From an altitude of 125 miles, Glenn read the planet like a roadmap, running a mental finger across familiar crossroads. He could "see" nothing else. But, at the edge of his first orbital sunrise, he found himself surrounded by "a big mass of some very small particles that are brilliantly lit up like they're luminescent." Twice more he migrated through the luminescent pasture—"similar to looking out across a field on a very dark night and seeing thousands of fireflies." He surmised that they might be the scraps of a recent air force needle-scattering experiment, but he quickly discarded this theory in favor of the idea that he had made a new discovery. Even when NASA scientists concluded that the particles probably originated in the spaceship itself, Glenn clung to the belief that he was indeed a new Columbus: "The particles were a mystery at the time, and they have remained one as far as I'm concerned."

As he approached the California coast for the first time, Glenn encountered another surprise. The automatic control system, designed to regulate the capsule position within the predetermined orbit, began to flip and roll. Glenn used the manual controls to conserve fuel. He became increasingly preoccupied with the erratic thrusts and counter-thrusts and then by inaccurate dial indicators. He abandoned a series of astronomical and weather experiments as well as a second snack. But, despite the complications, he took a pilot's pride in controlling the craft: "The idea that I was flying this thing myself and proving . . . that a man's capabilities are needed in space was one of the high spots of the day."

Unknown to Glenn, his independence was already limited by decisions made on the ground. On his second orbit he received an inquiry about the status of his landing-bag switch, and he returned the routine, "Roger. This is Friendship 7." He knew that the landing bag was connected to the heat shield that protected the capsule from the fires of reentry. He assumed, therefore, that Mercury Control wanted to double-check this most dangerous aspect of the mission. A few minutes later, however, fellow astronaut Gordon Cooper repeated the question and asked Glenn if he had heard "any banging noises or anything of this type at higher rates." "Negative," said Glenn. Cooper told him that was what they wanted to hear. When Mercury Control asked about the landing bag a third time, Glenn concluded that the scientists were seeking a clue for the luminescent particles.

Not until the last moments of flight, just twelve minutes before firing the retrorockets that would reduce velocity and bring the capsule down, did Glenn get a clear hint of serious trouble: He learned that the landing-bag deploy was transmitting a positive flash, indicating that the heat shield might have slipped. If that were the case, Friendship 7 and John Glenn were destined for flame and ash. "We suspect this is an erroneous signal," said ground control. Glenn decided that this was a good time to urinate, and he successfully passed 800 cubic centimeters of "clear, straw-colored urine." With less than a minute to retrofiring, astronaut Wally Schirra, stationed in California, advised Glenn to retain the retropack mechanism, which was wrapped around the heat shield and normally would be jettisoned after firing. "Roger," said Glenn as he raced toward the final fifteen seconds to retrosequence. "Roger, retros are firing. Are they ever. It feels like I'm going back to Hawaii."

Now that the retromaneuver was working, Glenn became nervous about the unjettisoned retropack: "This is Friendship 7. What is the reason for this? Do you have any reason?" From Texas, they told him to wait until he reached Florida. With only seconds to reentry, Glenn finally received a message from controller Alan Shepard: "We are not sure whether or not your landing bag has deployed. We feel it is possible to reenter with the retropackage on. We see no difficulty at this time in that type of reentry." Glenn, meanwhile, was so preoccupied with emergency details that he forgot—an automatic camera recorded his mistake—to close the faceplate on his pressurized suit. Hurriedly he cranked in the periscope and overrode the automatic controls to assure proper altitude. He received one final piece of advice from Mercury Control: "We recommend that you—." And then the rush of ionized particles that surrounded Friendship 7 produced a total voice blackout.

Plunging through the atmosphere, Glenn agonized at the loss of control. His imagination began to play tricks: "I think the pack just let go. . . . A real fireball outside." He saw chunks of the capsule burning: "This was a bad moment. But I knew that if the worst was really happening it would all be over shortly and there was nothing I could do about it. . . . I knew that if the shield was falling apart I would feel the heat pulse first at my back, and I waited for it. . . . Pieces of flaming material were still flying past the window . . . and the glow outside was still bright and orange. It lasted for only about a minute, but those few minutes ticked off inside the capsule like days on a calendar. I still waited for the heat. . . ."

Glenn's pulse zoomed to 134, the highest in the mission. To dampen the motion he attempted to release the drogue parachute. But before he could touch it the drogue exploded automatically, steadying the craft. Then the reef parachute snapped into place: "Beautiful chute. Chute looks good . . . the chute looks very good. . . . The chute looks very good." Splashing into the Atlantic, Glenn sweated out the recovery maneuver until a navy helicopter hooked the capsule and deposited it safely aboard the *Noa*. Within minutes President Kennedy hailed the achievement: "Some years ago, as a marine pilot, he raced the sun across this country—and lost. And today he won."

By the time Glenn had completed his debriefing, he had become a national symbol. "This is the new ocean," said Kennedy from the Rose Garden, "and I believe the United States must sail on it and be . . . second to none." In sheer jubilation, the sailors of the *Noa* voted Glenn an honorary member of the crew and awarded him the first of many prizes, Sailor of the Month. Glenn flew to the larger *Randolph* for a medical check and then to a NASA base on Grand Turk Island. "Well, it's been a long day," he said, "and an interesting one, too, I might add." But what he was unable to articulate was that he was happy!

Only gradually did he realize that his happiness was infectious. After the postflight tests, Kennedy dispatched Vice-President Lyndon Johnson to escort Glenn to Cape Canaveral, and in Florida the nation staged the first of many homecomings. John Glenn's family was already waiting, and their uninhibited joy spread around the country. Over 100,000 people lined the route from Patrick Air Force Base to the launching site, where Glenn shared the sunshine with President Kennedy. (What the hoopla really meant to Glenn surfaced briefly when he spotted a fellow named Carl Huss, the technician responsible for retrorockets: "Glad to be back; we had our moments, didn't we?") Kennedy pinned NASA's Distinguished Service Medal on Glenn's lapel and praised his "great professional skill . . . his unflinching courage and his extraordinary ability . . . under conditions of great physical stress and personal danger."

Glenn, sensing the shifting cameras, now knit together the crowd, the media, and the nation's honor: "We have stressed the team effort in Project Mercury. It goes across the board, I think, sort of a crosscut of Americana, of industry, and military, and civil service government workers, contractors—a crosscut of American effort in the technical field. . . . I would like to consider that I was sort of a figurehead for this whole tremendous effort." Then Glenn and his family departed for a private weekend vacation; it proved to be the quiet before the storm.

On a drizzly Monday morning, February 26, 1962—John Glenn Day—the astronaut and his family flew to Washington with President Kennedy. Despite the rain and the chill, a quarter million people lined Pennsylvania Avenue to watch his motorcade pass from the White House to Capitol Hill. The House of Representatives was packed with spectators, who came to hear him address a rare joint session of Congress.

Glenn spoke in the language of his past—New Concord, the Marine Corps, NASA: "I still get a hard-to-define feeling inside when the flag goes by. . . . Today . . . I got the same feeling all over again. Let us hope that none of us ever loses it." He introduced his parents and his wife's parents and his children and "the real rock," his wife Annie. "To even attempt to give proper credit to all the individuals on this team effort would be impossible," he said.

Beyond clichés, however, Glenn could not communicate the uniqueness of his experience. "It is a real fascinating feeling, needless to say," he remarked, attempting to describe the state of weightlessness. "The view from that altitude defies description." He struggled to express the one sentiment that he had never allowed himself to feel— the mystery of outer space—but he quickly abandoned the effort. Twenty-five times Glenn drew spontaneous applause from the nation's leaders. "As our knowledge of the universe increases," he concluded, bringing them to their feet, "God grant us the wisdom and guidance to use it wisely."

The next day four million people—equivalent to half the population of New York City—lined the streets of Lower Manhattan to produce the largest ticker-tape parade in history. "Freedom, devotion to God and country are not things of the past," Glenn assured a luncheon audience at the Waldorf Astoria. "They will never become old-fashioned. What has happened has jolted us back to reality, as to just what things are all-important." That night at a Broadway musical that was titled, with no small irony, *How to Succeed in Business Without Really Trying,* he received a standing ovation from the audience. The next day he spoke at the United Nations: "We have an infinite amount to learn both from nature and from each other." That evening he was in the audience at *Camelot.*

Overwhelmed by the public response, Glenn performed the one homecoming ritual that seemed to matter, greeting a crowd of fifty thousand that spread along the tree-lined streets of New Concord, Ohio. In these familiar surroundings Glenn's tired defenses softened, and he wept openly: "From swimming down over the hill in the college lake to outer space is a pretty big jump. Coming home, however, can be a very humbling experience." In the college gymnasium, recently named in his honor, he scanned the rows of faces that were familiar and forgotten: "It's great to be an American, and it's great to be home."

John Glenn's flight had captured the heart of the country. Everywhere, crowds and autograph hunters surrounded him. In a military ceremony at the Pentagon, he became the third astronaut to wear Astronaut Wings. In April 1962 NASA sponsored a scientific symposium to consider the implications of his flight: "This mission would almost certainly not have completed its three orbits, and might not have come back at all," said Glenn, "if a man had not been aboard." The National Geographic Society added his name to the pantheon of explorers, awarding him the Huddard Medal. He was named Father of the Year. On behalf of all the astronauts, he accepted the Celtic Cross from the Catholic War Veterans. He won the Marines Corps's Cunningham Award as best aviator of the year. Even the journalists and photographers who covered these ceremonies eventually broke ranks to ask for an autograph.

Glenn also became a friend of the Kennedys, attending the famous pool parties at Robert and Ethel Kennedy's Hickory Hill and sailing aboard the president's yacht. In this friendly atmosphere, he managed to divert public criticism of the astronauts' lucrative contract with *Life* magazine. In January 1963 NASA assigned Glenn to Project Apollo, the effort to place a man on the moon. At age forty-one he still dreamed of another mission into space. He did not know that President Kennedy, fearing the effects on public morale of a tragic accident, had ordered NASA to keep him on the ground.

Glenn's name was already immortal. On the anniversary of his flight, he presented the Smithsonian Institution with his regalia: the flight suit, helmet, a tiny American flag he had stowed aboard. The National Rocket Club awarded him the Robert H. Goddard Trophy;

the Daughters of the American Revolution saluted him "for demonstrating that patriotism is not old-fashioned." In May 1963 he journeyed to Japan to assist the flight of Gordon Cooper and stayed there
for a month as a goodwill ambassador.

Treated as a prophet of the space age, Glenn felt emboldened—
indeed, obligated—to offer his advice, opinions, and commentary on
a multitude of subjects. In answer to the question "why go?" he explained that "in space, one has the inescapable impression that here
is a virgin area of the universe in which civilized man, for the first time,
has the opportunity to learn and grow without the influence of ancient
pressures. Like the mind of a child, it is yet untainted with acquired
fears, hate, greed, or prejudice. In space, as yet, there is only one enemy
—space itself." He said that the orderliness of the universe proved the
existence of God: "This was a definite Plan. . . . Some Power put all
this into orbit and keeps it there." He urged the Nobel foundation to
create a Prize for space, and he recommended the establishment of a
national data center to disseminate new information. He endorsed the
Boy Scouts, the Boys Club, and the YMCA.

He was increasingly constrained, however, by his ceremonial assignments, and he felt insecure about his future in the space program.
He was willing to consider alternatives. The Kennedy brothers, appreciating his immense popularity, encouraged him to enter politics;
they even facilitated his entry into the Ohio campaign of 1964. But
Glenn hesitated to act; he worried about the insecurities of leaving
government work.

The assassination of President Kennedy magnified his dilemma.
Representing the astronauts at the funeral, Glenn first visited the
Lincoln Memorial, read with tears in his eyes the words of the second
inaugural speech ("with malice toward none") and the Gettysburg
Address. Just before midnight he and Annie entered the black-draped
north door of the Capitol to pay their respects to the president who
had befriended them. "What can you do for your country?" Glenn
wondered, allowing these words to determine his future. "That sounds
corny, I know," his attorney told the press, "but it's the way he feels
about it."

Jane
Seymour
Fonda
(II)

Aftcr three months in Paris, Jane
Fonda returned to America for a promotional visit in the winter of
1964: "I'm not a runaway actress," she said, "and I wouldn't want to
live there permanently. My home is New York." Yet, whatever her
conscious intentions, she already had begun to live the life of an exile.
She was now an international film star and could indulge an extravagent
way of life. Her social activities—and her wealth—insulated her from
the cultural changes that were occurring in the United States during the 1960s. She viewed these events from afar. It would be years
before she realized how much she had missed.

During her first months in France, Jane was preoccupied with
love. As the latest American beauty in Paris, she had caught the attention of the reigning connoisseur, film director Roger Vadim, the discov-
erer and sometime husband of Brigitte Bardot, Annette Stroyberg, and

Catherine Deneuve. Vadim's reputation as a lady's man matched his fame as a director. "I heard things about him that would curl your hair," Jane said of their first encounter in Paris in 1957; "that he was sadistic, vicious, cynical, perverted, that he was a manipulator of women." She wanted no part of him then and had rejected a later offer to work with him in Hollywood. But now, in 1964, when Vadim offered her a role in his film *La Ronde,* she was willing to take a chance: "I said to myself, 'Come on—be more adult.' "

They had met again at a masquerade ball, Vadim in the uniform of a Russian army officer, Jane dressed as Charlie Chaplin. "All night long we weaved around each other," Vadim recalled, "the clown seeking out and then rebuffing the soldier." But, when he came to the studio where she was filming *Joy House,* Jane quickly discarded her inhibitions, hurried in from the set (as Vadim captures the moment in his autobiography) "out of breath, wearing a raincoat that she had not taken the time to button . . . and stopped short, embarrassed at making her love so obvious, and then walked toward [me]. Her chest was heaving, her hair . . . had gotten wet and messed up . . . [and] her skin was flushed under her makeup."

Jane's infatuation simplified her career. In Vadim she found not only a lover but a mentor she could trust. She invited him to share her apartment, and together they commuted to the studios at Saint-Maurice where they filmed *La Ronde.* Cast as a "discreet and timid matron," Jane saw the movie as "a great big opportunity to do a beautiful visual comedy and my first costume picture." Vadim preferred the absence of costume, but Jane, at least at this stage of their romance, prevailed: "I am supposedly nude in bed, but I wear a bra and panties. . . . I never did and never will do a completely nude scene."

Her relationship with the French-born Vadim, himself a child of Russian émigrés (his true name was Roger Vladimir Plemiannikov), stimulated an international life-style. They became quintessential jet-setters, taking off to Amsterdam for dinner, to remote beaches, or to ski in the Alps. In 1964 they flew to Moscow on the eve of the May Day celebrations there. At midnight they were awakened by an enormous roar in the streets below. From their fifth-floor balcony they saw an immense caravan of military tanks, part of the armaments for the next day's parade. Jane, according to Vadim, turned a deathly white: "For the first time the idea of war had hit her as a reality." But when she was back in sunny Saint-Tropez, she managed to forget the terror she had felt in Moscow. All she would talk about was the friendliness of the Russian people. She thought that Americans who believed otherwise were victims of propaganda.

Despite her apparent sophistication Jane was still plagued by insecurities. She certainly loved Vadim, and as his lover she also assumed the role of sympathetic stepmother for his daughter, Nathalia. But she resisted a permanent attachment, fearing that a conventional marriage would only undermine their love affair.

She did attempt to establish roots of another sort. She purchased a 135-year-old stone and tile-roof farmhouse at Saint-Ouen-Marchfroy, twenty-five miles west of Paris. In its rural ambience she found a touch of America: "I fell in love with the color of the stone walls—a kind of beige honey color, like an Andrew Wyeth drawing." But its appeal lay in its incompletion, the work still to be done. In an outburst of creative effort similar to the labors of Frances Fonda at Tigertail Road, Jane embraced the task of redesigning and decorating the old structure and transforming the flat terrain that surrounded it. "I left the walls up but completely gutted the inside and modernized it," she said, meaning that she supervised the project. Her passion for organization assumed obsessive proportions. "The land was flat, and there weren't any trees, so I had a bulldozer come in to move the earth around and give it a more rolling effect." Jane shared her father's love of trees, but she lacked his patience to plant them and watch them grow. Instead she bought fully grown trees in Paris and ordered them planted in symmetrical rows: "It was wild—every morning you could see these lines of trees advancing up the road, like Birnam Wood coming to Dunsinane." When Vadim asked why she had not bought a house with trees in the first place, Jane replied, "I'd never find woods exactly like the one I want."

Once completed, the farmhouse became the stable center of her life. Usually she began her week by making up lists—"she had a mania for lists," said Vadim—shopping lists, menus, chores and projects, telephone calls, letters, gifts, and errands. She hired a family of Italian servants and instructed them about meals, housework, the gardening. To a growing collection of furniture and furnishings she added a menagerie of pets—dogs, cats, rabbits, chickens, ponies—none of which, she confessed, were housebroken. Here Jane entertained Vadim's two children, often his ex-wives, as well as a steady stream of film stars who came from Paris, New York, or Hollywood. (Henry Fonda, unamused by the cosmopolitans, was never among them.) "In spite of her career as an actress," noted the appreciative Vadim, "she was in fact an extremely good homemaker. . . . I thought it was what she liked." And so did Jane!

Yet she continued to pursue her career with determination. She returned to America in 1964 to play the title role in *Cat Ballou,* a spoof of westerns, and she won considerable praise for her deadpan performance: "Actress Fonda," said *Time* magazine, "does every preposterous thing demanded of her with a giddy sincerity that is at once beguiling, poignant, and hilarious." She followed this with a part in *The Chase,* a film that explored sin and prejudice in a southern town. "It's quite a part," she said in a comment that revealed much about her state of mind at the age of twenty-seven: "This woman Anna is all I think a woman should be. She has reasons to be frustrated, loving two different men in two different ways at the same time. But she can't stand pointlessness and dishonesty. She's one of those rare women who has put her life in perspective."

Her unorthodox life-style was a frequent topic of conversation in Hollywood, and she appeared as an authority on alternatives to marriage: "Women want to possess somebody, particularly in marriage. It's one of the main reasons I'm not married. I don't want to possess anyone . . . and I don't want to be possessed." Living with Vadim, she had learned that "women's concerns are quite different from those of men" —which may have been another way of saying that she was confused about Vadim's "extramural" activities. "When [women] feel a man is escaping from them they panic, they want to bring him back," she said. "The moment this happens the man feels trapped, and the woman feels frustrated." Fearing a repetition of her parents' marriage, she resolved to break the mold. She would strive not to feel jealous.

Her admiration of Vadim naturally embraced his outlook on the cinema. She became an avid student of his techniques and philosophy. "Jane thought she had no personality," Vadim later explained, "and was desperately trying to find her identity. . . . She was basically afraid of herself. . . . She thought that through hard work she could 'fabricate' a talent for herself but refused to admit that she already had something unique, infinitely rarer and more precious than fortitude and willpower." He tried to persuade her to stop searching for the underlying rationale of her roles; she must trust her feelings. "I learned more from Vadim about ridding myself of phony mannerisms and bad acting habits than from anyone else," she said. "For years I've been *showing* emotions. Vadim taught me how to let them happen."

Jane's success as an actress and her reputation for candor coincided with another development of the mid-sixties—the trend toward uninhibited sexuality. Her freedom of expression symbolized a liberation from the conventional "bourgeois" morality of the 1950s, though she herself did not always appreciate the role of liberator. When *La Ronde* opened in New York in 1965, for example, she was scandalized by a billboard photograph that showed her derrière, and she sued the distributor for the "anguish" and "shame" the photograph caused her. In a gesture of conciliation, the theater covered her backside with a swatch of white canvas. The imbroglio, useful for publicity, highlighted her plight: Jane was becoming what she could not hide, a body.

And, as a popular sex symbol, she felt obliged to promote her image. Like Vadim's other wives, she kept her hair long and blond; she used padded uplifts to fill her bosom. She was always on a diet, augmenting her powerful self-control with diuretics. "These pills," she would later complain, "turned what had been a really minor problem of fluid retention into a chronic one." She also continued to practice ballet: "I played a sort of game with myself. . . . I pretended I was a professional dancer who had to go on stage and perform no matter what. *Had* to. There were no excuses. None at all." Such self-discipline became an end unto itself. Besides preserving her slender figure, it provided a sense of accomplishment, a feeling of completion. "And at times when everything else in my life seemed to be falling apart," she explained, "ballet was the constant that ran through my life like a spinal cord, holding it all together, giving it consistency, pulling me through." Always aware of the fate of her mother—and the perils of physical deterioration—Jane would not allow her body to fail her.

Her concern about beauty and outward appearances, however, could not disguise her longings. The frequent disclaimers of possessiveness toward Vadim—what was probably a realistic fear that he might leave *her*!—belied her confidence in their relationship. When he returned to Paris without her in the midsummer of 1965 (she had to stay in California to finish *The Chase*), she suffered a sense of loss, and she decided precipitously to marry him. Vadim returned to America. Two days before the wedding, however, she decided to cancel it. Then she changed her mind again.

They chartered a private plane to take the wedding party to the Dunes Hotel in Las Vegas for the civil ceremony. Afterward they drifted through the gambling casinos, stepping outside in the morning to watch the sun rise above the desert. "I remember that day very well," Jane said. "I felt out of place . . . here I was, getting married, and saying to myself, 'I honestly don't know why I'm doing it.' I'll tell you, I was sleeping."

Marriage, accepted halfheartedly at best, undermined her peace of mind. Though she adored their social life together, traveling frequently between California, New York, and France, she was too self-conscious not to recognize a continuing fear: "People change after marriage," she declared. "They become very bourgeois. They're dead."

Jane struggled to avoid that fate, but because she was married she had to conceal her concern. "I know from my own experience," she admitted years later, "that women can have an external facade that appears frivolous and superficial, but can actually be serious people, behaving in a particular way to survive." She suffered from an unending ambivalence: "I guess I'm a kind of slave type," she concluded at the time. "I seem to function very well when someone puts me in a framework, and Vadim always knows exactly where he's going."

Her efforts to hide these doubts created a split reality: the visible world of headline names and continental sophistication, on the one hand; on the other, a detached posture from which she viewed the outward pleasure with skepticism and discomfort. With her cosmopolitan friends, she indulged in the latest fun of *haute* culture, which occasionally included drugs. "Used properly," she said of her brother's experiments with LSD, "it can be beautiful. The more we can see into ourselves, the more we can see outside ourselves." But her own reaction to drugs was illuminating for what they did *not* accomplish. Admitting that marijuana could make things "hysterically funny and brilliant," she acknowledged that its main effect on her was to make her "melancholy and boring." As Vadim explained, "Humor is not Jane's forte."

Her personal problems, what might be described as a psychological ache, became a controlling force in her career. "The identity I found as an actress is desperately important to me," she said. "I'm certain that deep down I still have no confidence. . . . So [I] go onto a stage, or a screen, and hide behind the mask of a character." Jane's choice of masks, however, remained fairly limited. Almost always she played a frustrated woman (usually an unhappy wife), searching for fulfillment.

After her marriage to Vadim, she returned to France to star in his film *La Curée* (known in America as *The Game Is Over*), in the role of the sensual young wife of a stodgy businessman. Then, back in America, she played, in *Any Wednesday,* a spirited young woman who must choose between remaining the mistress of an older man or settling down into a bourgeois marriage. In her next movie, Otto Preminger's *Hurry Sundown*, she was the passionate wife of an unemotional southern planter. Then came the film version of Neil Simon's *Barefoot in the Park*, yet another beautiful-angry wife situation that focused on the problems of marriage. These were her choices. Equally revealing were the films she rejected: *Bonnie and Clyde*, where she would have portrayed a loyal woman driven literally to death by her lover; and *Rosemary's Baby*, in which the theatrical ambitions of a young husband destroyed the integrity of marriage and corrupted his wife's pregnancy with evil.

Jane's preoccupation with personal problems distanced her from the political issues of the 1960s. She played no part in the civil rights movement or in the growing opposition to the Vietnam War. She seemed uninterested in or unaware of the ferment among American youth and the birth of a counterculture. Only as a tourist did she notice significant changes, commenting about the liberalization of social values and a loosening of everyday speech. She delighted in learning the latest slang.

While filming *Hurry Sundown* in Saint Francisville, Louisiana, in the summer of 1966, however, her political awareness increased. On the first day there, a black actor disrupted the tranquility by jumping into a segregated swimming pool. "There were reverberations all the way to New Orleans," Jane remembered. "People just stood and stared like they expected the water to turn black!" She joined the cast in urging director Preminger not to compromise with the local KKK. An uneasy truce settled over the company. But, near the end of the shooting, Jane was strolling along the streets when a young black boy gave her a flower. She thanked him with a kiss. Instantly a silence descended on the town, and within the hour the sheriff ordered the actors to leave.

Jane returned to the safety of Malibu but found herself in another legal scrape, linked not to politics but to her image. While she had been making *La Curée* with Vadim the previous year, a photographer had perched on the rafters above the set and had captured some revealing material (Fonda nude, except for flesh-colored panties), which he sold to *Playboy* magazine. "For all of ten seconds," Jane later said, "you saw my breasts." The pictures appeared in the August 1966 issue, causing, according to Jane's $9.5-million-dollar suit, considerable mental suffering: "It rocked me. It really did." But the lawsuit merely drew attention to her image (and after years of litigation, she lost the case).

"I think it's nice if people think I'm some kind of sex symbol," said Jane, "but I'm certainly not responsible." She denied any interest in prurient material. Yet her willingness to undress before the cameras placed her in the vanguard of the sexual revolution. *Newsweek* magazine featured her on its cover to advertise "the permissive society." It confirmed Jane's reputation. An Idaho school board promptly banned the magazine from its recommended-reading list.

Despite her fame for sexual exposure, she was careful to point out, "I'm not a physical exhibitionist." She insisted that her nudity on screen was always "necessary to the text, to achieve the proper dramatic effect." Yet her professional motivations suited a rebellious nature. Her attack on bourgeois hypocrisy was deliberate: "I was reacting against the attitudes of puritanism I was brought up with," she later said, "rejecting the values I considered artificial and guilt-ridden—with no firm conviction, I might add. I'm essentially a modest person."

In 1967 her dual identity as a shy exhibitionist turned Vadim's *Barbarella* into a smashing success. As the sexual superwoman of the future, Jane played her role with an unfailing humorlessness that seemed to mock itself. She embodied the future of sexuality: "As Barbarella, I overcame everything, because Barbarella's sexual potency was so dynamic it destroyed everything that stood in her way." Yet Jane denied an erotic intent. When critics questioned her personal values, she criticized the confusion of image and reality: "I'm no sex siren just because I believe in approaching sex and the human body with honesty. . . . I think the whole obsession with sex, and with the size of a girl's breasts, is a perversion. . . . Everyone fantasizes about doing things that they would be afraid to do in reality. That's not for me."

She fought to separate her personal identity from that conveyed in her movies. When a feminist interviewer asked her about the effect of *Barbarella* on her own personality, however, Jane could not answer. "My only thought was that no one had forced me to make the film. If I starved, dyed, and painted myself into that role, it was my own doing." Similarly, when she and her brother made a film with Vadim about romantic cousins, *Spirits of the Dead,* Jane had to deny its basis in fact: "Not that I am against incest," she declared, "but our style is more direct. When the time comes for incest we will do it head on and leave the titillating for others. Give us credit, at least, for honesty." Yet the parallels between Fonda the actress and Fonda the person were inescapable, even to her: "I always felt slightly out of focus. There was Jane, and there was this public figure. It was extremely alienating. I never liked it. I never felt comfortable with it." And its consequences were inevitable: "Year after year, movie after movie, the characters I was playing were little-bitty, one-dimensional girls, and this had its effect on me. After a while I stopped rebelling against my glossy, vacuous roles. The deeper, more complex, and exciting parts of me began to atrophy from lack of use."

Jane believed she was destined for better parts. "I'm ferociously ambitious," she admitted. "I must fulfill my potential. I don't believe in religion. I don't believe in an afterlife." She believed only in herself: "I can be a good actress, maybe a great one. But I'm not there yet—not with all the doors open, not with all the cannons going off."

As she approached her thirtieth birthday in December 1967, Jane and Vadim decided to have a baby. The decision aroused her anxieties about motherhood, not least of which was the fear of reproducing her own dismal childhood: "I was very aware of all the kinds of mistakes parents can make, and I was afraid I'd make them all too." But her worries reflected not only what she, as a mother, might do wrong but also what motherhood might do to her—to her image and to her body. Her fears were not unlike those of Frances Fonda: that pregnancy and birth would make her old and ugly, destroy not only her beauty but also her career. "But then I thought, 'Well, at forty you may be pretty damned sorry you didn't.' So I got pregnant."

Jane's pregnancy, begun in this climate of fear, was complicated by a case of mumps: "I felt so vulnerable. I realized how I had always . . . rejected femininity because it represented to me vulnerability, and a lot of things scared me." Her health obsessed her. She read books about nutrition; she eliminated salt and coffee from her diet; she gave up cigarettes. But her anxieties persisted.

Forced to slow down, she spent her time reading and watching French television. And she was drawn more and more to the major political issue of that time, the American war in Vietnam. "I was always defending the U.S. during those days," she later claimed. "I couldn't stand it if some Frenchman would come up and say, 'What do you think about destroying a Vietnamese village in order to save it?' I would say, 'It's not true.' " Vadim and some leftist friends tried to change her perspective. She could see on television the results of American bombing raids. She followed the testimony presented at Bertrand Russell's international tribunal investigating American war crimes in Vietnam. Slowly she began to perceive, in her words, "the split between what we were doing and what we said we were doing."

Her political evolution remained tentative, yet as inexorable as the birth of her baby: "It was all happening inside me, secretly, through various small things." In Paris she met American military deserters who confirmed stories of atrocities, and she gave them money for antiwar work. She visited members of the North Vietnamese National Liberation Front who were then in Paris negotiating with the United States about the shape of the treaty table. She saw a documentary film about the October 1967 march to the Pentagon—"boys with long hair and professors and radicals putting flowers into the guns of the guards"—and she approved their sincerity: "And I learned." When her father returned from an entertainment trip to Vietnam and denounced the antiwar movement for strengthening the morale of the enemy, she criticized his outlook. Yet her own commitment was still undeveloped: "The position I took then was signing petitions, going to rallies, working with the usual liberal things," she recalled. "Back in Hollywood I had been going to parties with all the other rich liberals. . . . It seemed so inadequate. It always seemed [to be] tokenism."

The outbreak of a student-workers revolution in France in May 1968 acted as a powerful catalyst in Jane's political growth. She supported the radicalization of the cinema workers and gave speeches to the technicians' union. But Vadim insisted that Paris was too dangerous for a pregnant woman. She was forced to spend her days at the farmhouse, watching history on television. "What was important about being in France," she later explained, "was that for the first time I realized that it really could all come down. There were days when we thought it was going to stop."

She also became more sensitive to events occurring in America. "I'm not sure what was more important: what was going on in France or what I saw on television about what was happening in the United States." She watched the police riots at the Democratic National Convention in Chicago and identified with the antiwar demonstrations. "It was a time of really tumultuous currents in world history," she said. "It was like rumblings going on inside all the time. . . . I just felt—let's get this baby out, I want to pack it up and go home, I want to get involved."

Jane was exhilarated by the birth of a daughter, Vanessa, named after another actress with strong political convictions, Vanessa Redgrave. Self-conscious about motherhood, she resolved to remain close to her baby: "I hate those actresses who say they can't nurse their babies because it ruins their breasts." Gradually she gained confidence in herself. "It's like preparing for a part," she concluded. "You worry and agonize and then you just go in and *do* it."

With motherhood Jane discovered a new coherence in the world. "For the first time in my life I felt confident as a human being and as a woman, and I'm sure it was because I was finally a mother. I began to feel a unity with people. I began to love people, to understand that we do not give life to a human being only to have it killed by B-52 bombs or to have it jailed by fascists or to have it destroyed by social injustice. When she was born—my baby—it was as if the sun had opened up for me. I felt whole. I became free."

Her sense of maternal fulfillment ironically intensified her desire for professional success. Through exercise and ballet she whipped her body into shape, and she eagerly accepted a new role that promised to transform her career. It meant that she had to stop nursing Vanessa after five and a half weeks. "I'm not afraid of my ambition anymore," she declared. "I've confronted my ambition head-on, and it's enormous. I'm out for the long haul. I don't want to disappear tomorrow."

To ensure her survival—professionally, psychologically, even, perhaps, literally—Jane, at thirty-one, took on the most demanding role of her career. In a film about marathon dancers during the Great Depression, *They Shoot Horses, Don't They?*, she prepared to play the part of Gloria, a tough victim of a world she could neither control nor accept. Jane saw Gloria as a loser, a woman who could never win, and she struggled to understand such a character—so different from herself —to combat her own frustrations.

Her first decisions were merely physical. To suit the style of the thirties, she discarded her falsies and decided to cut her hair: "You know what people said? 'Jane, *dahling,* you're out of your mind, don't cut off your hair!' I thought, 'Oh wow, so that's what I've become— a lotta goddam blond hair.' " Her hair was chopped off in a flapper's wavy style and her natural color appeared light brown: "I always had a deep-rooted psychological need to be a boy, and now I am one." She also prepared for the dance marathon with a program of strenuous exercise.

The film's political authenticity was especially important to her. She viewed the marathon contest as a metaphor for America in crisis: "The war we're going through now—well, our country has never gone through such a long, agonizing experience, except the Depression. The Depression is the closest . . . America ever came before to a national disaster, the kind of thing that unites people and reduces everything to basic questions—eat or not, live or die. Perhaps audiences—especially kids—will be able to come away from seeing *They Shoot Horses* with the feeling that, if we could pull out of the Depression, we can pull out of the mess we're in now." But her optimism about changing the flow of history was tempered by an appreciation of the inertia that worked against change: "It's about people dealing with problems created by society rather than by themselves. They are dealing with them the best they can, yet they are condemned for their solutions."

More profound for Jane than even these political issues was the film's psychological reality, a traumatic revelation about women that mirrored her most intimate and persistent horror. As Gloria, she played the role of a suicide. "The one, ultimate, final choice you have," Jane said about the movie, "is to take your own life, which is a very important choice. Everyone should have the right to do that." By taking this role—by becoming, at least temporarily, a suicide herself—Jane hoped to purge herself of that other suicide that had gripped her since the age of twelve. By duplicating the despair of her mother's life and the despair of her death, she expected to achieve transcendence. (Only much later would Jane acknowledge that Gloria's solution—handing the fatal gun to the man with whom she danced—was, as a political choice, "really something worse: She has a man kill her.")

Jane became possessed by the role: "I try to know pretty much how she would behave under different circumstances, and then to find ways of playing it that hook up with my own reality." To sustain the mood, she obtained a copy of a police murder manual, complete with pictures of gunshot wounds and decapitations, and kept it in her dressing room. She tried to understand other desperate people: "One day I heard on the radio that a seventeen-year-old woman who had just had a baby left the child in the middle of a busy intersection in downtown Los Angeles. I got information on the woman and read about her background." The physical strain, dancing fourteen hours a day, also enhanced the mood of despair. After the endurance race sequences, the entire company collapsed in a heap, gasping and weeping.

Jane sank deeper into Gloria, the suicide, her own secret shadow. "I became so unhealthily immersed in the role of Gloria, I couldn't tell reality from illusion," she admitted. "Big black wells of loneliness and depression fell over me. I became a manic-depressive." In her private life she started to talk like Gloria, "using a lotta bad English et cetera and so forth." Around Vadim she became hard, rough, brittle, and shameless about these emotions. "I discovered a black side to my character I didn't know about," said Jane. "It was like having a dead baby inside me, and I went around wondering why I couldn't give birth."

Unable to control her gloom, Jane stopped coming home after work. She moved into her dressing room, interrupting her self-exile only occasionally with visits from her infant daughter. Her goal was to become utterly bleak: "There could not be an inkling, a ray of hope." Everything had to end in Gloria's crucial lines: "The whole damn world's just like Central Casting. They've got it all rigged before we even show up. . . . I'm going to get off this merry-go-round."

Jane absorbed the mood, projecting it back to the cameras and inward into herself. The two images become self-reflective. "It was the perfect thing for her to pour all of her frustrations, her own disappointments in life, and all of her aspirations to want to achieve something meaningful," observed her director, Sydney Pollack. "There was no vanity in the performance, no self-preservation. There was no hiding in it. She went all the way." When the gun finally exploded, Gloria died —and so did some of Jane. "I had delivered Gloria. The symptoms of her character were gone. I was rid of her."

In the real world, however, the solution was not so easy. Gloria hovered in her imagination. So did Vadim, their marriage. Jane spoke about divorce and its liberating effects: "I wish I were crazier. Yeh, crazier! I mean, I simply cannot groove until errands are done, calls made, letters written. . . . I am constantly making *lists.* I envy people who can just say, 'Screw it all.' " She left Vadim and Vanessa in California and went to Hawaii to visit her brother, now famous for his own movie *Easy Rider.* She returned still unresolved. "If you start believing the screen," she remarked, "then one day you wake up and you are nothing inside, just another pretty face that isn't so pretty anymore. It takes a great deal of security to be a movie star and then go out on the street and be a slob. It takes guts."

George
Corley
Wallace
(II)

"It makes no difference who is the president," said Governor Wallace. "The issues are the same." In fact Lyndon Johnson was making things worse by linking civil rights legislation to the memory of President Kennedy. Wallace warned that passage of the civil rights bill "through a cloud of emotionalism" would cause "a dramatic change" in American government. By opposing the measure, he reasoned, he would save the country from "those who wanted to destroy human rights in the name of civil rights—and those who inspired hatred and chaos in the name of love and peace." Despite the moratorium on politics during the gloomy Christmas season of 1963, he dispatched his most trusted advisers to the West Coast to arrange a speaking tour.

Just after the New Year, Wallace led his entourage to the Pacific states, appeasing his fear of flight with brief stopovers, which also enabled him to experience western hospitality in the form of pickets, hecklers, and the announcement by the governor of Colorado that, in lieu of a greeting, he would send a charitable contribution to the bombed churches of Birmingham. "If people want to send money to our state, that's fine," Wallace said. "In fact it's becoming a promising new industry for Alabama." His speeches warned of a communist threat inherent in the civil rights bill—"the involuntary servitude act of 1964," he called it—because it allowed the federal government to intervene in private business. On this trip he also visited entrepreneurs and plant managers, trying to attract new industry and jobs to Alabama.

He returned home to a hornet's nest of racial disturbance. In Huntsville, at the NASA center, federal employees had already infiltrated the town with northern values, and Wallace could not prevent the desegregation of public schools there. In conservative Macon County, however, the governor used a white boycott as an excuse to close the only integrated high school. But his old nemesis, Federal Judge Frank Johnson, ordered Wallace to end such interference. "I think we are going to continue to have segregation in Alabama," Wallace replied, "as they have in most states in the union."

He enjoyed the comparison with the North, recognizing that he had considerable influence there. His mere mention of interest in the Ohio primary provoked Senator Stephen Young—already challenged by another fledgling candidate, John Glenn—to denounce the Alabamian as "a man who has defied the courts of the nation, who has abetted murder and violence in his state, and who has tarnished the image of our country throughout the world." Wallace threatened to sue for libel, but he found even greater satisfaction in the enthusiastic reception he received in Ohio. When reporters asked him questions about southern racial problems, Wallace deflected their curiosity: "The people of Alabama are very disturbed about the violence in Cleveland," he said with a straight face. "I'm glad we don't have problems like you have here in the North." The only problem he confronted in Ohio was the complicated electoral system, which made it impossible to get his name on the ballot.

In Wisconsin, however, Wallace found a simpler election machinery as well as an eager audience for his attack on the federal government. "My purpose," he explained upon entering the Democratic primary in March 1964, "is to tell the truth about the so-called civil rights bill and how it would destroy the private enterprise system in this country." For dramatic effect he launched his campaign against "the left-wing influence" in Appleton, Wisconsin, hometown of the late Joseph McCarthy: "Senator McCarthy gave some good warnings."

Despite pickets, hecklers, and the opposition of the Catholic hierarchy, Wallace remained a tenacious campaigner, seeking common ground with the dissatisfactions of the northern white middle class. He denied any racist intent: "Racism is evil. Racism is disliking God's handiwork because a person is another color." But he drew a sharp distinction: "If a man is convinced in his heart, and I am, that segregation is in the best interest of both races, there is nothing immoral or sinful about it." In his view the civil rights bill reflected alien ideals— the belief that "government can manage the people and, by management and manipulations, bring about a utopian life. . . . It is this way in Russia."

The ethnic voters of Milwaukee liked his message. They were willing to ignore the fact that Wallace had earlier contrasted the purity of the Anglo-Saxon South with the melting pot of the North, as he put it, "Poles, Italians, Germans, and other lesser breeds." At the Serbian Memorial Hall in South Milwaukee, three thousand voices sang "Dixie"—in Polish!

In the Wisconsin primary, Wallace received over a quarter of a million votes, one-third of the Democratic poll, and a quarter of the total vote. He promised to "carry on this fight . . . to break the trend toward centralized government." But he appeared indifferent to another statistic: "Governor Wallace got 25 percent of the votes," observed President Johnson, "and 75 percent voted against him."

In the Indiana primary, Wallace emphasized the similarity of racial feelings in the North and in the South: "A man who owns a home, which is his castle, ought to be able to sell it to people with blue hair and green eyes only. It's his home." He argued that the civil rights bill would not only invade the private sector but also increase the size of government bureaucracy: "The federal government in Washington is reaching into every facet of society and encroaching on the rightful powers of the states." Such arguments triggered a favorable response. At the very time that Democratic liberals were mustering votes in the Senate to break a southern filibuster against the civil rights bill, Indiana citizens registered an unmistakable protest. On primary day Wallace won 170,000 votes, 30 percent of the Democratic ballots, and swamped party regulars in the blue-collar counties near Gary. "We shook the eyeteeth of those people in Wisconsin," Wallace boasted, "and those noises you hear now are the teeth falling out in Indiana."

Emboldened by his success, he moved into Maryland. His presence in Cambridge provoked racial violence, and he received several death threats. But Wallace insisted that his position represented the will of the people, who, he said, "have been tranquilized into not speaking out, because of charges that you'd be a racist or immoral, or a bigot, or prejudiced, that you'd be biased if you oppose this movement." Now they spoke loudly, giving him over 200,000 votes, nearly 43 percent of the total. "People who supported me are called fanatics," he said, "but the liberals can't call us bad names anymore, because there are too many of us."

Wisconsin—33 percent; Indiana—29 percent; Maryland—43 percent. He began to dream of greater possibilities. To enhance his standing, he presented a formal speech to the National Press Club. (But the members snubbed him, refusing to bestow the traditional certificate of thanks, previously given to Khrushchev and Castro.) In June 1964 he announced his intention to qualify on as many presidential ballots as possible. He began a petition drive in North Carolina and collected one hundred thousand signatures in ten days. Dr. Bob Jones, head of the fundamentalist university of that name, described him as "a David warring against this giant, Tyranny." In Dallas the United States Junior Chamber of Commerce gave him a five-minute standing ovation.

Despite such spontaneous support, Wallace could not halt the passage of the Civil Rights Act of 1964. "This is a sad day for individual freedom and liberty," he said. To celebrate Independence Day, he accepted an invitation from Governor Lester Maddox to speak in Atlanta, where he invoked the spirit of the founding fathers against the forces of tyranny: "I intend to give the American people a clear choice," he declared, amid a rising chant of "George! George! George!" "I am in this race because I believe the American people have been pushed around long enough and that they, like you and I, are fed up with the continuing trend toward a socialist state which subjects the individual to the dictates of an all-powerful central government. I am running for president because I was born free. I want to remain free. I want your children and mine and our posterity to be unencumbered by the manipulations of a soulless state. . . . ."

Even as the crowd yelled his name, Wallace saw his power evaporate. A federal court prohibited his interference in the desegregation of public schools; another demanded the integration of Alabama state parks. With Lyndon Johnson certain of nomination, Wallace's allies—

Governors Faubus of Arkansas, Johnson of Mississippi, McKeithen of Louisiana—withdrew their support. The natural enemies of the Great Society, the Republicans of the South, rushed to Barry Goldwater. In a face-saving gesture, Wallace reluctantly announced his withdrawal from the presidential race on CBS's "Face the Nation": "Today we hear more states' rights talk than we have heard in the last quarter of a century. The principal reason for this resurgence . . . has been . . . the message sent to the leadership in both parties by the fine people. . . . I was the instrument through which this message was sent. . . . My mission has been accomplished."

Defeated on all fronts, Wallace substituted a rhetoric of defiance for any actual power, and his voice became more caustic and shrill: "We have no intention of surrendering our school system and the responsibility for the education of our children to bearded beatniks and faceless, spineless, power-hungry theorists and black-robed judicial anarchists." Yet he also conceded the futility of rejecting federal funds to build public schools. "We cannot rid ourselves of the power-hungry parasites by throwing their money back in their faces." And, when the Democratic party forced the Alabama delegation to sign a loyalty oath at the national convention, he presented an angry diatribe against the Great Society: "A so-called civil rights bill, an antipoverty bill, a no-win war, fiscal irresponsibility, a judiciary which initiates, executes, administers, prosecutes, and punishes—this is a revolution."

Wallace also searched for a way to save face. He considered a conversion to the Republican party, but Goldwater, already confident of carrying the South, rejected an alliance. Wallace then embarked on a "nonpolitical" speaking tour in the states where he had campaigned in the spring, but he failed to rally his supporters. In a surprise move, he called a special session of the Alabama legislature to propose a constitutional amendment "to keep the federal government out of our schools," and he suggested the summoning of a constitutional convention—something unheard of since 1787—to restore "home rule" and local government. "We are going to take this crusade across the country," he vowed. At his first stop, however, a conference of southern governors listened just long enough to bury the idea.

After Lyndon Johnson's victory over Goldwater, Wallace struggled to preserve a shadow of political influence. At the inauguration ceremonies he was heartened by the number of people who came to shake his hand. To Wallace such gestures demonstrated the similarity of northerners and southerners. He remained confident, therefore, that the arrival of northern business and industry in Alabama would pose no threat to the southern way of life. Even as the civil rights protest exploded in industrial Selma—at the very moment, in February 1965, that the Reverend Martin Luther King, Jr., sat in jail there for attempting to register black voters—Wallace arrived to speak on the topic "Selma's Bustin' Out All Over," and all he would discuss was industrial expansion, new plant investment, and the opening of the Alabama River to deep-water traffic. He uttered not a word about segregation, law and order, or the grass roots protest that was about to carve the name Selma indelibly on the American landscape.

But the pressure of nonviolent protest—daily parades, pickets, requests for registration forms—eventually provoked a violent counterattack, and Wallace, at last, intervened. He ordered the end of all night marches in Selma: "Mass demonstrations in the nighttime led by career and professional agitators with pro-communist affiliations and associations [are] not in the interest of any citizen." He pointed out that he was following the precedent of New York City during the Harlem riots of 1964. But his refusal to examine local voter registration procedures —his insistence that "no one can contest the right of anyone to register and vote in Alabama *if they are qualified*"—underscored his personal support of white supremacy. Martin Luther King promptly announced that the protesters would carry their grievance from Selma directly to the governor's mansion in Montgomery—on foot.

Wallace, who feared that such a protest would instigate racial violence and thus increase support of the civil rights movement, worked to prevent the march. After consulting with Colonel Al Lingo, director of public safety, he decided to approve the parade while denying the marchers any assistance from the state. But, when local officials refused to guarantee the safety of the marchers, Wallace reversed himself and ordered the protest halted at the Edmund Pettus Bridge in Selma: "Such a march can not and will not be tolerated. . . . Government must proceed in an orderly manner." And he instructed Lingo "to use whatever measures are necessary to prevent a march."

Despite these preparations—or precisely because of them—Wallace was surprised to discover how his words translated into plain English, at least to Colonel Lingo, who met the marchers with clubs, cattle prods, and tear gas. Wallace was furious at the horrible spectacle, which was broadcast around the country, and he castigated his peace officers for their brutal tactics. But in public he remained stubbornly defensive: "These folks in Selma have made this a seven-day-a-week job, but we can't give in one inch. We're going to enforce state laws."

Martin Luther King's decision to resume the march intensified the crisis. Wallace now appealed to the one man who might spare him another political defeat: "Voter registration and voting rights are not the issues involved in these street demonstrations," he declared in a telegram to President Johnson. "The activities of the civil rights leaders are directed toward a defiance of lawful . . . authority." Wallace requested an early meeting with the president and was pleased by Johnson's prompt invitation.

The president awaited him in the Oval Office. For three hours and seventeen minutes Wallace begged him to persuade civil rights leaders to stop the Selma march. Johnson, just as doggedly, asked Wallace to let the march proceed. The president urged him to change with the times, to accept the principles of universal suffrage, but Wallace insisted that "if I endorsed your views on suffrage, I could not return to Alabama and face my people."

"You know, George," Johnson said, "you can turn those [demonstrations] off in a minute. You go out there in front of those television cameras right now, and you announce you've decided to desegregate every school in Alabama."

"Oh, Mr. President," Wallace replied, "I can't do that, you know. The schools have got school boards, they're locally run. I haven't got the political power to do that."

Johnson leaned his face right at Wallace, and he growled, *"Don't you shit me, George Wallace."*

"If I hadn't left when I did," Wallace later admitted, "he'd have had me coming out for civil rights."

Undaunted by the Johnson "treatment," Wallace pleaded for understanding. "I'm against violence," he said, holding up a newspaper showing a police officer pouncing on a black protester. "That's not in Selma, that's in New York." He argued that the solution to the race problem would be found not in protest movements or the loosening of state literacy requirements but in "educational enhancement." He pointed with pride to his school-construction program, his free textbook program, the creation of opportunities that, he said, would reduce the number of dropouts among black students. But he refused to permit the march from Selma to Montgomery.

Judge Frank Johnson soon overturned the governor's ban. "A federal judge . . . prostitutes the law in favor of mob rule," Wallace replied in a televised address to the state legislature. "We see today a foreign philosophy that says to the people, 'You need not bother to work and meet the qualifications of a free man.' All you must do is demonstrate and cause chaos and create a situation whereby our propagandists, masquerading as newsmen, may destroy faith in local law enforcement . . . so that we may take all police powers into the central government." Yet, at the very moment Wallace condemned the growth of federal power, he demanded its presence in Alabama by formally requesting that President Johnson provide protection for the marchers. He also pleaded with Alabamians, as he had during the Tuscaloosa crisis of 1963, "to stay away from the points of tension." On the day the marchers were scheduled to arrive in Montgomery, he gave all female state employees the day off.

> I've never been to heaven, but I think I'm right
> You won't find George Wallace anywhere in sight
> Oh, keep your eyes on the prize.

Inside his office in the state capitol, Wallace struggled not to hear the reverberations from the throng outside. Martin Luther King was speaking:

> I know you are asking today, "How long will it take?" I come to say to you this afternoon, however difficult the moment, however frustrating the hour, it will not be long, because truth pressed to earth will rise again. How long? Not long, because no lie can live forever.
>   How long? Not long, because you still reap what you sow.
>   How long? Not long. Because the arm of the moral universe is long, but it bends toward justice.
>   How long? Not long, 'cause mine eyes have seen the glory of the coming of the Lord. . . .

He peeked through the venetian blinds, startled by the size of the crowd. He was told it was as big as the inaugural crowd. "In a few years that may be the way the inauguration crowd looks," he quipped. "Don't say that." When a formal delegation of protesters brought a petition to the mansion, Wallace refused to accept it.

He went to bed with the satisfaction of having thwarted any real concessions. At daylight, however, he learned that on a remote stretch of Alabama highway a white civil rights worker, Mrs. Viola Liuzzo, had been shot and killed. "Life simply should not be that cheap," Wallace said. But, despite his sympathy, he defended his administration from any culpability: "It's still safer on Highway 80 in Alabama than riding the subway in New York." By the time Wallace agreed to meet with the civil rights petitioners, Selma had become an inspiration for the single item that Wallace most feared—passage of the Voting Rights Act of 1965.

Besieged by national opinion, he was reduced to a series of rear guard retreats: another southern governor on the run. A Wall Street brokerage firm, taking Wallace at his word about Alabama's inability to bear the cost of protecting civil rights marchers, decided to reevaluate the state's credit rating. At the NASA center in Huntsville, the former Nazi scientist Wernher Von Braun told the governor that racial discord might force the closing of that federal facility. Antipoverty funds continued to reach Alabama counties, despite Wallace's occasional vetoes. And in the judicial system his efforts to block desegregation produced endless litigation and steady defeat. "Governors," he complained, "are getting to be high-paid ornaments."

Yet, for Wallace, the office of governor retained great potential. He relished political activity—not the desk work, which he abhorred, but the wheeling and dealing, the speeches, and most of all the applause. By July 1965 he had attracted $1 billion of new business, including seventy-five thousand jobs. He had established free textbooks through the eighth grade (as well as textbook selection committees that screened "writers with possible connections with communist-front organizations"). He had built more roads and highways than ever before (at generous rates for friendly contractors: "What you're talking about is chicken feed," he hushed a reporter. "It doesn't amount to anything at all. Just chicken feed. Chicken feed").

The office of governor, above all, represented even higher prospects. It was, for Wallace, the best of stepping-stones. It offered access to the national media. It enabled him to meet with national politicians. It gave him credibility on a national level.

By the summer of 1965, however, Wallace's horizons were diminishing with each passing day. Not for a minute could he forget that the Alabama state constitution forbade him to succeed himself, indeed, forbade him to seek any other state office for a full year. At the pinnacle of his fame, George Wallace faced a future without power, without even a job. In a grand understatement, he told the state legislature, "If you feel a need for me in the job I try to do, then I want you to know that I feel a need for you."

In October 1965 Wallace called an emergency session of the legislature to request a constitutional amendment to permit him to serve a second term. "The liberals say George Wallace wants to be president," he stated. "What is wrong with that?" He insisted that the only issue was the right of the people to choose their government: "Let the people speak! . . . I say let the people speak!" But, despite his audacity and political influence, Wallace encountered bedrock opposition in the state senate. He pleaded, cajoled, and attacked his enemies, but he could not gain the necessary votes. The failure to initiate a constitutional amendment darkened his prospects. His gloom was undisguised—and so was his anger. One day he hit a punching bag so hard that he broke his wrist.

Wallace's impending political demise soon paled in importance. In January 1966 Lurleen Wallace's doctors discovered an abdominal malignancy. After extensive surgery, they said she was cured. But, as she convalesced in the hospital, Lurleen and George viewed their future together with new eyes. For several weeks he had been talking about a change in their relationship. He watched her recovery closely. "Would you agree," he asked at last, "to run for governor?" She said, "Yes, George, I will," adding only that she wanted her doctors' consent. With their approval—and the sudden death of Wallace's only major rival, Ryan deGraffenreid—they prepared for the 1966 election.

The decision to have Lurleen run for governor revealed Wallace's immense popularity as an opponent of the political establishment. In the past he had attacked the federal judiciary, the White House, the bureaucracy, and the press. Now to this list of enemies he could add the conservative state senate that had ignored the will of the people. Once again he could invoke a populist spirit against an impersonal government.

The Wallaces appeared together in the legislative chamber to make their surprise announcement. Blond and thirty-nine, Lurleen dismissed her political inexperience and frail health. "I've been dying of cancer for five years," she said with a smile, "if you believe all the rumors." But it was Wallace who controlled the performance. "If my wife is elected," he declared, "we are frank and honest to say that I shall be by her side and shall make the policies and decisions affecting the next administration."

Aside from its legal necessity, the substitution of candidates of-

fered clear political advantages: Lurleen's campaign could at least pose
as an alternative to the past. In 1966, the first year after the passage
of the Voting Rights Act, Alabama Democrats worried about the
impact of black suffrage. As a gesture of conciliation, the party eliminated the "white supremacy" slogan from its ballot emblem. Wallace
even took the trouble to learn how to pronounce the word "Negro" so
that it didn't sound like *nigra*. With over one hundred thousand newly
registered blacks, race baiting had lost its appeal.

To the tune of hillbilly music, the Wallace campaign rolled
through the towns of Alabama. Sam and his Alabamians would warm
up the crowds while George and Lurleen mingled and shook hands.
"Now folks," Sam would say, "we want to play a little sacred number.
It's Governor and Mrs. Wallace's favorite, 'Just a Closer Walk with
Thee.' " The crowd would hush for the familiar hymn ("I am weak,
but Thou are strong") until the band switched to "Dixie" and Sam
introduced the candidates. Lurleen, shy as a schoolgirl, would accept
a bouquet of red roses, then present a four-minute talk about being
"humbled and grateful" to be "the instrument" through which her
husband might speak. When she had finished, the band would play
another round of "Dixie," which served as the signal for the incumbent, already striding to the microphone.

He would open on a note of disappointment, admitting that he
did not believe in flying saucers: "No, there ain't any flying saucers. It's
just the editors of those big northern newspapers having a running fit
because my wife is a candidate for governor." The crowd would hoot
in pleasure. And except for that reference to UFOs, Wallace scarcely
mentioned Lurleen's candidacy, considering it a "technicality." But it
reinforced his image as an enemy of the establishment: "I'm not
fighting the federal government; I'm fighting this outlaw beatnik crowd
in Washington that has just about destroyed the federal government,
and I'm trying to save it."

Nor did he hesitate to appeal to popular prejudices: "Of course,
I believe in segregation. Everybody does, when you get right down to
it." After a meeting with state school officials, he announced that
Alabama would not comply with the desegregation guidelines drawn up
in Washington. Just six days before the May primary, he halted the
integration of the state's mental hospitals, a decision that required
the transfer of inmates back to segregated facilities. Such acts assured the loss of the black vote. But on election day it made no
difference. In the largest turnout in Alabama history, including a dou-

bling of black participation, Lurleen Wallace drew over four hundred thousand votes, enough to defeat all her opponents combined and eliminate the need for a runoff.

Wallace's power had reached a zenith. Assured of control of the executive mansion for another four years, he had also purged the legislature of every single senator who the previous fall had opposed his own succession. In deference to Lurleen's landslide, he summoned the entire Alabama congressional delegation from Washington to create a united defiance of the "totalitarian" desegregation guidelines. Then he persuaded the state's college and university presidents to endorse a policy of noncompliance, and he pushed a measure through the legislature that declared the guidelines "null and void."

To demonstrate the absence of racist motives, Wallace sent his fourteen-year-old son, George, Jr., to an integrated junior high school in Montgomery. The example also underscored his own humble roots. "I ain't . . . The Club type myself," he said about the Birmingham elite. "Those folks . . . they got it all. . . . You go put a nigger in their school . . . [and] the rich folks can send their children to a private school." But he reminded school officials who had already desegregated in compliance with federal guidelines that they now violated state law. "Alabama is taking a historic step as an example," he explained. "That example is . . . telling the bureaucrats of power that they can take our federal money—and they know what they can do with it."

He lashed out at the national politicians: "There's not a bit of difference today in the national Democrats and the national Republicans," he stated on Labor Day of 1966. Robert Kennedy, Hubert Humphrey, and Lyndon Johnson on the one hand; Earl Warren, Nelson Rockefeller, George Romney, Richard Nixon, and Jacob Javits on the other: Put them all in a big sack and shake it up, he said, "and it wouldn't make any difference [who] comes out first, because they are all alike." He alone claimed to offer a clear alternative.

In November 1966 Lurleen won a huge victory, gaining 63 percent of the vote. She even attracted one-third of the black vote, largely because her opponent provided no significant difference. Her husband shared the glory: "I don't have any burning ambition to be president. My only interest is in the restoration of local government." But the day after the election he speculated more lavishly about 1968: "There's a chance of carrying a lot of states, especially industrial states. The working people are tired of this lawlessness—and that goes for working people of both races." By the time Wallace attended the national governors' conference in December, he had become comfortable with the idea: "You want to know my choice for head of the Democratic ticket? Well, it would be me."

Blue and white pennants fluttered from the lampposts along Montgomery's Dexter Avenue, and more than 100,000 people gathered to honor their new governor. The inaugural parade stretched ten miles and included not only black high school bands but also the integrated students from Huntsville. Lurleen Wallace, wearing a black cashmere suit and pillbox hat, waved occasionally to the happy crowd. But her "number-one" adviser got a bigger thrill, blowing kisses to the majorettes and beauty queens, shouting "hello" and "thanks" to passing county leaders. Even before she could speak, he stole the show with a speech about an Alabamian making just as good a president as someone from Texas.

Nipped by the presidential bug, Wallace predicted the issues for 1968: "Schools, that'll be one thing. . . . The people don't like this triflin' with their children, tellin' 'em which teachers to have to teach in which schools, and bussing little boys and girls half across a city just to achieve 'the proper racial mix.' . . . I'll give you another big one for 1968: law and order. Crime in the streets. The people are fed up with the sissy attitude of Lyndon Johnson and all the intellectual morons and theoreticians he has around him. . . . Vietnam? . . . Well, I think we've got to pour it on. We've got to win this war." He considered supporters of the Viet Cong to be traitors who, he said, should be dragged by their beards into court and then thrown *under* the jails.

Wallace's strength came from his position as a political outsider. At a time when voters worried about Vietnam, civil disobedience, and crime, he could attack the inadequacy of current programs and bemoan the failure of the regular party leaders. "I'm going over their heads," he said. "I'm going to the people." In the spring of 1967 he embarked on another speaking tour in the North, appealing to "small folks" against their natural enemies—bureaucrats (who "think they can sit there in their offices in Washington and tell us what time to go to bed and what time to get up"), college professors (who "sit up in those ivory towers and look down their noses at the rest of us and write a bunch of books"), federal judges ("the reason we have so much crime in our country is that we have a system of courts that tries to play God"), and professional politicians ("the people are going to run right over the politicians"). Asked about his own qualifications to shape foreign policy, Wallace glorified his ignorance: "I've read about foreign policy and studied—I know the number of continents. . . . We couldn't get in any worse position in our foreign policy."

In July 1967, however, he halted his political activities when a recurrence of Lurleen's cancer required prolonged treatment. Accompanying her to a clinic in Houston, he left her side only once in three weeks to denounce the "bureaucrats with beards." The suspension of speeches shielded him from charges of provoking the racial violence that burned American cities during the summer. Ignoring the angry demands for "black power," the Wallaces returned to Montgomery to push legislation that allowed schoolchildren to select the race of their teachers. "You know, there's nothing wrong with this country," Wallace said, "that we couldn't cure by turning it over to the police for a couple of years."

As Lurleen slowly recuperated, Wallace worked feverishly to qualify his American Independent party for the 1968 elections. "What we have done and what we stand for," she said to inspire him, "is bigger than my life and yours. Please go on with the fight." And when, just after the New Year, he announced his success, her prayer was as simple as it was pathetic: "I hope I can make it until November."

He made his formal announcement in February 1968. Admitting that the odds were against him, he sought something short of an absolute victory: He hoped instead to capture enough votes to control a balance of power in the electoral college. Then he could force one of the regular parties "to make a major concession to the people of our country, a solemn covenant" to protect local government, property rights, and the free enterprise system. "I would bring all these briefcase-toting bureaucrats in the Department of H.E.W. . . . and throw their briefcases in the Potomac River. . . . I would keep the peace [even] if I had to keep 30,000 troops standing on the streets, two feet apart and with two-foot-long bayonets."

As a southerner, himself a victim of federal power, Wallace appreciated the feeling of powerlessness among ordinary citizens, and he appealed to a growing hostility toward government authority. When President Johnson's commission on urban disorders described white racism as the cause of crime, Wallace called the report "an insult to the majority of the American people." He mentioned "some scum" who had recently lain down in front of the president's limousine: "When we get to be president and some anarchist lies down in front of our car, it'll be the last car he'll ever lie down in front of." Invariably his audiences shouted approval; invariably he reinforced their animosities: "A bearded professor . . . thinks he knows how to settle the Vietnam War . . . [but] hasn't got enough sense to park his bicycle straight."

Just as the campaign gathered momentum, it was abruptly stopped when Lurleen's health deteriorated. Wallace canceled his public appearances to remain at home. Then his primary target, President Johnson, withdrew from the race in March 1968. Preoccupied by Lurleen's illness, Wallace considered dropping out too. But the assassination of Martin Luther King, followed by riots in nearly every large city, increased the popularity of his law and order campaign. "I don't have any strategy," he said. "I don't sit up in some tower and theorize. . . . I'm just going ahead like I always have."

Lurleen died of cancer in May, at the age of forty-one. Red-eyed and haggard, dejected beyond expression, Wallace witnessed the swearing-in of his wife's successor, Albert Brewer. He could only sit in numbed grief. "The nights were worst of all for me," he confessed. He became listless, depressed, and morbid: "Nothing seemed to help me forget her terrible agony." But ironically it was death itself—the murder of Robert F. Kennedy—that resuscitated his political interests.

Wallace returned to the campaign trail in June, barely five weeks after Lurleen's death. He bore visible scars of grief, and the shooting of Robert Kennedy accentuated his own vulnerability. He viewed assassination, like flying in airplanes, as one of the risks of politics. At least he would go down fighting for his beliefs and doing what he enjoyed most in life. But wherever possible, he spoke from behind bulletproof glass or abruptly departed from an embattled stage.

Wallace tried to recover not only his dangling campaign, but also the threads of existence. Through politics he managed to staunch his sadness, but it was a slapdash therapy at best, and sometimes it failed. One night he ended an exhausting day by dialing a familiar phone number, only to drop the receiver like a hot coal when he realized Lurleen no longer waited for its ring.

His sense of personal loneliness mirrored his political isolation. He refused to shun endorsements from right-wing groups, described retiring Supreme Court Justice Earl Warren as an enemy of constitutional government, and proposed that the "anarchists" who disrupted his speeches needed "a good crease in the skull." He also gained unexpected help from the troubles of the establishment. When the Democratic National Convention in Chicago triggered street violence, Wallace said that the police "probably showed too much restraint." His candor—and his blunt style—won increasing support. By September, according to pollster Louis Harris, half the voters liked Wallace "for saying it the way it really is," and even more agreed that "liberals, intellectuals, and longhairs have run the country for too long."

As Wallace gained greater confidence, he ironically fell prey to his own illusions: He thought that he ought to appear "presidential." After months of searching, he chose as his vice-presidential running mate General Curtis LeMay. But that much-decorated soldier unwittingly destroyed Wallace's effort to appear respectable. In their first press conference together, LeMay expressed his willingness to use nuclear weapons in Vietnam. Wallace scrambled to the microphones to amend that statement: "We can win and defend in Vietnam without the use of nuclear weapons." LeMay's name also clashed with Wallace's deliberate rejection of professionalism. The release of formal position papers, the creation of an official platform, and the sheer exhaustion of the campaign gradually but inexorably weakened Wallace's vitality. He became brittle, actually dared hecklers to fight him, and he became more offensive. Organized labor, which backed the candidacy of Hubert Humphrey, denounced Wallace's claim to be a friend of working people.

Despite his skill at articulating the anger of the voters, Wallace's campaign collided with more powerful political forces: the inertia of patriotism and the sanctity of the two-party system. Public-opinion polls documented a dramatic decline in Wallace's popularity. According to Harris, his appeal as the best man to uphold law and order had reached a high point of 53 percent in September and then slid steadily from 43 to 33 to 24 to 21 percent. At the same time, his percentage of the total vote fell from 21 percent to 18 to 16 to 13 percent. In one week George Gallup detected a five-point slippage. Wallace lashed back: "They lie when they poll. They are trying to rig an election. Eastern money runs everything. They are going to be pointed out [as] the liars that they are." Five days before the election, however, he virtually conceded defeat: "Whoever becomes president of the United States . . . is going to be a better president because of this movement, because he's going to see . . . that there are other viewpoints that are to be incorporated in the attitude of the government."

Wallace returned to Clayton, Alabama, to vote, then took a stroll with reporters around the courthouse square. "The movement is highly successful already," he said. "Both parties are talking like we do. . . . We've shown that a southerner can be nominated for the presidency." He predicted a conservative tide that would sweep the country: "This is a people's movement, not my movement. I've been the spokesman. I will continue to speak for them." Later he sat in his campaign office, flicking the dials of the color television that reported his failure. "It's a fine popular vote," he said of the nine million people who had supported him. But, aside from forty-five electoral votes in the Deep South, he made no inroads in the electoral college. At midnight Wallace appeared at the cheerless Garrett Coliseum in Montgomery, where the Taylor Sisters—Mona and Lisa—entertained the diehards. "The election is not yet over," he stated. But, when California entered the Nixon column, it was.

He was buoyant the next day, saying farewell to the press at the Jefferson Davis Hotel: "The principles and philosophy that we espoused continue to live on . . . because the winner of the presidential campaign said almost identically the same things we were saying." He telegramed congratulations to Nixon: "After all . . . we've both lost a presidential race." And, like Nixon, Wallace refused to disappear: "Our movement of millions of people is still intact. . . . We will be around."

One month later a reporter found Wallace in his stark campaign office on Lee Street in Montgomery. The bunting had faded. "Stand Up for America" posters curled at the corners. He would not speak for the record, but it seemed that all he could do was speak, rambling in a political monologue that was interspersed with showings of news clippings and photographs. He talked about 1972, reentering the Democratic party, the prospects of the Nixon presidency. As he had in 1958, after his first political defeat, Wallace felt empty. But now his self-pity blurred with a more profound mourning. Lurleen was on his mind, entered his conversation at odd moments. "Just write," he told the reporter, "that you came in and looked at my pictures."

Phyllis
Stewart
Schlafly
(II)

"Mrs. Schlafly fights against communism": With these words, the *St. Louis Globe-Democrat* named her Woman of Achievement in Public Affairs for 1963. "Phyllis Schlafly stands for everything that has made America great and for those things which will keep it that way." From her mansion overlooking the Mississippi, she searched for signs of danger—and worried that peace with Soviet Russia would undermine her heritage: religion, family, and the free enterprise system. She also feared that the liberals would capture the Republican party in the next presidential election.

The succession of President Johnson emboldened her efforts for the conservative cause. In December 1963 she announced her candidacy for delegate to the Republican National Convention of 1964. She also started to write a book, *A Choice Not an Echo*, to arouse Republicans against the liberal tide: "History shows that mistakes can

be prevented by providing the people with facts and warnings in antici-
pation of a threatened event." Her target was not the Democratic party
but the enemy within: the "kingmakers" of the Republican establishment.

While writing her book at night, Mrs. Schlafly continued to fulfill
her varied obligations during the day. At a Lincoln Day luncheon, she
presented the keynote speech to the Missouri Federation of Republican Women. She served as chairman of the 1964 Easter Seal Mail
Campaign. She addressed the Missouri DAR about the dangers of
communist slogans—"like gelatin, 'peace' propaganda comes in many
delicious flavors"—and she warned that "the waters of history contain
the wrecks of countries which thought they could guarantee peace by
disarmament." She campaigned vigorously to attend the Republican
convention in San Francisco, running first in a field of four. She also
managed her household, took care of Fred and the five children, and
taught her six-year-old daughter to read. She was pregnant, too, and
expected the baby just after her fortieth birthday.

Her book, published privately by her own Père Marquette Press,
appeared in the spring of 1964. It soon demolished the tranquility of
the Republican party. In a saga of treachery, she accused the "secret
kingmakers" of the eastern establishment of rigging nominations and
adopting phony platforms in order to produce election defeats. Their
goal, she said, was to assure the continuation of an "America Last"
foreign policy.

"Who really picks your presidential candidates?" Mrs. Schlafly
asked.

"How are political conventions stolen?"

"How do 'hidden persuaders' and propaganda gimmicks influence
politics?"

Her charges reached the current election. "Will the Republicans
win in 1964?" Not if the kingmakers could prevent it, she said, because
they despised the one candidate who could win—Barry Goldwater.
"Just as one can predict with certainty that the sun will rise tomorrow,
so Republicans can bet their last dollar that the New York kingmakers
will use every weapon in the book . . . to defeat Barry Goldwater."

Mrs. Schlafly's instincts for conspiracy, finely honed in the war
against communism, served her well in the presidential race of 1964.
She predicted that New York Governor Nelson Rockefeller would fare
poorly in the primaries; she also predicted that the kingmakers would
sponsor a photogenic alternative, such as Governor William Scranton

of Pennsylvania, to lead the liberal faction. And just as her book appeared, on the eve of the California primary, the presidential contest seemed to follow her unlikely scenario. Rockefeller stumbled, Scranton rose, and Mrs. Schlafly emerged as a Republican prophet: "They saw the whole thing unfold exactly as I laid it out." Stimulated by gigantic purchases from Goldwater supporters—some businessmen bought thirty thousand copies!—her book saturated the Republican wards and precincts. Wherever it went, Goldwater's standing improved. "Cold water has the magic quality of leadership that is based on independence of thought and courage," Mrs. Schlafly declared. "He is the one candidate who will not pull his punches to please the kingmakers. . . . He is the only candidate who will truly offer the voters 'a choice, not an echo.' "

At the Cow Palace in San Francisco, Mrs. Schlafly received celebrity treatment. "Republican national conventions are the most fun things I can think of," she said. Everyone there had read her book. She attended parties at Nob Hill hotels. Strangers approached her to shake hands, although one liberal complained about receiving seventy unsolicited copies of her book! On the convention floor she cheered for ex-president Eisenhower. She cheered for Senator Everett Dirksen, who nominated Goldwater, "the peddler's grandson," for president. She cast her vote with the majority, and then she joined in the hysterical, self-confident laughter that heard only its own echo. It was, Mrs. Schlafly recalled, "the most exciting week of my life . . . a very exciting, victorious convention."

Back in Alton she spent the summer delivering boxes of books to the post office. "Putting up my own $3,000 to pay the printer was the biggest risk I'd ever taken," she later remarked. "It paid off. It sold and sold. I didn't need money from anyone." One million, two million, three million copies—at ten cents apiece, they made her economically secure and famous. Now she could add a triumphant epilogue to her saga of eastern conspiracies.

But the plots against her persisted: "Slogans have always been a part of politics, and we thought they were rough, until this year." The liberals called Goldwater a gunslinging cowboy. Mrs. Schlafly defended the image: "If you talk to any policeman, you know that they are taught to shoot from the hip—that is the way they protect society."

One afternoon in August a call from Honolulu interrupted her schedule. On the line was Admiral Chester Ward, USN retired, one-time judge advocate general, appealing to her for help. The survival of the nation was at stake, and he wanted her to write another book to thwart another conspiracy. She hesitated to accept, but her husband urged her—insisted, finally, that she undertake the project. She returned to the typewriter:

"Why is Khrushchev so confident of burying us, when Lenin thought Communism had only a 50/50 chance?"

"Do you know who is digging YOUR grave so that Khrushchev can fulfill his boast?"

"Do you know who is *really* risking nuclear war?"

For Mrs. Schlafly the enemy lurked not among communists but with "the gravediggers," "card-carrying liberals" like Secretary of Defense Robert Strange McNamara—she invariably used his middle name—Democratic defeatists who "day by day" labored to make us "weaker and weaker." Instead of building the nuclear arsenal, "they are diverting funds from defense muscle . . . [and] spending vast sums on non-military boondoggles, such as putting a man on the moon, and on purely political projects, such as the Poverty Bill." She chastised the lack of respect for engineering principles: "McNamara's failure to test properly the Edsel car was damaging only to Ford, but . . . his failure to test our missile warheads and defenses . . . will be fatal to the American Republic."

By September 1964 *The Gravediggers* joined *A Choice Not an Echo* in the campaign mails: "If our choice is wrong in 1964—there will be no second choice. . . . In 1964, General Barry Goldwater is the irreplaceable man. . . . Only he has the strength and leadership to turn the gravediggers out of office. Only he can give us PEACE WITH-OUT SURRENDER." In two months it sold two million copies.

Mrs. Schlafly's reputation spread through the GOP. The National Federation of Republican Women gave her a special citation for "dedicated service to Republican ideals and philosophy" and unanimously elected her first-vice-president, next in line for the presidency. She used this forum on behalf of Goldwater: "It looks as though the Johnson administration is determined to lose the nuclear arms race," she told the Republican women of St. Louis, "just as the same administration lost the Bay of Pigs invasion and is losing today in South Vietnam."

Her dissatisfaction with the Democratic foreign policy reflected an abiding suspicion of the Soviet Union. Where Presidents Kennedy and Johnson welcomed a thaw in the cold war and preferred to fight communism in Third World countries with technology, economic aid, and occasional military assistance, she steadfastly denied any weakening of the Soviet monolith. In her mind—and in Goldwater's—the ultimate enemy remained in Moscow. Thus the diversion of military spending for brushfire wars imperiled American military superiority. Yet it was precisely this thinking that alarmed the electorate. Having recently come close to war with the Soviets at the time of the Cuban Missile Crisis, the voters demanded greater security from a nuclear threat. They were eager to believe Johnson's promises of détente.

The opposition of conservatives to government spending also clashed with the economic optimism of the early 1960s. When Kennedy and Johnson espoused Keynesian principles—the idea that the federal government could assure economic growth by deficit spending or by altering the money supply—Goldwater supporters denounced such social engineering as a threat to the free enterprise system. Yet the tax cut of 1962 had helped stimulate the economy, and heavy military expenditures under Kennedy had reduced unemployment. Prosperity, in turn, provided greater confidence in economic tinkering. Even though few Americans understood the economic theories, most were prepared to vote their pocketbooks.

Given the economic upswing and the fear of the cold war, Johnson's landslide seemed inevitable. But to Mrs. Schlafly his victory confirmed her belief in conspiratorial politics. In a piece titled "The Lie That Won the Election," she acknowledged that "the decisive issue of the 1964 presidential election was nuclear war. The majority [voted] for Lyndon Johnson because . . . they were convinced by campaign oratory and television spots that LBJ would keep the peace better than Barry Goldwater." But she argued that such confidence was misplaced and that members of the Johnson administration, particularly McNamara, had testified falsely about the extent of American unilateral disarmament. Had voters known the truth, she said, "the election would have gone the other way."

Mrs. Schlafly also described other cabals against the Republicans, such as "the racial revolutionaries" who turned off "their violence like a faucet . . . after Goldwater was nominated" or the congressmen who stopped investigating the allegedly fraudulent TFX airplane contract to avoid embarrassing the administration. Such charges, even if they had been true, had had a small impact on the election. But Mrs. Schlafly emphasized these plots and machinations because she would not admit that her judgment about Goldwater had been wrong. Asked by a reporter her reaction to the election, she expressed an odd satisfac-

tion: "I'm thrilled to learn there are now twenty-six million conservatives in the Republican party."

" 'Sixty-four was a very big year for me," Mrs. Schlafly concluded:
two election campaigns, two books, dozens of speeches, weekly radio
broadcasts for the DAR, endless telephone calls. "But I was never gone
from home overnight, except when I went to the convention." One
week after the election she gave birth to her sixth and last child, a
daughter. Despite her enlarged family responsibilities, she soon
resumed her political work: "The only talent I really claim to have is
the ability to work in the midst of bedlam."

In the spring of 1965 Mrs. Schlafly and Admiral Ward began
another collaborative project, but she reserved her best energy for the
continuing partisan struggle. "The issue is not conservatism versus
liberalism," she insisted. "It is survival versus surrender. We have to
show what Lyndon Johnson is doing to advance Communism while
getting American boys killed under the guise of fighting it." In her eyes
Vietnam remained an unnecessary sideshow to the main theater of war
against Soviet communism. As first-vice-president of the National Federation of Republican Women, she traveled around the Midwest, giving as many as three speeches a week to strengthen her following.
"Many people in the organization have told me they would like to see
me run for the presidency," she said.

When the Republican women met in Washington, D.C., in 1965,
however, she received an unenthusiastic reception. The Goldwater
debacle had shifted the GOP back toward the center: "A few Republicans who did not support Goldwater now have the crust to tell the
Goldwater people to move aside. I don't think they are going to do it."
Instead of a direct challenge, Mrs. Schlafly encountered subtle parlia-
mentary maneuvers. The steering committee postponed the next elections to 1967 and voted to move the meeting closer to party headquarters. "My California following was just immense," Mrs. Schlafly
explained. "So that's why they postponed it and rigged up this notion
that no city in the United States could accommodate the convention
except Washington, D.C. Of course, I knew what was going on, but
I was powerless to do anything."

Keeping up appearances—"Mrs. Schlafly was her usual, good-
humored, lovely self," stated one delegate—she worked to protect her
base of support. In October 1965 she embarked on a speaking tour of
southern California. Her topic was national defense, and according to
her own count she drew crowds as large as 2,000. She also released one

of her talks, "What Are the Gravediggers Doing Now?" as a long-playing record. "An eloquent spokesman for a strong America here tells how the gravediggers are using the politicians to turn our country into a nuclear nudist colony," she wrote in self-promotion. "It includes Mrs. Schlafly's witty and musical descriptions of the gravediggers. You can inspire and activate your friends and neighbors . . . by inviting them to your home to hear this record."

Mrs. Schlafly published her third book with Admiral Ward, *Strike from Space,* in November 1965. She called it "a complete handbook to the best issues the Republicans have had since slavery," "a tool which can elect a pro-American Congress in 1966," "your scorecard to identify the men in Washington who are digging your grave"—a story "stranger than fiction" but one in which "the potential victims are real people, good Americans: you, your family, and your friends." As in her other books, the plot began in Moscow: "All true Communists . . . are dedicated to the Communist conquest of the world as the essential precondition to their other principal objectives." And she attempted to undermine criticism by claiming that the conspiracy was "so shocking to the non-Communist mind that, even if we prematurely discover it, we simply will not believe it."

As she explained it, the Gulf of Tonkin incident of 1964 typified the communist plot: "As a result of a deliberate provocation, carefully planned and exquisitely timed" to coincide with the presidential election, "the United States began the long fall into the trap of a shooting war" in Vietnam. "*Why* do the Communists want the United States fighting in Vietnam? Why did they deliberately provoke us into bombing North Vietnam?"

Her conclusion seemed as shocking as she had promised: "All the evidence screams the terrible conclusion that the Soviet strategy is *Make a Noise in Vietnam, but STRIKE FROM SPACE.* The Soviets deliberately trapped us in Vietnam to direct our attention and resources to a guerrilla-conventional war and away from the nuclear threat in space." While the United States had committed "the big money and huge national effort [into] prestige projects"—the "moondoggle," for example, in which "there is no military value"—the Soviets had developed orbital missiles that threatened "our survival and our freedom as well as peace on earth." (Remember, she cautioned, in the Russian language "Peace . . . means the condition *after* the communists have conquered the world!")

As the Vietnam War continued, Mrs. Schlafly found additional confirmation of the communist conspiracy. The liberal "gravediggers" had spread their influence among American youth. "The result is the disgusting demonstrations about Vietnam: the mobs halting troop trains, the burning of draft cards, and the anonymous phone calls to widows of our men killed in Vietnam saying, 'Your husband got what he deserved.' " In the face of the burgeoning antiwar movement, she pleaded for traditional patriotism: "We must have the will to run the strategic arms race, the courage to stand up to the scare-words . . . and the dedication to . . . win the only kind of peace we can preserve with freedom—*the peace of the brave.*"

Mrs. Schlafly continued to write articles and give speeches about national defense, and she prepared for battle within the Republican party. She now spent less time on DAR projects, abandoned the "America Wake Up!" radio show, and reduced her work for the Cardinal Mindszenty Foundation. "I just plain found the politics more fun," she has explained. In 1966 the National Federation of Republican Women awarded Mrs. Schlafly a silver bowl and another citation for "dedicated service," while the women of Illinois bestowed a gold charm with little dots for every crossroads at which she had addressed a Republican group. She had traveled a hundred thousand miles in Illinois alone.

Her goal was to be elected president of the National Federation of Republican Women, a position that would enable her to influence the choice of convention delegates in a conservative direction. As the last surviving Goldwater supporter in the Republican hierarchy, she expected opposition from the party leaders. But she refused to surrender quietly: "It was the principle of the thing; and conservatives are people of principle." When the Republican party leadership passed over her name and nominated a widow from Orange County, California, named Gladys O'Donnell, Mrs. Schlafly denounced the "New York liberals" for attempting "to purge" the party.

Republican women were soon fighting like cats. The incumbent president, Dorothy Elston, released a letter from Barry Goldwater that seemed to endorse Mrs. O'Donnell, but Mrs. Schlafly showed reporters an unexpurgated version of the same letter, which proved to be more neutral. Mrs. Elston said that Mrs. Schlafly would be a bad president because she had six children to raise. "My six children are the six reasons why I am in politics," Mrs. Schlafly replied. "They are my stake in the future of our country." Mrs. Elston said that whoever became the next president had to live in Washington, D.C. Mrs. Schlafly said she did not intend to become an office manager. Then Mrs. Elston said that the next president also had to live in the same office-apartment that she herself had been using. "Obviously," Mrs. Schlafly replied, "no normal, happily married woman with children could live in the one-bedroom Washington apartment." She knew that these objections concealed another political reality: "The men in the Republican National Committee know they can control Gladys O'Donnell, and they know that they can't control me."

> Phyllis exemplifies the finest in American womanhood, creating a beautiful home life for her family, successfully weaving all her interests into the total fabric of her life.

Her platform remained true to conservative principles: "I believe that our women are capable of making up their own minds, managing their own clubs, and electing their officers without outside interference. I believe that the big decisions in the Republican Party should be made by the grass roots [Republicans] who labor in the precincts." Her personal goals appeared self-effacing: "the satisfaction of knowing I did all in my power to give children the opportunity to grow up in a free and independent America."

Forty-five hundred Republican women convened in Washington, D.C., in May 1967. Here Mrs. Schlafly expected to prove her popularity among the rank and file. But the party leadership controlled the voting process and used its power to weaken hers. She could do nothing but protest, accusing the leaders of importing busloads of anti-Schlafly delegates and rigging the voting machines to reverse the actual tally. In the end the vote went 1,910 to 1,494 against her.

Soured by the ordeal, she now proposed the creation of a new Republican women's group that would be dedicated to conservative principles. "Strictly volunteers," she suggested, "not controlled from the top down and not loaded with political payrollers," but a "grass roots organization made up of just plain American women and mothers who believe in the cause of constitutional government and freedom." But when some of her supporters, including Maureen Reagan Sills, questioned a precipitous secession, Mrs. Schlafly reined in her ambition: "I am not going to lead you into anything you don't want to do. . . . Go home, think about it, pray about it, and write me in Alton."

She had come very close to victory, and, even though the National Federation of Republican Women lacked any real power, Mrs. Schlafly recognized its vast potential: "The political world I inhabit is a world of women. . . . This is a world where young mothers take their children with them to club meetings and when they do their precinct work, ringing doorbells and distributing literature." Such low-level workers formed the basis of her constituency. "They all want leadership," she said. "I will continue to give leadership and do as my supporters wish." A few weeks after her defeat, she wrote to the three thousand stalwarts who had followed her to Washington: "Dear and Loyal Friend, . . . You should banish any illusion that they will ever give conservatives their fair share of candidates, appointments, or legislation."

Yet she was reluctant to start a separate organization: "My object was not to be president of something. I just [wanted] to make a conservative voice felt in the Republican party and help conservative candidates. We've got to have somebody who offers a real change." She proposed instead a conservative network to coordinate political activities, and to handle contributions she established the Eagle Trust Fund in the summer of 1967: "Our overriding objective is to nominate and elect the right kind of president in 1968, [one] who can lead America in these perilous times."

In August 1967 her supporters received the first installment of a four-page newsletter called *The Phyllis Schlafly Report*. It kept alive the anger of her thwarted election, but more importantly it served as a personal forum for her conservative ideology. Through her newsletter Mrs. Schlafly would develop a coalition of supporters. She not only editorialized about current events but encouraged her readers to undertake specific political activities—a letter-writing campaign, for example, or a petition drive—to influence public policy. And she told them what kinds of issues they should be concerned about.

In the first newsletter she warned about "secret treaties" that "imperiled U.S. rights" to the Panama Canal: "The new Johnson giveaway will be a military defeat for our country even worse than the Kennedy-McNamara defeat at the Bay of Pigs." By the second issue she claimed credit for success in the headline "Shelving of Panama Canal Treaty Great Victory for America." But she also warned that "your life is no longer protected by the overwhelming strength that America had when McNamara took office." She demanded a prompt military buildup: "It is time we learned that we can never satisfy the Communists or the radical agitators *at any price*."

For the 1968 election, Mrs. Schlafly launched another campaign book, *Safe—Not Sorry*. "We have a no-win war in Vietnam, a noprosecute war on crime and communism, and a no-work war on poverty"—all were the result of cowardly leadership in the face of a massive communist conspiracy. She lamented the credulity of the public: "There are a few Americans who still cling to the naïve belief that there are no conspiracies and that events just spontaneously happen without anyone planning them that way." But she listed a series of public events, such as urban riots and violent crime, that did not "just happen"—instead, she claimed, they had been "organized by outside agitators and armed guerrillas, by various civil rights and New Left groups saturated with Communists and pro-Communists . . . by professional revolutionaries filled with hatred of Western civilization, and by federally-funded poverty workers and assorted do-gooders who think the only way to solve the problems of the 'ghetto' is to burn it down." That was why the blacks suffered the most: "It is a mark of Communist violence that Reds kill their own in order to make 'victims' to demonstrate about. . . . The Communists planned it that way . . . to make Negroes hate the whites, hate the police, and hate America."

In February 1968 she summoned supporters of the Eagle Trust Fund to St. Louis to attend a three-day Political Action Leadership Conference on the coming election. Two hundred fifty Republican women from thirty states, each wearing a gold eagle lapel pin, gathered beneath the banner THE EAGLES ARE FLYING. "This is not a new organization," Mrs. Schlafly said in opening the convention. "We already have an organization—the Republican party." She criticized the "socialistic" programs of the Johnson administration and the president's National Advisory Commission on Civil Disorders for blaming urban violence on white racism: "Guilt is *not* collective—guilt is personal." Then, behind closed doors, she organized workshops on such topics as "How to Prevent Liberal Control of Local Party Conventions," "How to Stand Up to the Rockefeller Blitz," and "How to Elect the Right Delegates to the Republican National Convention in Miami." In a vigorous finale, she exhorted the women to work aggressively at the local level. But they passed no resolutions, made no endorsements, and explicitly rebuffed the third-party possibility of Governor George Wallace. "I'm not for third alternatives," Mrs. Schlafly said.

Her political views left no ambiguities: "I believe there will always be bad guys in the world, and America must have nuclear strength or it will always be a temptation to other world powers." To the DAR of Webster Groves she stressed the indispensability of the ABM missile system to assure "American survival in the nuclear age." She saluted the rising star of California Governor Ronald Reagan, but as a political realist she went to the 1968 Republican National Convention as a delegate for Richard Nixon. "I supported Nixon because of his unequivocal pledge to restore our strategic superiority," she stated. "Nixon looked me in the eye. I heard him make his pledges."

Since four of the last five Democratic Presidents have involved us in four long, bloody wars, can the Democrats be depended on to give us peace?

Do you want to continue the Democratic policy of military weakness and indecision which cost us the *Pueblo* and crew and prolongs the Vietnam War?

Do you approve the Democrats giving away your money in foreign aid to Communist, pro-Communist and neutralist countries?

Elect Republicans in 1968!
PHYLLIS SCHLAFLY

As the only woman representative in the Illinois delegation at the Miami convention, Mrs. Schlafly mixed the serious business of national survival with partisan celebration. She cavorted on the beaches, attended buffet dinners, hosted an Eagle hospitality suite at the Deauville Hotel. "It's like being at a wonderful party," she said. "Oh, I never get bored. This is fun. I don't think there are more than a half dozen women in the country who have been a delegate as many times as I have. I've been on the credentials committee twice." In a formal eighteen-page statement, she testified to the platform committee about the twelve major gaps in the national defense: "The enemy is getting stronger and we're getting weaker." Then she joined the Republican majority in voting for Nixon and Spiro Agnew. "There are crises on so many fronts," she explained. "There is what I call the McNamara crisis. . . . I'm also concerned about law and order."

By the end of the summer Mrs. Schlafly and Admiral Ward had completed yet another campaign manifesto, *The Betrayers*. "Our cities have become more dangerous than the jungles infested by Viet Cong guerrillas," she wrote. "On all sides we witness a spineless surrender to violence—to rioters, looters, arsonists, murderers, rapists, street mobs, university students carrying obscene signs, 'peace' demonstrators, pornographers, revolutionaries, and blackmailers." To Mrs. Schlafly the problems of America in the 1960s revealed the signature of the communist conspiracy: "There must be betrayers in influential positions in order to bring America down so fast in so short a time." Ever the Republican, she called for "a complete housecleaning in the federal government in November 1968. It is the *only* thing we know we *can* accomplish this year."

After Nixon's victory Mrs. Schlafly expected a tangible reward for her loyalty, especially after Senator Dirksen recommended her for a position as "nonpaid consultant" on the president's Foreign Intelligence Advisory Board. "I didn't want a job in Washington," she recalled, "and that would have been right down my alley." But the Nixon White House was also listening to other advice. "They gave that job to Rockefeller, so you know it was an important job." Six weeks after Nixon's inauguration, Mrs. Schlafly pleaded with the president to replace incumbent bureaucrats with loyal Republicans: "This is the only way we can secure the change the American people voted for. . . . If Republicans fail to use this tool, no one will thank them for their gentlemanliness."

She was surprised, then angered, when Henry Kissinger continued the policies of his Democratic predecessors. "Richard Nixon ran on my platform," she liked to quote Governor George Wallace; "but after the election, he adopted Hubert Humphrey's." Even with a Republican in the White House, Mrs. Schlafly discovered that her brand of conservatism remained frozen out of power, betrayed not by her enemies but by friends.

John
Herschel
Glenn
(II)

"He seemed even more shaken by Kennedy's death than most of us," observed NASA psychologist Robert Voas. "It was as though a buddy had been shot down beside him." He mourned deeply. In the death of the president, John Glenn saw reminders of his own survivals—in World War II, in Korea, in the red smoke above the Atlantic—and he felt an obligation to justify the sacrifices of those less lucky than himself. With millions of other Americans, he "sat back and took stock of ourselves and our country and what our responsibilities might be and reassessed things."

With his future in the space program precarious, Glenn began to think seriously about politics, especially when he learned from the president's widow that Kennedy had approved his interest "in continuing public service." Yet the assassination had removed a powerful ally, and President Johnson showed no interest in supporting his aspirations.

Robert Kennedy, once the prime mover of Glenn's political fantasies, now discouraged the idea, emphasizing the difficulty of developing a professional organization.

But Glenn held a romantic view of the political process. Whereas the Kennedys and Johnson and George Wallace had studied politics all their lives, had learned the rules of brokerage in the courthouses, precincts, and cloakrooms of power, Glenn's lessons came from his civics class at New Concord High School and from occasional weekend visits to the congressional galleries. And his fame as an astronaut had catapulted him beyond traditional party organizations to a point where he did not seem to understand how essential they might be for anyone who seriously intended a career in American politics. "One of the fascinating things about the space program is that it gave me a chance to shape the future," he later said in a characteristic mix of candor and naïveté. "What an exciting, exhilarating thing for me! That's what's so exciting about politics. . . . You can help work out problems and plan for our future and, by God, that's exciting!"

Political inexperience was not his only handicap. Glenn's ideas about government appeared half-formed. He lacked a coherent philosophy and an agenda of action. He believed that personal qualities, patriotism, and virtue constituted sufficient criteria for leadership and that he could learn about politics from books. In his ranch-style house in one of the newly built suburbs of Houston, near the NASA space center, he sat in his den surrounded by trophies and put himself through a crash course in political theory. He read John Kennedy's *Profiles in Courage* and Theodore White's *The Making of the President 1960,* John Kenneth Galbraith's *The Affluent Society* and Barry Goldwater's *The Conscience of a Conservative.*

From this hodgepodge he extracted bland, non-ideological conclusions: "I think that a man can be conservative without being a reactionary and that he can be a liberal without being a radical, and that conservative and liberal can sit down and reason together without vituperation and without hate." He distrusted ideologues "so blinded by their beliefs they find the smallest disagreement and any opposition as evidence of treason. These black spirits line the main road of our nation's progress as a funeral mob shouting profanities at each other and all those that march steadily toward the future."

Glenn finally concluded that "to sit back and let fate play its hand out and never try to influence it at all is not the way man was meant to operate." He persuaded himself that his military and technical background, instead of limiting his political contribution, could provide a unique expertise for the space age. "If I don't have the guts to go ahead and try now," he said, "I'll regret it all my life."

His decision was complicated by the uncertainty of his political affiliation. Although his parents were lifelong Democrats, his wife was a Republican, and in the past he had voted across party lines. In the confusion, both parties claimed him. Republican leader Ray Bliss asked Glenn to run for the House of Representatives, as did presidential contenders George Romney and William Scranton. The Republicans even arranged for Glenn to be the guest of former president Eisenhower at the Rose Bowl football game, but the political conversation there was inconclusive. The Democrats, meanwhile, encouraged him to begin his political career in a less glamorous office, perhaps as lieutenant governor of Ohio.

His interest in government was taken seriously by so many professional politicians because there was a new ingredient in the electoral process. It was a time when political images and style had become paramount. President Kennedy had demonstrated the power of the media, and Glenn's face was familiar to everyone. After the assassination, moreover, anyone with the slightest connection to Kennedy could command instant attention. That was another political asset. Like Kennedy, he could project personal qualities that appealed to the public: health, vigor, and courage. And he appeared confident because he *was* confident. He had standing in his own right. Having been acclaimed an American hero, he believed in himself, and he felt entitled to a hero's perquisites, including the honor of public service.

Despite his inexperience, therefore, he intended to enter politics at the top—as a senator from Ohio. But before he could announce his decision to challenge the incumbent, Stephen Young, in the Democratic primary, he first had to resign from NASA and the marines. It was a difficult step. In January 1964, at the age of forty-two, Glenn believed that the first moon flights were seven years away—when he would be almost fifty—"not very old for most occupations, but on the edge of doubt for astronauts." Although he wanted desperately to make the first flight to the moon, he appreciated the diminishing possibility: "To be the oldest living astronaut in a permanent training status didn't seem to be ideal career planning. I began to wonder if I could perform a more active service for the U.S. in some other capacity."

Two months after the Kennedy assassination, he presented a formal request to be relieved of his assignment to NASA. Then he flew to the Ohio state capital, Columbus. "If there is one state in the union that has a little of everything of America in it, it is Ohio," he later said. "There are liberals and archconservatives, a wide spread of ethnic and religious groups, strip-mining areas in the east and, to the west, some of the richest farming land in the country." He believed he could embrace these differences, because he was, after all, a national hero.

At his first political press conference, Glenn exuded charm and confidence: "To serve in a body whose action can help mold the destiny of not only America but [of] the free world is certainly . . . a high challenge . . . [and] a great calling, too." Yet he was reluctant to talk about politics. Instead he hid behind the technicality of the Hatch Act, which forbade federal government employees to issue any political statements. "Please understand that I am unable to make any comment," he said about such matters as civil rights, tax cuts, federal aid to education, Medicare, Cuba, Panama, and the sale of wheat to Russia. "I have opinions, and you will definitely hear about them in the campaign." But for the moment he refused to comment.

He would offer only vague statements about his political beliefs: "Careful consideration of the current positions and leadership of both parties leads me to the choice of the Democratic party. I believe President Johnson has presented a program for our nation which a majority of Americans will support." (Annie Glenn, beaming nearby in a white pillbox hat and contrasting coral-colored dress, admitted a clash of loyalties: "I've been a Republican, but I think now I'm on the other side." Then, realizing the gaffe, she hastily added, "I *know* now I'm on the other side." Later some confused newsmen attributed these comments to her husband.) Glenn, meanwhile, dodged the question of his inexperience. He stressed that in twenty-two years of government service he had become "well acquainted" with military affairs, technology, and research and development, which constituted half of the federal budget: "I can make a valuable contribution here because I have practical experience in these fields. I can get political experience."

Convinced of his personal charisma—"Glenn's getting into the race," exulted one supporter, "is like finding out that Santa Claus is a Democrat"—Glenn was unprepared for the realities of politics. Three days after his announcement he confronted party regulars at the state Democratic convention in Columbus. "We had an amateur organization," he later admitted. "We were making mistakes"—not the least of which was his unwillingness to campaign. He refused even to make a tour of the hotel lobby to buy a newspaper, lest his presence appear to solicit an undeserved favor. He and Annie stayed in their hotel suite, greeting pilgrimages of Ohio Democrats who came for smiles, handshakes, and autographs. In these intimate groups Glenn appeared rather charming, but he made no promises; indeed he seemed unable to understand the special-interest representatives from organized labor, business, and minorities. Among the rank and file, however, his sheer fame proved sufficiently powerful to prevent an automatic endorsement of Stephen Young. The convention decided to endorse neither man. In fact it required an act of Glenn's will to stop short of total victory. A preemptive step, he feared, would split the party and weaken his chances in the general election.

To qualify for regular campaigning, he returned to Washington to apply for retirement from the Marine Corps, effective March 1, 1964. His pension, after twenty-two years' service, would be a modest $425 a month. At his farewell dinner with NASA, he was so overcome by the tributes to his character that he could not reply. ("No politician," one friend remarked, "can afford to remain speechless.") On George Washington's birthday, the Freedoms Foundation of Valley Forge (a nonprofit organization dedicated to advancing the American way of life) announced that Glenn would receive its highest award, a medal and $5,000, for "personifying the American way of life by sincere patriotic words and deeds in our country's hours of challenge." A hero on the road to politics could not have a better endorsement.

But he could not reckon with chance. Four days before his formal retirement, Glenn paused between political meetings for a shave and noticed that the sliding mirror on his medicine cabinet was stuck. He lifted the glass panel, but in his wet hands it slipped. As he shifted his weight, a small rug beneath him started to slide. "Suddenly I realized I was slipping, but I tried to hold on to the mirror and keep it from breaking, rather than let go and use one of my hands to break the fall. I began to spin in as I fell. . . . The mirror flew from my grip and crashed to the floor. Flying pieces of glass cut my hands and face." The back of Glenn's skull cracked against the metal edge of the bathtub: "It was the toughest wallop I've ever taken. They said it was a mild concussion. It didn't seem so mild to me."

Carried to bed, he remained dazed and frightened: "I didn't pass out, but I was in a state of shock." Only then did grave symptoms appear: "When I moved my head the least bit, it was as if the whole world were spinning upside down." He was diagnosed as suffering from severe labyrinthitis, an inflammation of the inner ear caused by blood pooling in the delicate semicircular canals that control balance and coordination. Unable to move, he suffered dizziness, nausea, vomiting, and a persistent ringing in the ears. His recovery seemed uncertain; the length of hospitalization was unknown. On March 1, Glenn postponed his retirement from the marines.

During the next few weeks, his doctors stressed the slightest signs of improvement. He was transferred to a hospital in San Antonio, Texas, nearer to his family and expert physicians. The headaches stopped, and the ringing in the ears became intermittent. But Glenn could barely move his head, and the persistent nausea killed his appetite. He lost seventeen pounds. There was no treatment either, except rest, and no certainty of a complete cure. "My recovery has been slower than the doctors and I had hoped for," said Glenn. "But I certainly plan no withdrawal from the campaign."

Unable to campaign for legal as well as medical reasons, Glenn allowed Annie to take his place. Because of an uncontrollable stutter, she took along another astronaut wife, Rene Carpenter, and together they spoke at informal social gatherings.

"Hello, I'm Annie Glenn," she would say. "You know, I stutter. So here's Rene."

The glamorous Mrs. Carpenter spoke briefly: "My husband and I consider John Glenn the most dedicated American we've ever known. You all can be proud Ohio produced and raised him—and I know he'll make you a wonderful senator!"

With such empty promises the wives kept the campaign alive. By the end of March, Glenn could sit up for two hours. He could also walk down the hospital corridors in small, unjostled steps, something like a duck walk, and with his head tilted forward at a 45° angle. With such disabilities he could not afford to retire from the marines. But, unless he did so soon, he would be unable to campaign in the Ohio primary.

He called a press conference in the hospital, where he lay sprawled in bed, keeping his head rigid. He admitted that he did not know how long it would take him to recover; he did not even know *if he would ever recover.* "No man has a right to ask for a seat in either branch of the Congress merely because of a specific event such as orbiting the earth in a spacecraft. . . . I believe every candidate should be judged on . . . what he stands for or what he proposes to do."

Since he could not appear before the voters, Glenn decided to withdraw from the election: "My interest in our country, the things that have and will make it great, and its future course as the world's leader are still my foremost interest. . . . It is better . . . to terminate these efforts now rather than carry on until the last moment . . . with any false hopes." In 1964, therefore, the people of Ohio never learned the nature of Glenn's politics or what it was he wanted to accomplish. But even after he left the hospital in mid-April, his name remained on the official ballot. In the May primary, with no campaign and no candidacy, Glenn captured more than two hundred thousand votes. Against his own wishes he had proved the potential power of his famous name.

It was small solace. In his home in Texas he moved through the rooms by the "wall-to-wall" method, his extended fingers providing a sense of balance while he held his head motionless. "If I told you I didn't suffer from anxiety and depression about the future, it would be far from the truth," he confessed. "I did plenty of wondering about the future and what I could do the rest of my life as a semi-invalid if my recovery went no further." His children were frightened by his helplessness. An unfamiliar fear spread through the family. Glenn's father was hospitalized with terminal cancer; Annie's father underwent two brain operations.

Annie, too, suffered from disturbing symptoms—a constant pain on her left side, a sore shoulder, and a lump on her knee—and underwent exploratory surgery. After a biopsy, the family waited several days for the result. The lump proved benign, and the Glenns encased the sample of cartilage in plastic, adding it to their souvenirs of survival. Glenn, meanwhile, continued to improve: "I'd reach a new level and think, 'Well, I'll learn to live with this much.'" When an interviewer from the JFK library mentioned that the slain president considered Glenn "an important asset to this country," the former astronaut responded with self-mockery: "I don't know what kind of a national asset I am."

The family crisis passed slowly. "To keep our minds off our troubles," they systematically went through their enormous correspondence—some half million letters and cards since the orbital flight two years before!—until every one was answered. "Although the letter is a facsimile, the above signature is not," read the usual postscript. "It is original." Glenn later published a representative sample to give inspiration to others; *"P.S. I Heard Your Heart Beat,"* a potpourri of odd questions and paternal advice, appeared in 1965.

Glenn's malaise worsened when he received a final accounting of the 1964 campaign: "I owe $9,473.46 for materials, and I am writing a personal check to pay it. I don't want any printer in Zanesville to get stuck on my bad luck." While on convalescent leave from the marines, his salary dropped below $10,000 a year, barely enough to pay the family bills. When his son enrolled as a freshman at Harvard, they used the last of the *Life* magazine money: "If our son, David, hadn't had a $1,000 scholarship, we could not have afforded his schooling." (He felt doubly honored when Harvard assigned David Glenn to a room once occupied by John Kennedy.) "If there is a war on poverty," said Glenn, "where do I go to surrender?" Yet a realistic appraisal of his situation did not diminish his sense of honor. In line for promotion to the rank of full colonel, he refused to apply "because . . . I'm going to leave the service, and I don't want to crowd out an officer who needs to move up." President Johnson promoted him anyway.

Describing himself as a "used astronaut," "ex-politician," and "depressed area," Glenn's efforts at self-improvement were stalled by the long convalescence. It was months before he could even eat with his family. By July 1964, Glenn had recovered his lost weight, but the prognosis remained vague. "We cannot predict total recovery," advised his neurologist. "We are optimistic, but, although his is a fairly typical case . . . it is worse than most."

As he waited for improvement, Glenn explored various business opportunities. He had already turned down a million-dollar offer to promote a breakfast cereal because he considered such a testimonial degrading to his image. But with new financial burdens and a dread of insecurity—for the first time in his life he would be off the government payroll—he considered any reasonable offer. Few tempted him. He knew exactly what he wanted—"something which will permit me to remain part-time with the space program, travel overseas, and keep up my interest in religious activities, the Boy Scouts, and the Freedoms Foundation. That sounds like a tall order, but if I can put it together I will."

His plans left no room for politics. He watched the 1964 national conventions on television and scorned Barry Goldwater's conservative politics. But he admitted that he "could feel at home in either party in Ohio." The idealism of the post-assassination shock was subsumed by more elemental concerns: "I want to get better. Then we'll see what happens."

By September 1964 Glenn was healthy enough to nod—both literally and in the corporate sense. For a salary of approximately $50,000 and additional stock options, he joined the board of directors of the Royal Crown Cola Company, the third largest bottler of soft drinks in the United States. It was the only job offer he received, he later confessed, that did not require him to make commercials. Besides soothing his pride and his pocketbook, Royal Crown appealed to Glenn's sense of mission: "I hadn't been able to get the memories of our trip to Japan out of my mind," he said, recalling his brief stint as goodwill ambassador in 1963. "Perhaps if I had other opportunities to visit other countries I could learn a lot myself and also perhaps project some of the excitement that I feel about our country, space exploration, and how much it's going to mean to the whole world." At Royal Crown he assumed responsibility for "development and expansion of the company's international operations," which consisted of seventy-five franchised bottling plants in twenty countries. He was specifically exempted from corporate advertising and public relations.

Glenn jogged into shape along the country roads near his home. He resumed water-skiing and for the first time in six months drove his Corvair convertible. But he craved one final proof of his recovery— "the one that would really satisfy me that I was cured—flying. I wanted to get up in the cockpit of a very fast plane and see what happened." After passing a physical examination that enabled him to retire without disability, he obtained permission to fly. He soon reported for a jet refresher course and flew for a week with a copilot. Then he went up alone: "Unless you have been flat on your back with an uncertain future, you can't possibly imagine what this meant."

On a chill January morning in 1965—the same day that the United States Senate welcomed such new members as New York's Robert F. Kennedy—Glenn was attending a brief and cheerless military ceremony at the nearby Arlington Navy Annex. Flanked by Annie, in her white pillbox hat, and his children, Colonel Glenn bade farewell to the marines after nearly twenty-three years of service. The very privacy of the affair—light-years away from the ticker tape and the throngs—mirrored his somber mood. He offered no words of advice, none of reflection. He stayed in the national capital only long enough to visit the newest Senator Kennedy. Then he flew to Columbus, Ohio, where he put on the uniform of Royal Crown Cola.

Responsible for increasing the company's number of foreign bottling franchises, he made what one corporate colleague called an "excellent transition." He also took a position on the board of directors of the Questor Corporation, an auto parts and sporting goods manufacturer. It expanded his connections in the Ohio business community and increased his income by several thousand dollars. In exchange, he had to give little more than his name.

Glenn's business career left ample time for his other activities. For the Freedoms Foundation, he headed a Freedom Roll Call educational campaign to arouse public interest in traditional values. He addressed the National Space Club on the third anniversary of his orbital flight and said that the goal of landing an American on the moon by 1970 was less important than "the tremendously exciting exploration of the universe . . . even if there were no such country as Russia." He took a consulting job with NASA, serving as a celebrity delegate at astronautic conventions, presenting speeches, and contributing to Project Apollo. He and his Soviet counterpart, Yuri Gagarin, were elected honorary members of the International Astronautical Academy in Paris. He received a Silver Buffalo award from the Boy Scouts of America for his "outstanding service to boyhood." He attended NASA headquarters to observe the telemetry of spaceflight Gemini 4, featuring the first "space walk," by American Ed White. "Too often religion resists the new," he told a conference of Southern Baptist pastors in Dallas, recalling the story of the "little old lady" who complained: "There shouldn't be a space program. We should all stay home and watch TV the way the good Lord intended."

With his interest in international business, Glenn accepted an invitation from Washington to embark on a goodwill tour of Western Europe in the autumn of 1965. It began in West Germany, where he inspected the rockets and spacecraft of the European space program. He received a hero's welcome in Berlin, attended an industrial fair, and chatted with Chancellor Ludwig Erhard in Bonn. "It's my first visit to Europe," he told Pope Paul VI in a private meeting at the Vatican. "Ah," replied the pontiff, "but you have seen it all before from on high." He was honored in Holland, applauded in Great Britain, and received the Italian Order of Merit from Prime Minister Aldo Moro. Crowds cheered him in Spain and Portugal. The press hailed the tour as a "diplomatic triumph."

He returned to his desk in Houston to apply the lessons of diplomacy to his corporate advancement. At a time when American business, flushed with the prosperity of the 1960s, worked aggressively to open new world markets, especially in Asia, Africa, and Latin America, Glenn's fame proved a valuable asset. Royal Crown elected him vice-president in charge of expansion. Then, in a major reorganization, the corporation created a new subsidiary, Royal Crown Cola International

Limited, and named Glenn to head it. He proceeded to use his international connections to obtain franchises in every corner of the world. He also enjoyed executive perquisites, including a corporate-owned luxury apartment in mid-Manhattan. "Up to that time," he later remarked, "I really didn't have any money." So satisfying was his business career that Glenn rebuffed several overtures to enter the race for governor of Ohio in 1966, saying he had no political plans "at this time."

Glenn's voluntary activities and frequent honors kept his face in the public eye, but he cherished his privacy. To escape well-wishers, he liked to go camping with his family. In the summer of 1966 they joined Robert and Ethel Kennedy on a dangerous rafting expedition down the middle fork of the Salmon River—"the river of no return." Flown into the wilderness by single-engine planes that had to stand on their wings to clear the trees, shooting white-water rapids between narrow rock walls, amid roasting heat and torrential thunderstorms, Glenn found tangible evidence of his continuing vitality. But he especially relished the conversations around the campfire. Robert Kennedy led the discussions, ranging from the naming of Friendship 7 to the "components of real friendship." Glenn was somewhat awed in Kennedy's presence. He respected his intensity, and he took great pride in counting himself among Kennedy's close friends.

Just after Glenn's forty-fifth birthday he began to experience the painful losses of middle age. John Glenn, Sr., member of the Masons, Odd Fellows, and the American Legion, died of cancer in New Concord at the age of seventy-one. A fiery explosion at Cape Kennedy took the lives of astronauts Gus Grissom, Ed White, and Roger Chaffee. On a bright, frosty February morning at Arlington National Cemetery, a stony-faced Glenn helped carry Grissom's flag-draped coffin as tears ran down his face. The next month, he mourned the loss of another pioneer, the Soviet cosmonaut Yuri Gagarin, killed in a plane crash. "Man tries something, and sometimes he succeeds and sometimes he fails," said Glenn in a speech to the National Space Club on the fifth anniversary of his flight. "We hate to lose good friends, but we think that they went in a good cause." He scoffed at the idea of "some great cosmic drag race" with the Soviet Union: "The really important part of the manned space program is exploration in the greatest sense of the word."

In his own life, however, exploration assumed mundane proportions. He agreed to participate in a television series, "Great Explorations," which would chronicle the great discoveries of world history.

"We do not plan this as just another travelogue showing places and artifacts. . . . We plan also to cover in some depth the 'why' and 'later effect' that show their true importance in history." In the premiere show, Glenn retraced the thousand-mile trail of Stanley and Livingston through modern Tanzania. By foot, by rail, mostly by Land Rover, his entourage lived partly off the land during the filming of the landscape and its unfamiliar people. For the camera, Glenn tried to master the art of throwing the knobkerrie, a local throwing stick, but he proved more adept with a Winchester 70, helping to kill a massive rogue elephant. "There was cause for destruction," he said. "But I'm not proud of killing this great beast." Broadcast in January 1968, Glenn's performance won few plaudits, though most reviewers commented favorably on his compassion for the African people.

These same instincts explained his enthusiasm for Robert Kennedy's presidential campaign in 1968. In backing the insurgent candidate, however, Glenn aroused the displeasure of his corporate colleagues, who drafted a resolution forbidding any director of Royal Crown Cola to participate in the election. Glenn accepted their challenge. At a closed-door meeting, he swore to defy the resolution: "The fact is Bobby Kennedy is my friend, and I intend to campaign for him." Passage of the resolution would force his resignation, but he dared them to proceed, threatening to hold a press conference to expose the proceedings. Royal Crown Cola quietly dropped the matter.

Still, Glenn's political feelings remained hidden by his glamour. While Robert Kennedy deplored the war in Vietnam, Glenn restricted his comments to touting his friend. He joined Kennedy on the first campaign swing, trying to transfer his aura to Kennedy. In the small ethnic towns of Nebraska, Glenn described Kennedy as "a man you can trust" and warned about political power "sliding into fewer and fewer hands." But when he drew warm applause, Kennedy interjected: "Don't give him a hand. I'm the candidate. . . . Now if you don't help me, you'll be letting down one of America's greatest heroes." Glenn loved the attention and enjoyed doubling as part of the flying wedge that swept the candidate through the crowds.

He stayed with Kennedy in bleak times too. Walking together in California "through a very poor area where several hundred people, mostly children, black, brown and white," surrounded the candidate, Glenn studied Kennedy's responses. It was as if Glenn were making mental notes for his own life. "Every American must be able to realize his full potential," said Glenn, "unrestrained by race, creed, color, or lack of opportunity." He accompanied Kennedy to a late-night meeting with black leaders in Oakland, California, home of the Black Panther party, and found himself denied entrance because of the color of his skin. Later, when he was admitted, Glenn listened "while the Negro leadership poured out their spectrum of thoughts, complaints, suggestions, frustrations, and plans." His observations revealed much about his own political thoughts: "From moderate leadership came constructive suggestions and plans. From extreme militants came a vitriolic torrent of threats and calls for armed action that were frightening in their implication." Kennedy impressed Glenn with his ability to leap across these differences, to embrace opposites with a broad compassion.

Glenn went to Los Angeles with Kennedy, savoring victory at a small party in the Ambassador Hotel, while the candidate went downstairs to face the cameras. Kennedy mentioned Glenn's support in what was practically his last breath. After the shooting, Glenn accompanied him to the hospital, interrupting his vigil only when Ethel Kennedy asked John and Annie to stay with the young Kennedy children. "It was my awful duty to wait for six of his children to wake from their sleep," Glenn said, "wait to tell them their father had been shot." At Ethel's request the Glenns escorted the children back to Hickory Hill, Virginia, and spent another night with them. Robert Kennedy died that night. In the morning, Glenn broke the news to each of the children.

While Kennedy's body lay in state at Saint Patrick's Cathedral in New York, Glenn gathered with the senator's friends to plan the funeral. He stood at attention the next morning near the flag-covered coffin, watching as Cardinal Cushing performed the religious ceremony. As Andy Williams sang "The Battle Hymn of the Republic," Glenn grasped the coffin and then, to the sound of the Hallelujah Chorus, helped to carry it slowly up the aisle. On the sweltering eight-hour train ride from New York to Washington, he remained close to the body. He carried his share once again at Arlington, and, as the American flag was removed from the coffin, he completed the traditional rolling and gave it to Edward Kennedy. Of his few friends in the world, said Glenn, "I can now count one less."

The second Kennedy assassination triggered another pang of civic responsibility. With his multitude of business and political associations, Glenn organized a bipartisan Emergency Committee for Gun Control and agreed to serve as its chairman. "The family of my friend, Robert F. Kennedy, was but one family among thousands who must suffer each year the agony of a senseless loss caused by a gun," he testified to a Senate subcommittee three weeks later. "We simply cannot permit such senseless killing to continue. We must do all we can to prevent those who should not have guns from getting them." Unable to understand the opposition to gun control, Glenn placed his hope in public opinion: "We are coming to the end of the battle of the silent many against the vocal few." But his political efforts went no further. During the ensuing summer he and Annie were frequent visitors at Hickory Hill, and they tried to help the Kennedy children overcome their loss. Glenn was proud to be named a trustee of the newly formed Robert F. Kennedy Foundation.

Late one night he sat in Robert Kennedy's library leafing through a volume of Emerson's essays: "It was all marked up in the margins and underlined. Bobby did that a lot. I read a passage that he had underscored heavily, and I've never forgotten it." So powerful was its impact on Glenn that his daughter, Lyn, embroidered the text on linen and hung it in a frame at the entry of their home: "If there is any period one would desire to be born in, is it not the Age of Revolution, when the old and the new stand side by side and admit of being compared?"

These thoughts ennobled Glenn's spirits, rekindled his passion for great achievement. Just as surely, they reminded him of the impoverishment of his own life. "Evoking our memories of him in cold eulogy would be a mockery," Glenn wrote about Robert Kennedy, "if not followed by resolve to quicken the future he sought. . . . His role as catalyst in the mixture of our times will go far beyond his times." In a eulogy, Glenn recalled a gift that Kennedy had given to his son, David, an inscription to his book *To Seek a Newer World*. "If we don't find it," wrote Kennedy, "you must." Glenn paused for effect: "Now —we must."

He returned to that volume by Emerson and found another passage, also underlined in Kennedy's hand, that pressed even closer to his sense of destiny: "The characteristic of heroism is its persistency." The words described his own tenacity and self-discipline, the stuff of marines and astronauts. "When you have chosen your part, abide by it, and do not weakly try to reconcile yourself with the world. . . . If you would serve your brother, because it is fit for you to serve him, do not take back your words when you find that prudent people do not commend you." The message etched like a diamond. Glenn knew what he must do, and he quoted from Emerson: "Always do what you are afraid to do."

Jane
Seymour
Fonda
(III)

Her search for identity intensified in the summer of 1969. She was thirty-one and recognized as a star, but she felt incomplete and unhappy. She tried changing her appearance—wore blue denims and short hair—and busied herself with self-improvement projects: speed-reading, self-hypnosis to stop smoking. Then, unwilling to change too much, she returned to France with Vadim and Vanessa.

The farmhouse, built as her island of peace, shrank into a cloister. On the twentieth of July, the family gathered at the television for word of the moon landing, only to be diverted from Neil Armstrong by the marvelous sight of their baby walking for the first time. For Jane those first steps exaggerated the inertia of her own life. "From the beginning," she has remarked about her daughter, "I watched her—listening, learning, perceiving—and I thought, 'Why her and not me? Why is it that in growing old we lose the ability to see, smell, touch, and feel?' " She believed it was a matter of will: "I suppose I could have gone on like that forever, superficial and numb and somehow very old in my young skin."

Her first impulse was to run away, and she returned to southern California. But the atmosphere there was as unsettled as she herself. By the summer of 1969 opposition to the Vietnam War had reached the respectable middle class. Jane's closest friends, Donald and Shirley Sutherland, had become outspoken dissenters, reinforcing the antiwar arguments she had first heard in Paris in 1968.

The war, by then, had also disrupted the consensus of values. Young people had grown increasingly disaffected from the established culture. Their music, sexual habits, drugs, clothing, and hairstyles all reflected a spreading defiance, and this, too, had penetrated affluent Hollywood. Jane saw these changes in her brother, Peter, and in such friends as Roman Polanski and Sharon Tate. But she was too embroiled in her own problems to be affected, at least so far. She returned to France. A few weeks later she learned that Tate had been murdered. People such as the writer Joan Didion, closer than Jane to the new life-style, remembered that "no one was surprised." But the news shocked her—and deepened her depression. "I have always done things with a passion," she would later say, "whether it was trying to make a marriage work or worrying about babies or planting trees. And suddenly everything that I had been pouring my energies into seemed unimportant." She craved a larger sense of purpose.

In Paris Jane heard that one of her friends was going to India, and she decided to go along. Perhaps she, like the Beatles and Mia Farrow, might find nirvana there: "I needed to go away and put myself in a totally new environment in order to understand myself." After Vanessa's first birthday, in September 1969, she departed. "And India overwhelmed me." The romance of gurus and Zen provided no warning of the stark reality. "I had never seen people die from starvation, a boy begging with the corpse of his brother in his arms. It struck me. I couldn't accept it as the Westerners do when they go to India to study astrology or metaphysics." She was shocked by the indifference of American hippies, who "were *getting off* on India." She realized that she would have to go somewhere else to find meaning for her life.

From India Jane flew to California to begin publicity for *They Shoot Horses*. She arrived dead-tired at night and went directly to a Beverly Hills hotel. The contrast shocked her. "I still had in my eyes the crowds of Bombay, in my nose the smell of Bombay, in my ears the noise of Bombay. . . . India was urine, noise, color, misery, disease, masses of people teeming." The view in southern California was so different. "I saw those houses of Beverly Hills, those immaculate gardens, those neat, silent streets where the rich drive their big cars and send their children to the psychoanalyst. . . . Beverly Hills was as silent and empty and antiseptic as a church, and I kept wondering, 'Where is everybody?' "

In the autumn of 1969 masses of people took to the streets to protest the Vietnam War. Jane was beginning to articulate her dissent, but she took no action to join them. She seemed preoccupied with family obligations. She returned to France, then flew back to New York, and then to California, Hawaii, and New York again. "I can't bear to stay in one place too long," she explained. But each departure from America reinforced the futility of running away from home and reawakened her fear of becoming, as she put it, "a married woman on a farm in France."

At the end of 1969 she learned that the New York Film Critics had named her Best Actress for her performance in *They Shoot Horses*. It boosted her spirits, for the moment. "I'm very optimistic about the world tonight." But personal success did not ease a deeper discontent. The realities of the outside world had to be noticed. "We'll always be pouring money into military war," she said. "I'm not happy about the political situation either. . . . Come to think of it, I take back what I said earlier about the world getting better. The only thing I'm optimistic about is *me.*"

Jane's willingness to flaunt convention—the use of four-letter improprieties ("I don't say intercourse") and smoking marijuana in front of reporters—suggested a subterranean change, but she hesitated to make a direct statement. She was looking for something concrete. Thumbing through the pages of *Ramparts* magazine, she was struck by an article about fourteen American Indian college students who had invaded Alcatraz island in the first part of November:

> They told the press that they had come there because Alcatraz already had all the necessary features of a reservation: dangerously uninhabitable buildings; no fresh water; inadequate sanitation; and the certainty of total unemployment. They said they were planning to make the five full-time caretakers wards of a Bureau of Caucasian Affairs. . . .

The story touched her conscience. She telephoned the author and asked him to take her to Alcatraz. "I'm here to learn what's going on," she said. "I've been gone so long. I feel so ignorant about what has happened in this country. I want to get involved." It was her first step. The second followed more easily. She arrived at the San Francisco waterfront wearing tight jeans and clipped hair and climbed aboard a small boat that took her to the besieged island. Her sincerity overcame her fear. After conversations with the militants there, she perceived for the first time the connections between the pioneering spirit and the war in Vietnam.

From Alcatraz, Jane's search for commitment led toward another militant group, the Black Panthers, who in recent months had engaged in virtual warfare with police and the FBI. Mark Lane, a radical lawyer, arranged a meeting. "It was the first time I had met black militants with a political ideology, a political discipline." She was impressed by their revolutionary ardor, and when she described them she expressed their point of view: "The Panthers aren't racists. Those who kill them are racists! Of course I like the Panthers; of course I totally support the Panthers; of course I say that any black man who hasn't a gun today in this country is a fool. Fighting for the Panthers is not violence; it is self-defense."

Jane continued to seek a political commitment. At a Hollywood party she met an antiwar activist, Fred Gardner, who had been working to organize soldiers against the military establishment. He had helped build a network of off-base coffeehouses for disaffected servicemen. Jane soon enlisted in his cause.

One Sunday morning, in March 1970, she went to Fort Lawton in the state of Washington to shout encouragement to militant Indians who scaled the fences to claim the federal property as an Indian cultural center. Shoved by the MPs, she managed to avoid arrest, but the violence outraged her. She drove to nearby Fort Lewis to protest. At the local coffeehouse the radical GIs asked her to distribute antiwar leaflets on the base. Given the rules of military conduct, it was a task for civilians. "I knew the importance of doing it," Jane admitted, but she told them that she was "not ready yet to do that." Instead she entered the base to hand out printed invitations to meet her at the coffeehouse that evening. Such activity was legal. But Jane was arrested anyway and detained for several hours before receiving a formal expulsion from the base. "Well, it was something of a turning point for me," she stated. "The very fact that I was arrested for doing nothing except exercising my constitutional rights started me off in a new direction."

Her first skirmish—unwanted, uninvited, and unexpected—accelerated her political evolution. "Anybody in this country who gets arrested for doing something he knows is right will never be the same again." She flew to New York to meet with leaders of the GI protest and appeared on the Dick Cavett talk show with one of the Alcatraz militants. As she left the studio, Jane was spat on by an unidentified man. The incident accentuated her alienation—another step in her political development.

She returned to the West Coast with renewed zeal. She walked picket lines with Indians in Washington, attended meetings with GI radicals in southern California, and met with Black Panthers about raising bail money. She confronted her father with testimony of American atrocities in Vietnam, but she failed to change his mind about the war. She toured the movie studios to raise money for radical causes.

In April 1970 she embarked on a cross-country tour with an older woman friend from France to obtain firsthand information about the antiwar movement. "There is so much to learn," Jane wrote. They visited the Pyramid Lake reservation, in northern Nevada, where local tribes were fighting a federal irrigation project. She was appalled by the poverty there. Then she headed east into Idaho and then to Salt Lake City. But she interrupted the journey to fly back to Hollywood to attend the Academy Awards ceremony, where she hoped to use her nomination for best actress as an opportunity for a political speech. Instead she attended a losers' party at the home of Elizabeth Taylor and Richard Burton and solicited contributions for the Panther bail fund. The next day she returned to Utah and drove on to Denver, where she joined a thirty-six-hour Fast for Peace with Dr. Benjamin Spock. "The hardest thing in the world," she observed, "is to make white, middle-class liberals aware of oppression."

She also tried to visit the stockade at Fort Carson where three Black Panthers were purportedly held incommunicado for antiwar activity. Denied admission, she sneaked onto the base to distribute political literature. When the MPs arrived, Jane tried to escape. But, in what became a familiar ritual, she was arrested, detained, and expelled. "I could be on my ass in Beverly Hills enjoying myself," she assured a sympathetic crowd off-base, "but I have to face myself in the morning." She drove south. In Santa Fe she heard President Nixon offer a new plan for peace in Vietnam, via a short incursion into Cambodia, and she denounced him in a televised interview. Then she arranged to give an antiwar talk at the University of New Mexico a few days later.

She arrived in Albuquerque on the day that four students were killed at Kent State University. For the first time Jane spoke to a public gathering, spoke for herself. "People think actresses do that easily," she later said, "and it's not easy at all; we're used to hiding behind masks." No role could now contain her. An articulate, if unpolished, rhetoric rose from her voice. "You suddenly open up the floodgates, and you have no words to express what it is you're . . . feeling—rage; the rage people feel when they've been lied to and suddenly realize it. The rage of someone who was, despite the cynicism and everything else, very idealistic about her country."

Determined to deepen her involvement, Jane flew to Los Angeles to cosponsor a nationwide protest against the war. Then she went back to New Mexico and then to Fort Hood in Texas. No sooner did she arrive than she departed for Washington, D.C., to participate in a mass protest against Cambodia and Kent State. "Greetings, fellow bums," she saluted the one hundred thousand protesters who jammed the Ellipse on a 90° day. She raised her fist: "Power to the People!" Then she went back to Fort Hood to distribute antiwar messages. She was quickly intercepted, finger-printed, and expelled.

She resumed her overland journey, aiming to arrive at Fort Bragg, North Carolina, in time for antiwar demonstrations on Armed Forces Day in mid-May. In South Carolina she stopped for another university protest and here got her first exposure to tear gas. At Fort Bragg she was arrested for leafleting. Then, she joined Mark Lane in lobbying congressmen in Washington, shared a podium at the University of Maryland ("Who's getting rich off this war?" she shouted), and tried to enter Fort Meade. In New York City she appeared at an antiwar rally on the Lower East Side and addressed a Peace Action crowd in Central Park on Memorial Day.

"When I left the West Coast I was a liberal," she said. "When I landed in New York I was a revolutionary." Jane's rapid metamorphosis—three frenzied months of travel, public appearances, and undisciplined rage—extinguished her illusions about personal happiness. It also brought, at last, a coherence to her private life, eliminated the dilemmas about marriage, family, and stardom. "I realized that they were treating me as a person," she said of her introduction to the radicals. "This was so beautiful that I began to feel uncomfortable with people who still considered me a doll. And it completed my revolution, and Vadim was the first victim of such revolution." During the summer of 1970, with hardly a struggle, Jane and Vadim drifted apart. "It was hard to shake hands and say good-bye," she said, "but it was absolutely essential."

To reduce her responsibility for ending the marriage, Jane viewed the decision as a social and political act. "Do you know why marriage can be wrong?" she asked. "Because the normal process of a human being is to change, and marriage prevents people from changing. Women, especially. They don't want to change because they are afraid to be independent, to be lonely, to have confidence in themselves." She saw the condition of women in America as a state of exploitation. "Why should a woman only wash her husband's socks and cook her husband's meals and deny herself new horizons? Why should a girl pay for a night of love by having a child?"

> The new Jane Fonda has her light-brown hair cut short, brushed down to eye level, hugged to her small, fragile face.
>
> *Vogue,* June 1970

Her new image reflected a new identity. If Vadim was the first victim of the revolution, the second was herself, "Jane Fonda the doll." She defined herself now as a woman in time, a person with a past and also a future, a before and an after. "I was proud to be a good cook; I was proud to be an understanding wife; I was proud to say that being happy means to make someone else happy," she explained. "But now I am free, and it is such a good feeling."

What Jane lost in the personal sphere—security, stability, and intimacy—she obtained in the movement. Whereas once she had thought her problems were purely psychological, the result of a miserable upbringing, now she formed a political identity that provided coherence and comfort: "I suddenly felt that I . . . that I had come home! And it was the most explosive and wonderful feeling." As part of her conversion Jane became an apostle, using her access to the media as a way of promoting causes and winning converts. Although her enthusiasm sometimes exceeded her knowledge of politics, she took pleasure in exploiting her fame for political purposes: "What society has done is to say [that] certain people have made it, are special," she explained. "And what the star system represents is a typical sickness of our society —competition." For this reason she refused to sign autographs for her fans.

She still wanted an acting career, however. In the summer of 1970 she accepted the part of Bree Daniels, a call girl, in Alan Pakula's film *Klute*. Jane defined her role politically as the "inevitable product of a society that places ultimate importance on money, possessions, and competition." To prepare for the movie, she visited the "hierarchy of the prostitute world," talked to call girls, streetwalkers, madames, and pimps, and spent a night in a New York City courtroom watching the legal process. "I made Bree much more vulnerable than a real prostitute would be. A real character would have been difficult to make sympathetic."

She continued to work for radical causes. With Mark Lane she sponsored a GI office in Washington, D.C., to protest the harassment of military personnel for their political views. Together with Lane and Donald Sutherland, she welcomed Black Panther leader Huey Newton when he came east for a reunion with Bobby Seale in a New Haven courtroom. "Huey Newton is a great, great, gentle man," said Jane. "He is the only man I've ever met who approaches sainthood." She gave him her rented penthouse to hold a press conference. For her audacity she began to receive death threats.

Hostility became a basic element in her life. During the making of *Klute* the technical crew refused to talk to her: "They thought I was unpatriotic, a traitor." Yet she treated her job professionally and even persuaded the director to rewrite the ending to create greater ambiguity. "I'm not a cynical person, as Bree was," Jane later explained. "I'm not a loser. I don't get frightened. I am not somebody who needs to rely on a man for my identity anymore, if I ever was."

After completing *Klute* in late 1970, she launched a campus speaking tour to raise money for the Winter Soldier Investigations, a Nuremberg-type tribunal sponsored by veterans opposed to the Vietnam War. As she traveled between Ontario, Canada, and Bowling Green, Ohio, to speak about "Alternatives to Vietnam," she confronted yet another dimension of her radical identity. At the customs desk in the Cleveland airport, the inspector ordered her to step aside. Something was wrong. "Listen," she said, "your job is to open my bag, not make me step out of line!" To which he replied, "Shut up." When Inspector Lawrence Troiano did open her bags, he was intrigued by Jane's address book. He put it aside and continued the inspection. Soon he found an enormous cache of pill bottles that were labeled B, L, and D.

"B-L-D," he said.

"Yes," she answered. "B-L-D means breakfast, lunch, and dinner."

Troiano ordered her detained while he called a supervisor. After examination of the 102 plastic vials, this senior official escorted Jane into his office while he contacted *his* supervisor. She complained of discomfort from her menstrual period and asked to use the bathroom. He told her to wait for police matrons, but when he turned his back, Jane headed for the lavatory. The police chased her, provoking a noisy pushing match that ended with her sitting in handcuffs and facing additional criminal charges of assaulting a policeman. And when the matrons did arrive for a strip search, they found a few prescription tranquilizers and a bottle of Dexedrine in her handbag.

"Here is another commie," they announced, delivering Jane to the Cuyahoga County jail. She spent a sleepless night talking with prisoners and yelling at the jailers. Mark Lane arrived the next day and escorted his handcuffed client to a hearing in federal district court (Jane turned her back on the bench when the judge challenged her legal representation), and she was finally released on $10,000 bail on charges of smuggling drugs. She was promptly re-arrested on assault charges and had to post another, $500 bond. She also received a civil suit from the assaulted policeman. "I was never hassled until I started talking against the war," she declared. "It was a political arrest." (Years later the United States Senate Select Committee on Intelligence would reveal that Jane, as one of Nixon's "enemies," had been under surveillance by the National Security Administration, which intercepted her long-distance telephone calls and telegrams, marked some of her file "confidential," stamped other documents "top secret," and circulated transcriptions through the highest echelons of government. The committee also discovered that FBI director J. Edgar Hoover personally drafted a letter claiming Jane had led a Black Panther meeting in chanting, "We will kill Richard Nixon and any other mother-fucker who stands in our way" and that Hoover sent this disinformation to a Hollywood reporter to discredit Jane in the industry.)

"America is a sinking ship unless we try to remember what it stands for," said Jane as she resumed her political crusade. She flew to New Orleans to join a protest for the Black Panthers and later loaned them four rented cars that were used in an escape attempt from a police blockade. She attended a Black Panther national convention in Washington, D.C. She traveled to Atlanta, Chicago, Los Angeles, Texas, North Carolina, and Florida, trying to obtain money for political trials. "Very few people believe me. . . . They think it's a phase I'm going through, a psychic trauma. Others think I'm trying to be important or that I do it for publicity. . . . But I do it," she asserted. "And I am committed to go on doing it for the rest of my life."

Despite her sense of commitment, Jane's political development remained rudimentary: "Don't ask me to define myself politically. I am not ready. All I can say is that through the [people] I've met, the experiences I've had, the reading I've done, I see an alternative to the usual way of living." She described this alternative as "a total change of structures through socialism. Of course I am a socialist. But without a theory, without an ideology." Jane, who was so perfectionist about her professional work—and in private life was thorough to the point of obsession—felt dissatisfied with this ambiguity. Whatever her political beliefs, she knew that she was not a leader.

Viewing herself primarily as an actress, she resolved to stay in show business; she would dedicate her talent to various radical causes. Early in 1971 Jane joined actors Donald Sutherland and Peter Boyle, comedian Dick Gregory, writer Jules Feiffer, and other antiwar entertainers in an anti-establishment stage show aimed at American servicemen. "It's been very disconcerting for many of us in Hollywood to see that Bob Hope, Martha Raye, and other companies of their political ilk have cornered the market," she told a press conference. "A lot of us who have different points of view about the war . . . have decided the time has come to speak to the forgotten soldiers." The show was called FTA, and the polite press translated the F as Free—Free the Army!

In the Haymarket coffeehouse in Fayetteville, North Carolina, near Fort Bragg, Mrs. Richard Nixon, played by Jane, rushed into the Oval Office to announce a massive protest demonstration outside:

"I'd better call the army," suggested the president.

"You *can't*, Richard."

"Why not?"

"It *is* the army!"

"What we are doing," explained Jane, "is underlining what the soldiers already know. *They* know that the war is insane. They know what GIs have to contend with better than we do." Denied permission to appear on military bases, FTA traveled the coffeehouse circuit, trying to connect regular army grievances to radical protest: "When the time comes for these guys to make a decision, will they allow themselves to be used in riot control? Will they allow themselves to be used to break strikes? Or will they kill people in Vietnam? When the time comes for them to take an active position, they know they will not be doing it as isolated, vulnerable individuals. . . . Because, after all," she pointed out, "we didn't tell them anything they didn't know."

Though she preferred the stage, Jane remained involved in street politics. In North Carolina she walked a picket line to support Cesar Chavez's national boycott of non-union grapes; in Las Vegas, Nevada, she led two thousand welfare protesters in a four-mile march down Sunset Strip and into Caesar's Palace to challenge cuts in the rolls; in California she visited black radical Angela Davis in prison and then addressed a rally to support thirteen nuns and priests accused of a plot to kidnap Henry Kissinger. "I'm not here as a do-gooder," she declared. "I'm here as a revolutionary, a revolutionary woman," and she expressed her willingness to "lay my life on the line." With Donald Sutherland, Jane founded an organization, Entertainment Industry for Peace and Justice, and at a public meeting in Los Angeles she called for the victory of the Vietcong. "I would hope that my career would never be separate from my life," said Jane, aware of a possible blacklist. "But if, because of my political activities, I were prevented from working in Hollywood . . . I would work elsewhere." She won vindication in the spring of 1971, when the federal government dropped the drug charges. On principle, she refused to receive the confiscated pills, but she insisted that, as a condition for accepting her personal tape recordings, they must be played in front of FBI agents, who therefore had to listen, once again, to the voices of veterans denouncing the Vietnam War. After a brief appearance at a Cleveland police court, the assault charge was also dismissed.

Jane then went to California to produce another attack on the establishment, *Steelyard Blues*, "a film which says stealing is not theft, property is theft." More important than her performance was the impact of new friends on Jane's political evolution. While living in Berkeley she visited the radical Red Family, a political collective that had recently expelled one of its founders, Tom Hayden. Jane enrolled her daughter in the group's Blue Fairyland nursery program and later lived in one of their houses. Here she first encountered radical feminism: "I began to realize that this particular revolution is not only their revolution," she said of women's liberation, "it's my revolution too. . . . Suddenly I could view my entire life in a totally social context. I was able to understand, for the first time, my mother . . . my sister, myself." Emboldened by these revelations, Jane agreed to play a six-role television drama, "Fascinating Women," in which she passed in stages from Playboy bunny to housewife: "We put ourselves into roles and play roles that have been fitted out for us. . . . And most of these roles, because they are defined by men, are oppressive for women."

After joining the FTA troupe on a Christmas tour of the Pacific in 1971, Jane went to Paris just after the New Year to work with director Jean-Luc Godard in a film about the 1968 uprising in France, *Tout Va Bien* ("Everything's Okay"). "We work for the consciousness industry," she told a reporter. "Masses of people go to the movies every Friday night, they think to be entertained. What is happening in fact is that they are passively sitting there, and what is being determined is what they think about themselves, what they want to buy or think they should buy or look like, who they should love and how they should live, [and that] they should forget the pain and numbness that has existed over the past week." She herself had no intention of altering the relationship between a passive audience and the media; she only wanted to change the content of the message they received.

Her role in this movie, however, greatly accelerated her professional transformation. Playing the part of a middle-class news reporter who chooses to become a revolutionary woman—a role that closely followed her own awakening—Jane discovered a way to express her political development in film. In the role, as in reality, she emerged as a new person, a convert never again to be the same. This personal change—from innocence to awareness—would become the dominant theme in nearly all her subsequent movies. Hereafter Jane Fonda would play herself.

In April 1972 she won an Academy Award for her part in *Klute*. "It's a grotesque ceremony that pits people against each other," she said. But she appreciated its symbolic value: "The Oscar is what working people relate to when they think of people in the movies. That's what the masses of America, who think I'm a freak and who think that people who support the Panthers and speak out against the war are all some kind of monsters, relate to. It's important for us to get that kind of acclaim. It means we're legitimized in the eyes of those working people."

With that satisfaction, Jane resolved never again to make a movie that was incompatible with her politics: "It's very hard to make a progressive movie—a movie that doesn't make the Third World look bad, that doesn't make women look bad." And so she developed a slide show that she brought to union halls, churches, and community centers. In these artless surroundings Jane had to struggle against the very image she had spent two decades creating: "As soon as you say 'Jane

Fonda,' I take over and they become little yellow people again." On the screen, she projected scenes of devastated villages, bombed buildings, the terror of the maimed.

Despite her passion, however, Jane made few personal friends on the left: "I was tired. I was tired and raw. . . . It was the lowest period." One evening in 1972 she shared an audience with another media show presented by Tom Hayden. Its images were new and unexpected to her: "In one section there were pictures of Vietnamese women having plastic surgery to make their eyes round and their breasts bigger. I was stunned. I thought . . . that same phony Playboy image that made me wear falsies for ten years, that made millions of American women dissatisfied with their own bodies, has been transported thousands of miles to another culture." She could see her own role in this cultural imperialism, a personal responsibility for perpetuating sexual stereotypes. She was doubly impressed that a man would reach such feminist insights. "I was so impressed. . . . I fell in love with him right away."

Through Tom Hayden, Jane's political perspective matured. Long a militant activist, a civil rights worker in the South, founder of Students for a Democratic Society, a community organizer, and one of the Chicago Seven defendants after the riots at the Democratic convention of 1968, Hayden understood the difficulty of building a movement. He expected no sudden apocalypse. His philosophy of a steady struggle reinforced Jane's enthusiasm. "It's going to be a slow process of organizing and educating until people become aware that they are on a treadmill running nowhere," she said in mid-1972. "You have to be prepared to work fifty, seventy-five years for a different society, work for the rest of your life, then pass the task on." This vision of continuing activity gave her a unique role. As she saw it, "somebody out front must show that you can hold opposing opinions and still continue to work."

With Hayden's support Jane departed on another adventure. In July 1972 she flew to Paris and then to North Vietnam. She brought with her letters from home for American POWs and a desire to see for herself the impact of the war: "more destruction to hospitals, churches, villages, schools, and cities than I care to think about." In her shame and outrage she offered to help, agreeing to give tape-recorded interviews for rebroadcast to American soldiers and pilots:

> I implore you, I beg you to consider what you are doing. In the area where I went it was easy to see there were no military targets,

there is no important highway, there is no communication network.

Tonight, when you are alone, ask yourselves what are you
doing.

Accept no ready answer fed to you by rote in basic training.
. . . I know that, if you saw and if you knew the Vietnamese under
peaceful conditions, you would hate the men who are sending you
on bombing missions.

Have you any idea what your bombs are doing when you pull
the levers and push the buttons?

Should you allow these same people and same liars define for
you who your enemy is?

Can we fight this kind of war and continue to call ourselves
Americans?

Upon returning to Paris, Jane reported that the POWs supported
the election of George McGovern: "They fear if Nixon stays in office
they will be prisoners forever." She showed a silent color film of healthy
POWs and appeared in it herself wearing a black Vietcong uniform
and a helmet strapped to her chin. When she was told that some
Americans considered her a traitor, Hanoi Jane, she attacked Nixon
instead: "Given the things that America stands for, a war of aggression
against the Vietnamese people is a betrayal of the American people.
There is the treason." Congressman Fletcher Thompson demanded an
investigation of her broadcasts.

"The people who are speaking out against the war are patriots,"
Jane replied. "I cried every day for America. The bombs are falling on
North Vietnam, but it is an American tragedy." Politicians, veterans'
groups, and conservatives urged a boycott of her films. "Genocide," she
said, "is more important than anyone's career. People [who] are considered radical today will be considered normal years from today." Despite
the clamor, the House Internal Security Committee could find no
crime and closed the case. A few days later columnist Jack Anderson
gave the Senate Banking Committee FBI files containing her private
financial transactions. And the other covert operations—wiretaps, surveillance, mail intercepts—continued.

Jane returned to Tom Hayden more devoted than before. She had
memorized portions of a Vietnamese poem,—"we'll fight you with all
the joy of a woman in childbirth." They decided to have a baby:
"Vietnam rekindled an enormous amount of hope in me," she said.

Through the Indochina Peace Campaign, Jane and Tom continued to protest the war in Vietnam. In the fall of 1972 they launched a nine-week, ninety-city pre-election tour to protest the policies of the Nixon administration. (In Congress, meanwhile, Richard Ichord introduced legislation to limit the "travel of people like Jane Fonda"; in Minneapolis the Veterans of Foreign Wars voted that Jane be prosecuted for treason; in Oswego, New York, the local school board barred her from the school auditorium. "Don't forget that Nixon was trying to get elected as a man who was winding down the war," Jane later commented about this harassment. "That's why there were all the shouts of treason. It was a Nixon tactic that he's used since the fifties to discredit his critics.")

After Nixon's election in November, Jane and Tom went to Roros, Norway, where she would play the lead in Joseph Losey's film of Ibsen's *A Doll's House.* Her politics soon interfered with the shooting: "I discovered that the male characters, who are somewhat shadowy, had been built up, and the women were shaved down." Jane demanded revisions of her part: "Nora was an intelligent and vital woman waiting to explode all the way through her life," said Jane, in what seemed almost an autobiographical statement. "In my version she took on sexuality as a subterfuge to get what she wanted." When Losey rejected her suggestions, Jane used other tactics: "I found I had to become Nora with Losey, bat my eyelashes, and make it seem as though it was his idea."

During the filming, Jane confirmed that she was pregnant and announced her plans to marry Hayden: "We decided to do it for two reasons. One is that for Tom and me it's a deepening of the commitment. . . . And the other is that I had enough problems. Having a kid without being married was all I needed!" Their announcement in Norway appeared strictly political: "We are campaigning for peace together. . . . Our relationship is a very private thing, and we don't intend to let it interfere with our activities in the movement." After the filming they went to Stockholm to protest at the American Embassy against the Christmas bombing of North Vietnam. "The U.S. election," Jane told the crowd, "did not give Nixon a mandate to carry on the war." An unidentified woman attacked her with red paint.

In January 1973 "Mrs. Jane S. Plemiannikov" flew to the Dominican Republic to divorce Vadim. A few weeks later she and Tom were married at her Laurel Canyon home by an Episcopal priest. They celebrated with Irish jigs and Vietnamese songs. Two days later the priest was suspended by his bishop for marrying a divorced person without permission. Instead of a honeymoon, the newlyweds embarked on a political tour through New England to protest the continuing war in Indochina.

When the Nixon administration staged elaborate homecoming ceremonies for POWs in February 1973, Jane called the freed pilots "hypocrites and liars." (The General Assembly of Maryland promptly passed a resolution naming her persona non grata.) And when some of the POWs reported being tortured in North Vietnam, Jane denounced their charges. (The state senate of Indiana voted to censure her.) "I'm quite sure that there were incidents of torture," Jane conceded in a television interview. "But the pilots who are saying . . . that it was systematic, I believe that that's a lie. . . . These men were bombing and strafing and napalming the country." (Students at the University of Southern California burned her in effigy.) "We have no reason to believe that U.S. Air Force officers tell the truth," she insisted. "They are professional killers. Never in the history of the United States have POWs come home looking like football players." Later in 1973, as the Watergate revelations unfolded, Jane advocated impeachment "not simply because of [Nixon's] criminal activities"—the burglary, the spying, the harassment of civilians, crimes that she herself had experienced —"but because his first administration was responsible for six million people being killed, wounded, or made refugees in Indochina."

After the birth of their son, Troy, Jane and Tom endeavored to live like ordinary people (but without the economic burdens). They moved into the upper half of a small house in Santa Monica, where they shared the housework, slept on a mattress on the floor, used the *Klute* Oscar as a bookend (it was consequently unmolested in a burglary), and enrolled Vanessa in an "experimental" public kindergarten. "Possessions used to be very important to me," said Jane, in her before-and-after grammatical style. "They were like a fortress; it was a kind of security to have a lot of things. But I've given away or sold most everything . . . out of a need to be unburdened."

Aside from her family obligations, Jane worked for the Indochina Peace Campaign, wrote political pamphlets, and produced woman-oriented slide shows on Vietnam. "Some people think I hate the country and try to tear it down," she stated. "We should not allow right-wingers, of the likes of the Nixon administration, to take our American flag away from us." Informed by journalist Jack Anderson of the contents of her FBI file—copies of her address book, financial statements from her personal bank accounts, surveillance reports of Vanessa in nursery school, all material that predated her trip to Hanoi—Jane filed a multimillion-dollar suit against members of the Nixon administration for conspiracy to violate her constitutional rights.

She continued to defend the Hanoi regime. With Hayden she embarked on a twenty-five-city tour to mobilize public opinion against American support of South Vietnam. They also planned a documentary film about the reconstruction of the North. With cinematographer Haskell Wexler and their eight-month-old son, Jane and Tom returned to Hanoi in the spring of 1974. She was shocked by the damage, so much greater than it had appeared in 1972, and she remarked that the historical debate about whether or not the Pentagon "intended" to bomb civilian targets "will not change the fact that nearly everything was bombed." After arranging to leave Troy with Vietnamese caretakers—"we were somewhat anxious," Jane admitted, "but we reminded each other that many Vietnamese families had been separated for months or years at a time"—they drove into South Vietnam. "How many wars will it take," asked Jane, for "us to learn that the defense budget can be increased and missile systems perfected till all our cities rot, but as long as the U.S. pits itself against the wishes of people who want to be their own masters . . . then the U.S. will fail." Their film, *Introduction to the Enemy,* appeared in 1974. Jane called it "a first step in tearing away the mask that the Pentagon has given these people."

When the Vietnam War officially ended in April 1975, Jane and Tom revised their political agenda: Hayden would run for political office; Jane would support his efforts. She was very much the spectator when he went to Sacramento to announce his intention to challenge Senator John Tunney in the 1976 Democratic primary. It was Jane's first political campaign, and she preferred to stand on the sidelines. But he failed to win a following and lost the primary by a large margin. Afterward she supported his decision to remain in politics. With the Vietnam War no longer an issue, they transformed the Indochina Peace Campaign into a new organization, the Campaign for Economic Democracy, which would be concerned with the problems of disadvantaged groups in California. In July 1976 Jane accompanied Hayden to the Democratic National Convention that nominated Jimmy Carter for president. "People say to me, 'What a sacrifice you've made! How brave you are! How much you gave up!' " she said. "And it makes me want to laugh, because I have given up nothing. Nothing. Nothing except irrelevance."

As Hayden entered the political mainstream, Jane decided to resume her career in Hollywood. She had not abandoned her political commitment, but like her husband she chose to work within the traditional system. It would be a division of labor. While Hayden worked to create a political organization, she would attempt to merge her politics and art in the movies—and make films that were politically significant. She would also use her substantial earnings to finance their political projects.

In her first major movie since *Klute,* she played the part of Jane Harper, wife of an unemployed aerospace executive in the ironic comedy *Fun with Dick and Jane.* To maintain their suburban life-style, the two characters become thieves. Jane Fonda had no trouble understanding the motives of a frustrated, affluent housewife. For all its frivolity, moreover, the role paralleled her personal transformation: the before and the after, the old passivity and the new urgency to act.

With this formula in mind, Jane created her own production company, IPC Films, and began to plan projects that would bear such titles as *Coming Home* and *The China Syndrome.* "I've changed tremendously in the last three years," she said. But the times, too, had changed. "So much is possible now. It was a long, hard winter, but now there's a new wave out there, and it has nothing to do with people who play it safe. . . . I think the only way to survive as an artist is to be in step with history . . . to be plugged into *life,* and to always be open to changing."

Her passion for political awareness—the dramatic passage from innocence to commitment—emerged in her next role, in the highly romanticized film version of Lillian Hellman's *Julia.* Jane played the young Hellman, whose love for another woman accelerated her political development. "I'm reaching middle age rapidly," Jane said on the eve of her thirty-ninth birthday, "and I've never had a chance to show real feeling for another woman, a feeling that was not neurotic, not erotic." Through risk and moral commitment, she could fulfill her potential: "It is very important to make movies about women who grow and become ideological human beings and totally committed people."

As part of her political rebirth, Jane stressed the importance of reconciling herself to her female identity: "The alienation that I felt growing up is gone—completely gone. . . . The deep scars will never go away," she confessed. "But essentially what I lost was cynicism. I moved from my sex-kitten image to a very different place, and I feel that if *I* could change, anyone can." She was optimistic, full of hope: "I am a very happy person," she said in her fortieth year, "and that's something I never thought I'd be able to say about myself."

George
Corley
Wallace
(III)

During January 1969, the month
Richard Nixon became president, the ex-governor of Alabama suffered
on the sidelines of power. He employed a skeleton staff at the campaign
headquarters, published a monthly *George Wallace Newsletter*, and
opened a post office box numbered 1972. But his concentration was
weak. He would abruptly leave the office to visit Lurleen's grave or take
a somber drive along the state highways he had had built for his
constituents. "If this administration will be sensitive to the feelings of
the people of my region," he declared about the Nixon White House,
"I'd be happy to be isolated forever." But his mind was still very much
on those ten million votes he had won in 1968. They "represented only
the tip of an iceberg"; there was no telling how deep his support might
run, or in what direction. "We shall continue . . . to keep the move-

ment alive." It was only a glimmer, but he had to follow it to feel alive himself.

Soon he was striking at the federal government, especially at Nixon, who had carried the South in 1968. At every opportunity he reminded the president of his campaign promises, not the least of which was a commitment to restore local control of the public schools. On Nixon's actions hinged Wallace's future. "I don't have any special plans," he said in a voice riddled with sarcasm, "but this administration has made many commitments. I *hope* in 1972 there will be peace and domestic tranquility. I *hope* the federal government recognizes the right of the states to run their own schools and their own affairs. I *hope* the tax burden on the masses of people will have been greatly eased. Then most everything our movement stands for will have been achieved. . . . But," he sighed, "we'll just have to wait and see."

In September 1969 his attention focused again, as it did each autumn, on the desegregation of the public schools. Trying to bait the Nixon administration into making a political mistake, he advised Alabamians to defy the federal courts: "Take your children wherever you want," he urged, borrowing a tactic from the late Martin Luther King, "regardless [of] where the courts say, and stay there until you get what you want." His efforts could not prevent court-ordered busing; nonetheless he succeeded in staking out an independent position. "I'm just reminding the president of what he said he would do if he were elected."

Despite his southern pride, Wallace appreciated the liabilities of his regional identity. In the fall of 1969 he decided to broaden his horizons—or at least create a semblance of doing so—by embarking on a fact-finding mission to Asia. He was fifty years old. It was his first trip outside North America since World War II. Three weeks after the vast moratorium-day protests against the Vietnam War, he arrived in Saigon to meet a military constituency that in 1968 had cast more ballots for Wallace than for any other candidate. The troops greeted him enthusiastically. But, because of direct orders from Washington, he was denied access to the South Vietnamese leadership. He settled for low-level briefings and then went on to Thailand, Taiwan, and South Korea. He returned to America more hawkish than ever. "Vietnamization," he said of Nixon's strategy for troop withdrawals, "is not going to end the fighting. . . . There's no way to withdraw combat forces until the enemy is crushed. . . . It would take [fewer] casualties to win the war." As for the dissent on the home front, he remained unyielding:

"I wish I had copyrighted or patented my speeches. I would be drawing immense royalties from Mr. Nixon and especially Mr. Agnew." Later Wallace corrected himself: "When I was saying what Agnew's now saying, Mr. Nixon said I was unfit for public office."

The time had come to take the fight back to the people. One evening in February 1970 he stood on a Coca Cola crate behind the microphones in the ballroom of the Jefferson Davis Hotel and admitted the inevitable: George Wallace was running again for governor. His enemies, as always, outnumbered him. With a wink he lifted the tablecloth from the speaker's table. "I look under the sheet and I see some strange bedfellows," he declared, resurrecting a guest list of foes. "I see all the Humphrey-Muskie Democrats. There's the chairman of the Democratic executive committee. And I declare there's a member of the president's Cabinet in there. There's a group of militants. And 'way back in the corner there's some of the big newspapers of Alabama. And there are the special interests." In Mobile he added to the list of enemies Governor Albert Brewer (once his protégé), the Department of H.E.W., the Alabama Power Company, and the telephone company. But when local cartoonists invented a bed of their own showing the Citizens Councils, the KKK, and Wallace under the same covers, he finally put aside the old gimmick. "This ain't any little governor's race," he told a reporter. "I know that and Nixon knows that. You know he's trying as hard as he can to beat me."

It's Johnny Dollar and his Three Dollar Bills loosening up the folks with the "Truck Driver's Lament" and "Okie from Muskogee" and those pretty girls carrying plastic buckets for cash donations and offering bumper stickers that say, not "Wallace for Governor," but just "WALLACE" (because maybe they can use any leftovers for some other campaign), and then to the yip of the rebel yell comes "Dixie" and then the spry candidate himself. The small hands grip the lectern, the chin thrusts forward, the dark eyes flash. Wallace is in his element, alive, and brave with promises. Better roads, he says. More medical schools. Lower utility rates and cheaper health insurance. Pensions for the old and a vow to reopen "every school closed" by the federal courts. All that's fine, says Wallace, but don't be fooled. There's only one issue this year, and he repeats it from the Gulf of Mexico to the Tennessee Valley. "If the people of Alabama don't elect me Governor," he cries, "it will be a sign to the rest of the country that Alabama has quit fighting."

As the campaign began, Wallace encountered a new federal enemy, the "dirty tricks" of Nixon's White House. Large sums of money poured into the coffers of the opposition. (Later, the White House counsel, John Dean, placed the amount spent on trying to defeat Wallace at $400,000.) The president also unleashed the IRS against Wallace's brother, Gerald, allegedly involved in kickback payments. (Nothing was ever proved.) And even more ominous was the arrival from John Mitchell's Justice Department of twenty-five federal registrars to enforce the Voting Rights Act, or, as Wallace put it, "to register the bloc vote that's trying to beat me." With three hundred thousand new black voters on the rolls, the Alabama segregationist faced a major fight. "If I'm out of the way," he asked the white voters, "who is going to be left to speak for you?"

The first primary was held on May 5, 1970. Wallace watched the returns in his Montgomery home, jumping between the couch and the TV channel selector. "Goddam niggers," he grumbled, as the tallies came in. "That's the nigger vote. . . . That's all nigger votes. That's all that is." All night the numbers arrived, and all night he swore in frustration. By morning he was haggard and tense and stuck in second place behind the victorious Albert Brewer. They would meet again in a special runoff. "It's going to be tough," Wallace declared, "but we will win." He knew what to do.

IF YOU WANT TO SAVE
ALABAMA AS YOU KNOW ALABAMA,
REMEMBER!
THE BLOC VOTE (NEGROES AND THEIR
WHITE FRIENDS) NEARLY NOMINATED
GOV. BREWER ON MAY 5TH. THIS
BLACK AND WHITE
SOCIAL-POLITICAL ALLIANCE
MUST NOT DOMINATE
THE PEOPLE OF ALABAMA!
THIS SPOTTED ALLIANCE MUST BE DEFEATED!
THIS MAY BE YOUR LAST CHANCE.
VOTE RIGHT—
VOTE WALLACE

He sat in the back of his big car as it sped along the sixty miles of rolling green country between Montgomery and the county seat at

Clayton, where he would vote. In the gray drizzly day he appeared nervous about the size of the vote: "Sure are a lot of black faces in town . . . I mean, these niggers are really turning out, ain't they?" He headed straight for the polling booth, and for the eighth time in twelve years voted for himself. "Now don't let them niggers beat us, you hear?" he said, patting a friend on the back. "I'm telling you now, if I don't win, them niggers are going to control this state." He paid a social call on his eighty-three-year-old stepgrandma, Mama Mae, widow of the beloved Dr. George Wallace, and then he stepped into his favorite café for lunch. "Wouldn't you use the bloc-vote tactic if you were me?" he asked the reporters who followed him. "I mean, all these niggers being told how to vote by a few ain't the right way, now is it?" When the press inquired about his plans in case of defeat, Wallace exuded southern charm: "If I lose, in my statement tonight I'm going to say, 'Well, I won't have you boys to kick around anymore.' "

He won by thirty-five thousand votes. "Alabama still keeps her place in the sun," he declared the next day, "and Alabama will continue to be heard from. We'll see all you national newsmen again." Buoyed by his victory, Wallace promptly challenged President Nixon to fulfill the pledges of the "southern strategy." "The president says he's against busing, but he keeps right on busing," Wallace protested. "These platitudes will no longer satisfy us." Besides, he added, the best way for the Republicans to get rid of George Wallace in 1972 would be to steal his program. That was fine with him: "Because that means they would satisfy the people." Yet he remained a loyal supporter of the president's policy in Indochina, including the incursion into Cambodia: "There wasn't anything for the president to do—if he wants to get out of Vietnam—except to do what he's doing."

Rejuvenated by his comeback victory, Wallace rose from the rut of personal depression. During the primaries, he had taken a fancy to a young dark-haired beauty, a divorcée named Cornelia Snively. Bred in a political family—she was a niece of Big Jim Folsom—she shared Wallace's prime interest. He invited her to join him on a family vacation near Key West. They both had suffered recent personal losses, by death and divorce, and their conversations, as Cornelia later described them, "became somewhat like therapy sessions for both of us." They talked of marriage, but Wallace was skeptical about the nineteen-year difference in their ages: "You don't want to marry me, someday I'll be in a wheelchair."

On Labor Day of 1970 Wallace returned to the campaign, fighting to win the general election. "They's people who can't stand me, and they's people for me 100 percent. They's no middle ground on George Wallace. . . . If I'm defeated, you watch out. They gonna ruin the public schools. . . . They gonna make the workers pay through the nose. . . . If this black bloc vote determines who will be governor of Alabama this year, they'll determine every governor of Alabama for the next fifty years. . . . Don't let this happen, because then who will stand up for you? They want your voice stilled and silent," he said. "It's up to y'all." The voters took heed. In November Wallace won in a landslide.

The victory spirit overcame his caution. Just after New Year's Day, 1971, Wallace and Cornelia were married at Montgomery's Trinity Presbyterian Church. "People's wives help 'em," he later explained to reporter Sally Quinn. "It's good to have 'em around. And I have children and they needed a mother." To her delight, Cornelia became the beneficiary of Wallace's old remorse. "I think he transferred his affection from Lurleen to me," she remarked. "He treats me the way he wishes he had treated her." She overlooked the fact that he still referred to Lurleen as "my wife."

Cornelia soon lightened him up: "She tells me how to dress, get my tie matched up with my shirt. She watches me on television and tells me to smile more. She boosts my morale." Out went the blue suits and slim-jim ties. He took to wearing Edwardian suits, wide ties, and bright color-coordinated shirts. Hair spray replaced the slick brillian- tine; sideburns crawled down his cheeks. "I don't dye it you know," he said about his brownish tint, "I just touch it up; it's gettin' a little gray here at the sideburns." Whether it was sex appeal he was after or just respectability wasn't clear, but Wallace felt sufficiently self-conscious about his appearance to bring an elevated platform when he spoke in public, so that his new wife wouldn't tower above him. He had prom- ised Cornelia, so his friends claimed, that he would make her "the Jacqueline Kennedy of the red-necks."

As part of the new image, the Wallaces attended a pre-inaugural concert, where they sat in an integrated audience for a musical program that included ballet and opera. The next day Wallace's inauguration rhetoric was in obvious contrast to his militancy of eight years before. "Alabama belongs to all of us," he declared in 1971, "black and white, young and old, rich and poor alike." The key issue was not race but rather "an illegal abuse of federal governmental power . . . the despotic tyranny of a federal government . . . [that] can and will destroy America."

Wallace's timidity reflected not only a yearning for respectability but also his shaky hold on the Alabama power structure. His narrow margin of victory in the Democratic primary had weakened his control of the legislature. He also respected the potential power of the new black vote. Yet he retained a keen sense of public opinion in the South. When a military court convicted Lieutenant William Calley of war crimes at My Lai, Wallace proposed—to no avail—that the Alabama branch of the selective service suspend the draft, and he showed his own sympathies by visiting the incarcerated soldier at Fort Benning, Georgia. "There was no hue and cry when civilians were killed in World War II," he told a rally of Calley supporters. "The Silent Majority is not going to be silent anymore."

In 1971 he arranged out-of-state "Appreciation" dinners, which, at $50 a plate, helped line his campaign purse. "They'll tell you that the South has changed," he said, brushing off that possibility. "But these new governors everybody talks about—Jimmy Carter in Georgia and Dale Bumpers in Arkansas—they all called my name in their campaigns and it helped them." But he avoided the old issues of race, hippies, and the liberal press. "That banking crowd in Wall Street and the foundations," he explained, "are more dangerous to the United States than any militant group I ever heard of." When President Nixon announced an impending visit to China, Wallace called it "a colossal mistake" to negotiate with any country whose main interest was "exporting heroin [and] subversion."

During the summer of 1971 he became embroiled in another controversy with Nixon. It began over the president's southern strategy. Nixon hoped to close the school-busing debate by canceling a federal plan for Austin, Texas. Wallace did not want busing either. But he saw in the president's action an inconsistency that he could exploit politically. In a telegram sent to the White House, he asked Nixon to clarify "the conflicts between your recent statements opposing the busing of schoolchildren and the action of federal departments directly under your control." When Nixon responded by ordering his administration to "hold busing to the minimum," Wallace promptly told the Alabama school boards to ignore the federal courts. "All I'm trying to do," he explained, "is help the president and the attorney general and his wife—what's her name? Martha?—to do what they say they all want to do, and that's stop busing. Just make these judges stop toting our kids all over creation." By forcing Nixon to take a stand, Wallace had ensured that busing would remain a major issue in the 1972 election.

He arrived in Tallahassee, Florida, just after the New Year, 1972, to announce his return to the Democratic fold: "Too long, this party has been controlled by the so-called intellectual snobs who feel that big government should control the lives of American citizens from the cradle to the grave." As a candidate in the presidential primary, he offered a populist platform filled with small-government intentions and short on the particulars: "Peace through strength . . . a fair tax system . . . the discontinuance of foreign-aid programs . . . continued withdrawal from Vietnam. . . ." He saved the best for last: "a complete halt to involuntary busing."

Thus, in a field that would include Hubert Humphrey, Edmund Muskie, George McGovern, John Lindsay, and Shirley Chisholm, George Wallace set the main agenda. His slogan challenged them all: "Send 'Em a Message." Through the towns and cities of Florida, he concentrated on big nighttime rallies, a latter-day mix of rural evangelism, country music, and crackerjack oratory. He knew how to reach the people. In Orlando, for example, he told them that when Nixon was in China "the president asked Mousy Tongue for advice on busing and Mousy Tongue said, 'I can't advise you on busing 'cause when I take a notion to bus 'em and they don't like it I just bus 'em anyhow.' And," said Wallace, pausing for effect, "that's just the way we're doing it here."

As he surged ahead in the popularity polls, his opinions become increasingly subject to public scrutiny. Asked about the SALT negotiations with the Russians, he described his preferred modus operandi: "I'd say, 'Look, goddammit, you done broke every agreement we ever made. Now you wanna let us set up a team of observers and electronic devices, okay. But if not, the hell with it. We'll all burn up together.' "

On the subject of women's rights he made finer distinctions: "I put 'em on a pedestal. I don't want to bring 'em down to equality. Women and men are different. I don't believe women should be drafted, but I'm for equal rights and equal pay."

As for blacks: "I never was a racist. I just never was against black folks. I was unfairly labeled by the . . . liberals who don't know the difference between a racist and a man who believes in states' rights." It was all crystal clear: "I know a lot of folks like to let on that I've changed," he told seven thousand supporters in Jacksonville, "but the truth of the matter is that I'm the only man running . . . who hasn't changed."

Wallace, consequently, appeared the least surprised when he defeated the entire field in Florida with a 42 percent plurality. Then he moved into the North, opening his campaign in Milwaukee "on a night so cold and snowy," he recalled, "that those of us from Alabama couldn't understand why everything didn't just shut down." As Billy Grammer's bluegrass band, a fixture in his campaign, switched from "Alabamy Bound" to "On, Wisconsin," Wallace welcomed the cheering response: "It's people who like country music who are gonna save this country. These folks can poke fun at themselves, and they don't go around so serious like the other folks do."

His rustic candor appealed to northern farmers and blue-collar workers. After only nine days in Wisconsin, Wallace ran second in the vote. He returned to Montgomery happy enough to quote Martin Luther King: "We're going to keep on keeping on." As the anti-establishment candidate, he relished the predicament of his rivals. When Humphrey, Muskie, McGovern—all onetime supporters of U.S. involvement in Vietnam—acknowledged that the war was a mistake, he questioned their competence: "But what kind of a mistake did they make? A mistake that cost fifty thousand American lives and two hundred thousand wounded and $120 billion of your money—and I don't think that entitles a man to be president of the United States." Snubbed by the Democratic leadership at the Jefferson-Jackson Day celebration in Detroit, Wallace scheduled a counterrally that so far outdrew the regular meeting he had to hold two sessions to accommodate the throng, and then he proceeded to defend Nixon's bombing of Haiphong.

Yet Wallace overestimated his popularity in the North. He neglected to field slates of delegates and left just one day for the Pennsylvania primary. He hoped that his mass appeal would overcome these organizational weaknesses.

Heading for a meeting in Boston, Cornelia asked him what he would say about the Kennedys there. "I'm going to say they're one of the most attractive political families in the country."

"And what will you say about the Saltonstalls?"

"Oh, they're not even in it anymore. They let a nigger beat them. Or was that the Peabodys?"

Wallace apparently was referring to black Senator Edward Brooke. But when a *New York Times* reporter quoted this dialogue, Wallace denied it. "He was changing," the reporter would later observe. "In 1968 he would have admitted he said it."

On the April night of the Pennsylvania primary, Wallace went to bed satisfied that he would run "a pretty good fourth up there." He woke up the next day to learn he had come in second. He followed Pennsylvania with a strong showing in Indiana and then carried Tennessee, Alabama, and North Carolina. "Every dog has its day," he boasted, "and ours is next." He thrived on the screaming and the cheers, responsive to the multitudes that grabbed at his hands. "They say I'm an evil man, a demagogue," he suggested to a reporter. "Well, I don't play on people's emotions, I just reflect them." To a question about his interests outside politics, he replied: "Sure, I have outside interests. Why, I love archery, and I spend a lot of time down at the shootin' range, and of course there's mini-golf and tennis and Ping-Pong like the Chinese do, and I do find fishin' very relaxin'. . . ." Then a burst of laughter belied all these possibilities, and Wallace grabbed the reporter's pencil. "I'm just jokin', honey," said this strictly political creature, "don't put none of that stuff down."

In May 1972 he took his campaign into Maryland, a state whose racial turmoils he understood and could exploit. "We've accepted nondiscrimination and freedom of choice in Alabama," he assured a country club audience on the conservative Eastern Shore. "But that has not been enough for the social schemers. They want ratios and balances, and they're busing our children hither and thither into kingdom come to get it—and that's what I'm against." No longer an archsegregationist—"It's just a passé issue"—Wallace supported "quality education for everybody, regardless of race, creed, or color." But not everyone was persuaded by the change. In Frederick, on the penultimate night of the campaign, he met an obstreperous crowd that surprised him with a hail of rocks and bricks, one of which grazed his chest.

He returned to Montgomery for Mother's Day, visited Mozelle, who was recovering from surgery, and stopped at Lurleen's grave. Leading the polls in Maryland, he considered canceling his last appearances. But Monday morning came, the schedule was fixed, and he could not resist another moment in the sun. At Wheaton, Maryland, however, a hostile crowd greeted him with tomatoes, eggs, and soap studded with nails, and the Secret Service had to shelter him behind bulletproof glass. It had no effect on his appetite. At a luncheon banquet his place was set with the usual grilled ground meat. Then he went on to Laurel, where he found a friendly shopping-center crowd that wanted to shake his hand. "I like the touch of hand to hand," he remarked, "because I receive a pleasant satisfaction of confidence and force."

Reaching for a hand, Wallace heard five quick loud bursts, found himself sprawled on the pavement, his legs limp beneath him. "This must be the end," he thought. "I'll start feeling faint and pass out, and that will be the end." Cornelia hovered above, protecting him from other imagined assassins. "I can't move my legs," he groaned. He saw a .45 aimed at his head. "Who are you?" he gasped.

"Secret Service."

"Well, you can put your gun up. I've been shot enough for one day."

Now the numbness turned to pain, excruciating pain that was not stilled, even for a second, by any lapse of consciousness. He was hoisted aboard an ambulance and rushed toward a hospital. "I was convinced that I was fatally wounded," he would later recall, "and I was trying to be as gritty as possible to the end." Images careened through his mind, the oldest ones most vividly. "My mind flashed the memories of the last few lucid moments of my first wife's life, when with her weak, tired voice she reminded me, 'We will all meet in heaven.' " He moaned in agony. "Knock me out!" he pleaded. "Please knock me out. I don't mind dying, but please don't make me suffer like this."

At Holy Cross Hospital in Silver Springs, the medics tore through his clothing to reach the mangled body. Five bullets had struck. There were superficial wounds in the right forearm and upper arm and a flesh wound at the front of his right shoulder. One bullet had lodged in the spinal column, causing paralysis, and another had blasted into his full stomach, dangerously splattering intestines through his abdominal cavity. Wallace, at last, was freed of the immediate pain, sedated for a five-hour operation. The less threatening injury, the one to his spine, awaited later attention.

As he rested in intensive care, Wallace received good news about his victories in Maryland and Michigan. But his state of complete helplessness overwhelmed him. "What am I going to do?" he asked Cornelia. "Why has this happened to me? If I were a mean man, maybe I could understand it, but I've never done anything to hurt anybody. I didn't deserve it." Amazed at his survival, he pondered the prospect of a half-existence: "This may be more of a burden than I can bear." He found comfort and pride as the VIPs came to visit him: President Nixon (who noted in his diary Wallace's joy at the recent primary victories, his "sentimental" patriotism, his military salute to the commander-in-chief); Spiro Agnew and Strom Thurmond; Edward Kennedy and Ethel Kennedy; Muskie and Humphrey and McGovern; and Shirley Chisholm, with whom he prayed. When he met reporters for the first time ten days after the shooting, Wallace appeared reedy and thin-voiced, still slightly dazed, and he made an uncharacteristic slip by suggesting that his campaign was finished. "The campaign is not over or anything like that," he quickly corrected himself. "Why, I ran second in Oregon without even going there."

A huge abscess in his abdomen imperiled his life. He lost over thirty pounds. Feverish and weak, he drifted in and out of depression. By mid-June the doctors found substantial denervation in his legs, and the operation to remove the bullet from his spinal column offered a bleak prognosis about his ability ever to walk again. Wallace hung on grimly, defiantly. Within two weeks he could sit in a wheelchair, lift weights, and move on his arms along parallel bars. He received an overnight pass to visit Cornelia at the local Holiday Inn, and the two of them clutched like teenagers. "It wasn't politics that made him push that chair," his wife said. "It was the same thing that motivated Adam." After fifty-four days in the hospital, he participated in a teary farewell mass with the doctors and nurses who had saved his life. As he read aloud Psalm 23, his voice broke into a long rolling sob.

President Nixon provided a medical evacuation plane that carried him first to Montgomery, where he resumed his official powers as governor, and then to Miami for the Democratic National Convention. He appeared as a shadow of himself. At a convention dominated by young affluent liberals, Wallace pleaded for a conservative platform on busing, tax reform, and law and order—in his words, "really the majority report as far as the American people are concerned"—and he warned that the Democratic party "cannot win the election without the support of those who supported me." For his troubles, he was ignored. George McGovern won the Democratic nomination, and Wallace left the convention in despair.

The discovery of another abdominal infection forced further surgery, and his long recuperation now served as a convenient refuge from the political wars. He thought of resurrecting a third party. But the arrival of a special emissary from President Nixon, John Connally, persuaded him to quit the campaign. "And all he really wants from you," Connally reported to the president, "is to be sure that his message on the issues was heard." Nixon reciprocated with words of spiritual uplift and sent the governor the inspirational film about FDR, *Sunrise at Campobello.* Wallace, meanwhile, ignored McGovern's request for an endorsement. In the end he backed Democratic candidates on the state and local levels and stubbornly refused to be drawn into the presidential contest. He expressed no surprise at Nixon's landslide in November: "If [the Democrats] had accepted my proposals on welfare, busing, and law and order, it would have been a much closer race. . . . I told them the future of the Democratic party lies in the hands of the average citizen of this country."

After the election Wallace sat in a wheelchair at the state capitol, calm, subdued, almost tranquil about the drastic transformation of his life. "It's difficult to accept, but life has to go on," he said in a flat, listless tone. "There are still a lot of things I can do, and I'm lucky to be alive at all. Naturally, there are times when I get despondent, but that's beginning to go away. I don't have those real bad periods of depression anymore."

Paradoxically, while his lower limbs hung immobile he suffered sharp, stabbing pains along the ghost nerves and at the sensitive borders of tissue where the paralysis began. Willing to try any remedy, he consulted with a faith healer, but he held few illusions: "It's like gravity. I could pray all day and jump off the state Capitol and still fall. God has laws that He set."

To alleviate his physical misery he did daily exercises and felt proud as any athlete about his ability to lift heavy weights. But the psychological discomforts, that uneasy acceptance of reality, persisted and bedeviled him. He denied any bitterness toward his would-be assassin, Arthur Bremer; at the same time he believed in the existence of an undiscovered conspiracy against him. He read and reread Bremer's diary—"and something about it does not ring true." In moments of depression, he chattered about his childhood and youth, his early religious experiences in Clio, in which he "came to know and accept Jesus Christ as my personal savior," but he remained perplexed about the arbitrariness of his fate: "I accept—with normal human petulance—the fact that what happened was in all likelihood God's incomprehensible way of testing my faith and my forbearance, no matter how often I may wonder wryly if I was really worth all the attention."

Wallace touched emotional bottom on January 20, 1973, a brisk day in Washington, D.C., when he sat in his wheelchair and watched Richard Nixon take the oath of the presidency: "The thought crossed my mind that if I had not been shot it could have been me standing there." Once that winter, watching television, he inadvertently saw a rerun of his own shooting and plunged further into self-pity. He clung more to Cornelia, teary-eyed, called her mama, and swore he could not live without his family. But he worried, too, that he might lose her. "He's got this terrible jealousy of Cornelia," one of her friends asserted. "Every time she gets out of his sight he thinks she's running around on him." He was resigned to his future only in the most limited way. "But if I could *walk* the next minute and be *whole* again," he declared, "I would have no problem in the world."

In the winter of 1973 Wallace returned to the hospital for additional surgery—his sixth operation since the shooting—and the recuperation proved much slower than expected. His long absence from Alabama politics dismayed his allies and foes alike. Word reached him that prominent men were discussing the necessity of his retirement. Ironically it was just the tonic he needed, the political goad to recover. He saw himself once again as the underdog, and he was determined to prevail, almost out of spite. "You know, when you've been shot up like I have, it takes time to recover," he declared. "I've been doing my therapy. I can get well." Time allowed healthy scars to form, reducing his dependence on drugs, and Wallace began a series of acupuncture treatments to restore color and muscle tone to his extremities.

He reentered the public world in small ways, attending the funeral of Governor Winthrop Rockefeller in Arkansas, greeting high school students at a YMCA Youth Legislature, addressing a fund raiser in Dallas to pay his campaign debts. He welcomed recently returned POWs at the state mansion, and in a gesture of reconciliation he traveled to the town of Eufaula to honor one of them, a black sergeant.

Fifty weeks after the shooting, Wallace stood on his own feet, strapped to a special lectern, and presented a half-hour televised speech to the state legislature, mostly about local issues, in order to demonstrate unambiguously his recovery. The performance won thunderous applause, brought tears to cynical men, and enabled him, once again, to jut his jaw proudly. "I can't exactly run upstairs or jump over fences and holler hurray," he said afterward. "But I can run this office, and I can campaign for reelection next year, and I feel I still represent a lot of folks across this nation." His future, as ever, was entirely political.

Having survived his personal tragedy, Wallace assumed a new place in American politics; no longer quite the pariah of old, yet not fully acceptable. He required, beyond public sympathy, some further respectability, a move toward the political middle. Whatever spiritual mellowing his injuries might have brought, he knew, too, that it was in his interest to seek accommodation with moderates and with blacks.

To celebrate July 4, 1973, he eagerly accepted an invitation to share the podium at the "Spirit of America" festival in Decatur with another prominent political survivor, who for ambitions of his own, felt he too must move toward the political center, though from the opposite direction: Senator Edward Kennedy. (Before their meeting, however, Wallace prudently arranged for any sudden medical emergency, ordering a helicopter, a speedboat, standby surgeons and nurses, and an abundance of blood.) "This is the finest thing that has happened to me this year," said Wallace in accepting the Audie Murphy Patriotism Award before ten thousand cheering supporters. "I can't walk yet, Senator," he added, with an eye toward their shared future, "but I hope you won't think me immodest when I say you can't keep a good man down." After celebrating his fifty-fourth birthday in August 1973, he vetoed a legislative bill that offered a pension to any governor disabled in office.

Wallace's search for respectability brought him back to the University of Alabama at Tuscaloosa, where ten years earlier he had attempted to prevent the admission of black students. On the Thanksgiving weekend of 1973 he proudly crowned the annual homecoming queen, who for the first time was a black student. He also visited a meeting of southern black mayors at Tuskegee and received a standing ovation. "All of us are God's children," he declared. "I don't think anyone would be against somebody for the way God made them. My position has been against central government meddling in local affairs." Asked about this recent turnaround, Wallace denied its existence. "This is nothing new. . . . There have been some differences on powerful, federal bureaucratic control, but I've been meeting with blacks for years."

Seeking an unprecedented third term as governor in 1974, Wallace endeavored not only to solidify his political base but also to prove his personal vitality. As in past campaigns, the bunting-covered flatbed trucks rolled from one courthouse square to the next, bringing country and western bands that invariably played "Dixie" just before the governor's appearance. But now Wallace could not bounce through the crowds; he was pushed by a pair of state troopers. As he was strapped into a lectern that was wrapped in protective glass, the crowd would come to a sudden awkward hush. Yet he still knew how to draw a laugh, lambasting "those federal bureaucrats up in Washington with nothing but peanut butter sandwiches in their briefcases, trying to tell us a thousand miles away down here in Alabama how to run our business." He knew they loved him for what he represented, and he played to their

sympathy. "They come to me and they say, 'Wallace, you're changing,'" he declared, invoking some imaginary idiots. "I say, 'No, I
haven't changed. You didn't listen.'" Looking at his chrome wheelchair that glinted in the sunshine, they appreciated the price he had
paid.

Wallace campaigned in 1974 with a fistful of political debts, most
based on his virtual monopoly of state government for over a decade.
Many obligations resided within the black community. Now he called
them in. Convinced that Wallace would win, the newly enfranchised
black leaders rushed to the bandwagon. And Wallace reinforced their
reasoning: "Not long before the election," explained the black mayor
of Hobson City, "George saw to it that we got $153,000 in road funds.
Everybody in town remembered that, instead of all that he had done
before."

Bragging about his support among Alabama blacks, Wallace
coasted to victory in the Democratic primary, capturing 64 percent of
the vote, the largest margin in history, and he claimed over 20 percent
of the black vote too. In gratitude he vowed to be "the governor of all
the people," to help "whites and blacks . . . achieve the American
dream." He was proud, too, to stand beside Reverend Ralph Abernathy
as they both received honorary doctor of law degrees from the predomi-
nantly black Alabama State University. "Because of his good judgment
and official restraint," read Wallace's citation, "no freedom-loving and
freedom-seeking student . . . met violence at the hands of the law on
the Alabama State campus during the civil rights struggles of the
1960s."

A few months later Wallace made a surprise, unpublicized appearance at the Dexter Avenue Baptist Church, the very pulpit where
Martin Luther King had first pronounced the doctrine of nonviolent
civil disobedience. "As far as I was concerned," Wallace assured the
assemblage of black pastors, "there never was a race question; it was
a question of big government." As he was wheeled from the sanctuary,
they rose in his honor to sing "The Battle Hymn of the Republic." In
this way Wallace accomplished a profound reconciliation of the races,
on the surface at least, which was no small achievement.

He also became the beneficiary of Watergate. In his view the
scandal was "the symptom, not the disease"; the true cause of it was
"naked power unchecked by moral restraint." Wallace liked Nixon and
respected his political skill but obviously felt no sorrow at his departure.
When Nixon himself begged the governor to speak against impeach-

ment, Wallace refused to help. "He said he hadn't examined the evidence," the president noted, summarizing Wallace's evasion. "That he prayed for me. That he was sorry this had to be brought upon me. That he didn't think it was proper for him to [act]."

In the aftermath of Watergate the issues belonged to Wallace. Mistrust of the federal government spread around the country, reinforcing his appeal. As a southerner, moreover, he could articulate the frustrations of powerlessness: "Let me tell you," he said at the Southern Governors Conference, "the New South is just as tired of this central government flimflam—of giveaways and bureaucracies—as the Old South was." When Edward Kennedy formally withdrew from the 1976 elections, Wallace found himself leading the Gallup poll. "They're thinking what I've been preaching for years now," he said of public opinion. "The average man is swelling up, bursting out because he's been flouted. He knows you're not being a racist when you talk about welfare and busing and law and order and the like."

Wallace's third inauguration, in January 1975, underscored the massive social upheaval that had changed both the fifty-five-year-old governor and the citizens who heard him speak. A black choir stood conspicuously as a backdrop. "The people in government in this state are concerned with all our citizens, whether they be black or white," he said. "It shall continue to be that way." He found satisfaction in this state of affairs, so different from the days of segregation. It seemed to validate his personal mission, perhaps explained the purpose for which he had miraculously been saved. "I shall continue my interest in national affairs," he vowed, his voice rising as he departed from the prepared text. "Not to do so would be a dereliction of my duties. Those who don't like it can do what they will."

Beneath the bravado, Wallace harbored doubts about his ability to endure another national campaign. At a private meeting with his advisers, the governor listened as one after another urged him to run, climaxed by a fervent plea from his brother. "Gerald," said the unimpressed Wallace, "why don't you go out and get your ass shot at, get bricks thrown at you, with your wife at one end of the country and you at the other. You give me your list of girls you see at all the bars in town, and I'll stay home." But the lure of the presidency remained more powerful: "As long as we have this iniquitous income tax that's grinding the middle class out of existence, I'll be alive and well and around."

He flourished as the eternal outsider, enjoying the spectacle of established politicians clamoring to end his career. In their hostility he

saw irony and vindication: "I'm one of the few [candidates] who has
a constituency that does not contain many members of the hierarchy
of the Democratic party, many members of Congress, many party
leaders, many of the intelligentsia, many of the bureaucracy, many of
the nonproducers. And those are the people that the great mass of
people today resent and are blaming for their ills and the troubles they
now face." Wallace knew nonetheless that he could not win without
respectability, and he continued to seek a broad spectrum of support.
He even welcomed Martin Luther King, Sr., in Montgomery and
expressed belated condolences for the death of his son.

Wallace never doubted his appeal to the populace, but he also
sought to establish his credentials as a statesman. To gain firsthand
experience—and also to show off his robust health—he arranged for a
five-nation goodwill tour of Western Europe, his first trip across the
Atlantic. He met with conservative leader Margaret Thatcher ("a
lovely talk with a lovely woman"), chatted with Italian premier Aldo
Moro, and visited the Berlin Wall. After what he called a "sentimental
visit" to Scotland, home of the Wallace forebears, he returned to
Montgomery. He seemed remarkably unaffected by the experience:
"I've seen Europe on television . . . so really it was nothing new to me.
You can learn as much about going abroad by watching and reading
news, and reading books and stories and publications, as you can by
seeing some concrete walls, a few automobiles in traffic jams, and some
scenery."

Wallace promptly announced his entry into the 1976 presidential
campaign. "Trust the People," read the banner behind him, as he
called for "a political revolution" among "that great mass of Americans
who pay their taxes, fight our wars, make our cars, grow our crops, and
try to live decent, law-abiding lives." At issue, he insisted, was "the
survival of the middle class," the backbone of his constituency. "Being
a southerner is not as much geographical now as it is a state of mind,"
he explained; "we have as many southerners in Illinois as we have in
Alabama. When I say 'southern' I mean this: People are beginning to
realize that big government is not good for the people."

Well financed by mail order solicitations and leading all Democrats in the opinion surveys, Wallace entered the election year with
undisguised optimism. "President Wallace invited reporters into the
Oval Office today," he mimicked the voice of David Brinkley, "and
told them to get out of town." As a program, he offered the same
agenda as in 1968: law and order, lower taxes, local self-control, and a

strong military defense: "This country's got a bad spiritual problem. . . . We've got a whole lot of people in this country who've been stomped on and hit on so long by the government that they just don't know what to think."

At first the campaign did well, drawing large crowds in areas, such as Boston, where busing remained a bitter issue. But soon another trend became apparent: a pervasive, unshakable suspicion among his supporters that Wallace was too weak physically to function as a president. In Florida, the first major primary state, Jimmy Carter played on these fears. There, Carter paraphrased the "send 'em a message" slogan of 1972: "Send 'em a president!"

Wallace's efforts to dispel the so-called health issue was complicated when one of his state troopers accidentally dropped him, forcing him to wear a cast. "You're not president with your feet," exclaimed Wallace. "You're president with your head." He worked desperately to restore his constituency. In Key West he attacked busing ("quit all this social experimentation with little children"); in Hialeah he denounced welfare for "those who won't work"; at Palm Beach he suggested that lawbreakers go to prison "until their hair turns white or they go to the electric chair." He promised the elderly more social security, assured the Cubans that Castro was "an international bandit," and appealed to Catholics by opposing abortion. They applauded him and cheered him and encouraged him, but in the polling booths they voted for Jimmy Carter.

Shocked by his defeat on southern soil, Wallace attacked the "phony health issue." More than ever, he needed to bypass the media, to reach the people, to touch the flesh. But now confinement to the wheelchair, the obsession with his physical security, became an insurmountable barrier. Instead of parading through city streets, he had to settle for airport rallies and expensive television advertising. To compound matters, as his support waned, so did the campaign contributions. In Illinois he again finished second, well behind Carter.

They would meet next in North Carolina. "Nothing's that tough," said Wallace, ever the realist. "After you've been shot five times and suffered the loss of walking, what's a loss? . . . So losing a campaign—my goodness, that's not your life. That's not the right to look at the sky, the trees, your wife, and your family, enjoy your friends. Of course I would like to win," he continued, "but I've lost some pretty tough battles. You don't win every time, but the election is not over." Now he attacked Carter for stealing his program and robbing him of his constituency. To lose to a southerner wounded his pride: "I'm the reason some of them are running—because I proved they could do well in other parts of the country."

They loved Wallace dearly in North Carolina; but, in 1976, they loved Carter more. In defeat, Wallace resolved to continue the campaign, but his optimism had vanished. "All the other candidates are now saying what I've been saying all along," he complained. "I have no positions of my own left." But he knew it was not the issues that were hurting him. It was his image: "All they can see is the spokes of my wheelchair. The television catches every one. You've got a man standing up saying, 'Big government is eating you up.' And you've got a man in a wheelchair, all humped over, saying the same thing. It's hard to beat." He was a man without illusions: "I guess you could say that Arthur Bremer really messed me up politically with that gun."

Still he stayed with the failing struggle, led a patchwork crusade into Wisconsin, Pennsylvania, Texas, and Indiana, all former strongholds that fell one by one. He could only rationalize his declining fortunes: "The people I have represented are today the majority of the United States." The old fires were banked, the anger reduced to a whisper. But when Carter threatened to invade Alabama, Wallace stirred to save his self-respect. "I don't know if I'll be making any more political speeches," he told a crowd in Muscle Shoals. "But I want to thank you all for letting me speak for you, for letting me represent your viewpoint. . . . Remember when we were looked down upon as some subculture?" At Birmingham Southern College his appeal to nostalgia was the only thing left: "We have shared a lot of history, a lot of hardship, a lot of crops." In mid-June, Wallace signed a truce, giving all his political forces to Jimmy Carter. "I lost. The people voted for Carter," he declared. "That was it."

One week after the national bicentennial, Wallace went to New York City for the Democratic National Convention. He sat in his hotel suite eating alone. Cornelia returned from one of the splashy private parties. "They were all asking about you," she said, trying to cheer his spirits. Wallace leaned forward, peering over his dark-framed glasses. "Yeah," he said, "I'll bet they were."

He was preoccupied with the next day, what might well be his last chance to address a national audience. "They tell me they'll give me six minutes," he said. "What do you say in six minutes? And when you speak from a wheelchair it's not the same. Now if you were standing. . . ."

Wheeled into Madison Square Garden, Wallace offered a final defiance: "The monster bureaucracy is driving people in this country nuts. It should get off their backs and out of their pocketbooks." He looked out at the throng that had come to anoint his successor. "Some of you laughed at me," he asserted, putting it politely. "But now you're saying it."

He was tired, almost glad that it was all over. "Every hotel has no bathroom I can get into, doors that aren't wide enough," he said. "Finally that gets old." But he clung to the future. George Wallace would admit only that this year, 1976, was "my last *presidential* campaign. It may or may not be my last campaign."

Phyllis
Stewart
Schlafly
(III)

Phyllis Schlafly knew, of course, that Richard Nixon was no liberal, but neither was he, in her estimation, a conservative. Three months after his inauguration, she felt almost as powerless as she had when the Democrats were in office. "The trouble is that conservative women do not carry the political clout in the Republican party to which their tremendous work entitles them," she complained. "This is wrong. Politics is too important to be left to politicians."

Her remedy—given her later position—was most surprising: she called for a feminization of American politics. "More women," she said, "should strive for the elected positions now held by men, and more women should support those who do." But Phyllis Schlafly was certainly no feminist; her suggestion reflected a conservative image of women. In her view, women in politics would not alter the structure of government but rather would serve as guardians of virtue: "Women can raise the moral tone of politics. They keep their ideals while playing the game."

Her own ideals focused on the national defense, a subject she felt Nixon was neglecting. She spent the spring of 1969 trying to gain support for an antiballistic missile (ABM) system to prevent a Soviet attack. She wrote letters to the press, gave speeches to conservative groups, and testified before the Senate Armed Services Committee in Washington. "I am the mother of six children," she said, listing her qualifications, "[and] so I have a substantial stake in the future of America." She criticized the idea of "parity" with the communists and denied the existence of technological obstacles: "If the United States is capable of solving the problems involved in sending men around the moon . . . surely we can solve the problems of defending ourselves against a nuclear missile attack! If we want to, that is." In an open letter to the president, she requested the release of secret archives that, she claimed, would expose the communist plan to destroy the United States.

When the Senate finally did approve the ABM in August 1969, Mrs. Schlafly drew another moral conclusion: "The vote on the ABM gives all Americans the black-and-white proof of which senators believe in the defense of America against Communist aggression—and which senators are for appeasement of the Communists." For her efforts, she was named Woman of the Year by the Illinois Federation of Republican Women. She was forty-five years old.

Mrs. Schlafly's patriotism usually served to promote her conservative ideology. For example, in a welcoming speech to newly naturalized citizens in 1969 (for which she later won a George Washington Honor Medal from the Freedoms Foundation of Valley Forge), she extolled the laissez-faire tradition and denounced its critics: "America has been able to give more good things to more people than any nation in the history of the world—NOT because government solved our problems —but because government stayed out of the way and let the initiative and inventiveness of man solve our problems instead." She itemized the contributions of American inventors—the "magnificent" walk on the moon, the work of Ford, Edison, Westinghouse, even George Washington Carver ("Where but in America," she asked, "could a sickly boy of slave parents rise to such heights? . . ."). But she characterized political dissenters as "native parasites . . . unwashed, ungrateful for the privilege of living in America. . . . Don't confuse them with the great majority of Americans, who are good, law-abiding, and generous."

At a time when antiwar protests were erupting on college campuses, Mrs. Schlafly appealed to Young Americans for Freedom to become "a voice for victory in Vietnam." She praised the alliterative wit of Vice-President Spiro Agnew, especially "his magnificent speeches on biased television reporting. . . . We back him 100 percent for saying what most of us have known for a long time." She attacked the Supreme Court for liberalizing standards of pornography, and she attacked the Senate for rejecting President Nixon's conservative nominations to the Court. When Senator Everett Dirksen died, she joined the Republican Women of Illinois in urging an anti-obscenity bill as "a living memorial."

In the fall of 1969 she was proud to learn that she, too, was the object of a Republican conspiracy. Fifteen party leaders had met secretly to name a candidate for the twenty-third congressional district of Illinois, and they asked her to run. She accepted at once: "Only with a responsible Congress can President Nixon achieve the goals that the silent majority of America supports." Her agenda was clear: "Our citizens are concerned about high taxes, inflation, high interest rates, and the shrinking value of the dollar . . . fed up with campus riots, revolution in the streets, and the breakdown of law and order."

> YOUR HOME
>
> NEEDS A
>
> HOUSEKEEPER

As the Republican candidate for the House of Representatives in 1970, Mrs. Schlafly promised to "start Housekeeping." With bounteous campaign contributions—including $33,492 from industrialist W. Clement Stone—and prominent endorsements ("The reason I like Phyllis is that she talks straight," said John Wayne), she saturated the district with billboards, television tapes, and broadcasts of conversations with "representative citizens." She criticized welfare, which drained tax dollars from hardworking citizens to subsidize "freeloaders." She denounced foreign aid, which caused inflation, high interest rates, and soaring taxes.

She used the campaign not only to find votes but also to spread the conservative gospel. In the aftermath of the shootings at Kent State University, Mrs. Schlafly testified to a special legislative committee and

condemned the activities of "professional agitators," left-wing professors, and "spineless" college presidents. "I reject the idea that our
colleges and universities are the private domain of the faculty and
students," she asserted. "The taxpayers have prior rights"—and so did
hardworking parents who "scrimped and saved to send our children off
to college. . . . We have a right to a guarantee that they will not be
taught revolution, criminal acts, drug use, or immorality."

Mrs. Schlafly proved an avid campaigner, traveling, by her count,
thirty-five thousand miles to "shake all those strangers' hands, eat all
those third-rate chicken suppers, attend political meetings every night
and weekend, subject [herself] to press and political attacks that im-
pugn [her] integrity and motives, and face probes into personal life and
finances." ("Do you know how bad it is to campaign for office?" she
would later say. "Heavens! It's just hideous. I wouldn't wish it on Betty
Friedan.") Mrs. Schlafly accused her opponent, the incumbent, George
E. Shipley, of "building roads in Yugoslavia," which upon further
examination turned out to be her indirect way of saying that he had
voted for the International Development Association, an affiliate of
McNamara's World Bank. "The road situation in this district is terrible," she said. "I don't see why we build roads in Yugoslavia when we
have bad roads here." At a luncheon in Shelbyville she sought the
women's vote: "My opponent says a woman's place is in the home. But
my husband replies that a woman's place is in the House—the United
States House of Representatives."

Mrs. Schlafly's genteel conservatism appealed to Republican en-
claves—civic clubs, luncheon groups, and party organizations—but to
her dismay she failed to locate the elusive Silent Majority. "Examining
the demographics of the district I was in, we figured there had to be
a Wallace constituency there," she later explained, "and I was never
able to decipher those people at all. I was never able to make contact
with them. I was never able to get their vote." In 1970 ideological issues
were less important to the voters than closed plants, mass layoffs, and
the decline of home building.

She lost by 3 percent—in a year the Democrats carried the nation.
She cried in private, but publicly Mrs. Schlafly denied a personal
failure. It was not the unpopularity of her conservative platform that
had defeated her; rather, she believed the voters rejected the program
of the national leadership in Washington. "In Illinois the fault cannot
be placed on . . . the usual factors that cost elections . . . good candidates, good organization, good advertising, and a united party. The

overriding issue in the 1970 election was the economy—but many Republicans didn't seem to know this until after the ballots were counted." Once again she would blame the Republican hierarchy for neglecting the interests of the grass roots. As in 1952, therefore, she had no reason to reexamine her political beliefs: "Give up? Never! It is our country which is at stake. We must redouble our efforts to build the kind of America we want for our families and children. We should have no regrets . . . because we did it for the right cause."

Her distrust of the Republican establishment intensified when President Nixon announced the strategy of détente. The sudden death in December 1970 of her friend General Thomas Power, former head of the Strategic Air Command, underscored her sense of betrayal: Mrs. Schlafly believed he "died of a broken heart"—literally—because the president had broken his 1968 campaign pledge to restore American military superiority. Her disappointment with Nixon turned to anger, the rage of misplaced confidence. She attacked the improvement of relations with Red China: "Will Ping-Pong Propaganda Erase History?" she asked in an essay that won another George Washington Honor Medal from the Freedoms Foundation: "Those who think that a ping-pong game can turn murderers into gentlemen or convert a Communist into a friend show they have learned nothing from the past. . . . Civilized people don't dine with murderers and criminals, and that is what the Chinese Reds are."

Mrs. Schlafly circulated an opinion survey among conservatives— "How Do You Rate President Nixon?"—and in June 1971 she reported the results. One-third of the Republican respondents would not vote for Nixon again: "Republicans in increasing numbers are coming to . . . [one] conclusion: President Nixon is too liberal!" She criticized the president's isolation from the conservative wing: "The White House staff has erected such a barrier around the president that a constructive warning of trouble cannot get through." (Mrs. Schlafly would later claim that her survey had a catalytic effect on the White House: "I know for a fact that Nixon was always having someone monitor what I was doing," she said. "And I always felt that that [poll] . . . was an element in his paranoia that led him to do all those outrageous things he did, which he thought were going to plug every hole and assure his reelection in '72.")

As Nixon announced plans to visit Peking, Mrs. Schlafly warned him that one of the most precious American freedoms unfortunately included "the freedom to commit suicide." She listed the contradic-

tions between his policies and the promises of the Republican platform
—"military inferiority," deficit spending, aid to communist countries,
SALT, and tolerance of communists in Cuba. "Is there anyone still so
foolish as to think we can put our hope for peace in a treaty with the
Soviets?" With her husband she conducted a survey of television news
broadcasting and concluded that the media were conspiring to keep the
public ignorant of the Soviet threat. Backed by an organization called
Defenders of American Liberty, Mrs. Schlafly initiated a media program to counter such misinformation.

Nixon's détente, meanwhile, brought sad consequences to her
hero, Cardinal Mindszenty, who had lived in the American Embassy
in Budapest since 1956. "The new U.S. policy calling for 'an era of
negotiation,' made Cardinal Mindszenty no longer a welcome guest."
When he fled to Vienna in 1971, she went there to meet him. In
Vienna she also tried to interview American representatives at the
SALT talks, but was denied entry. This "paranoiac secrecy" confirmed
her conspiracy theories about détente. But she was received warmly by
the cardinal, with whom she discussed the perils of communism. She
returned home with a plan to publish an English-language edition of
his biography—*Mindszenty the Man*, which appeared in 1972.

She also prepared for the presidential election of 1972. "The
crying need of our times is for noble leaders," Mrs. Schlafly declared,
"for men and women who have the courage to stand fast against false
propaganda, who persevere in their principles when they reach high
positions, who remain loyal to the people who look up to them." On
these grounds Nixon failed to qualify. She attempted to build a right-
wing coalition within the Republican party: "We must teach the
Republican-incumbent-turned-liberal the lesson that when he betrays
his promises the consequences are defeat at the polls."

Her rallying cry against Nixon remained national defense. And so
when, in December 1971, a woman from Connecticut invited her to
participate in a debate about domestic issues—specifically, the Equal
Rights Amendment, which was sailing through the Congress—Mrs.
Schlafly countered with a proposal to debate military affairs. As for the
ERA, she would later recall, "I thought it was somewhere between
innocuous and mildly helpful." Besides, she added, "I didn't know if
I really was on the other side." To which her conservative friend
replied, "Let me send you the material and when you read it I know
you'll be on the other side." The information did not alter Mrs.
Schlafly's opinions; but it changed the entire course of her life.

SECTION 1: Equality of rights under the law shall not be denied or abridged by the United States or by any State on account of sex.
SECTION 2: The Congress shall have the power to enforce, by appropriate legislation, the provisions of this article.
SECTION 3: This amendment shall take effect two years after the date of ratification.

Mrs. Schlafly published her response, "What's Wrong With 'Equal Rights' For Women?" in February 1972: "Of all the classes of people who ever lived, the American woman is the most privileged. . . . We have the most rights and rewards and the fewest duties." Protected by the traditional family system ("a woman can enjoy real satisfaction when she is young—by having a baby"), honored by the tradition of chivalry ("in America a man's first significant purchase is a diamond for his bride"), freed from back-breaking drudgery by the genius of American technology (Edison, Howe, Ford, and Westinghouse), the American woman, according to Mrs. Schlafly, enjoyed the best of all worlds—the choice of whether or not to work, traditional awards of child support, custody, and alimony, and exemption from the military draft. "The claim that American women are downtrodden and unfairly treated is the fraud of the century," she said. "The truth is American women never had it so good."

Having exposed the supposed fallacies of the ERA, Mrs. Schlafly returned to her first passion—the military defense. In 1972 she traveled around the country to make film interviews of experts on nuclear weapons strategy and then distributed them to television stations as public service announcements: "I did the whole thing myself. I raised the money. I hired the crew. I went out and interviewed them. I edited it. I packaged it. I got the stations to take it."

For her essay "Our Moral Duty to Build Nuclear Weapons," Mrs. Schlafly won another George Washington Honor Medal from the Freedoms Foundation. And, when Nixon returned from Moscow with the SALT treaty in May 1972, she volunteered to represent the National Association of Pro America and testified before the Senate Foreign Relations Committee against ratification. "No more unequal, craven, and degrading agreement has ever been signed by any nation," she stated. "History proves that weakness invites aggression." Feeling betrayed by Nixon, she supported the presidential candidacy of conservative Representative John Ashbrook. For the first time in sixteen years she did not run as a delegate to the Republican National Conven-

tion, but she went to Miami anyway to rally her supporters. Then she
"just sat it out."

With less to occupy her in the Republican party, Mrs. Schlafly
became more involved in the ERA debate. "The ERA thing really kind
of fell in on me," she later recalled. "I did the report in February
[1972]. I thought I had said my piece. And then I got a lot of mail."
In March 1972 Congress approved the ERA and sent it to the states
for ratification. The question of women's status became a major topic
of discussion. As an outspoken opponent of the amendment, Mrs.
Schlafly was invited frequently to participate in public debates. She
proved a fierce advocate: "It took practice and, well, just courage." Her
opposition to the ERA fit perfectly with her conservative ideas and a
laissez-faire theory of government.

In October 1972 Mrs. Schlafly announced the creation of a lobby
group, STOP-ERA, and appointed herself the national leader. She had
few illusions about immediate success: "Girls, there is something you
have to understand. This is one battle we cannot win." But she softened the bad news with a homey aphorism, as soothing as it was
inspirational: Women are like tea bags; you just don't know how strong
they are until you dunk them into hot water!

For the battle against the ERA Mrs. Schlafly could draw upon her
experience fighting communism, particularly her understanding of
propaganda. "The psychology of winning is a very important element
in any political campaign," she would say of the women's liberation
movement. "They had the slogans. They had the semantics. They had
the psychology of inevitable victory. They had the power and prestige
of all-important people. . . . They had umpteen organizations." And
she believed that feminists, like communists, had revolutionary incen-
tives: "Their motive is totally radical. They hate men, marriage, and
children. They are out to destroy morality and the family. They look
upon husbands as exploiters, children as an evil to be avoided (by
abortion if necessary), and the family as an institution which keeps
women in 'second-class citizenship' or even 'slavery.' "

Her defense of marriage and the family partly reflected the hidden
drama of her own personality. First there were her fears that the natural
order of male priority and female dependence might abruptly be top-
pled, as it had been years before for her parents. Second was a genuine
pride that in her own marriage she had found a bulwark against such
insecurity. Her insistence that American inventors (whom her father
had adored and imitated) had already liberated American housewives,

and her visceral hostility to feminists as a threat to the jobs of the male providers—these two recurrent themes in her writing suggested the existence of a deep anxiety about the disruption of the American family. It was this emotional reservoir, repressed from any conscious view, that provided the bottomless energy for her war against the ERA.

Her first task was to change public opinion—to show that beneath the innocent sound of "equal rights" lay a sinister purpose. To do that she needed an audience. She also had to overcome the inertia of conservatives, particularly conservative women. Feminists, many of whom had gained experience in the civil rights movement or the antiwar movement, had seized the political initiative. As Phyllis Schlafly put it, "The women libbers are people who like to agitate, and the women I deal with are not the kind who normally like to make themselves obnoxious." But she was quite willing to fill the breach. She launched the anti-ERA movement in the unratified states, held press conferences, drafted petitions, and testified to the state legislatures: "The U.S. Constitution is not the place for symbols or slogans, and it is not the proper vehicle to alleviate psychological inferiority." She said that "it would be a tragic mistake for our nation to succumb to the tirades and demands of a few women who are seeking a constitutional cure for their personal problems."

She campaigned in Indianapolis; led one thousand women in Richmond, Virginia; assured Missouri lawmakers that "there are always going to be women who can sweet-talk their husbands into doing nice things for them." Her monthly newsletter doubled its output and attacked ERA on multiple fronts: the draft, income tax, child-care centers, homosexuality, and abortion. "The world has not devised a better deal for women than marriage, or a better place to bring up children than the home."

In 1973 she debated the ERA with one of its most famous advocates, Betty Friedan, at the University of Illinois. "I consider you a traitor to your sex, an Aunt Tom," said Friedan. "I'd like to burn you at the stake."

"I'm glad you said that," replied Mrs. Schlafly, "because it just shows the intemperate nature of proponents of ERA."

"I'm having a ball," Mrs. Schlafly exclaimed. "It's a fun fight. I've been in a lot of fights that have been grim and bitter and tiresome and tedious. But this is a fun fight. The girls really enjoy it." After twenty-five years of thankless protest and public scorn, the frustrations of powerlessness and the defeat of conservative candidates, she relished her recent victories. "The Equal Rights Amendment is a terminal case," she said in 1973. "The only question remaining is whether its sponsors will let it die peacefully, and with dignity, or . . . engage in massive bloodletting in a vain attempt to save their offspring." By the end of the year, the trend appeared unmistakable: four more states had ratified the amendment; thirteen had refused; one voted to rescind. "Not too bad a track record for an amateur."

Mrs. Schlafly could bring a new confidence into the fight for a strong national defense. "Home and Country," the DAR slogan, became her watchword. "Whereas the Equal Rights Amendment is probably the number-one threat to our homes today, it is just as important that we direct our attention to the number-one threat to our country," the "international criminals who are envious of America—who want to control or destroy us in order to control the world." She listed "The Seven Deadly Deceptions of Disarmament": "America is big and rich. We must have the expensive weapons to protect ourselves. . . . If we don't, we will be at the mercy of ambitious aggressors."

She worked assiduously to spread the alarm—through her newsletter, as contributing editor to the magazine *Human Events,* and in a regular radio series for CBS's *Spectrum.* She criticized President Nixon for allowing American military strength to lag behind that of the Soviet Union. She also blamed Nixon's détente for trade agreements that produced an inflation of food prices in 1973. "Now we have hippies, drug addicts, wiretappers, burglars, influence peddlars, armed robbers, and sadistic murderers," she said during the summer of the Watergate revelations. "There is much evidence of a sad deterioration in the moral fabric of our country." She warned against "enemies and termites working to undermine our country."

Having abandoned hope for a conservative revival in the White House, Mrs. Schlafly cultivated support among the right wing. She criticized Governor Ronald Reagan for blurring his differences with Nixon. "The trouble with conservatives today," she wrote in 1974, "is that, having been fishing for the past ten years and not having elected a real conservative as president, they have no faith to let down their nets again." Amid the cry for impeachment, however, she saw signs of political renewal. If nothing else, Nixon had proved once, twice, that a conservative Republican could be elected president, and he had proved, thirdly, "the folly of our voting for . . . 'the lesser of two evils.' " She denied that his resignation was "any great disaster"—just the opposite: "The conservative American, anti-Communist ideology has the brightest future it has ever had, not only because events have proved us right on every issue, but also because events have proved the socialists and the big-government-spending, Communist-appeasing, unilateral-disarming politicians wrong, a thousand times wrong."

The search for a conservative coalition conveniently reinforced the drive against the ERA. The *Phyllis Schlafly Report* published countless exposés of liberal foibles: "Playboy and Rockefeller Foundation Finance ERA", "How ERA Will Hurt Divorced Women"; "The Fraud Called Détente." Mrs. Schlafly also used her familiar forums: "It isn't enough to teach reading, writing, and arithmetic," she advised the St. Louis chapter of the Freedoms Foundation, as she accepted two more George Washington medals. "Schools ought to be teaching right from wrong." For the Illinois DAR, she exhorted "good citizen" girls about "A Woman's Place." In a speech to a National Town Meeting at the Kennedy Center in Washington, D.C., she attacked the ERA as a power grab by federal politicians and bureaucrats. "We women," she told a convention of state legislators, "have the right to be supported by our husbands and not work."

Standing at the forefront of confrontation, Mrs. Schlafly attracted considerable abuse from supporters of the ERA: "They always come to hiss at me. They're such slobs." She claimed to be unaffected by these tactics and insisted that her own groups avoided "emotional generalities or vulgar attacks." Yet she became a master of emotional weaponry, irritating her opponents into fury. She especially enjoyed flaunting her self-proclaimed independence. "It's obvious that I'm fully liberated," she would boast. "That's what drives them up the wall. That's what drives them up the wall. I've got a lovely husband, six children—I breast-fed them all—and I do what I want to do." Even Karen DeCrow, president of the National Organization for Women, acknowledged her power. "If I had a daughter," said DeCrow, "I'd want her to be a housewife just like Phyllis Schlafly."

Meanwhile, with the resignation of President Nixon, she renewed her efforts to change American foreign policy. She had hoped that the conservative Gerald Ford would reverse détente. But when he announced his intention to continue that policy Mrs. Schlafly concluded that the real threat to American security was not the president but his chief adviser, Secretary of State Henry Kissinger, who remained in office. With her coauthor, Admiral Ward, she therefore undertook to write another book—*Kissinger on the Couch*—which argued that there was a master plan to disarm the United States. Its chief architect was

Kissinger, and its purpose was to pave the way for a communist take-
over. "No president could knowingly do such a thing," they admitted;
but Kissinger, a foreigner by birth, "apparently has no care about our
safety." The book was 785 pages long—a magnum opus on nuclear
strategy. But its argument was so unusual that few paid any attention.
"But since it came out," Mrs. Schlafly observed, "I've noticed people
don't defend Kissinger anymore."

Amid her immense labors—the fight against the ERA, the crusade against détente, the monthly newsletter, meetings, radio shows,
and speeches—Mrs. Schlafly decided to enroll in law school at Washington University in St. Louis. "I was trying to get one of my children
to go to law school," she explained, "and I said, 'If you don't go I'll
go.'" On the principle of the double dare, she passed the entrance
examinations and was admitted. "I've debated all the lawyers they've
had on the other side," said the fifty-one-year-old freshman, "and I felt
I got the better of all of them." Now they would not be able to pull
rank!

Mrs. Schlafly also moved to consolidate her support by creating
a formal organization, the Eagle Forum, in October 1975. It would
serve as "the voice of the home-loving, family-oriented American
woman who needs to be heard in opposition to the quarrelsome agitators." She named herself president. As in her other activities, she
maintained her personal leadership: "I am articulating what the majority of women in this country believe. . . . What has never occurred to
these women's libbers is that women don't like their silly amendment."
She appealed as much to fear as to pride, prejudice no less than piety.
"NOW is for pro-lesbian legislation," she reported, "so that perverts
will be given the same legal rights as husbands and wives . . . to adopt
children and the right to teach school."

Her ideas about sexual politics crystallized in her book *The Power
of the Positive Woman.* She saw herself as an archetype, her life as a
model others might follow. "It is self-evident to the Positive Woman,"
she wrote, "that the female body with its baby-producing organs was
not designed by a conspiracy of men but by the Divine Architect of
the human race. . . . The Positive Woman . . . rejoices that she has a
capability for creativity that men can never have. . . . The women's
liberationists . . . who try to tell each other that the sexual drive of men
and women is really the same . . . are doomed to frustration forever.
. . . The new morality . . . is a cheat and a thief. It robs the woman
of her virtue, her youth, her beauty, and her love—for nothing, just

nothing." In this light the ERA was not only immoral but unnatural: "The fundamental error of the Equal Rights Amendment . . . is that it will mandate the gender-free, rigid, absolute equality of treatment of men and women. . . . The moral, social, and legal evil of ERA is that it proclaims as a constitutional mandate that the husband no longer has the primary duty to support his wife and child."

As the opposition to the ERA gained momentum, Mrs. Schlafly tried to harness her influence for the presidential election of 1976. Her villains remained the leadership of the eastern establishment: "For the first time in our two-hundred-year history the United States lost a war," she said, blaming Kissinger and Rockefeller for the defeat. "Kissinger has trapped Ford in an artificial world so far divorced from reality that it has expunged from his memory more than twenty years of history through which Ford himself has lived." To reverse this liberal drift, Mrs. Schlafly and her coauthor, Admiral Ward, published a new election-year manifesto, *Ambush at Vladivostock*. It claimed that President Ford, through a combination of physical exhaustion, mild brainwashing, and sheer stupidity, had been tricked into accepting America's second-class status in the nuclear arms race. They therefore endorsed the election of a true conservative, Governor Ronald Reagan: "The crisis confronting America in our bicentennial year is not a crisis of technology, or a crisis of resources, or a crisis of production, or even a crisis of funding. It is a crisis of leadership."

In August 1976 Mrs. Schlafly went to Kansas City to testify against the ERA before the platform committee of the Republican National Convention. The Democrats had already endorsed Jimmy Carter, Walter Mondale, and the ERA, and she argued that "religious and family-oriented Americans" would gladly support an anti-ERA platform. When the question came to a voice vote, she thought that she had won; but the chair ruled otherwise. She considered carrying the fight to the convention floor, then decided against it: "I felt it would be bad politics. . . . The big issue of the Republican convention was who was going to be the nominee." Besides, she pointed out, if Reagan won the nomination the platform would be irrelevant "because Reagan is against ERA and Mrs. Reagan is against ERA. If Reagan is nominated, we've won." And if Reagan did not win, "we would have been blamed for his defeat, even though it was not our fault. So we refrained from making waves on the ERA."

The nomination of Gerald Ford in 1976 represented another defeat at the hands of the liberal Republican establishment. But she found hope in Reagan's unyielding concession speech—"one of the most dramatic moments in political history"—in which he "demonstrated he needs neither ghostwriter nor prompters . . . to deliver a masterful, meaty, relevant, and eloquent speech." She underscored Reagan's refusal to mention Gerald Ford by name—a "conspicuous omission," which suggested "that the survival of America" depended on neither of the presidential candidates. Since Mrs. Schlafly could not support Carter either, she worked instead on the congressional races: "If we just had another fifty conservative congressmen in Washington, it wouldn't make any difference who is president."

By November 1976 the Eagle Forum claimed a membership of fifty thousand supporters in forty-two states. But it could not prevent the election of Jimmy Carter or the Democratic control of Congress. Mrs. Schlafly remained undaunted: "Surveying America after our bicentennial, it would be easy to conclude that we may become another of the many civilizations that perished after discarding the moral standards that bound their people together." She saw her world surrounded by crime and vice, divorce and abortions, violence, perversion, and pornography. But the task of a conservative woman was "to resist these trends and mend the rips in the fabric of civilization." And she was optimistic about the future: "I don't think Rosalynn will have any more impact than Betty Ford," she said. "I feel the prospects are excellent for holding the line."

John
Herschel
Glenn
(III)

As Apollo 11, the first American moonship, approached a landing in July 1969, John Glenn appeared at Mission Control in Houston feeling as "ancient" as the Wright brothers. "I'm green with envy," he admitted. "I'd give anything to be up there right now. Who wouldn't?" As nostalgic as any pioneer in retirement—"It is as though the first wagon train had just crossed the Great Plains," he said about the voyage—Glenn contemplated the "long series of personal qualifications and opportunities" that had led him from New Concord to NASA to Royal Crown Cola: "And there is much luck involved," he said. He was almost forty-eight.

The success of Project Apollo dramatized his own inertia. "One reason why man is driven to explore the universe, to reach for the pinnacle, to master the unknown, may be that by doing so he gains better control over his future," Glenn wrote. But for him the future was rapidly receding. His children had grown up; his daughter would soon be married. Despite his success in business, he still yearned for public service. Instead he was always being honored for what he had done in the past. To almost everyone but himself, John Glenn was a "former astronaut."

The old mission haunted him. Finally, it forced him to act. In the autumn of 1969 Glenn quietly resigned from his executive positions at Royal Crown Cola (he remained on the board of directors) and moved back to Columbus, Ohio. Two weeks before Christmas he announced that he had put away the "easy" life of a businessman. He would take his chances in the Democratic primary for the United States Senate. "No other pursuit can be more important," he declared, and he reaffirmed his "dedication to my country and sincerity in wanting to solve its problems."

As in the ill-fated campaign of 1964, Glenn refused to define himself either as liberal or conservative. He hoped, rather, to rise above political strife. He would run for office as a patriot and a hero. With a name-recognition rating of 95 percent—his major opponent, Howard Metzenbaum, scored less than 12 percent—he anticipated no trouble in reaching the electorate.

He failed to realize that, by 1970, image alone was not enough. Since the days of John F. Kennedy, voters had become more sophisticated about political issues—and less trustful of politicians. They were unwilling to settle for an earnest smile or a record of military valor. Vietnam, civil rights, the environment—these issues could not be ignored. But, even when Glenn addressed them, he sought the middle ground. He endorsed Nixon's policy of Vietnamization, but asked that it move faster. He urged "meaningful" land reform in South Vietnam, but mainly as an incentive for the anti-communist soldiers. Metzenbaum delighted in calling him Ivory Soap.

Glenn predicted that his candidacy would "guarantee excitement and involve more people"—which it certainly did, although not in the manner he had intended. He spoke about the risks of ABM missiles. He criticized inflation ("above 6 percent . . . and holding"). He condemned Nixon's "cynical southern strategy, holding back the hard-won gains of integration in the South." And, in the style of the Kennedys, he embraced progress and growth: "We have to realize that the world is changing fast and we have to adapt to that change, not resist it. We have to welcome dissent and not repress it." Wherever he went voters surrounded him—to ask for his autograph.

Few listened to his words. "Rightly or wrongly, there was an air of the space program about me," he would remember. "I had studied the issues and prepared what I thought were good positions, but I'd walk into a meeting and the first question I'd hear would be, 'Do astronauts really drink Tang?'" In the midst of the campaign a near-disaster aboard the Apollo 13 moonship focused public interest on the space program. At a typical press conference five out of six questions dealt with outer space. And the candidate encouraged this emphasis. On Earth Day, April 20, 1970, he told students at Ohio State University that "our planet [is] a big spacecraft," and he stressed his familiarity with technology.

Glenn misunderstood the nature of his popularity. Expecting only slight competition in the primary, he neglected the traditional Democratic constituency in the cities. He concentrated on the Kiwanis circuit, appealing to rural voters, Republicans, and independents, whose help he would need in the general election in November against the son of Robert Taft. Metzenbaum, meanwhile, spent huge personal sums on advertising, which overcame his initial obscurity. Glenn complained that such expenditures had corrupted the electoral process and only proved that a millionaire "can buy an election." Despite his own fame—because of it—he had difficulty raising money: "Everyone assumed if I was well-known I must be well off."

Nor was he helped by the eruption of tumultuous issues that did not lend themselves to his congenial platitudes. "Everyone is losing confidence in everything," he observed, "our foreign policy, our universities, our electoral system—all because we haven't changed things that need changing, and we haven't told people the truth." The killing of four students by National Guardsmen at Kent State the day before the primary dramatized the deep fissures in Ohio politics. "I was there ten days ago," said Glenn, shaken by the tragedy. "When I finished the question-and-answer period, a nice kid with bushy hair followed me out to the car. He kept saying, 'People have got to listen to us, hear our point of view, or everything will blow up. Can't anyone help us?'"

As the father of young adults, Glenn appreciated the disaffection of American youth: "Today's young people are the most idealistic in the nation's history. That idealism should be used to help guide the present political system." He endorsed an all-volunteer army and supported lowering the voting age to eighteen. "Anyone can throw a brick through a window," he explained. "It takes some guts to work for change within the system. I think the kids have the guts. But the system has to show them . . . they are welcome within it." He tried to identify with the Kennedy élan and its emphasis on youth. He persuaded Ethel Kennedy to campaign for him. He reminded voters of his friendship with Robert Kennedy: "I was in California with him when he was shot. I want to work on some of the ideas he embraced."

The aura of the hero attracted the voters. Glenn carried seventy-six of Ohio's eighty-eight counties, but he failed to reach the urban Democrats. In a surprise conclusion, he lost to Metzenbaum by thirteen thousand votes. It stunned him. He felt outraged and humiliated: "Two wars, cross-country speed run, orbital flight, and then to be rejected by my home state. It wasn't very pleasant." He could hardly bring himself to make a perfunctory speech for the media the next day. "The American people always turn their backs on their heroes," he said privately.

Having personalized the contest, Glenn promised himself vindication. He learned to muffle his hatred of Metzenbaum, at least in public, and he resolved to work within the Democratic organization to establish his party credentials. In the general election, he campaigned for gubernatorial candidate John Gilligan and led an effective Citizens for Gilligan committee that triumphed in November. "I don't think anyone besides the governor has spoken at more [Jefferson-Jackson Day] dinners or fund-raising events," said Glenn. "I did more TV spots for him than anyone else, and he knew it. What's more, I know from polls and ratings that I came across well on TV." Glenn could also find some satisfaction in the fact that in November Howard Metzenbaum lost to Taft.

After the election, Glenn attempted to solidify his place by taking charge of the Buckeye Executive Club, a Democratic fund-raising group for large donors. Gilligan reciprocated by appointing him to head a citizens' task force on environmental problems. After months of testimony Glenn's committee reported that Ohio enjoyed the "unique and dubious distinction" of having every type of environmental pollution possible: "This kind of degradation must stop." The task force then submitted proposals that would form the basis of Ohio's first environmental protection laws.

Glenn also emerged from the 1970 campaign with a large personal debt—and a passionate desire never again to face impoverishment. "I had no law practice or established business to fall back on," he said, explaining the economic consequences of defeat. "I had severed my ties. We just didn't have much money, [and] so I set out to gain some stability for us." To pay political bills that reached $163,000, he organized "An Evening with the Stars," calling upon such celebrities as Andy Williams, Henry Mancini, and Art Buchwald, friends from the Kennedy days, to stage a benefit performance. But, even with the debts largely settled and a meager inheritance after the death of his mother, Glenn conceded that he "really didn't have any money."

To build his fortune he summoned the same personal attributes that served him so well in the past—determination, self-discipline, and integrity. He also profited from the help of friends with connections. Since his days at Cape Canaveral, Glenn had become close to one of the local hotel keepers, Henri Landwirth, a Jewish survivor of a Nazi concentration camp. From Landwirth, Glenn learned about promising investments in two Holiday Inn hotels that were planned to open near Disney World, in Orlando, Florida. A businessman named Robinson Callen, who apparently liked to be associated with people of Glenn's fame, invited him to join the venture as part-owner. Glenn quickly gave himself a crash course in the hotel business, and the partners competed aggressively to win the Holiday Inn franchise.

Besides demonstrating a plan of operation, Glenn also needed a sound financial package. His experience at Royal Crown paid off. He had already established valuable contacts with Cleveland bankers, who provided a loan for the construction of the hotel. With generous arrangements from the major investors, and with Landwirth's management, Glenn entered the partnership for $37,500, then used the early returns to capitalize on two other hotels in Florida. "Those inns are a good business, man," he later said. With reinvestments in state and local bonds and in blue chip stocks, his assets by 1974 exceeded $750,000: "I have more money than I ever thought an old rhubarb peddler from New Concord would ever have!"

Glenn continued to reign as a national monument. On Memorial Day of 1971 he rode in the pace car at the Indianapolis 500—until it crashed into the grandstand (he emerged unhurt). In 1972, on the tenth anniversary of his space flight, he returned to Cape Kennedy to unveil a plaque in his honor and expressed surprise at "what elementary questions we were trying to answer at that time: What happens to a man's senses in orbit? Would your eyeballs change shape and distort your vision? Could a man control his spacecraft?" He remained a strong proponent of the space program and criticized the dwindling of public support: "Many have regarded it as a race to the moon with Russia and are saying now, 'We've won, so let's quit.' But it's deeper than that.

It's very basic research helping to solve our problems right here on earth. No one knows what the benefits will be."

Glenn appeared frequently in public forums. He traveled a campus lecture circuit, advising students to work within the political system. With television producer David Wolper, he prepared a documentary series called "Here Comes Tomorrow," which showed how science and technology could be applied to social problems. He remained the object of immense private interest, still receiving thirty to forty letters each week for autographs and pictures, and with "people writing for all sorts of advice and weird things. . . . They have medical problems the doctors have not been able to solve. They want to know where to send their children to school or what investment to make." He answered most of them. They reminded him of his days of glory, as did the many souvenirs he kept in his spacious home in Columbus: a replica of El Cid's sword, given by the people of Toledo, Spain; a plate from Willy Brandt; a pair of chintah birds from Burma; the tusk of the elephant shot in Africa. "We're doing well, and I have no complaints at all," he said.

But he would not live in the past. He intended to return to public affairs: "I don't rule anything in or out." Loyal to the Gilligan Democrats in Ohio, Glenn supported the presidential hopes of Senator Edmund Muskie, the front-runner in 1972. He expected to attend the Democratic National Convention in Miami—but his plans were scuttled when Muskie withdrew from the contest. From the experience, Glenn obtained a memorable lesson on the fallibility of the Ohio establishment.

Describing himself as a liberal Democrat who refused "to sit back and just let things go," he began to plan another race for the Senate, two full years before the 1974 election. He neglected to reckon with the Ohio machine, however, and with the ambitions of Governor John Gilligan. For Gilligan had manufactured fantasies of his own, including a reelection victory in 1974 that would enhance his chances for the national ticket two years later. When Glenn asked Gilligan to endorse him for 1974, the governor countered with a proposal of his own—suggesting that Glenn run with him for lieutenant governor. The Senate seat would go to Howard Metzenbaum. The idea offended Glenn, who thought he deserved greater recognition. But when he rejected it Gilligan arranged a private meeting of Democrats and labor leaders that gave Glenn the choice between submission to party discipline or obscurity. Glenn became enraged: "I warned him that we were either going to come to a peaceable agreement or I was going to come out swinging. The governor's people evidently thought I was going to knuckle under, but I didn't."

He relished the personal combat. At a meeting of the Democratic state executive committee in the autumn of 1973, he read an eleven-page indictment of "pure political blackmail": "Suddenly, inexplicably, I am alone and a target marked for political extinction. . . . I never pulled out high over targets. I was the one that went in low and got them—and as a result was known as 'Old Magnet Tail' because I happened to pick up more flak than anybody else doing it!" He would not run from trouble now: "It's quite obvious that this can either be the dusk or dawn of my political career"—but he would not "let them put me in a box." Yet, as Glenn later remarked, "seldom was heard an encouraging word." When, because of Watergate, President Nixon appointed Senator William Saxbe attorney general, creating an immediate vacancy for an Ohio senator, Gilligan named Glenn's major rival, Howard Metzenbaum, to complete the unexpired term.

Glenn reacted with two unprintable expletives. Then, more calmly, he explained his feelings to a reporter: "The bond between the people and the elected leaders in this country is a sacred trust, and without that trust we're in trouble. . . . Now people feel that their lives are slipping away from them, that events control them rather than the other way around. This is made even worse when they see that they are being lied to, when mendacity and duplicity are refined to a high art in Washington. Well . . . I've lived my life on principles of honesty, decency, and integrity, and I'm proud of it," he said. "I know I sound awfully red, white, and blue, but that's the way I feel, dammit. That's the way I've always felt."

Glenn launched "Announcement Week" just before Christmas of 1973. "Politics should be the most honorable of professions," he said. "But what it often gets to be is quite [the] opposite. To a lot of people politics is an ego-building thing. . . . I've had all the honors I need." But that week he campaigned vigorously—drove from Lima to Piqua, stumped a supermarket in Dayton, shook hands at Youngstown Steel and Tube, chatted with customers at the Eva Gabor Wig Boutique in Steubenville, and visited all-black Wilberforce College—all to gain public attention. He wished it could be otherwise: "I respect people's privacy. Maybe it's because I've had so little privacy all my life."

Glenn's sincerity appealed to the political climate after Watergate. In contrast to the campaign of 1970, voters were less concerned about specific issues than with finding leaders to trust. Glenn played to that wish: "The main issue . . . is the integrity of our public officials." To establish his honesty he released a 183-page statement of his financial assets, showing his personal worth to be $767,000. He challenged Metzenbaum to put aside "cosmetic press agentry" and do the same. But when Metzenbaum released his own tax records, including a pending appeal with the Internal Revenue Service, and then appeared on television to defend his claims, Glenn dismissed the performance: "I don't need to buy TV time to tell people I'm honest." A bumper sticker spoke volumes:

> NIXON/METZENBAUM
> —TAX CONSULTANTS

Glenn exploited this single issue: "If he has nothing to hide, why doesn't he release everything? Are there conflicts of interest? That's what our suspicion has to be. If there's nothing to be ashamed of, why doesn't he bring it out?" (Metzenbaum would eventually win his case against the IRS, but not until 1975.) Meanwhile, the candidates traded insults about tax shelters and business loans. Glenn also appealed to the Kennedys for help, but to his amazement and everlasting rage Ethel Kennedy listened first to her brother-in-law, Edward Kennedy, a supporter of Metzenbaum, and turned Glenn down. Jacqueline Onassis broke a precedent to make a commercial: "John Glenn's leadership would be a shining light in the United States Senate. I have never done anything political for anyone before, but I feel that both I and the country have an obligation to John Glenn."

He saved his most potent weapon for a final televised debate with Metzenbaum at the City Club in Cleveland, four days before the primary election. Ever since he had heard that Metzenbaum accused him of never holding a proper job, Glenn had nursed a private fury: "Howard, I can't believe you said that," declared Glenn in a tone that instantly quieted the packed theater. He mentioned his twenty-three years of service in the Marine Corps—two wars, 149 missions, twelve times hit by antiaircraft fire—and his well-known career as an astronaut with "my life . . . on the line.

"I ask you to go with me," he suggested, turning to Metzenbaum on the stage, "as I went the other day, to a veterans hospital and look at those men, with their mangled bodies, in the eye and tell them they didn't hold a job.

"You go with me to any gold star mother, and you look her in the eye and tell her that her son did not hold a job.

"You go with me to the space program, and you go as I have gone to the widows and orphans of Ed White and Gus Grissom and Roger Chaffee, and you look those kids in the eye and tell them their dad didn't hold a job.

"You go with me on Memorial Day . . . and you stand in Arlington National Cemetery—where I have more friends than I like to remember—and you watch those waving flags and you stand there and you think about this nation and you tell me that those people didn't have a job.

"I tell you, Howard Metzenbaum, you should be on your knees every day of your life thanking God that there are some men —some men—who held a job. . . .

"I've held a job, Howard."

Glenn carried every single county in the state, winning the Democratic primary in May 1974 by ninety-four thousand votes. "People are disgruntled," he said, explaining the result. "They're not happy about the way things are going. . . . Maybe people are looking for something new. Maybe it's the desire for change. Whatever it is, they don't like what they see today."

He brought the same momentum into the general election, the first held after the resignation of President Nixon. At county fairs, fund-raising dinners, and the huge Labor Day picnic near Akron, Glenn promised to help heal the wounds of Watergate and restore confidence between the people and their leaders: "There is a dissatisfaction in the country that is frightening, and I stand before you today because of that dissatisfaction. A year ago I had the party arrayed against me, and I decided I was going directly to the people." His independence was now his greatest asset. He even rejected help from Edward Kennedy—partly out of pride, but also because he doubted the value of old names. And, despite his outrage at Watergate, Glenn spent over $1 million on the campaign, among the highest expenditures in the country that year.

In November he won the election by nearly one million votes: "Who would have thought that the whole Ohio Democratic party could go against me—the governor, labor, all that money—and I could still win? I thought maybe, just maybe, it could be done—but, good Lord, I'd have settled for a five-vote edge!" The two-to-one margin of victory catapulted his name into the national arena, where he was mentioned frequently as a possible vice-president. "I just want to be the best senator Ohio ever had," he insisted. But his ambition would not rest. "Honesty is a passive thing," he remarked in a revealing statement, "unless you have the ideas and will to take action."

Senator John Glenn went to Washington in January 1975, bought a large house on two acres of land, and resolved to overcome the stereotypes that had marked him a political innocent with an electable face. He turned down assignments to the Aeronautical and Space Science Committee and the Armed Services Committee. He chose instead to serve on the Interior and Insular Affairs Committee, with jurisdiction over energy legislation, and on the Government Operations Committee, which supervised nuclear power and nuclear weaponry. Both were technical fields, and Glenn enjoyed the complex calculations required in these areas. He worked hard, shunning the limelight. He made no junkets in his freshman year.

His diligence contrasted with the creaky structure of the Senate: "You sit in caucus and watch these old-timers fuss and fume and fight over little procedural matters when their jurisdiction is being stepped on just a hair, just a tiny bit—instead of everybody thinking, 'God, the country needs this and, sure, take it and do it and I'll take the next one.' They're very protective of their jurisdictions. Now that needs to be changed." During a prolonged caucus about emergency assistance for Vietnam, he stalked out of the room. And, when his colleagues exulted at the rescue of the *Mayaguez* crew in Cambodia in May 1975, he reminded them "that a few [marines] have died . . . representing . . . the best 'Semper Fidelis' tradition."

He nevertheless established a remarkable legislative record, especially for a neophyte. He gained numerous amendments on floor votes; he wrote effective "Dear Colleague" letters that circumvented defeats in committee; he was even successful in challenging the Majority Whip on a vote about fuel cells. "I think there might have been a question in some people's minds whether, because of my background, I might come here with one big eye in the middle of my forehead, or pointed ears, or something. . . . My only regret is that I'm not six people and don't have a five-hundred-man staff, so as to be able to get into more things that I'm interested in."

1938: Henry and Frances Fonda, and six-week-old Jane (in basket), boarding train in New York for Los Angeles.

ABOVE
1952: Phyllis Schlafly, at home at the stove, the day after winning Republican nomination for Congress.

LEFT
World War II: Sgt. George Wallace with Lurleen and daughter Bobbie Jo.

ABOVE
*1960: John and Annie Glenn and their two children, on
vacation in New Concord, Ohio.*

RIGHT
February 20, 1962: the astronaut.

ABOVE
January 14, 1963: the Governor, at his first inauguration.

BELOW
1967: Glenn, with Robert and Ethel Kennedy, at a Democratic fund-raiser, the Plaza, New York City.

LEFT
1959: Jane Fonda, stretching her legs between scenes of her first movie, Tall Story.

RIGHT
1970: *Phyllis Schlafly, again a Republican candidate for Congress.*

BELOW
1968: *Jane Fonda and Roger Vadim with their daughter, Vanessa.*

© JAMES ANDANSON/SYGMA

RIGHT
1972: Jane Fonda after her return from Hanoi.

BELOW
1971: the Governor and Cornelia, his second wife.

SYGMA

ABOVE
1977: the foe of E.R.A., Mrs. Schlafly, with her husband, J. Fred, and two of their six children.

RIGHT
May 1979: Phyllis Schlafly, under a photo of the Capitol at the National Press Club, claiming the death of E.R.A.

RIGHT
1980: campaigning for a fourth term as governor.

BELOW
1980: Jane Fonda working out.

OWEN FRANKEN/SY

ABOVE
1983: Annie and John Glenn,
announcing his presidential
campaign, in New Concord, Ohio.

RIGHT
1979: Annie Glenn, with the Senator,
christening the U.S.S. Ohio.

UPI/BETTMANN NEWSP

Although he described himself as a moderate, Glenn's early legislative record leaned slightly to the left. He supported campaign reform laws, a consumer protection agency, national health insurance, funding of medical research, and larger appropriations for education. He favored the right to abortion, the Equal Rights Amendment, and the H.E.W. plan to eliminate sex distinctions in physical education. He urged price controls on oil, improved distribution of natural gas, and suggested drilling offshore for new deposits. "I like to look over open ocean, too," he said about the opposition of environmentalists, "but, if the option is between drilling and thousands of people out of work, I am going to opt for jobs." On foreign policy he tended to be more conservative.

As his reputation improved, so did the possibility of reaching even higher office. But at first Glenn reacted modestly: "If I'm picked for anything else anytime, I want it to be because I was doing the best job I knew how to do right here, and I'm not running around the countryside trying to pick up brownie points here and there. I'm neither campaigning for nor shirking . . . whatever happens." When Ohio Democrats encouraged him to run for president as a favorite son in 1976, he rejected the idea, calling it "a throwback to the politics of the past, which we are trying to get away from." Yet he would not rule out a reversal of course: "You can't help but be glad that people like you. . . . If there's a deadlock, well, I'd consider the situation."

Glenn's success in the Senate also magnified his stature in the Democratic party. Robert Strauss, the party's national chairman, asked him to present the keynote speech at the 1976 convention in Madison Square Garden. Then Jimmy Carter invited him to Plains, Georgia, to discuss the vice-presidency. They walked together through the Carter peanut patch, visited the family cemetery, sipped cokes and iced tea: "I don't know that anybody could feel fully qualified to serve in the presidency," Glenn admitted after the meeting. "That's the biggest job in the world. I think all you can bring to that, really, is a dedication to doing everything you can absolutely do."

Along with Walter Mondale he was still a prime contender for the vice-presidency when the Democratic convention opened in New York City in July 1976. To bypass the crowded hotel switchboard, Glenn installed a special telephone in his suite. If it did not ring, he joked, at least "I don't have to abort out the top." He worked on the keynote speech until the last minute, fixing words, adjusting the breath marks, worrying about the angle of the cameras.

Then the gavel fell, and the Peter Duchin orchestra played "Fan-fare for the Common Man." John Glenn stood at the lectern, sur-rounded by bunting, and addressed the delegates. But he aimed his speech at the television audience, especially at the presidential candi-date who was watching intently in the hotel room upstairs. Glenn was the same man whose speech, fourteen years earlier, had brought the entire federal government to its feet.

Now, however, his words juxtaposed with the visual images of television—and the effect was dreadful: "The key to restored confi-dence (*milling, talking, laughing people jostled together on the floor*), to restored control for each of us, to restored freedoms (*Mayor Daley spoke to his delegates by telephone*) lies in renewed partnership be-tween citizens and their government. Now is the time (*Hubert Horatio Humphrey entered the convention, waved*) for bold and re-sponsive government to forge that partnership. A time to harness quickly (*Humphrey moved into the presidential box, where Rosalynn whispered to Amy*) the spirit of renewal we saw expressed so vividly (*Humphrey waved again to the happy warriors, who loved him still*). A time to reestablish the people's faith in government (*Peter Rodino walked to the New Jersey delegation*). And, more importantly, a time to demonstrate government's faith in the people (*Mondale explaining something to an interviewer, the milling crowd*). It is time to bring decision making into the open with the pros and cons made clear (*Senator Frank Church, chin in hand, listened*). We must select new leaders, leaders with vision, leaders who will set a different tone for this nation, a tone of opportunities sought and seized, a tone of na-tional purpose (*then the broadcast cut to a commercial for 'new extra-strength Tylenol'*)."

He felt insulted, then angered, by the noise and confusion on the convention floor, but he remained hopeful of his chances. With Annie he dined at the panoramic Sky Club in Manhattan and returned to his suite to learn that the call from Jimmy Carter would come on the special telephone at eight-thirty the next morning. He awakened early. But the phone did not ring—would not ring. Carter was about to dispatch a special messenger to Glenn when at last it did ring, but then President Ford was on the other line and Glenn was put on hold while the presidential candidates chatted for three minutes.

"John," Carter's voice drawled at last, "I've called to let you know that I've picked someone else. I enjoyed meeting you, John, and I want you to be my lifelong friend. I'd also like to count on your help in the campaign."

"I'll do whatever I can."

He turned to Annie: "Well, we wondered who was going to cut the grass at home this weekend. It's going to be me."

Jane
Seymour
Fonda
(IV)

Her career as an independent movie-maker began with *Coming Home*. It was set in 1968, the year of her own awakening, and it told the story of Mrs. Sally Hyde, the wife of a marine officer who went to Vietnam to prove his manhood. "One of the subliminal undercurrents of the film, in my mind," said Jane, "has to do with what is strength? what is masculinity?" As the woman left behind, Sally moved cautiously from political innocence into passionate involvement with a crippled antiwar veteran: "All we wanted to do in this movie [was] to show this woman moving from point A to point B. . . . It would have been phony to have her undergo some liberal conversion." But, although Sally Hyde committed adultery, it was not she who was punished in the film. Rather, the absent soldier-husband bore the ultimate responsibility—and escaped from his guilt by committing suicide in the end. This reversal of values—the adulterous wife

217

as victim—suited Jane's feminist goals. It also justified her opposition to the war: "The degree to which I can render that woman real has a whole political implication for me personally, because those are the kinds of people who hate me, who thought I was a traitor."

After completing *Coming Home*, Jane bought a 120-acre mountaintop ranch in the Los Prados National Forest, just north of Santa Barbara, which she and Tom Hayden planned as a retreat for the Campaign for Economic Democracy. "We had no intention of fading away after Tom's campaign, the way so many candidates do. You have to build a human community, and that's what the camp is all about." Beginning in the summer of 1977, they provided sun, swimming, and sports for sixty children, including "scholarship" campers from the farm workers union and the Delancey Street drug rehabilitation project. Their camp offered special features: lessons in solar energy; trips to the Diablo Valley nuclear power plant and to the antinuclear Abalone Alliance; and "Political Day," during which the campers learned to vote, make speeches, and organize politically.

Hiring a professional staff, Jane returned to acting—and made *Comes a Horseman*, a movie that pitted the rugged individualism of the Old West against the invasion of greedy oil investors. "All my life has been privilege," she admitted. "You can be a privileged movie star, or you can commit yourself to the idea that people can change their lives and can change history. I want to make films that will make people feel stronger, understand more clearly, and make the move forward." Outside her roles, she emphasized the satisfaction of her career: "I'm still working, and a lot of those people who called me a traitor are out of a job—or serving jail terms."

As mass magazines welcomed Jane's return to Hollywood—"The rebel has mellowed," said *Time*—she joined Hayden on a campus tour that upset the equilibrium. At Central Michigan University she attacked the nearby Dow Chemical Company, which had contributed money to the local college. Dow retaliated by suspending its assistance. "I am not proposing communism, and I am not proposing destruction," she replied angrily. "I am proposing that we extend democracy to our economy and put the quality of life, jobs, and safety above corporate greed." The skirmish reaffirmed her radical identity: "I hate the isn't-it-wonderful-she's-come-back-to-her-senses-and-joined-the-fold. I'm more profoundly committed to what I believe in now than in the days when I was considered a traitor. Today I'm polite because it's possible. You couldn't be polite six years ago. It wasn't until Watergate began to be exposed that we could work through the system." But she had no intention of accepting exile again. Instead she would use her notoriety against her enemies. When the Hollywood Press Club belatedly recognized her achievement, she accepted their award from archconservative John Wayne. ("I'm surprised to find you at the right of me," he quipped.) Despite her radical commitment—because of her commitment—she demanded the full attention of the media.

Her next movie was *The China Syndrome,* made in 1978. Here, too, politics and entertainment reinforced each other. Jane played the part of Kimberly Wells, a television news reporter who discovers a nuclear accident as well as a corporate cover-up to conceal it. "I saw Kimberly as a woman with a real stake in opting for the company line, in needing job security," explained Jane, who studied for the role by going on assignments with TV newswomen in Los Angeles. She deleted any obvious preaching from the script, saying, "You can't make movies on a soapbox." To add realism she dyed her hair red: "Only one of the featured female TV reporters in Los Angeles doesn't have dyed hair. I don't think it's a personal proclivity. It's part of the reason these women are hired. They are supposed to be startling." Why red? "I was going to dye my hair blond, but my husband said he had never had a relationship with a redhead and had always wanted one."

While completing the movie, Jane fell on a rocky hillside and broke her foot. It created a problem because in two months she had to wear a bikini in Neil Simon's *California Suite:* "I was out of shape, I hadn't done ballet for over a month, I'd put on weight—I wouldn't have worn a bikini in front of my kids! But the director refused to cut the scene, so I had to do something *fast!*" Henry Fonda's fifth wife, Shirlee, introduced her to an exercise class run by Leni Cazden. "And within two weeks," said Jane, "the entire shape of my body changed." In the movie, Jane detested the role she played: "She's the kind of person that George Wallace would describe as a pointy-headed East Coast intellectual who thinks that Californians have scrambled brains!" But she stole the show anyway with her muscular torso tucked inside a purple bikini.

Hollywood movies gave her a vast potential following. In her next film, *The Electric Horseman,* she played another innocent news reporter having to confront the greed of big corporations. "I look for things that will make an audience better, stronger, even angrier than before they came into a theater," she explained. "I don't, however, want them to be more cynical, bitter, or bored. I want them to be moved. I want my films to be about *something.*" She saw her fans not only as paying customers but as a political resource.

While filming in Saint George, Utah, Jane began to institutionalize a program of physical fitness. Persuading the owners of a spa there to allow her to start an exercise class, she invited other women to join the calisthenics. Her personal obsession about stamina and self-discipline soon spread into a larger movement: "I discovered that working out had a definite effect on their attitudes about themselves. They felt better about themselves." She began to think about an exercise program for masses of working women.

Jane won the Golden Globe Award as best actress for her part in *Coming Home* and received the 1979 Female World Film Favorite Award, based on an international survey by Reuters. "I guess I'm back," she said, "but so is Nixon; only I'm getting paid and he's not." After an award ceremony in Los Angeles, her father left in a Lincoln limousine, her brother departed in a Cadillac limousine, and Jane drove away in her Volvo station wagon. Her consistency facilitated the dual identity as actress and activist. But she welcomed the tranquility of the Carter years: "I've reached the conclusion that rallies and speeches aren't necessarily as effective as making one hell of a good movie!"

The China Syndrome opened in the winter of 1979 and soon disrupted the peace. When news broadcaster Barbara Walters scheduled an interview with Jane, the General Electric Corporation withdrew its sponsorship, claiming that the program would contain "material that could cause undue public concern about nuclear power." Jane countercharged that GE was trying to suppress criticism in the media. At issue was Jane's credibility: Who could believe her? But, few could still doubt her sincerity when the avuncular face of Walter Cronkite appeared on television screens in March 1979:

> Good evening. The world has never known a day quite like today. It faced the considerable uncertainties and dangers of the worst nuclear power plant accident of the atomic age. And the horror tonight is that it could get much worse. It is not an atomic explosion that is feared; the experts say that is impossible. But the specter was raised that perhaps the next-most-serious kind of nuclear catastrophe, a massive release of radioactivity . . .

Three Mile Island brought her back into the political arena. "Reality has a way of destroying the imaginary," Jane and Tom Hayden wrote in the aftermath of the crisis, "in this case, the myth of nuclear safety." At a press conference, they denounced President Carter's support of nuclear energy: "The Three Mile Island affair ends a generation of corporate cover-ups and false government assurances. . . . There is now a Vietnam-style credibility gap between Americans and their government." Committed to the solar alternative, they redesigned their own house to accommodate the new technology, and Tom took a job with Solar Cal in the administration of Governor Jerry Brown.

Amid the controversy, Jane won her second Oscar as best actress for her performance in *Coming Home.* Her comeback seemed certain. The ABC television network now agreed to underwrite her favorite project, *The Dollmaker,* although it would not be aired until 1984. Governor Brown asked her to sit on the California Arts Council. She had no desire to run for public office, but she was eager to serve in government. She also continued to speak in public. With Hayden and Brown, she addressed a crowd of one hundred thousand in Washington, D.C., about the risks of nuclear power: "If we continue to place our health and safety in the hands of utility executives whose main goal in life is to maximize profits, we will see more Harrisburgs, we will see more leaks, and we will see an increase in the cancer epidemic that is already running rampant in this country." When she returned to Los Angeles, she announced a settlement of her six-year-old suit against the FBI. For the first time in its history, the agency admitted its legal error and promised to respect the laws of privacy in the future.

Her return to respectability, however, now confronted a conservative backlash. When pacifist Joan Baez circulated an open letter condemning the treatment of political prisoners in Vietnam, Jane refused to sign it, and she asked Baez to "reconsider the assertion of your ad that the Vietnamese people are 'waiting to die.' Such rhetoric only aligns you with the most narrow, negative elements in our country, who continue to believe that Communism is worse than death." At a time when the media dramatized the plight of Vietnamese "boat people," Jane's stridency ignited an old rage. California conservatives retaliated by rejecting her nomination to the Arts Council.

"How can I express the sorrow and outrage I feel on learning that the spirit of the witch-hunts of the 1950s . . . still smoulders in our state senate? . . . Is it not a function of art to hold a mirror up to society? Must the mirror reflect only the images that reassure our politicians?

"As for me, I intend to continue following the dictates of my conscience as an actress and as a political woman, recognizing that there will always be those who, ignoring the meaning of democracy, will call this treason."

Her colleagues supported her. By a unanimous vote the Screen Actors Guild bought a full-page advertisement in the *Los Angeles Times:* "What is at stake is not the civil liberties of one woman but the rights of us all." Instead of backing down, Jane became more active. She reaffirmed her support of Vietnamese refugees, sponsored a fund raiser to provide medical assistance, and called for full civil liberties in Vietnam. She also encouraged striking farm workers in California: "We can not only do what we did in the 1960s, but we can do it better, stronger, and we will win."

With Hayden at her side, she addressed two hundred thousand antinuclear protesters in New York's Battery Park: "We believe all of us against nuclear energy have to think of ourselves as Paul Reveres and Pauline Reveres, going through our country town by town, city by city, warning people about the dangers." The couple then announced a fifty-city tour on behalf of the Campaign for Economic Democracy to build a national grass roots organization against large corporations and big government.

Their first stop was Harrisburg, Pennsylvania, near Three Mile Island, where Jane defended her patriotism against pickets from the American Legion. The couple posed in front of the radioactive towers and then departed on a whirlwind tour that reached from executive suites in Atlanta to the sidewalks of New York, from American University in Washington, D.C., to UCLA. They packed their days with TV and radio talk shows and back room meetings, outdoor rallies, and campus lectures. Everywhere, they backed local causes—rent control, the farm workers' lettuce boycott, solar energy, and the rights of working women—what they called, in sum, the principles of economic democracy. "We do all this because we *have* to win," said Jane. "We're running out of air, water, money, resources, and hope." Over two hundred thousand people, some carrying picket signs—HANOI JANE— heard them speak. "Obviously there are large numbers who come out of curiosity," she admitted. "But there are a whole lot of people who feel their lives lack direction."

By the time the couple reached California, Jane herself was ready for a change: "I'm not a political leader. I'm an actress." In a surprise move, she announced her withdrawal from politics. "Nowadays you have to be a millionaire to run for any high office," she explained. "But they never banked on people like Tom Hayden marrying someone like me. I don't apologize for putting my tremendous salary at the disposal of people who are poor. And he's one of them."

She also endorsed the cause of working women, which would be the subject of her next film, *Nine to Five.* In a silly plot that might be called "the secretaries' revenge," Jane again played a female innocent, a middle-aged reentry clerical worker who is awakened to the harshness of office politics. "It is *unbelievable* what is happening," she explained. "The office structure . . . pits women against each other very viciously: older women versus young, black and brown versus white, pretty versus ugly, thin versus fat. It's important who dresses better than who. The sexual tensions, the pay problem, the lack of promotion . . ."

The crusade for economic democracy coincided with capitalist schemes of her own. Up to this time, Jane showed little entrepreneurial ambition. But she was rich; she commanded $2 million per film by the late 1970s. "I make all this money, see," she explained. "I wanted to invest it in a business that would provide some kind of real service for people. I don't play the stock market or invest in huge corporations. I criticize them, [and] so I'm not going to put my money in them." Her advisers told her to invest in something she understood. "Then it occurred to me that there's one thing I do know, and that's physical fitness."

The Jane Fonda Workout studio opened its doors in Beverly Hills in December 1979. For $5.50 (later $6), it offered a regimen of aerobatic muscle-stretching exercises, lunch, and a shower—a package aimed at the busy working woman who wanted to keep fit. It appealed to the new enthusiasm for health. It helped people help themselves. But it also provided a distinct social objective. "The business isn't *mine,*" Jane explained; "all the profits go to . . . things I believe in." The Workout program was owned by the Campaign for Economic Democracy and, as a sign in the lobby attested, the earnings went "to promote alternative sources of energy, stop environmental cancer, fight for women's rights, justice for tenants, and other causes related to environmental protection, social justice, and world peace." Jane could be a capitalist and a reformer at the same time.

"Discipline," she proclaimed, "is liberation." The regimen of physical fitness altered her self-image: "I am no longer Jane Fonda, the actress, wife, mother, activist. I am an athlete. I *have* to push myself to my limit and beyond because I'm preparing for competition. But the competition is with myself."

Perhaps it was no coincidence that this latest preoccupation with her body—its health, image, and beauty—commenced on the eve of her forty-second birthday (the same age, almost to the day, that Frances Fonda decided that her body was too ugly to keep). Asked if she had inherited her physical endowment, Jane believed otherwise: "I like to think a lot of my body is my own doing and my own blood and guts. It's my responsibility." She also denied narcissistic motives. "I don't pretend to be devoid of vanity, but I try to fight against it, and I do know that what's important to me is how I feel about myself rather than how I look to other people."

Her economic success facilitated a reconciliation with the Hollywood establishment. She and Hayden moved closer to the liberal mainstream. In 1980 Jane endorsed Jerry Brown for president and joined a star-laden cast that performed on his behalf. She became a featured commencement speaker, pleading for the extension of democracy into the corporate boardroom. She went to Israel on a "nonpolitical" trip to raise money for the Haifa Theater (and, accident-prone as ever, she fell down a flight of stairs and broke her foot). When the Screen Actors Guild went on strike, Jane co-hosted a fund raiser in the Hollywood Bowl, and she was later honored by her mentor, Lee Strasberg, with an Actors Studio award for career achievement.

Reconciliation culminated, for Jane, in an expensive valentine she bought for her father—the movie rights to the Broadway play *On Golden Pond.* She would work with him for the first time since she was a teenager doing summer stock in Omaha. In her movie role as Henry Fonda's daughter, Jane again confronted the angry, distant father of her real life. "I actually reexperienced all those horrible feelings that come when you have an extremely strong, domineering, tough parent who can, with a look or a word, make you feel *that* big," she said, pointing to a speck of dust. "I was, as a daughter, again feeling that awful, powerless, misunderstood, sick-in-the-stomach place." At Squam Lake, New Hampshire, the serene setting for the film about parents at the twilight of life, Jane arrived for work, in her words, "like a blithering nincompoop, like I'd never acted before." She vomited. She tripped on her feet. She overacted and, even worse, overheard her father complain about her performance: "The first day I was so bad, I was so scared." But even in these moments of anxiety, she remained a professional, studying her own psychological responses as a way of understanding the character she played. "What was so great about this was that while on the one hand I was suffering from insecurity and nerves—deeply suffering—the other half of my brain, the actor's part, was saying: 'Wonderful! Use it! This is exactly what the character should be feeling!' That," said Jane, "is just the sort of thing that works for me."

As Jane and Henry Fonda read the script together, they realized how little they were acting. Jane had no trouble identifying with the daughter: "I knew what that woman in the movie was feeling. My father could still evoke the same feeling in me." Less certain was the possibility of reaching a personal accommodation, moving from the film back to reality: "I knew that for it to work," said Jane, "we had to be naked, as it were, prepared to reveal ourselves." She wanted that moment. It would be her last chance to know her father.

"It's the hardest thing I ever had to say as an actress," she confessed. "He has just said something hateful to my character, just hateful." It was the speech of old man Thayer, but it reached her in the voice of Henry Fonda: "I didn't know we were mad. I just thought we didn't like each other." To which she was supposed to reply—almost autobiographically—"I want to be your friend." As they rehearsed the scene, Henry Fonda refused to make eye contact, playing as an actor, not as a father. Jane searched for a way to pierce his armor, to touch the man. As she completed her line—"I want to be your friend"—she pressed her palm against his chest. "I could see his body start to shake as he fought to control his emotions," she recalled. "There was an element of absolute reality to it, that I want to be his friend and he's hard to be friends with." Afterward they would not speak a word about the scene.

Jane then took a role that was modeled, in part, after her mother. As a brusque businesswoman in the movie *Rollover,* she tried to introduce the American public to the dangers of Arab petrodollars and a coming collapse on Wall Street: "We took a reality that exists and is not even contested these days and then spun a hypothetical melodrama around it. . . . We've got a problem and people had better start thinking about it." The movie proved to be one of her few box-office failures —yet she saw no alternative to such politicized roles.

She would remain at the forefront of controversy. She addressed a rally to defend Soviet dissidents. She marched in a pro-Israel parade in Los Angeles but was forced to leave because Jewish leftists attacked her alleged sympathy for the PLO. She attempted to visit South Africa, but she was stopped at the border. When Hayden announced his candidacy for the state legislature in 1981, Jane donated huge sums for his campaign. Later she made an unlikely couple with Senator Barry Goldwater, defending the First Amendment on Norman Lear's televised broadside against the Moral Majority. She received the Crystal Award for promoting the role of women in Hollywood business. "We're trying to use whatever we have—money, power, influence— to make things better, not for our own self-aggrandizement," she maintained. "We're idealists in a world that's becoming more and more cynical. We're trying to keep idealism alive on this mountaintop."

On Golden Pond opened in December 1981, the same month she published *Jane Fonda's Workout Book.* Both were instant hits. She attributed her success to self-discipline: "I have a frantically busy schedule, with long erratic hours of work, plus children, a husband, a house to run—the works. But for the past fifteen years I have made fitness a priority." Her book also addressed larger questions of nutrition, pollution, and the ecological balance. "She wants to change the world," Jane said of herself. "But there is still a long way to go. As a nation our consciousness is not only primitive, it is downright primeval."

With her fame, Jane's ventures needed little promotion. She herself could offer ample proof that the product worked. Her sinewy body stretched across the cover of the Workout book as it climbed to the top of the best-seller lists, reaching 1.25 million sales in two years. She then produced a sequel about pregnancy and birth, based on the Jane Fonda Workout program for expectant mothers. After the books, she introduced videotapes and records (selling two million of these), developed the Jane Fonda calendar, which included health food recipes, and presented a new line of Jane Fonda gymnastic clothing. All the proceeds went to the Campaign for Economic Democracy, which helped to finance Hayden's political fortunes. "When you're a movie star, everything becomes totally out of whack," Jane explained. "You're always being made to feel that you're special. . . . Tom knows what's real. And I want him to respect me, to like me. I would be ashamed if he ever thought I was falling for it. So even if, in my heart, sometimes I feel a little cocky, it doesn't last long because I come home and get in bed with a guy who is doing stuff that's so much more important than what I do."

She took pride in her family, despite the time she spent away from home. She was strict with her children: "The very things that used to annoy me most about my mother, I find myself repeating, to my horror. Nagging. Being overly rigid about organization." She supervised a

$300,000 reconversion project for her new house. "I feel very uncomfortable sometimes when I'm made to look like a superwoman who does all these things at once and does a great job at all of them," she admitted. "I don't. It's hard, and something gets sacrificed in every area."

Jane felt pleasure, nevertheless, about the integrity of her life, her ability "to blend personal values and beliefs directly with the money-making aspects" of her career. She preferred popularity to the old hostility, but she held few illusions about its continuation. She opposed the political climate under Reagan: "The public opinion polls indicate that basically we're a good people. We don't want to be in El Salvador. We don't want the neutron bomb. We think there's too much money being put into the defense budget. We want social security. We're a good people," she said, "we're a brave people, [but] we're confused."

On a wintry day in January 1982, the temperature −13°, Jane went to Omaha, Nebraska, Henry Fonda's hometown, for a benefit premiere of *On Golden Pond.* On Henry and Jane Fonda Day, she accepted the keys to the city. Their relationship preoccupied her thoughts. As Oscar time approached in the spring, she hoped the Hollywood prize would assure their reconciliation: "If my father were to win, it would be the stuff that dreams are made of, that I could provide for him the vehicle for which he would win the Academy Award. . . . How often does a kid get a chance to give a gift like that to a parent?"

At last, she accepted the trophy in his absence—"Oh Dad, I'm so happy and proud for you"—and she rushed to his bedside to deliver it. "Reconciliation is what *On Golden Pond . . .* was about," she said. "It makes you think about all those unsaid things you want to say to people you love." Thus she would ease her grief when, just a few months later, he was dead. She was forty-four years old and entering her own middle age.

George
Corley
Wallace
(IV)

After the nomination of Jimmy Carter in July 1976, Wallace retreated to the solitude of the governor's mansion. He still suffered from extreme pain that jumped sporadically along his damaged nerves. He also suffered an embarrassing impotence —not sexually, but in having lost his grip on power. His frustration was made worse by his loneliness. During that hot summer, his wife was frequently absent—to get her face lifted, to promote her book, *C'nelia*, and to enjoy a social life he could not endure. Left with his old cronies, he expressed suspicion about her wanderings; he spoke about her with others on the telephone.

His candor left him vulnerable. When Cornelia went to Washington in August 1976, he received an anonymous tip. It led to the discovery of a homemade telephone wiretap that went from the master bedroom of the mansion to a tape recorder in the basement. Hundreds of hours of private conversations had been recorded and the tapes placed in the mansion safe. "He exploded, it just absolutely grabbed him," reported one of the governor's associates. "He was so mad about the tapes being made that he not only had the tapes burned, but had a sledgehammer taken to the taping device, and it was worth $4,000. He supervised the smashing of it."

When Cornelia returned home, a trooper blocked her at the front door, but she coaxed her way inside. She admitted tapping the telephone. She claimed that she was trying to find out who had spread rumors about alleged extramarital activities. She denied any other wrongdoing: "All I was ever trying to do was to hold this marriage together." Wallace allowed himself to be appeased, for the time at least. He let Cornelia slice his fifty-seventh birthday cake, collect the presents, pose for the cameras. But soon, to his dismay, the gossip touched his reputation.

"Being in politics is very difficult," Wallace told a hastily called press conference just after Labor Day. "Of course, it's been more difficult since I was shot in 1972." He could only confirm the worst rumors—wiretapping in his own bedroom, the mistrust of his wife, awkward revelations of matrimonial discord. "A purely domestic matter," he insisted. "There were no politics involved at all. No one was hurt; no one has been harmed." He swallowed his pride, even volunteered to support Cornelia should she, like Lurleen, desire to succeed him in the governor's office when the current term expired. "There ain't any questions for you to ask," he said at last, cutting off further disclosures. "If you folks in the press would leave us alone in our domestic matters, we'll solve it a lot quicker."

Drained by his domestic turmoil, Wallace welcomed the distractions of politics. With Jimmy Carter as the Democratic candidate, he ended his quarrel with the party leadership, stumped the state with his fellow southerner, and shared the satisfaction of Carter's victory in November. "He's my friend," said a happy Wallace; "he'd have to be a good man because he beat me in the primaries." In a gesture of truce, Wallace ordered the flag of the United States restored to its preeminence above the stars and bars of the Confederacy at the state capitol. He also halted forty-five years of sectional discord when, through his executive power of clemency, he issued a pardon for Clarence Norris, the last survivor of the Scottsboro boys, those Depression-era symbols of racial injustice in the Old South. "We are not in utopia," Wallace assured the former fugitive in a tearful ceremony in Montgomery.

"We've got a long way to go as does every place else, but we don't have to go as far as most others—I'm glad for it, I praise the Lord for it. . . . This is one of the best places in the country for whites and blacks to live, whether some people believe it or not."

As he chatted with Norris, Wallace revealed how easy it was for a southerner to accept racial peace. He was unashamed of the stereotypes that had defined race relations in the South. There black and white could share a common language. He spoke familiarly and without bitterness: "How do you stay so young—black folks stay young, white folks get old—how do you stay so young?"

"That's because we eat a lot of soul food," interjected a black reporter, "fried chicken, collard greens—you whites eat a lot of beef steaks."

"I like collards as well as you do," replied the governor from Clio. "I used to eat cold corn and collard for breakfast."

Within a year Wallace brought the history of criminal extradition in Alabama full circle by asking the governor of Georgia to return a white man, J. B. Stoner, for prosecution on charges of bombing a church in Birmingham in which four black girls had been killed in September 1963. He gave no explanation of the long delay.

He was proud to be invited to the White House on the first day of the Carter administration. But he was not too proud to bring the president one personal request: He asked for support of research to help the nation's paraplegics. He felt comfortable in Carter's Washington and even considered living there. Since the state constitution of Alabama forbade him to succeed himself in 1979, Wallace set his eyes on another government job—the expected vacancy in the United States Senate when the aging John Sparkman would retire. "If I decide to run, it doesn't matter who else will be in there," said Wallace. "If I decide not to run, that will depend on who is running."

As he prepared for another statewide election, his personal troubles took their toll. In August 1977 an anonymous woman advised news reporters to visit a supermarket and look beneath the bell peppers. There they discovered a swatch of papers that proved to be the unsigned documentation of George Wallace's impending divorce. Everyone who knew about the matter denied its authenticity. But the plot unraveled rapidly one September morning when Cornelia announced that she could "no longer endure the vulgarity, threats, and abuse" and moved out of the mansion. "It's a private matter, and I trust our friends will treat it as such," said Wallace. Within a week he filed for divorce, claiming that "there exists such a complete incompatibility of temperament the parties can no longer live together as man and wife."

Cornelia countersued: "The reason for the breakup of this marriage was not incompatibility, but the commission of actual violence and cruelty." She claimed that Wallace not only beat her but tried to strangle her, and for her safety she had begun to sleep with a gun. "George wanted the divorce. I didn't. I fought it a long time. I just couldn't fight any longer," she stated. "There were other people influencing him. That's all I can say. People who wanted to be close to George's power fought to get me out of the picture." Whatever his motives, Wallace considered the case "private and personal." He refused absolutely to discuss it. He hoped that his silence would limit the political damage. "The people have been good to me," he explained. "I want to keep paying them back."

On their seventh wedding anniversary, George Wallace, aged fifty-eight, and Cornelia Wallace, aged thirty-eight, were scheduled to meet in court. She claimed that Wallace or one of his associates had hidden millions of dollars in leftover campaign money. But, since she could not prove these charges, she accepted a much smaller out-of-court settlement: $75,000, a small cabin at a lake resort, and a few personal items. Wallace expressed no regrets: "My wife and I, in my judgment, are still friends." (Within eight weeks he had received about fifty proposals of marriage.) But he worried about the political repercussions. "Anything can be used in a campaign," he admitted. "I'm sure the people of this state, who supported me so generously and have made me a national figure, will not give up that investment now."

Living alone, he settled into a rigid routine about which he had little choice. He rose at seven and had a black valet bring him "whatever I want" for breakfast. He was carried for a bath and then for a half hour of exercise, followed by a massage and electric shock therapy to stimulate his legs and prevent atrophy. Then he worked the telephones, which, because of the deterioration of his hearing, had been fitted with special amplifiers. (For face-to-face talk, he became adept at lipreading, but he also counted on his aides to repeat questions directly into his ear.) By noon Wallace was ready for one of his scheduled trips to the toilet. Then he went to his office for the afternoon. He left around six and returned home to bed to work the phone into the night. For diversion he watched "Hee-Haw" or football. "I've been in a lot of tight situations, and I always knew I might get shot," he said. "But shot dead. Not this! I never thought I'd be a paraplegic."

As he entered the final year of his governorship, in 1978, Wallace anticipated the luxury of serving as an elder statesman: "Crusading is for the young. Middle age is just hanging on. . . . The Senate would be good for me. I'd be active and feel like I'm contributing something." In the early spring he began to campaign again, assuring the voters that "we don't need no people from Yale to tell us who we are. . . . I've been from San Francisco to Ithaca, New York, telling every part of the country what you sent me to tell 'em—that the South is just as good as any place else." He dismissed rumors of his declining popularity: "I'm going to win. I know a lot of those folks in Washington. I can help the state. I'm not out of place anymore."

Despite his bold front, Wallace did indeed worry about living in the national capital. As a precondition for running, he had persuaded the Alabama legislature to pass a special law, providing him with two full-time bodyguards to accompany him to the Senate. Even then, he had his doubts. To sort things out he decided to take a brief vacation at his beach house on the Gulf shore. For three days, away from the ringing telephones, he soaked in the sun, cultivated a tan, and dreamed of life beyond politics. It was a sobering prospect, not untempting.

As he rehearsed the words of his next speech, he argued with himself about whether to include the one phrase that would surely change his life, perhaps forever. "I even got to the point in my speech where I was going to make that statement," he later admitted; "then I almost did not make it." But then he did. "Having thought all day yesterday, and last night and today," he told a gathering of local government officials in Mobile, "I've decided . . . I will not be a candidate for the United States Senate." His political career seemed finally finished, although even as his listeners gave him a standing ovation he thought about taking it back. "I did not say I was necessarily retiring from politics," he added, "and I did not say I am not."

About his motives, Wallace remained, as ever, coy and sketchy. He denied any fear of losing the election, denied, too, any problems of popularity or raising campaign funds, or even ill health. "Maybe a little fairy talked to me while I was asleep," he teased reporters. "Maybe I got to thinking about all the pointed-head guideline writers in Washington who might run me crazy." Beneath his saucy banter Wallace concealed more fear than he dared confront—a fear of isolation, a fear of loneliness, and a deeper anxiety as well, a terror not much different from his notorious fear of flying. It was, at bottom, a fear, understandable in any paralytic, of total helplessness. "Well, I just got to thinkin' about bein' up there in Washington, a strange town 'n' all, and with my condition," he would later explain, "I'll tell you the truth . . . I just didn't want to be up there all by myself."

For all his talk about the equality of the South, moreover, Wallace worried about the stigma of regional inferiority, of being considered provincial and a hick. A master of sarcasm, he dreaded the laughter of others, perhaps feared also the shame of self-exposure, of appearing foolish even to himself. He couched these fears in the language of paralysis and drew a peculiar and unconvincing comparison with the one man who really did overcome the handicap. "I used to think there wasn't much difference between my being in a wheelchair and Franklin D. Roosevelt's using one, but there is a difference," Wallace asserted. "My needs are harmonious with my duties as governor, and the people of Alabama understand the nature of my handicap and my limitations. But it might have been an entirely different case in a different city, serving in a different office. So it is not the first time the wheelchair has played a part in my political fortunes." This time, he admitted, with no small regret, "it meant closing a chapter, if not the book."

Bidding farewell to Washington politics, Wallace boasted of his achievement. "The one overarching accomplishment . . . the legacy that I am proudest of having had a hand in passing on," he declared, "was the long-due recognition of the middle class as the forgotten infantryman of this country." He condemned the national press for distorting his record, for seeing "something racist and ugly in my espousal of relief and rescue for the middle class and in their swelling response to my attacks on their abandonment." He still spoke for "the people," reminded the Washington leadership of a widespread "disgust with the lessening of the nation's defense strength . . . that this country has given away much that was won in hard-fought battles . . . by conceding much to world communism."

"At any event," said Wallace, making a final swing, "I take leave for the moment of my old friends the pointy-heads, the professors who flunked bicycle parking, the fearless regulators with their huge brief-cases, and all the other bizarre specimens that gave zest to my work.

"It isn't an irrevocable good-bye," he said, "just 'so long' while I take a rest under the fifty-mission rule of rotation."

No sooner did Wallace shut the door than it flew open in his face at the news of the unexpected death of Alabama Senator James Allen, which caused a second major vacancy in the political scene. There was now practically no way he would lose an election for the Senate. Never precipitous, Wallace mulled over the prospects for three weeks, before announcing his decision: He would not run for either seat. But he emphasized that he was not retiring from politics: "I expect to remain politically active for years to come."

Such aspirations seemed unrealistic, even to him. In the summer he was hospitalized again with a urinary tract infection, one of the chronic infirmities that afflicted his body. His spirits sank into another depression. At the annual Labor Day picnic in Mobile, a political event he had missed only once in twenty-one years (and that was when he was close to death from peritonitis), Wallace sat morosely in the backseat of his limousine, stretching his hand through the window to greet hundreds of well-wishers, until, at last, even the sight of "the people" repelled him. "I just don't want to see any more of them," he confided. "What you don't seem to understand is that most of these folks'll be delighted to git shed of me."

Since World War II, Wallace had lived almost exclusively on the state payroll, and now for the first time he had to worry about an income. He talked about it all the time. With personal assets of about $200,000, he estimated his annual cost of living at $75,000. But he was reluctant to ask for handouts "because," as he explained, "of all the handicapped people out there who get along on so much less. I don't want them to be discouraged, you know." For an undisclosed sum, he agreed to serve as a tour host for a holiday trip to Jerusalem and Tel Aviv, but he never went.

"I just don't know what I'm going to do," he said, sounding like a broken record. " 'Course, I got to keep active, you know. I've always been active, so I've got to keep on being active." He contemplated following in the footsteps of the retired governor of California, Ronald Reagan. "Well," Wallace asked, "you reckon anybody'd want to hear what I'd say on the radio?" He agreed to write a regular column for an editorial syndicate in South Carolina, but after one attempt he canceled the deal. What in the end saved his future and his dignity was his friends in high places, who arranged for him to become director of development for rehabilitation resources at the University of Alabama in Birmingham at a salary of nearly $70,000. In this job, he assumed responsibility for consulting about rehabilitation, working with government agencies, and fund raising: "I know I will be working in an area of great interest and concern to me, and I feel I can make a meaningful contribution."

As the curtain descended, Wallace sought a truce with the verdict of history, strove to clarify, if not actually revise, his record on the issues. "I was not an enemy of blacks in those days," he claimed, discussing the turbulence of the civil rights movement. For the first time publicly, he accused the commander of the Alabama state troopers of defying his direct orders on Selma's Bloody Sunday, and he admitted that the large number of racial killings—the bombing of the Birmingham church, the fatal beating of Reverend James Reeb, the shooting of Mrs. Viola Liuzzo, the dozens of unsolved homicides that plagued the state during his long tenure—these, he said, "broke my heart." "I made mistakes in the sense that I should've clarified my position more," he asserted in a partial concession of error. "I was young and brash and didn't do so. I was never saying anything that reflected on black people, and I'm sorry it was taken that way." After all, he explained, "the first people I saw when I opened my eyes when I came into the world and could see were black people. I've lived among them all my life. Some of my finest friends—" The phrase drew him up short. "You laugh when you make that statement, you know," he went on, "but the people of Alabama never did dislike black people, and that's one reason the transition was so easy. It was the legal battles where we did the fighting. We were fighting against politicians, not black people."

In this mood of reconciliation, Wallace was glad to bid farewell to Jim Crow. "It's good that it's been changed," he said. "It's good that the civil rights bill has passed. It hasn't been the evil that we thought in attacking property rights. That's what we were against it for." And yet, for all this mighty revisionism, he swore he would "do it all over again," even if he had to survive as a cripple. "I would do it all over again," he repeated, "because I get a lot of satisfaction out of hearing a president . . . sound like I did in 1963. . . . Don't they talk about the asinine tax structure—the very word Jimmy Carter uses I used to use?"

As he prepared for a Wallace Appreciation Day rally at Garrett Coliseum on a frosty afternoon in January 1979, the governor worried about the turnout: "It's the wrong time of the year, and I'm going out. . . . Everybody has his day, and I've had mine." Fifteen hundred supporters, few of them black, came to say good-bye and to cheer as a hillbilly band plucked an old southern ditty, "You've Fought All the Way, Johnny Reb." "I do love you," Wallace responded, with tears in his eyes. "I'll still be around. I don't know what my future will be . . . whether there will be any political future. So I'll just say so long for a while. God bless you, my friends." In a formal farewell to the

Alabama legislature a few days later, he praised the state's "splendid racial relations." There he received another prolonged standing ovation. "I suppose my political career is over," he said, almost hoping that someone would yet contradict him. "I'm not going to say 'never, never,' because you can paint yourself in a corner that way." On January 15, 1979, on what would have been the fiftieth birthday of Reverend Martin Luther King, Jr., Wallace rode unsmiling at the back of a converted yellow school bus as it moved slowly down Montgomery's Dexter Avenue, part of the inauguration parade of his successor, Governor Forrest "Fob" James.

Wallace satisfied his pride elsewhere. He felt good about helping paraplegics—he was a celebrity among them—and enjoyed giving lectures to a class studying third-party movements at Auburn University. "Oh, I ain't sayin' I ain't gonna run again," he assured an interviewer who visited him in his suburban house. "But it's awful hard to get around like this. Maybe if it was something that you could win pretty easy, without much of a campaign. But if it was gonna be a hard race, I just wouldn't be up for it." Wallace kept his options open, he explained, because some presidential contender might yet offer him a chance at the vice-presidency: "I might be agreeable. I'm still alive. Maybe it's not all over, maybe it is."

At his sixtieth birthday, in August 1979, Wallace proposed an appropriate epitaph: "I told you so!" "We warned that someday it'll be like it is in Los Angeles," he said about the continuing opposition to school busing outside the South. "The same hue and cry. Why, even Governor [Jerry] Brown is running for president and complaining about this big government up in Washington. Ain't that what Carter says about it? And ain't that what everybody says about it?" He demanded recognition for his past efforts: "Maybe if all of them had looked at really what I was trying to tell them in '63, instead of concocting in their own minds racism because [I am] a southerner, then we might not be in as bad shape today." As a birthday present, Fob James appointed him a special "governor's counsellor," an honorary title he shared with Big Jim Folsom that paid $18,000 a year. "I have no political ambitions," Wallace insisted. "I never say 'never.'" But when Governor James dismissed some of Wallace's supporters, the ex-governor offered private consolation: "Just you hang around for three more years. I'll be back."

Wallace flourished as the elder statesman of Alabama politics. He waited for a personal telephone call from Rosalynn Carter before agree-

ing to serve as the star guest at a presidential fund raiser. He proudly
shared a spotlight with Ethel Kennedy at the inauguration of the first
black mayor of Birmingham. Yet Wallace never wavered in his loyalty
to the South, and he backed Carter in 1980 over the insurgency of
Edward Kennedy.

His political enthusiasm during these months mirrored his personal condition; the discomforts of paralysis matched the inertia of
retirement. "I'm out of it," he said during a period of great pain.
"People don't want to hear what I have to say." He required twenty-six
stitches in his side to close a festering bed sore. So excruciating were
his torments that he checked into an Oregon hospital to try an experimental chemical therapy, but the effect was uncertain.

He received comfort from loyal supporters, among them a young
blond divorcée named Lisa Taylor, who with her sister, Mona, had
formed half of the country and western Mona-Lisa duet that accompanied Wallace on the campaign trails in 1968. For Christmas he gave
her a diamond solitaire. And when Cornelia predicted a reconciliation
with her former husband, Wallace publicly announced his forthcoming
marriage to thirty-three-year-old Lisa, daughter of a coal millionaire
from Jasper, Alabama. "I'm very happy to have as my wife one with
such high values, honesty, integrity, and intelligence," said the sixty-
two-year-old bridegroom. "She is a fine woman."

With his batteries recharged, Wallace began to test the political
waters in earnest—making speeches, cutting ribbons, accepting honors
and awards that bolstered his spirits, and kept his name in the public
eye. "Now, you know, I'm not campaigning for anything," he insisted,
after heading the pre-Christmas parade at Auburn. "I'm just traveling
around." When the Alabama Ethics Commission ruled in 1982 that
the ex-governor held one too many jobs in state government, Wallace
resigned as Fob James's consultant. It made his political choices that
much easier. "I now realize the frailty of human life," he commented
about his suffering. "I may not be here tomorrow. I may not be here
this afternoon."

But, for as long as he was around, Wallace decided to make the
most of it. With music supplied by a group called The Southbound
Glory, and plenty of barbecued ribs and chicken, baked beans and cole
slaw, his new wife at his side, Wallace hailed two thousand supporters
—small businessmen and state government employees, jobless steel-
workers and dirt farmers down on their luck—and he promised to set
things right. "Regardless of your color, we're all in the same fix," he

said about the second year of Reaganomics. "We can't pay our bills, so we must join together and see [that] all black and white Alabamians have opportunities in schools and jobs." With the blessings of his doctors, he would seek an unprecedented fourth term as governor of Alabama: "I promise you I will not be paralyzed in the head."

In the summer of 1982 he went to Birmingham to pay a call on the twenty-fifth annual convention of the Southern Christian Leadership Conference, once headed by Martin Luther King, Jr., and to a sea of black faces he apologized for all the mistakes of the past. "We in Alabama are all together now," he said. "All of us in the same fix. Only a very few can make ends meet." Asked if he had changed his attitude toward blacks, Wallace denied it: "No, I have respected them and loved them always. . . . I was *for* school segregation in those days," he admitted. "I've had black leaders say to me, 'We know why you said what you said.' And I tell them, 'No, you're wrong. I wasn't saying that for expediency. I believed in segregation.' " Now, however, Wallace maintained, "I believe that segregation is wrong. And I don't want it to come back. I see now that we couldn't live in a society like that."

In the small town of Dothan, mostly white folks crowd into the dusty farm shed where the temperature exceeds 100°, swat at the flies and gnats, sweat, sip cokes, laugh at the fat man at the microphone who prepares them for the grand entrance of GEORGE (Yahoo!!) Ceee. WALLACE. "I'm glad we're putting on such a good show," says the happy candidate with a deliberate nod toward the front rows, " 'cause we're having this rally covered by the Washington Post, the New York Times, and Reuters. They come to see if you going to get rid of George Wallace. But I'm here to tell 'em, 'No such luck!' " Just another country boy who's hoisted himself up from poverty, Wallace appeals to the desperation of the moment, the grievous unemployment rate that flashes around 15 percent. He promises to bring new jobs into the state through his numerous contacts with those he calls "the captains of industry." He foreswears any presidential ambitions—"six shots is enough," he states grimly—and then they swarm forward to touch him, to get another autograph, to tell him their problems.

Later, with Tammy Wynette wearing shimmering silver belts and singing "Stand by Your Man," Wallace openly courts the black vote, the crucial balance of power in the first Democratic primary. "I'm not apologizing for anything," he maintains. "I stood for what I stood for because I believed, like most white people in Alabama at the time, that

segregation was right. . . . Some of my attitudes were mistaken, but I
haven't been an evil man." He stresses his evangelical rebirth, asks for
Christian forgiveness. "I never advocated anything for the devil," he
explains. "But every man has sinned and come short of the glory of
God."

The black political leadership, spurred by the outcry of Mrs. Coretta
Scott King, denounced his campaign. But Wallace's humility appealed
to an abiding thirst for reconciliation. The memory of his populist
programs—free textbooks, schools and roads, help for the needy—this
record of past concern remained alive in the black community. In his
hometown of Clayton, where Wallace made the usual pilgrimage to
vote for himself, he posed with the black people who came to embrace
him and to pull the Wallace lever. He won the first Democratic primary, with 42 percent of the total vote and one-third of the black
turnout. "I am very proud," he said.

In the second primary of 1982 he defined the election as a contest
between rich and poor, between archconservatives and populist moderates, between Birmingham aristocrats and "the people." "I'm the only
governor you'll have who can talk to heads of corporations, who will
be quoted by the national press, and who will get Alabama publicity
and jobs," he explained. He called for "victims' rights" in criminal
cases, attacked "tax loopholes for the rich," and charged that "a few
federal judges and thugs run the country." It was a close election, too
hard for the pundits to predict, and it hinged, finally, on a powerful
black minority that rejected the advice of its political leaders and voted
its conscience, voted for Wallace, and yet, curiously, remained too
embarrassed by this assertion of independence to tell the truth to the
pollsters who flocked around the voting booths to make the exit surveys.
"I'm very humbled by this win," declared Wallace of his upset victory.
But when his wife, Lisa, moved to raise his hand in triumph, he shooed
her away. "Oh, no," he exclaimed, "they'll say you had to hold it up.
One paper up the country wrote that Wallace was so weak the night
of the election that his wife had to hold his hand up."

He ran in the general election against Republican Emory Folmar
—a man regarded by the voters as so conservative as to make George
Wallace appear a veritable liberal. "When you have people starving to
death and not eating properly in this state and you're having . . .
$100-a-plate dinners," scoffed Wallace, "I tell you in my judgment
that's going to be one of the issues in this campaign—that the rich are

getting richer and the poor poorer." He held up a book—rare prop indeed in his bag of political tricks—James Agee's *Let Us Now Praise Famous Men,* with its photographs, by Walker Evans, of the Great Depression years, of starving, worried faces, of bleak, bleak prospects. "When the Republicans were in power before," Wallace attested, "we had people like this all over the state of Alabama, and if they stay in Washington very much longer there'll be people like this all over Alabama again." Creating a coalition of poor whites and poor blacks, of country people with long memories and a small future—the kind of populist alliance about which Martin Luther King once dreamed— Wallace won 60 percent of the vote and his fourth term in office.

On a cold January morning in Montgomery, twenty years to the day of his first inauguration, Wallace wheeled past the bronze star embedded in the marble floor of the state capitol to commemorate the spot where Jefferson Davis took his oath of office to the Confederacy. There were no marching bands this day, no parades, on direct orders from the governor, lest he appear to trifle at a time when unemployment was running at 15.3 percent. He placed his hand on the red family Bible, repeated the oath of office to his brother, Judge Jack Wallace. A black man led the Pledge of Allegiance; a black man pronounced the benediction. And then, as the band played "Dixie," Wallace rolled his chair toward the lectern. "For God's sake, let us hear the sighs of the hungry and the cold among us," he stated in his most solemn voice. "No one can be rich, as long as there are those among us who are hungry. Any nation that forgets its poor will lose its soul." He offered only the simplest of hope. "In times like these," said Governor George Corley Wallace, "we must turn to one another and not away from and against one another. . . . Some of you have summoned me in your weakness. Now all of you must sustain me by your strength."

"I'm a born-again Christian, and I'm reaching the eveningtide of life," he explained to a reporter who remained doubtful about his resurrection. "At my age there's no reason to say one thing and mean another."

"I feel good," he remarked, passing his sixty-fourth birthday. "Oh, I have some discomfort all the time. But I have had for twelve years. I've been governor longer sitting down than I have standing up."

Phyllis
Stewart
Schlafly
(IV)

Soon after the Carters moved to Pennsylvania Avenue, Mrs. Schlafly arrived at the White House gates to protest the First Lady's involvement with ERA: "Rosalynn Carter is part of the Executive branch," she said, explaining what she considered an abuse of feminine wiles. "She wakes up every morning on an Executive branch bed. She [makes] calls to a number of state legislators on an Executive branch telephone. . . . The Executive branch has nothing to do with [the ERA]." Mrs. Schlafly resisted any government interference in family affairs. When the Supreme Court denied disability benefits for maternity, she praised this defense of traditional marriage: "I think the father should have to support the baby," she said.

Her arguments against the ERA won widespread support, particularly in the state legislatures that had not yet ratified it. Whereas, in the early 1970s, the ERA had seemed certain to pass, the momentum had now shifted. And, as it did so, the debate became more heated and acrimonious. Mrs. Schlafly was attacked frequently—once with an apple pie thrown in her face. But she showed that she, too, could fight tenaciously. She viewed her opponents with contempt, believing them to be failures not only as politicians but as women: "My husband lets me do what I want to do," she maintained. "Why, if these women's libbers were nice to their husbands, their husbands would let them do what they want to do, too. They just don't want to be nice." She also knew how to enrage them. Once, on her radio show, she defended the black market in baby adoptions—"a victimless crime"—and when feminists objected she attacked them for what she thought a worse evil: abortion.

With Democrats in the White House, she also protested a weakening of the national defense: "The most dramatic news event of the last decade is not the presidential election, not exchange visits of foreign heads of state, not Watergate, not space flight, not the Vietnam War, not even New York's financial default. It is the shift in the strategic balance of power from the United States to the Soviet Union." She deplored détente as well as President Carter's preachings about human rights. In a speech to the Cardinal Mindszenty Foundation, she said communism was "the greatest invasion of human rights in history." She also opposed the transfer of the Panama Canal: "If President Carter is so interested in human rights, he might start by defending the thirty-five hundred American citizens who live in the U.S. Canal Zone."

In 1977 she was chosen by the Daughters of the American Revolution to serve as national chairman of national defense, which allowed her to attack détente in another monthly column. "Is our situation hopeless in the face of . . . Soviet nuclear superiority?" she asked on the twentieth anniversary of Sputnik. "Of course not. The great productive American private enterprise economy that successfully fought a two-front war in World War II, and then put a man on the moon, can certainly stay ahead of the Soviet Union *if* we want to. It's a matter of national will, national determination, and national priorities." For her defense of the free enterprise system, she won her ninth George Washington Medal from the Freedoms Foundation of Valley Forge. For her fight against the ERA, the Associated Press named her one of the ten most powerful people in Illinois.

With such accolades, she decided to confront the women's liberation movement when it converged in Houston in November 1977 to celebrate International Woman's Year. "These are the most sexist women in the world, who cannot solve their own problems and want the government to do it for them," she said in a speech entitled "International Woman's Year: A Front for Lesbians and Radicals." She organized a countermeeting of "pro-family" supporters at the Houston Astrodome. To twenty thousand women who protested feminist reform, she promised imminent victory: "God is on our side. We have somebody on our side who is more powerful than the president of the United States."

By the end of 1977 her growing fame brought her to a crossroads. The campaign against the ERA had proven her effectiveness, and she had built a large personal following among conservative women. Some suggested that she challenge Senator Charles Percy's bid for reelection in 1978. Mrs. Schlafly admitted that being "the only woman in that exclusive club of a hundred men would . . . [be] exciting." It would also increase her power and influence. But there were also disadvantages. Twice before she had run for office and lost: "Illinois is a big state, and it's a real killer." She also weighed the consequences of abandoning the fight against the ERA in order to become, as she put it, "one minority vote in the United States Senate."

What finally settled the matter had nothing to do with politics: "Fred kept saying it was my decision. And I knew it was, as long as I made the decision he wanted."

She asked Fred if he would accompany her to Washington.

"Certainly not."

"It's just plain different for a man leaving his wife home in the district to go to Washington than it is for a woman to leave her husband," Mrs. Schlafly concluded. "It's just plain different." Her independence ended there: "A man has to feel he has a function. And I want my husband to know I need him. I don't want to become so self-sufficient he thinks I don't."

Besides, the fight against the ERA had stiffened. "The football game is in the last quarter and your team is winning," she reported in the spring of 1978. "Suddenly the coach of the losing team demands that the game be extended to give them time to catch up." As the ERA approached the seven-year deadline for ratification in 1979, feminists demanded an unprecedented time extension to gain passage in a few more states. Mrs. Schlafly protested such a change to a subcommittee of the House of Representatives. But the Democratic majority ignored her. Their decision forced her to continue the fight in the state legislatures, where she expected to win: "Our final victory . . . is within our grasp. When that happens, you will share in the most remarkable victory of our time because you . . . will have proved that the truth is more powerful than the White House, the press, and the left-wing foundations combined!"

She returned to Springfield, Illinois, to explain her objections to ERA—the threat of government-funded abortions, homosexual schoolteachers, women in combat, men refusing to support their wives—and conceded under oath that she could indeed support an equal rights amendment, though not the one under consideration. "There are no exceptions," she explained. "It's rigid. It's absolute." When President Carter lobbied for the amendment, she attacked his meddling in state affairs. She also dismissed the role of Hollywood celebrities who made pro-ERA advertisements. What was important, she said, was the power of the vote. In Illinois, ERA failed for the seventh time.

She continued to cultivate her support. For the 1978 elections, she created a STOP-ERA political action committee that donated $90,000 to conservative candidates. She believed that these expenditures assured the triumph of democracy. She never doubted that, contrary to public opinion polls, the majority opposed the ERA: "How can you explain why President Carter, being a Christian and all, supports the ERA? It can only be that he's so completely out of touch with the grass roots and what women of this country want."

In addition to her activism, Mrs. Schlafly remained a full-time student. In December 1978 she earned a diploma from the law school of Washington University, ranking twenty-seventh in her class. At age fifty-four, however, she was not at the brink of a new career. She preferred being a lawyer's wife to becoming a successful lawyer. Nor did she ever lament a missed opportunity. She passed the state bar examinations the first time: "Of course I'm thrilled. I've become the country's authority on the Equal Rights Amendment and . . . I'm glad the expert is on our side." She wrote a scholarly legal analysis, "The Effects of Equal Rights Amendments in State Constitutions," that was published by the conservative Heritage Foundation. It documented her case: "Where the ERA made a unique constitutional difference, it always resulted in a loss to the woman."

Amid popping champagne corks and a telephoned bomb threat, Mrs. Schlafly proclaimed March 22, 1979, the seventh anniversary of the passage of the ERA by Congress, as the date of its official defeat

—"the greatest victory that American women have had since the ratification of the women's suffrage amendment in 1920." Although Congress had authorized the ERA extension, allowing until 1982 for ratification, she insisted that the amendment was "legally, morally, and constitutionally dead." At a celebration for her supporters, at the Shoreham Hotel in Washington, she predicted further success: "We are the most powerful positive force in America today. . . . What is now inevitable is that our side is going to come out on top. . . . I've always said women would rather be loved than liberated."

She introduced the ERA Follies, songs and skits that parodied the feminists:

"Who's goin' to open the door?" sang the Gloria Steinem look-alike.

"No one," answered the woman in the Bella Abzug hat.

Who's goin' to give up seats on the bus for us? Who's goin' to buy houses in our names? Who's goin' to give us insurance policies? Who's goin' to pay our alimony?

"No one."

And to the tune of "Old-Fashioned Girl," the ladies laughed at the words, "I want a person, just like the person that married dear old person."

"We like to have fun," Mrs. Schlafly told a reporter.

She remained a prudent campaigner, nonetheless, visiting un-ratified states to solidify support. When the Carter administration proposed reopening the military draft and including women in conscription, Mrs. Schlafly countered on Father's Day with an advertising blitz called Dads Against Drafting Daughters. She demanded that the administration refrain from changing the laws that exempted women from draft registration and combat assignments.

Her letter-writing lobby in 1979 coincided with an increasing concern about American military defense. "The news photo of Mrs. John Glenn christening the new Trident submarine called the *Ohio* in Groton, Connecticut . . . may have misled some Americans into believing that the U.S. Navy is still the greatest and most up-to-date in the world," she warned. "It isn't. One boat does not make a navy." Even worse was the signing of SALT II, which, according to Mrs. Schlafly, restricted American missiles to a status of perpetual inferiority: "SALT stands for Surrender A Little at a Time." No longer did the Russians need to cheat: "It allows the Soviets to build everything they need to achieve a first-strike capability, decisive nuclear superiority, and control of the world. . . . They can do it all legally under SALT II." Nor, she observed, did Carter even claim that the treaty was verifiable, only "adequately verifiable." "Would you be satisfied," she asked, "if your spouse was 'adequately faithful'? "

As a member of the board of directors of the American Conservative Union, she testified against SALT before the Senate Foreign Relations Committee. Here she linked the treaty to the international communist conspiracy: "Many people seem to assume that the only utility of nuclear weapons is to kill millions of people. Nothing could be further from the truth." She suggested other uses for nuclear weapons, such as blackmailing our allies in the Third World. She pleaded for nuclear superiority and urged a change from the strategy of Mutual Assured Destruction (MAD) deterrence to launch-on-warning. She demanded the construction of the B-1 bomber, the MX missile, more Minuteman III weapons, cruise missiles, and Trident submarines. Otherwise, she advised, "our entire population . . . will be sitting ducks for mass murder, nuclear blackmail, or economic disaster, at the will or caprice of the Kremlin."

With an eye toward the 1980 presidential election, Mrs. Schlafly summoned her followers to the eighth annual strategy session in St. Louis, where, beneath a banner that proclaimed "With God's help, the end of an ERA," she exhorted them "to pray as though it's all up to God, but . . . to work as though it's all up to us." In the three-day workshop, she gave instructions about public images, counseled on makeup and speech writing, and used video recordings to teach effective gestures. She offered seminars on how to get elected, how to influence politicians, and how to reach the media. "If there is one word that best describes us," she said, "it is that we are the believers. We believe that God is in His heaven, that eternal life awaits us . . . in eternal principles that do not change." She asked for perseverance and self-discipline to win "the battle for God, family, and country."

She intensified her attacks on Jimmy Carter, linking the administration's support of ERA to the failures of its foreign policy. The president had devoted his best energy to lobbying the North Carolina legislature, she said, and neglected American problems in Iran. In November 1979 she testified again before the Senate Foreign Relations Committee against Carter's human rights treaties. With an eye for the fine print, she explained that the ideal of universal equality trespassed on the United States Constitution: It could justify the drafting of women, exempt men from alimony payments, and attack the principles of private property. "We cannot gain the respect of others by placing our own rights in jeopardy." Vigilant against an invasion of ERA principles, she urged a House Armed Services subcommittee not to repeal male-only combat laws. She won the immediate point and also gained an important congressional precedent for subsequent arguments in the courts.

Her warnings about the military consequences of ERA seemed prophetic when in January 1980 President Carter responded to the Soviet invasion of Afghanistan by requesting draft registration for men and women alike. "For seven years they've been accusing me of seeing something under the bed," she said. "But now we're finding out it can happen." To her way of thinking, the drafting of women represented part of an ERA conspiracy: a way to circumvent the moral objections to the proposed constitutional amendment. "President Carter did everything his wife told him to do," she declared, explaining the sexual politics of the cold war. "Rosalynn had embraced the entire ideology of ERA, and the ERA-feminist-women's lib strategy demanded the drafting of women. So Jimmy Carter was led down the primrose path." In Mrs. Schlafly's view Carter's submission to women confirmed his overall weakness: "If this administration can't stand up to women's lib, they can't stand up to the Russians." She promptly established the Coalition Against Drafting Women to lobby on Capitol Hill, organized a nationwide petition campaign, and filed a lawsuit in federal court on behalf of young women opposed to the draft. "The purpose of our armed forces," she reminded the Kiwanis Club of St. Louis, "is not to serve as an equal-opportunity employer. Its only purpose is to defend the United States of America."

ERA and military defense—two incompatible entities in Phyllis Schlafly's politics—determined her election plans in 1980. She approached the one presidential candidate she believed was right on both issues: opposed to the ERA and tough enough to face the Russians. She was respectful but blunt:

"You did promise, didn't you, that you would not reappoint Henry Kissinger?" she asked Ronald Reagan.

"That's right, I did."

"Reagan," Mrs. Schlafly concluded, in offering him her allegiance, "should never be allowed to forget that promise."

She was chosen an alternate delegate to the Republican National Convention of 1980. "I've worked hard for everything I've gotten," she said, "and I doubt very much most women would want to work that hard." Wearing a large Reagan button, a STOP-ERA emblem, and the ubiquitous gold eagle pin, she testified before the Republican platform committee, persuading it to repudiate the ERA for the first time since 1940: "We realized that if we didn't get out and defend our values, this little feminist pressure group was going to end up changing our schools, our laws, our textbooks, our Constitution, our military, everything— and end up taking our husband's job away." After the convention, she defended the rejection of the ERA as "the finest statement of women's rights in history. It supports women's rights without taking away tradi- tional rights such as exemption from the draft." She also praised the disavowal of abortions and school busing and the support of the ABM missile and nuclear superiority. "There has been a persistent effort . . . to propagate the myth that the Republican party platform . . . is somehow the most 'conservative' ever," she said. "It is the country, not the Republican party, which has moved to the right."

Through her political action committees she contributed funds to conservative candidates. But she also sought higher inspiration: God "certainly blessed America more than any other country. And I think when you are the recipient of lots of blessings, responsibility goes along with it." Asked about what she had prayed for, Mrs. Schlafly men- tioned the defeat of ERA in Iowa: "That was quite a surprise for everybody." Anything else? she was asked. "Well, Ronald Reagan's victory."

"I'm on top of the world," she exclaimed the next day. The president-elect appreciated her support and appointed her to a forty- member Defense Policy Advisory Group. Here, during the weeks of the presidential transition, she pleaded for nuclear superiority, new weap- ons, and elimination of the plan to draft women. Inside these citadels of power, she allowed her fantasies to roam—admitted interest in a Supreme Court appointment; considered, as she put it, "the idea of letting people recommend me for Secretary of Defense." Reagan, however, showed no interest in her—and so, "after prayerful considera- tion," she let the matter drop. Her relationship with Reagan continued to be friendly, but she remained outside the administration.

"What we have been working for for twenty years," she said "has been established as the mainstream of American political thinking." As Reagan moved into the White House, Mrs. Schlafly opened her own office on Pennsylvania Avenue, from which the Eagle Forum could "let Congress know . . . the views of the grass roots." Her agenda itemized her lifelong antipathy to liberal reform—opposition to the drafting of women, opposition to the ERA, opposition to sex education in the schools ("what you have left is a how-to-do-it course from which all moral values have been taken away and in which the children are not told about the alternative of virtue"), opposition to federal spending ("I'm in favor of cuts, cuts, cuts . . . they can cut everywhere . . . without qualification"), opposition to library censorship ("There is no excuse for every . . . library not having an anti-ERA book written by the leader of the STOP-ERA movements . . . and the biography of the leader of the . . . movement"), opposition to abortion, opposition to affirmative action.

She testified to the House subcommittee on social security to defend the rights of homemakers, widows, and mothers: "By bearing and nurturing six children who have grown into educated and well-adjusted citizens . . . I have done vastly more financially for the Social Security system than any worker."

She testified to a Senate Labor subcommittee on sexual harassment in the workplace, denying the existence of a problem: "The most cruel and damaging sexual harassment taking place today is the harassment by feminists and their federal government allies against the role of motherhood and the role of the dependent wife." Sexual harassment was not a problem for the "virtuous woman," she said, "except in the rarest of cases. When a woman walks across a room, she speaks with a universal body language that most men intuitively understand. Men hardly ever ask sexual favors of a woman from whom the certain answer is no."

She testified to a House subcommittee on education about teaching youngsters to read by the phonics method, as she had done for her own children, and to use traditional textbooks to impart moral values. Through the Eagle Forum, she launched a Headstart Reading Project, "an adult-to-child volunteer program," to hasten its acceptance.

She celebrated "a tremendous victory for everything we've been fighting for" when, in June 1981, the Supreme Court upheld the exemption of women from the draft on the grounds that Congress already distinguished military obligations along gender lines (the result of an earlier Phyllis Schlafly lobby). "It's perfectly obvious that if ERA were in the Constitution," she observed, "the decision would have gone the other way.

"Women were honored until the women's liberation movement came along and told them they were second-class citizens," she maintained. "I never felt second-class." She contrasted the obligations of privilege, her sense of personal responsibility, with the attitudes of liberals who placed their faith in politics: "My opponents' idea of compassion is to set up another government bureaucracy. . . . I've spent a lifetime doing volunteer work of one kind or another." She had no regrets: "As I travel about the country," she said in an open letter to American teenagers, "I meet hundreds of attractive young women in their thirties who, ten years ago, freely and enthusiastically chose to follow the Pied Piper of feminism. They have good jobs with high salaries, but they aren't happy. They have an ailment described as 'baby hunger.' Their biological clock is ticking away." Through her oldest son she became a grandmother for the first time.

Mrs. Schlafly stepped down the carpeted staircase into a halo of television lights. A band played "Somewhere over the Rainbow." It was June 30, 1982, and the ERA was dead. "Thanks," she said with tears in her eyes; "we made it." With steak and champagne toasts, with speeches by Jerry Falwell, Jesse Helms, and James Watt, she savored "the most remarkable political victory of the twentieth century." But only briefly, for she was already planning her agenda for the "new era" ahead: the end of sex education ("a principal cause of teenage pregnancy"), opposition to the nuclear freeze ("the atomic bomb is a marvelous gift that was given to our country by a wise God"), the elimination of feminism from textbooks ("the way it is now, you can't show a picture of a woman washing the dishes"), and the introduction of more "pro-family" books in American libraries. "I've always been achievement-oriented," she admitted, "very industrious, and I know how to use my time."

As she approached her sixtieth birthday, she appeared as a paragon of efficiency and self-discipline. She rose at seven each morning and worked until midnight, rationing her time with the parsimony of any careful housewife. "I am into nutrition," she said, as her weight remained unchanged since her youth. "We eat a lot of fresh produce, few sweets." At Fred's prodding, she agreed "under duress" to maintain her physical fitness. "I lie down in front of the TV set during the evening news and do my exercise routine."

In the prime of her power, she saw her life as a model for others. "A woman should spend the first twenty years of her life growing up," she said, "the next twenty raising the next generation, and the third saving the world." She was immodest about her achievement and unembarrassed about her pride: "I'm very satisfied with the division of my life into a couple of different careers."

Her calendar was still full. "I talk on the telephone. I meet with reporters. I do two newspaper columns a week. I do five commentaries for Cable News Network. I write my monthly report. I run my organization. I'm interested. I'm alive. Gosh," Phyllis Schlafly exclaimed, "isn't life great?"

John
Herschel
Glenn
(IV)

As Jimmy Carter moved into the White House in January 1977, John Glenn set aside his ambitions for higher office: "If I can have an impact on leaving the whole world a little better place some way through efforts in the Senate, I can't think of any greater challenge for the next fifteen years." He sat on the Government Operations committee, where he worked on the problems of nuclear power; and in the Foreign Relations committee he presided over the subcommittee on East Asia and the Pacific. Both assignments focused on national security; both required mastery of intricate detail —the ratio of kilowatts to spent plutonium, for example, or analysis of photographs sent from orbiting satellites. It was the kind of work he loved—and did well.

Although Glenn, as a Democrat, supported the new administration, he qualified the extent of his loyalty. He did not like to play politics. He thought of himself as an idealist, a man of principles. If pressed by conscience, he would be unafraid to break ranks. Among his colleagues, such traits translated into stubbornness. "All his adult life he has been fooling with complicated machines, and he thinks everything can be fixed mechanically," observed one senator. "Some things can't be fixed that way, and the government is one of those things."

Glenn concentrated on building a legislative record. He sponsored innovative measures to desegregate public schools. He visited the People's Republic of China to help pave the way for a normalization of relations. He journeyed with a congressional delegation to the Middle East, where he met leaders of Israel, Egypt, Jordan, and Iran, as well as representatives of the Palestine Liberation Organization. He held hearings on safety standards in the nuclear power industry. (And, while he was working late in his senate office one evening, thieves broke into his house and stole many of his mementos.)

For his legislative efforts in 1976, the liberal lobby, Americans for Democratic Action, gave him a fifty rating, dead center in the political spectrum. He remained there in subsequent years. He was a keen defender of the free enterprise system. But when President Carter defined the energy crisis as the moral equivalent of war, Glenn advocated a program of national "planning"—"I hate to use that word because all sorts of communistic vapors get into the air"—and he insisted that "in any commonsense business in the country, a businessman looks ahead and tries to see . . . his options for the future." He even fought for the appointment of an energy "czar" to regulate the price of fuel. When, instead, Congress created the Department of Energy, Glenn criticized its weakness—"a big, amorphous, gooey area where nobody has authority."

He remained optimistic about American technology and particularly about nuclear power. But he took a very cautious position on its sale abroad, fearing that the increase in the number of reactors would encourage more weapons. He had no such doubts about American arms. He opposed President Carter's cancellation of the B-1 bomber. His was a pilot's perspective. Although Glenn doubted the value of the B-1 as a nuclear deterrent, he appreciated its aeronautical superiority. It would give the United States an edge in conventional warfare— where, he believed, "any future combat scenario" was more likely to begin; "we hope, we pray to God, that it never escalates beyond that."

His personal memories of World War II and Korea provoked disagreements with Carter's foreign policy in Asia. In the aftermath of

Vietnam, he warned the president against "inducing even greater skepticism with regard to our reliability for a long-term U.S. commitment." He opposed a plan to reduce American forces in South Korea. He fought to retain air bases in the Philippines and demanded guarantees of the military umbrella for Japan. His positions reflected a distrust of diplomatic bargains; he preferred the certainty of military strength.

He was also doubtful about détente and disarmament: "The SALT process is not a panacea," he said in 1977; it was only "our best hope in enhancing mutual security." His suspicion of the communists ran deep. He refused to accept Soviet promises. Instead he demanded absolute verification of any arms control agreements. In the absence of trust, verification would depend on the quality of American technology. He was confident, at least in the beginning, that listening posts in northern Iran would provide sufficient information.

He expressed a similar caution about domestic issues. "Now is not the time to relax, to lower the guard," he told the American Civil Liberties Union, which honored his record: "To live up to the American dream, to make it a reality not at some far future data, but in our time, in our day, that is your challenge, that is my challenge." He took pride in his 100 percent voting record on civil rights issues. More than that, he construed the subject in its broadest terms. He sponsored legislation to control arson, for example, not only because it cost $2 billion each year, but also because its primary victims were members of minority groups.

Nor was Glenn reluctant to challenge the most conservative bastion of racism in the country: his own United States Senate, which traditionally exempted itself from civil rights legislation. After reading Senate employment specifications—"no blacks," "white only," no secretaries who wear "pantsuits"—he demanded an end to job discrimination on Capitol Hill: "Perhaps this is the most difficult time of all in this struggle because now is the time when these laws have to be put into effect in men's and women's hearts all over the country." But he could not overcome the ensuing filibuster.

Complexity did not frighten him. He worked tirelessly to master the details of nuclear technology. Then, in 1978, he introduced pioneering legislation to promote the sale of nuclear power—"without bombs, without the spread of nuclear weaponry that too easily could follow, indeed, without the haunting specter of a future mushroom-cloud holocaust." The nuclear nonproliferation act of 1978 proved the crowning achievement of his first term in office.

More than most politicians, Glenn held a moral view of power that seemed almost archaic in the Senate. "We have only one weapon —truth," he said, upon learning of mass atrocities in Cambodia. "Moral indignation must be our starting point. Morality . . . should not be divorced from politics." He was, consequently, unafraid of negative public opinion. He supported the sale of F-15 fighter jets to Saudi Arabia in 1978, for example, despite the objections of his influential Jewish constituents.

In November 1978 Glenn journeyed with a special delegation to the Soviet Union to discuss human rights, SALT, and military expansion. At the Kremlin he met members of the ruling Politburo and listened to a rambling monologue by Leonid Brezhnev. Despite diplomatic propriety, he asked impolite questions on behalf of Ohio's Eastern European immigrants who, he said, wanted to know when Moscow intended to liberate Hungary, Czechoslovakia, and Poland. The question drew a smile from Russian faces—until Glenn assured them he was serious. A Soviet spokesman then explained that they were smiling because they had not heard such questions since the days of the cold war. To which Glenn replied that the Soviet military buildup had not been seen since the cold war either.

Two months later, in January 1979, he attended a sumptuous dinner at the Great Hall of the People in Peking to celebrate the normalization of relations with China. But he was not very happy there either. He was especially angry that President Carter had failed to consult with the Senate about this dramatic reversal of American foreign policy. "Let there be no doubt: Informing some of us two hours before the public announcement cannot be considered consultation. . . . Regrettably, the administration's failure to consult Congress on important issues has become, I am afraid, too much of a pattern." His trust of Carter diminished; he resolved never again to be caught by surprise.

He made sure to visit Taiwan on his way home and supported the sale of advanced jet aircraft to the traditional ally "to insure Taiwan's continued freedom to decide its fate." His suspicion of the communist menace intensified two weeks later, when China invaded Vietnam. "You can draw up all sorts of doomsday scenarios as to what might happen along the northern Chinese border," he warned. He also questioned President Carter's response to the revolution in Iran and condemned the failure to protect secret military technology. He believed that the loss of control in the area imperiled the ability to monitor Soviet missiles.

These breaches of security alarmed him, arousing mistrust not only of Russians, Chinese, and the Ayatollah Khomeini, but also of President Carter himself. At the conclusion of the SALT II negotiations, Glenn decided to speak out. His opportunity came on a gray morning in April 1979 at the naval base in Groton, Connecticut, where the nuclear submarine, *Ohio,* would be launched. Annie Glenn had been invited to perform the christening. Glenn drafted a speech about the problems of SALT II.

As they prepared to leave their home, Glenn received an unexpected telephone call from the Oval Office. The president was asking him to soften his remarks about the treaty. Glenn declined. The president asked him again, but Glenn still refused. For a half hour they argued, destroying any patina of propriety: "I have never talked to a president that way before, and no president has talked that way to me before." Glenn finally capitulated to the presidential honor and presented a clumsily edited speech about arms control: "Verification must be better designed and agreed to prior to submission to the Senate"; SALT II would not be acceptable "on the basis of just statements of 'good faith' in Soviet intentions." He had accommodated Carter for the occasion, but he had no intention of remaining compliant on a matter he considered so essential to the national defense: "I guess the idea was that I should be reasonable and just go along with this hope that we could get something worked out. I wasn't willing to do that."

After the president submitted SALT II to the Senate for ratification in the summer of 1979, Glenn assumed a preeminent role in its consideration. His experience as a military pilot and his familiarity with the technological issues gave him special credibility among his colleagues. As a Democrat, moreover, his disagreement with Carter carried great weight. He quickly protested the weakness of assured verification in SALT II, and he questioned the ability to detect treaty violations or to monitor improvements of existing missiles. These charges assumed greater importance when the Carter administration admitted belatedly the presence of a Soviet military brigade in Cuba. Glenn challenged the reliability of United States intelligence: "When we don't know something like this, it is obviously an intelligence error." The persistent failure of American satellites—"we were blind for the better part of two years," he would later explain—assured his opposition to SALT. In the foreign relations committee, he introduced amendments to modify the treaty. When they failed, he voted against ratification in committee. He was prepared to fight the treaty on the Senate floor, but then the issue never came to a vote.

Glenn's opposition to Carter did not end until the president changed his foreign policy. Facing an election challenge from Edward Kennedy and feeling betrayed by the Soviet invasion of Afghanistan, Carter gained Glenn's support by rekindling the cold war. In January 1980 the president asked for a postponement of the vote on SALT II. Then he proposed a boycott of the Moscow Olympics. Glenn gladly supported it: "The Soviet invasion of Afghanistan is not consistent with the principles associated with the Olympic Games, and the Soviets should not benefit from the attention and prestige associated with hosting this important event." Later, when Republican candidate Ronald Reagan cited Glenn's opposition to SALT in an attack on Carter, the senator repudiated the charge: "I'm not opposed to the SALT treaty," he claimed. "There are just some details about verification I'm concerned about."

Sharing Carter's hostility to the Soviet Union—and feeling little sympathy for the insurgency of Edward Kennedy—Glenn endorsed the reelection of the president. "The complexity and scope of today's problems ensure that there will be no quick answers, no easy solutions," he explained. "In these uneasy times, we need all the patience, dedication, intelligence, and courage that the American people can muster." When Carter arranged a campaign rally on the eve of the Ohio primary, Glenn canceled a foreign-policy speech to stand at his side. "There have been some disappointments," he admitted, but he urged the voters "to close ranks." Four days later Carter's victory in Ohio clinched the nomination.

Glenn himself ran for reelection in 1980, standing as a candidate "who understands war but who loves peace." With a grueling campaign, he built a coalition of blacks, Jews, and organized labor, as well as his traditional supporters in the rural districts of Ohio. The results were impressive. On the presidential level Reagan carried Ohio by a half million votes, but Glenn won his own race by a margin of 1.6 million, gaining 69 percent of the total vote, and he captured all but one of Ohio's eighty-eight counties. "I'm Annie Glenn's husband," he exulted, using the self-effacing expression that President Kennedy had once uttered in Paris. "Tonight we celebrate a great victory." He expressed no remorse at Carter's defeat, nor sympathy for Walter Mondale who had beaten him to the vice-presidency four years earlier: "They ran as a team, were elected as a team, and were defeated as a team."

The political climate after the election suited his conservative instincts. "You could say that the success of the Democratic party led to our demise in this election," he observed. "We were so successful that we have created a great new middle class of people with better incomes, better homes, and better opportunities for their kids. These people are now concerned that they not regress—a fear that has created perhaps a whole new wave toward traditional Republicanism." Glenn adopted the language of the victors. He talked about balanced budgets, stimulating productivity, and rejuvenating private enterprise: "We can't interfere, by too much taxation and regulation, with business's ability to be competitive." He also emphasized the importance of strengthening the national defense. Unlike many Democrats, he seemed comfortable in the age of Reagan.

His popularity encouraged him. Having demonstrated his independence of Jimmy Carter, he believed he could run on his own record in 1984. Even if the former administration controlled the nominating process in the Democratic party, he thought he could reach the voters directly. He would offer a unique position—neither the liberal past nor the explicit conservatism of President Reagan. Three weeks after his reelection in 1980, Glenn received a confidential memorandum from a member of his staff: "Define a vision, play an active role in the formation of centrist Democratic policy, highlight and expand Senate experience."

Glenn determined to strike an independent course. But because he was not by nature a passionate man—indeed, just the opposite—his efforts were difficult to see. His passion was too easily lost in a sea of mathematical reasoning: "Right now there are 247 nuclear power reactors in the world," he explained in 1981. "Each develops about 146 gigawatts (one gigawatt equals 1 billion watts) of power. Each of these gigawatts develops about 250 kilograms of plutonium each year. A nation with fairly low sophistication in nuclear matters can make a bomb from ten kilograms of plutonium. . . . If you multiply all that, the potential from 247 peaceful nuclear reactors is between four thousand and eight thousand bombs per year. That's what we're trying to prevent," he said at last. "That's why we passed the Nuclear Nonproliferation Act." His insistence that the United States stop supplying Israel with nuclear materials clearly separated him from the policies of the Reagan administration. But his reasons for distrusting that ally often appeared obscure to the voters.

Glenn's attempt to run an issue-oriented campaign also clashed with voter expectations of political images. In an ironic way, he became a victim of his earlier popularity. His fame as an astronaut had been unexpected. He had not needed to project an image—he was an image! But, as a presidential candidate in an era of mass communications, Glenn needed to create a presence, a presidential aura that would reach voters who were not necessarily interested in the issues at all. For this task, he had no experience.

He could only run on his record, most of which reflected his interest in technology. He remained fiercely loyal to the space program, viewing its technological triumphs as an ingredient of economic recovery. He deplored a lagging interest in research and development: "We have always been well advised in this country to put some money into research even in poor times," he said. "The fact is we get back far more from the space program that we put into it."

Aware that the state of the economy would play a major role in the 1984 election, Glenn hesitated to support Reaganomics. "In the military, you're trained to wait and wait before you make a commitment of your forces," he explained. "In government, you have a lot of pressures, the push of the press and everything else. But I think you want to get everything you need to know first. There's no need to take a position until that time." His reluctance to lead the Democratic opposition in the Senate reflected his partial approval of the president's program. He, too, supported tax cuts for business to stimulate investment, improve productivity, and then, through the trickle-down effect, create jobs. But he opposed the president's selective approach to free enterprise. He argued for consumer protection. He preferred socially directed tax measures to discourage pollution and increase civilian research. In the end he voted for the administration package. Asked later about the popularity of conservatism, he acknowledged a shift in public opinion: "Government still has a role. But I think we as Democrats are going to hesitate a bit before we favor establishing a lot of new programs from Washington."

As he passed his sixtieth birthday, in July 1981, Glenn emerged as a major force in the Democratic party, running third in the polls behind the liberals Walter Mondale and Edward Kennedy. But here, too, he hesitated to commit himself and lagged behind other candidates in building an organization: "Some things about politics take some getting used to. Asking for money. . . . I'd rather wrestle a gorilla than ask for fifty cents." But he went through the necessary appearances to keep his name in the public eye. Unlike the other candidates, he did not worry about name recognition. He knew how to attract a crowd. On the twentieth anniversary of his space flight, for example, his picture appeared in newspapers around the country. The release of a Hollywood movie about the astronauts, *The Right Stuff,* would provide more publicity. Glenn thought, consequently, that he could go over the heads of party leaders to the people themselves. If he was confident in nothing else, he was certain of his fame.

His connection to the space program also helped to define his political position. He became a strong advocate of national regeneration through technology. He recommended basic research in space, science, and industry. "To say that smaller and simpler is better and more beautiful is nice," he said about the military reforms proposed by Senator Gary Hart, "but it's not true. We can't give up technological superiority, because then we'd have to match the Soviets tank-tube for tank-tube, and we can't. We have to make our technology work." He conducted a poll of American Nobel Prize winners in chemistry and medicine since World War II; it showed, to his satisfaction, the importance of federal funding. "When we cut off inquiry into the unknown, we're eating our seed corn. It doesn't make any sense. But if you give Americans the proper tools, they can outproduce and outcompete anybody, head and shoulders."

Glenn's enthusiasm for science coexisted with his fear of runaway technology. He worried about the Bomb—"wrapping even more fingers around the nuclear trigger"—and he cosponsored resolutions in the Senate to revive SALT II. "In some ways nuclear power may have replaced . . . big steel capacities that fifteen years ago were almost a status symbol for developing nations," he said about the pressure for nuclear proliferation, "but . . . unless we're willing to really take a tough stand on this issue and try to lead the world, time may be running out for us." The birth of his first grandchild—the son of his son—symbolized his obligations to the future: "I would like to think that my children, my great-grandchildren, and probably my great-great-grandchildren might have a hope of living in a world free from nuclear dangers and that there would be a comprehensive test ban somehow, some way in the future." He pleaded for ratification of the limited agreements reached a decade earlier.

Against the backdrop of such moral issues, Glenn resented the effluvia of politics—the constant talk about style, presence, and the dullness of his speeches. Despite the importance of his image, he seemed to have difficulty generating enthusiasm. "I felt very passionately about my country when I was on top of that booster, and in two world wars," he said, dismissing any lack of personal fervor. "It wasn't rhetoric or gobbledygook on the line, it was me. But I don't see any need to hoot and holler about it." Reluctantly he hired a coach: "If Ted Kennedy can lose weight, I can learn to speak." But, in fact, he never did learn to relax in public, although he sometimes succeeded in using his shortcoming to good effect: "I'm glad to be here," he said, slapping a lectern with both hands, "because the Democratic party needs a magnetic, charismatic, and electrifying speaker."

Glenn went on the campaign trail in 1982, stumped thirty-six states on behalf of ninety Democratic candidates. He focused on his own pockets of strength—the South, the border states, nonurban areas elsewhere: "Small-town Ohio relates to small-town Iowa and small-town New Hampshire," he said, explaining his strategy. With Mondale and Kennedy controlling the liberal flank, Glenn occupied the political center: "I'm naturally pretty much in the middle, and people know it." In the off-year elections, 80 percent of the candidates he supported were successful. He concluded that the American people wanted "stability and a sense of hope, not radical change."

His speeches reached for tradition—offered the same vision as his address to the joint session of Congress twenty years before: "Whatever other problems we have, this nation remains today exactly what it was at the time of its founding—a land of unparalleled blessing, of unparalleled hope, of unparalleled opportunity. We remain that beacon of freedom that stands before the rest of the world." Often he recited from the Pledge of Allegiance—"one nation . . . under God . . . indivisible," pausing after each phrase to explicate the familiar text—or he quoted from Emerson, as Robert Kennedy did, about "new horizons, the future that . . . can eclipse anything we have ever known in the past."

He sought to be presidential, to rise above the objections of the party establishment: "That's what I did back home in Ohio when they said they were going to oppose me." He appealed to consensus, hoping in his personification of American dreams to transcend differences of class, race, and region. He hoped to personalize the political spectrum in order to make it disappear. "I have a big ego," he admitted. "But for me the glitter, the glamour, the attention mean very little now, I've had it all. I've had the ticker-tape parades."

In the warm April sunshine, schoolchildren waved American flags along the edge of John Glenn Highway, which led into New Concord, Ohio. He waved as he passed them and moved to the podium in the gymnasium of John Glenn High School. He wore a charcoal-gray suit and red silk tie, carrying at least ten pounds more than he had in the days of Project Mercury; his hair was thinner, mostly gray. He was almost sixty-two. "Being back home here with all of you brings with it a flood of memories," he told the townspeople who had come to hear the announcement of his candidacy. "We were taught honesty and fairness and compassion for those who had less, and a confidence and faith in the future that in this land a young person from this small town could aspire to anything." Those values still lived; they were, he said, "truly the heart of the American experiment, and they must be the soul of government as well.

"My own life in some ways is what this country is all about. . . . My ambition is really for the country. You may think that's just talk, but it's what drove me in combat, it's what drove me in the space program, and it's what drives me to be president."

Epilogue

It would be presumptuous to write a finale to these careers: Each remains active and unfinished.

In 1984 John Glenn ran for president. But, after defeats in the early primaries, he ran out of money and withdrew from the campaign. He continued to serve as the senior senator from Ohio.

In 1984 Jane Fonda won critical and commercial acclaim for her first television film, *The Dollmaker;* published another book, *Women Coming of Age,* which became an immediate best-seller; and introduced her own line of gymnastic clothing.

In 1984 Phyllis Schlafly served on the platform committee of the Republican National Convention, which approved her conservative agenda regarding abortion, school prayer, and "Star Wars" space missiles. She remained the driving force of the Eagle Forum lobby.

In 1984 George Wallace greeted all the Democratic presidential contenders on the steps of the state capitol in Montgomery, where he advised them to avoid being shot. Later he endorsed Walter Mondale and Geraldine Ferraro. He was serving an unprecedented fourth term as governor of Alabama.

A sense of destiny rests at their center of being. They are ambitious people—and aggressive. Each of them pursued power relentlessly. Their militance represents a basic element of their public identities. They appeal to a fighting spirit: "the fighting judge"; "the MIG-mad marine"; "Saint Jane"; the woman who said that God's greatest gift to America was the atom bomb.

Anger is another common denominator. Because of an accepted decorum in politics and because they are proficient at self-control, they seldom permit anger to erupt in public. But there are enough examples of rage to establish its presence. Anger may explain the often-stated desire to destroy their opposition. They sought through power not only to "show off" their strength but also to "show" their opponents. In the four careers there are unmistakable, recurrent themes of vengeance.

Ambition, aggression, anger—these are clues for understanding success in America. But whatever the psychological truth, such impulses lack any content in themselves; they are energy without matter. What shapes ambition and gives it substance is the historical reality that surrounds every individual life.

Fonda, Wallace, Schlafly, and Glenn succeeded by embracing the world as they found it. Whether as politician, actress, lobbyist, soldier, or entrepreneur, they worked best within existing institutions. Even when they protested specific policies, they did so within the limits of the law. None, in other words, challenged the basic structure of society.

This pragmatic spirit enabled them to survive the dramatic changes of their lifetimes. For in the quarter of a century between 1958 and 1983, the nation underwent a major transformation of values: The principle of separate but equal gave way to a multiracial society; the feminine mystique passed on to the two-paycheck household; the belief in American technology confronted international competition and ecological limits; the idea of military hegemony faced pluralistic communism and the rise of the Third World.

These changes have touched the life of every American, but especially those who emerged as public figures. The careers of Fonda, Wallace, Schlafly, and Glenn make no sense outside this historical context. But, at the same time, the course of history appears equally absurd without the lives of those who made it—and were made by it.

Consider the changes they embody:

George Wallace began his career in the world of Jim Crow as a southern populist, the candidate of the NAACP. The civil rights movement of the late 1950s pushed him to the right as he defended segregation and states' rights. He earned a national reputation by defying the federal government—but only to the limit of the law. Then, he carried his appeal into the North, where he proved that the race question was not a southern problem but a national crisis. He ran for president four times, losing finally to Jimmy Carter, another southerner, who offered the voters a more sanitized version of his own program. He returned to Alabama to preside over a new atmosphere of racial accommodation.

Jane Fonda's acting career typified the transformation of sexual values. Her early roles reflected a prevailing fear of sexuality: She played the parts of flirts, sexual victims, or frustrated wives. After moving to France in the mid-1960s, her roles symbolized a loosening of values: the acceptance of nudity, adultery, and obscenity. Her personal attitude toward marriage reflected larger social trends—openness about sex, increasing divorce, and the rise in two-parent childrearing. After 1970 her own politicization served as a model for her roles. She portrayed women as independent people. As a businesswoman, moreover, she epitomized the female entrepreneur of the 1970s, merging career, family, and social involvement. By the 1980s sexual freedom and beauty appeared less important than concern about fitness, health, and aging.

Phyllis Schlafly remained consistent to conservative principles. What changed dramatically in her career was the place of conservatism in American society. Her staunch anti-communism of the late 1950s appeared as a "fringe" movement (so characterized in *The New York Times* Index), far from the political mainstream. The candidacy of Barry Goldwater in 1964 offered a wider audience for her views, but his defeat greatly diminished her opportunities. She broke with Nixon and then with Ford. Meanwhile, she developed her own following among conservatives and used it to defeat the ERA. By the late 1970s she had emerged as a central figure in the conservative movement. When Ronald Reagan defeated the liberal consensus in 1980, she could ride his coattails into national politics. For twenty-five years she had kept the faith; the conservative revival mirrored her own.

John Glenn was a soldier first, a cold warrior in the marines and NASA. His life had depended on the superiority of American technology. After his flight into space, he entered the Kennedy orbit, where he imbibed a cautious brand of liberalism. In the mid-1960s he became a business executive in a multinational corporation and a strong proponent of traditional values. The second Kennedy assassination rekindled his interest in politics, but by then the values he represented had lost their popularity. Not until Watergate had destroyed public confidence in the political establishment could he win an election. His career in the Senate reflected his lifelong commitments: moderate reform, suspicion of foreign powers, and respect for technology. Such values, despite his unsuccessful presidential campaign, typified the national mood of the early 1980s.

The changes of these four lives serve as paradigms for the period.

To summarize them so quickly, however, eviscerates their meaning. In retrospect it is seductive to emphasize the logic and fluidity of these careers: their development appears natural, perhaps predestined. It is too tidy. What is apparent from their biographies is just the opposite. Nothing was ever inevitable. At crucial times in their lives each chose to act in a certain way. Why and how they chose depended on a variety of factors—personal will, ideology, ambition, the circumstances of the moment. The consequences, for better or worse, came later. For in the end it is always choice—human choice—that becomes the stuff of history.

Bibliographic Note

Perhaps the most obvious, yet startling aspect of fame in America today is the insatiable thirst for information about the private lives of public figures. There is, quite simply, an astonishing abundance of material relating to the subjects of this book. Indeed, one suspects that the willingness to reveal personal information to the general public represents a basic ingredient of the personality of success in a democratic society, what might be viewed as an umbilical relationship between leaders and followers, celebrities and fans. For, if fame is its own reward, it hinges nonetheless on the continued feeding of the public maw. In any case, the availability of this "public" archive greatly facilitated the research of this book.

The life of Jane Fonda is amply documented in the countless interviews she and her family have given to the press. The best study of her life is Thomas Kiernan, *Jane Fonda: Heroine for Our Time* (New

271

York, 1982), which represents a substantial revision of his earlier book, *Jane: An Intimate Biography of Jane Fonda* (New York, 1973). Also helpful is James Brough, *The Fabulous Fondas* (New York, 1973); Fred Lawrence Guiles, *Jane Fonda: The Actress in Her Time* (Garden City, N.Y., 1982); and the autobiography of her father, Henry Fonda, written with Howard Teichmann, *Fonda: My Life* (New York, 1981). Jane Fonda has written autobiographical fragments in Lillian Ross and Helen Ross, *The Player: A Profile of an Art* (New York, 1962); *Jane Fonda's Workout Book* (New York, 1981); and Femmy DeLyser, *The Jane Fonda Workout Book for Pregnancy, Birth and Recovery* (New York, 1982). For a complete description of her films, see George Haddad-Garcia, *The Films of Jane Fonda* (Secaucus, N.J., 1981).

For George Wallace, the best study is Marshall Frady's *Wallace* (New York, 1968), which may be supplemented by Wallace's autobiography, *Stand Up for America* (Garden City, N.Y., 1976). Wallace's emergence as a national politician is well documented in Bill Jones, *The Wallace Story* (Northport, Ala., 1966). Other useful books include Jody Carlson, *George C. Wallace and the Politics of Powerlessness* (New Brunswick, N.J., 1981); Wayne Greenhaw, *Watch Out for George Wallace* (Englewood Cliffs, N.J., 1976); and Michael Dorman, *The George Wallace Myth* (New York, 1976). For revealing personal stories, see also two family histories: Cornelia Wallace, *C'nelia* (Philadelphia, 1976), and George Wallace, Jr., *The Wallaces of Alabama* (Chicago, 1975).

The career of Phyllis Schlafly is best elucidated in her own voluminous writings—nine books, the monthly *Phyllis Schlafly Report* (published since 1967), and numerous articles and speeches. Carol Felsenthal's study, *The Sweetheart of the Silent Majority: The Biography of Phyllis Schlafly* (Garden City, N.Y., 1981) offers a balanced overview. In addition to these published works, Mrs. Schlafly granted an extended interview in October 1983 and, even more important, offered selected unpublished material for this book. These items are marked in the Sources section as "Schlafly Papers." They have been donated to the Stanford University Library in Palo Alto, California.

The most complete biography of John Glenn is Frank Van Riper, *Glenn: The Astronaut Who Would Be President* (New York, 1983). It should be supplemented by an older study, Philip N. Pierce, *John H. Glenn: Astronaut* (New York, 1962) as well as Glenn's autobiographical writings in a collection assembled by the original astronauts, *We Seven* (New York, 1963). Tom Wolfe's entertaining and astute

The Right Stuff (New York, 1979) places Glenn's early career in historical context. For the transcript of Glenn's flight into space, see the National Aeronautics and Space Administration's *Results of the First U.S. Manned Orbital Space Flight* (Washington, D.C., 1962). The psychiatric profile of the astronauts appears in George E. Ruff and Edwin Z. Levy, "Psychiatric Evaluation of Candidates for Space Flight," *American Journal of Psychiatry* 116 (November 1959), pp. 285–91. Glenn's career in the Senate is documented in the *Congressional Record*.

Sources

JANE SEYMOUR FONDA (I)

Page

5   "You could feel": quoted in Thomas Kiernan, *Jane Fonda: Heroine for Our Time* (New York, 1982), p. 73.

6   "The only thing": Alfred Aronowitz, "Lady Jane," *Saturday Evening Post,* March 23, 1963, p. 24.

8   "a sort of New England": Lillian Ross and Helen Ross, eds., *The Player: A Profile of an Art* (New York, 1962), p. 93.

8   "an eagle eye": [Henry Fonda], *Fonda: My Life* (New York, 1981), p. 199.

8   "It's not natural": *Ibid.,* pp. 163–64.

8   "a woman standing": *Ibid.,* pp. 164–65.

8   "I was scared": Ross and Ross, *Player,* p. 93.

9   "we'd all pour": Brooke Hayward, *Haywire* (New York, 1977), p. 159.

9   "Whenever Jane, and later": quoted in Kiernan, *Jane Fonda* [1982], p. 14.

9   "From as early": Jane Fonda, *Jane Fonda's Workout Book* (New York, 1981), p. 9.

10   "found that his kids": quoted in Kiernan, *Jane Fonda* [1982], p. 16.

10   "I don't remember": Ross and Ross, *Player,* p. 93.

10   "I've spent [my childhood]": Aronowitz, "Lady Jane," p. 24.

11   "He got furious": Oriana Fallaci, "Jane Fonda: 'I'm Coming into Focus,'" *McCall's,* February 1971, p. 147.

11   "They just cut": quoted in Fred Lawrence Guiles, *Jane Fonda: The Actress in Her Time* (Garden City, N.Y., 1982), p. 33.

12   "If anybody mentions": [Henry Fonda], *My Life,* p. 211.

12   "the delicate intricacies": Kiernan, *Jane Fonda* [1982], p. 24.

12   "We were all eating": [Henry Fonda], *My Life,* p. 212.

12   "Just look at me!": Guiles, *Jane Fonda,* p. 39.

12   "Very sorry": *Ibid.,* p. 40.

12   "I sat on the edge": [Henry Fonda], *My Life,* p. 219.

13   "If you lose your mother": Ross and Ross, *Player,* p. 92.

13   "Is it true?": [Henry Fonda], *My Life,* p. 225.

13   "I was brought up": Kiernan, *Jane Fonda* [1982], p. 61.

14   "If you let him": [Henry Fonda], *My Life,* p. 231.

14   "Jane would wake up": *Ibid.,* p. 225.

14   "As a young girl": Thomas Kiernan, *Jane: An Intimate Biography* (New York, 1973), p. 36.

14   "By the time": *Ibid.,* p. 51.

15   "I felt that a different": Jane Fonda, *Workout,* p. 13.

15   "Eating binges": *Ibid.,* pp. 13–14.

15   Jane did not menstruate: Aimée Lee Ball, "The Unofficial Jane Fonda," *Redbook,* January 1982, p. 28.

15   "It's a phase": Martha Weinman Lear, "Whatever Happened to Mr. Fonda's Baby Jane?" *Redbook,* August 1969, p. 130.

15   "It was a bit": Ross and Ross, *Player,* p. 95.

15   "I had no technique": [Henry Fonda], *My Life,* p. 256.

15   "I never went": Ross and Ross, *Player,* p. 96.

16   "When I discovered": Aronowitz, "Lady Jane," p. 24.

16   "a reputation for being": quoted in Kiernan, *Jane Fonda* [1982], p. 61.

16   "suddenly turned into": *Ibid.*

16   "pep pills": Jane Fonda, *Workout*, p. 14.

16   "They sat up": [Henry Fonda], *My Life*, p. 270.

16   "knew almost nothing": Ross and Ross, *Player*, p. 96.

16   "Everyone was in such : Kiernan, *Jane Fonda* [1982], p. 56.

17   "I was eighteen": Thomas Thompson, "A Place in the Sun All Her Own," *Life*, March 29, 1968, p. 70.

17   "After a month": Ross and Ross, *Player*, p. 96.

17   "I wanted to jump in": *Ibid.*, p. 97.

17   "It's the last thing": James Brough, *The Fabulous Fondas* (New York, 1973), pp. 169–70.

17   "a beauty with the dazzle": "Miss Jane Fonda," *Vogue* (April 1, 1958), p. 107.

17   "an uptown beatnik": Brough, *Fabulous Fondas*, p. 170.

17   "I was feeling": Ross and Ross, *Player*, p. 98.

18   "For the first time": *Ibid.*

18   "panic in the eyes": Aronowitz, "Lady Jane," p. 24.

18   "Are you a human": Susan Strasberg, *Bitter Sweet* (New York, 1980), p. 15.

18   "I didn't believe": Kiernan, *Jane Fonda* [1982], p. 75.

18   "The first impression": *Ibid.*

18   "You are sensitive": Aronowitz, "Lady Jane," p. 24.

18   "he saw a tremendous": Guiles, *Jane Fonda*, p. 71.

18   "Before, I'd been scared": Kiernan, *Jane Fonda* [1982], p. 76.

19   "The light bulb": Thompson, "A Place," p. 70.

19   "Now I know": Helen Markel, "Henry Fonda's Daughter Goes into Orbit," *Good Housekeeping*, March 1960, p. 36.

19   "inevitable discovery": "The Inevitable Discovery of Jane Fonda," *Look*, November 10, 1959, p. 122.

19   "The reason I loved it": "Playboy Interview: Jane Fonda and Tom Hayden," *Playboy*, April, 1974, p. 85.

19   "Acting gave her": Kiernan, *Jane Fonda* [1982], p. 80.

19   "Acting is holy hell": Markel, "Henry Fonda's Daughter," p. 36.

19   "Control is what I'm after": *Ibid.*, p. 40.

20   "It's scary what's going": *Ibid.*

20   "I have grown up": Kiernan, *Jane Fonda* [1982], p. 90.

20 "I think marriage": *Ibid.*, p. 109.

20 "The thing I object": Guiles, *Jane Fonda*, p. 91.

20 "had any bad effects": Markel, "Henry Fonda's Daughter," p. 38.

20 "I was brought up": Aronowitz, "Lady Jane," p. 25.

20 "I wouldn't be anywhere": Jon Whitcomb, "A Father's Daughter," *Cosmopolitan*, July 1960, p. 10.

20 "like a squirrel": Brough, *The Fabulous Fondas*, p. 178.

21 "Nothing could possibly": George Haddad-Garcia, *The Films of Jane Fonda* (Secaucus, N.J., 1981), p. 74.

21 "I enjoyed making myself": Ross and Ross, *Player*, pp. 100–101.

21 "I began to see": *Ibid.*

21 "She could be": Aronowitz, "Lady Jane," p. 23.

22 "I never would have thought": Haddad-Garcia, *Films of Jane Fonda*, p. 80.

22 "Jane Fonda cops": John Springer, *The Fondas: The Films and Careers of Henry, Jane and Peter Fonda* (New York, 1970), p. 179.

22 "To do it": Ross and Ross, *Player*, pp. 99–100.

22 "an American original": Aronowitz, "Lady Jane," p. 23.

22 "A stage career": Haddad-Garcia, *Films of Jane Fonda*, p. 89.

22 "Here were two women": Hayward, *Haywire*, p. 285.

23 "My whole childhood": Kiernan, *Jane Fonda* [1982], pp. 118–19.

23 "It's like her life": Aronowitz, "Lady Jane," p. 23.

23 "strangely familiar": Springer, *The Fondas*, p. 186.

23 "the enormous thing": Guiles, *Jane Fonda*, p. 108.

23 "Yeah, yeah, I always": Aronowitz, "Lady Jane," p. 23.

23 "Now a new talent": *The New Republic*, November 24, 1962, p. 26.

23 "I have star quality": Aronowitz, "Lady Jane," p. 23.

23 "Now . . . all I want": Kiernan, *Jane Fonda* [1982], p. 118.

24 "The girl's look": "A U.S. Jane Conquers Paris," *Life*, January 10, 1964, p. 75.

24 "My rebellion against": [Henry Fonda], *My Life*, p. 324.

24 "One can't make films": Pierre Kast, "Jane," *Cahiers du Cinéma*, December 1963–January 1964, p. 187.

GEORGE CORLEY WALLACE (I)

Page

25   "I'm as happy": *Wall Street Journal,* May 6, 1958, p. 1.

26   "the handshakingest candidate": *Montgomery Advertiser,* January 24, 1958, p. 5A.

26   "get a living": *Montgomery Advertiser,* February 19, 1958, p. 8A.

26   "our way of life": *Montgomery Advertiser,* February 16, 1958, pp. 1–2.

27   "area of this country": George C. Wallace, *Stand Up for America* (Garden City, N.Y., 1976), p. 10.

27   "a sort of Tom Sawyer": *Ibid.,* pp. 11–12.

27   "I must have been born": *Ibid.,* p. 16.

28   "Dr. Wallace tried": Marshall Frady, *Wallace* (New York, 1968), pp. 55–56.

28   "I made up in aggressiveness": George Wallace, *Stand Up,* pp. 17–18.

29   "I wasn't but about ten": Frady, *Wallace,* p. 59.

29   "Winning that page's election": George Wallace, *Stand Up,* p. 21.

29   "stood on that bottom": Wayne Greenhaw, *Watch Out for George Wallace* (Englewood Cliffs, N.J., 1976), p. 94.

30   "people dying for a cause": Robert Sherrill, *Gothic Politics in the Deep South* (New York, 1968), p. 269.

30   "I did it just": Frady, *Wallace,* pp. 59–60.

30   "best sport on campus": *Ibid.,* p. 83.

30   "I hung on by": George Wallace, *Stand Up,* p. 26.

30   "I preferred to start": *Ibid.,* p. 31.

30   "the appearance of a somewhat": *Ibid.,* p. 33.

31   "This practical demonstration": *Ibid.,* p. 36.

31   "I wasn't really awake": Greenhaw, *Watch Out,* p. 229.

31   "I tried to maintain": George Wallace, *Stand Up,* p. 41.

32   "You'd see all them": Frady, *Wallace,* p. 86.

32   "flight fatigue, anxiety": Michael Dorman, *The George Wallace Myth* (New York, 1976), p. 123.

32   "Hell, I was too glad": Frady, *Wallace,* pp. 87–88.

32   "Call it fear": George Wallace, *Stand Up,* pp. 47–48.

32   "severe anxiety state": Greenhaw, *Watch Out,* p. 238.

32   "Never again would Lurleen": George Wallace, *Stand Up*,
        p. 49.

33   "I had seen enough": *Ibid.*, p. 52.

33   "Energetic, ambitious, liberal": Frady, *Wallace*, p. 98.

33–34   "to get out": Carl Solberg, *Hubert Humphrey* (New York,
        1984), p. 17.

34   "racial prejudice . . . but my": George Wallace, *Stand Up*,
        p. 57.

35   "You've got to have": Greenhaw, *Watch Out*, p. 18.

35   "I was away": George C. Wallace, "Introduction" in George
        Wallace, Jr., *The Wallaces of Alabama* (Chicago, 1975), p.
        xiv.

35   "I remember . . . that he": *Ibid.*, pp. 40–41.

35   "He was tense": Greenhaw, *Watch Out*, p. 238.

36   "The dual school": George Wallace, *Stand Up*, p. 128.

36   "Gestapo methods": Jody Carlson, *George C. Wallace and
        the Politics of Powerlessness* (New Brunswick, N.J., 1981), p.
        21.

36   "every member of the FBI": Frady, *Wallace*, pp. 121–22.

37   "To my good friend": George Wallace, *Stand Up*, p. 162.

37   "Mr. Eisenhower, who": Dorman, *George Wallace Myth*, p.
        25.

37   "which has made it": Bill Jones, *The Wallace Story*
        (Northport, Ala., 1966), p. 8.

37   "Never succumb to the idea": *Montgomery Advertiser*, Janu-
        ary 28, 1958, p. 1.

38   "total resistance to the efforts": *Montgomery Advertiser*,
        February 14, 1958, p. 1.

38   "more jobs, higher living": *Montgomery Advertiser*, February
        5, 1958, p. 2A.

38   "the shameful educational": *Montgomery Advertiser*, Febru-
        ary 7, 1958, p. 4D.

38   "absolute and complete. . . . We can": *Montgomery Adver-
        tiser*, March 2, 1958, p. 1G.

38   "KEEP ALABAMA SOUTHERN": *Montgomery Advertiser*, May 4,
        1958, p. 3A.

38   "more worn than washed": *Montgomery Advertiser*, May 29,
        1958, p. 2A.

38   "Out-litigate 'em": *Montgomery Advertiser*, March 17, 1958,
        p. 2A.

38   "Fair play for all": Jones, *Wallace Story*, p. 14.
38   "Sure, I'm sorta tense": *Montgomery Advertiser*, May 5, 1958, pp. 1–2A.
39   "neither my children": *Montgomery Advertiser*, June 3, 1958, p. 1A.
39   "Where is John Patterson?": Greenhaw, *Watch Out*, pp. 114–15.
40   "John Patterson out-niggahed": Frady, *Wallace*, p. 127.
40   "I had set my heart": George Wallace, *Stand Up*, p. 71.
40   "You'd see him": Frady, *Wallace*, p. 130.
40   "The days were long": Greenhaw, *Watch Out*, p. 198.
40   "my favorite hero": George Wallace, *Stand Up*, p. 72.
40   "to keep pace": Jones, *Wallace Story*, pp. 38–39.
40   "I couldn't make": Carl M. Brauer, *John F. Kennedy and the Second Reconstruction* (New York, 1977), p. 141.
41   "those lily-livered": Greenhaw, *Watch Out*, pp. 120–21.
41   "a low-down carpetbaggin' ": Frady, *Wallace*, p. 179.
41   "a judicial dictatorship": George C. Wallace, *"Hear Me Out"* (Anderson, S.C., 1968), p. 84.
41   "will firmly resist": *Ibid.*, p. 57.
41   "As your governor": *Ibid.*, p. 130.
41   "the ultimate purpose": Jones, *Wallace Story*, p. 80.
41   "I pledge to": George Wallace, *"Hear Me Out"*, pp. 80–81.
41   "How can you": *Time*, June 8, 1962, pp. 25–26.
41   "It's been the same": *Ibid.*
42   "Those federal courts": Jones, *Wallace Story*, p. 50.
42   "Millions of Americans": *Ibid.*, p. 52.
42   "Those people who want": George Wallace, *"Hear Me Out"*, pp. 137–38.
42   "I'm gonna make race": Frady, *Wallace*, p. 140.
42   "I'm so glad": George Wallace, *Stand Up*, p. 74.
42   "Today I have stood": Frady, *Wallace*, pp. 141–42.
43   "I never had money": *New York Times*, May 14, 1963, p. 26.
43   "I don't know how": Ray Jenkins, "Mr. & Mrs. Wallace Run for Governor of Alabama," *New York Times Magazine*, April 24, 1966, p. 92.
43   "Almost instantly": Greenhaw, *Watch Out*, p. 200.
44   "This is a fine city": Frady, *Wallace*, pp. 151–63.
44   "a phony and a fraud": *Ibid.*, p. 161.

44   "This military dictatorship": *New York Times,* May 16, 1963, p. 23.

45   "Mr. President": George Wallace, *Stand Up,* pp. 77–78.

45   "who could go to bed": Brauer, *John F. Kennedy,* pp. 255–56.

45   "Your guess is as good": *New York Times,* May 20, 1963, p. 20.

45   "I embody the sovereignty": George Wallace, *"Hear Me Out",* p. 133.

45   "If Martin Luther King": *Newsweek,* June 10, 1963, p. 30.

45   "Down South . . . at least": *New York Times,* June 3, 1963, p. 16.

45   "basic inherent question": *U.S. News and World Report,* June 17, 1963, p. 19.

46   "All they wanted": Greenhaw, *Watch Out,* p. 3.

46   "I intend to be present": *New York Times,* June 9, 1963, p. 50.

46   "I have kept": *New York Times,* June 10, 1963, p. 1.

46   "The unwelcomed, unwanted": Greenhaw, *Watch Out,* p. 141.

46   "This is a bitter": George Wallace, *Stand Up,* p. 81.

47   "I want the Supreme Court": *New York Times,* August 6, 1963, p. 17.

47   "We will win": *New York Times,* September 5, 1963, p. 20.

47   "The society is coming apart": *New York Times,* September 6, 1963, p. 14.

47   "It would do the nation": *Wall Street Journal,* September 11, 1963, p. 14.

47   "They go to Africa": *New York Times,* October 11, 1963, p. 24.

48   "the real African": George Wallace, *"Hear Me Out",* pp. 134, 51–52; Frady, *Wallace,* p. 172.

48   "We may disagree": *New York Times,* November 23, 1963, p. 8.

48   "Are you glad": George Wallace, *Stand Up,* p. 84.

48   "Do you think": Sherrill, *Gothic Politics,* p. 261.

PHYLLIS STEWART SCHLAFLY (I)

Page

49   "I think you're a product": Interview, October 31, 1983; Schlafly Papers.

50   "We had a happy": *Ibid.*

50   "I grew up": *Ibid.*

50   "There were hard years": *New York Times,* January 24, 1980, p. C2.

50   "The true stories": "Titles of American History Month Essays," November 15, 1968; Schlafly Papers.

50   "a very strong woman": Interview, October 31, 1983; Schlafly Papers.

51   "would much rather": *Ibid.*

51   "We had less": *Ibid.*

51   "I never had a bicycle": *New York Times,* January 24, 1980, p. C2.

51   "I felt a compulsion": Carol Felsenthal, *The Sweetheart of the Silent Majority: The Biography of Phyllis Schlafly* (Garden City, N.Y., 1981), pp. 24–25.

51   "I've been very lucky": *Ibid.,* p. 32.

51   "The sexual desire": Phyllis Schlafly, *The Power of the Positive Woman* (New Rochelle, N.Y., 1977), p. 17.

52   "The best thing": Dale Wittner, " 'All Women's Liberationists Hate Men and Children,' " *Chicago Tribune Magazine,* May 20, 1973, p. 22.

52   "I didn't belong": *New York Times,* January 24, 1980, p. C2.

52   "Take advantage": Felsenthal, *Sweetheart,* p. 30.

52   "I read all the novels": Interview, October 31, 1983; Schlafly Papers.

53   "We believe that the people": Felsenthal, *Sweetheart,* p. 80.

54   "blond banking expert": *St. Louis Globe-Democrat,* March 6, 1949.

54   "Before the meaning": Felsenthal, *Sweetheart,* p. 82.

54   "it was love": Linda Witt, "Equal Rights at the Schlaflys," *People Weekly,* March 30, 1981, p. 104.

54   "Cover girl with executive": *Ibid.,* p. 103.

54   "Fred . . . rescued me": Felsenthal, *Sweetheart,* p. 79.

54   "a profusion of white": *St. Louis Globe-Democrat,* October 20, 1949.

55 "A family cannot be run": Schlafly, *Positive Woman,* p. 50.

55 "A Positive Woman cannot": *Ibid.,* p. 17.

55 "Whereas a woman's chief": *Ibid.,* p. 54.

55 "No. I did": Barbara Grizzuti Harrison, "The Woman Who Is Fighting the Law That Most Women Want," *McCall's* (April 1982), p. 101.

56 "There are thousands": *St. Louis Post Dispatch,* March 3, 1952, p. 2D.

56 "As a housewife": *Alton Evening Telegraph,* January 22, 1952.

56 "flapped around the district": Interview, October 31, 1983; Schlafly Papers.

56 "I never ran out": *St. Louis Globe-Democrat,* April 10, 1952.

56 "as a tribute . . . to the": *Illinois State Register,* June 17, 1952, p. 3.

56 "A woman's place": Proceedings of the Illinois State Republican Convention, 1952, p. 43; Schlafly Papers.

57 "I never had a chance": Interview, October 31, 1983; Schlafly Papers.

57 "sex had nothing": Felsenthal, *Sweetheart,* p. 161.

57 "My career rose": Interview, October 31, 1983; Schlafly Papers.

58 "one of the very best": "Study Outline: The Korean War"; Schlafly Papers.

58 "The eggheads like": "Adlai Stevenson"; Schlafly Papers.

58 "Which New Deal": "Information Please for Republicans"; Schlafly Papers.

58 "Had Americans understood": Phyllis Schlafly, "Teach About Communism in Catholic Schools," *Catholic Educator,* November 1960, p. 224.

58 "Most great leaders": Joseph Vecsey and Phyllis Schlafly, *Mindszenty the Man* (St. Louis, 1972), p. 5.

59 "battle of ideas": *Chicago Tribune,* March 11, 1958, II, p. 2.

59 "What prominent Fair Deal": "Quiz on Communism: Who Said That?"; Schlafly Papers.

60 "Do you support": *DAR Magazine,* September 1958, p. 789.

60 "If you have a good": *Chicago Tribune,* March 11, 1958, II, p. 2.

60   "discipline, hard work": *DAR Magazine,* September 1958, p. 789.

60   "No woman would ever": Schlafly, *Positive Woman,* p. 19.

60   "When I started": Interview, October 31, 1983; Schlafly Papers.

61   "We particularly agree": *New York Times,* December 15, 1975, p. 44.

61   "too few people": Schlafly, "Teach About Communism," p. 220.

61   "unique pitch": Interview, October 31, 1983; Schlafly Papers.

61   "designed to combat": Schlafly, "Teach About Communism," p. 221.

61   "world ignorance of Communist": Felsenthal, *Sweetheart,* p. 167.

61   "threaten the right": *Ibid.*

61   "that any teacher": Schlafly, "Teach About Communism," p. 220.

62   "I was approaching things": Interview, October 31, 1983; Schlafly Papers.

62   "one of our most loyal": Felsenthal, *Sweetheart,* p. xviii.

62   "fifteen years of sustained": Schlafly, "Teach About Communism," pp. 221–26.

62   "You can't stop": Interview, October 31, 1983; Schlafly Papers.

62   "While I believe": *Alton Evening Telegraph,* April 23, 1960, p. 1.

63   "It was a hopeless": Interview, October 31, 1983; Schlafly Papers.

63   "I believe this to be": Phyllis Schlafly, *A Choice Not an Echo* (Alton, Ill., 1964), p. 75.

63   "a pink dress": *Chicago Tribune,* July 27, 1960, II, p. 1.

63   "Goldwater was exciting": Interview, October 31, 1983; Schlafly Papers.

63   "I made speeches": *Ibid.*

63   "We had the firsthand": *Ibid.*

63   "the most terrible": *Ibid.*

64   "They have infiltrated": *Alton Evening Telegraph,* November 17, 1961.

64   "Disarmament in the face": *Alton Evening Telegraph*, February 6, 1962, p. 4.

64   "Our opposition is committed": *Chicago Tribune*, April 17, 1962, p. 7.

64   "victory over this godless": *Alton Evening Telegraph*, April 24, 1962, p. 1.

64   "you only need": *New York Times*, December 15, 1975, p. 44.

64   "Civilization progresses, freedom": Schlafly, *A Choice*, p. 90.

65   "The Monroe Doctrine": *St. Louis Globe-Democrat*, July 2, 1963.

65   "We should not submit": Schlafly, *A Choice*, pp. 91–92.

65   "official confirmation of the . . . master": *St. Louis Globe-Democrat*, July 12, 1963.

65   "I appear here": *Nuclear Test Ban Treaty. Hearings Before the Committee on Foreign Relations. United States Senate. 88th Congress, First Session* (Washington, D.C., 1963), pp. 911–12, 916.

65   "I insisted on Barry": Felsenthal, *Sweetheart*, p. 169.

66   "No one who lived": Phyllis Schlafly and Chester Ward, *Kissinger on the Couch* (New Rochelle, N.Y., 1975), pp. 542, 545.

66   "it was inappropriate": Interview, October 31, 1983; Schlafly Papers.

JOHN HERSCHEL GLENN (I)

Page

67   "There should be": George E. Ruff and Edwin Z. Levy, "Psychiatric Evaluation of Candidates for Space Flight," *American Journal of Psychiatry* 116 (November 1959), pp. 385–86.

68   "It's the kind of place": Betty Garrett, "Annie and John Glenn: A Love Story," *McCall's*, March 1975, p. 26.

68   "We're a Christian": *New York Times*, February 21, 1962, p. 25.

68   "She feels that our relationship": [The Astronauts], *We Seven* (New York, 1963), p. 241.

68   "I do not happen": *Ibid.*

68   "having a family": *Ibid.*

69   "wasn't what you would call": Philip N. Pierce, *John H. Glenn: Astronaut* (New York, 1962), p. 12.

69   "NCHS Senior Airways": *We Seven,* p. 34.

69   "One of the most disturbing": Michael Kramer, "John Glenn: The Right Stuff?" *New York,* January 31, 1983, p. 20.

69   "I was the chief": *Ibid.*

69   "Both his mother": Pierce, *Glenn,* p. 17.

69   "aviation had a wonderful": *We Seven,* p. 35.

70   "But none came": *Ibid.*

70   "Well, I'm going down": *Life,* March 2, 1962, p. 31.

70   "Despite intense heavy": Pierce, *Glenn,* p. 32.

71   "It means going around": Kramer, "John Glenn," p. 20.

71   "You do all kinds": *We Seven,* p. 39.

71   "Today, I finally got": Pierce, *Glenn,* p. 38.

71   "Now, you may think": Kramer, "John Glenn," p. 19.

72   "Just about the time": Pierce, *Glenn,* p. 60.

72   "maybe enough . . . to circle": *New York Times,* July 17, 1957, p. 5.

72   "I didn't have time": Pierce, *Glenn,* p. 60.

73   "The flight was real fine": *New York Times,* July 17, 1957, p. 5.

73   "I [knew] that space": *We Seven,* pp. 41–42.

73   "I enjoyed this stint": *Ibid.*

73   "I didn't know the human": W. R. Lovelace, II, "Duckings, Probings, Checks That Proved Fliers' Fitness," *Life,* April 20, 1959, p. 26.

74   "From some of the strange": *We Seven,* p. 42.

74   "I am a man": *Ibid.,* p. 43.

74   "thinks I'm just about": *Time,* April 20, 1959, p. 18.

74   "I don't think any": Tom Wolfe, *The Right Stuff* (New York, 1979), pp. 115–16.

75   "Although relationships with their families": Ruff, "Psychiatric Evaluation," p. 389.

75   "On Sunday nights": Anna Glenn, "Seven Brave Women," *Life,* September 21, 1959, p. 149.

75   "I have had a lot": John Glenn, "Space Is at the Frontier of My Profession," *Life,* September 14, 1959, p. 38.

75 "John tries to behave": *We Seven*, p. 16.

75 "I did not deny": Walter Cunningham, *The All-American Boys* (New York, 1977), pp. 167–68.

76 "You don't climb": *We Seven*, p. 103.

76 "What [are] we to do": Mark Goodman, "John Glenn Takes an Earth Walk Again," *New Times*, January 11, 1974, p. 30.

76 "This past eight or nine": Loyd S. Swenson, et. al., *This New Ocean: A History of Project Mercury* (Washington, D.C., 1966), pp. 238–39.

77 "Contrary to this being": *Ibid.*

77 "We're anxious to get": *New York Times*, September 17, 1960, p. 8.

77 "if a man orbits": Swenson, *This New Ocean*, p. 284.

77 "If you don't know": *New York Times*, November 30, 1961, p. 20.

77 "When the time comes": John Glenn, "We're Going Places No One Has Ever Traveled . . . ," *Life*, January 27, 1961, p. 50.

77 "Anyone who doesn't": *We Seven*, p. 25.

77 "It's an understatement": *New York Times*, February 22, 1961, p. 8.

78 "He was real, real shook": *Life*, February 2, 1962, p. 28.

78 "This really hit": Shirley Thomas, *Men of Space* 5 (Philadelphia, 1962), pp. 28–29.

78 "Those were pretty": *We Seven*, p. 231.

78 "I am, naturally": Swenson, *This New Ocean*, p. 335.

78 "It seems incredible": John Glenn, "I'll Have to Hit a Keyhole in the Sky," *Life*, December 8, 1961, p. 50.

79 "I learned very early": Swenson, *This New Ocean*, p. 412.

79 "as one guy": John Glenn, recorded interview, June 12, 1964, Oral History Program, John F. Kennedy Library, Boston, Massachusetts.

79 "dozing, light sleep": [National Aeronautics and Space Administration], *Results of the First U.S. Manned Orbital Space Flight* (Washington, D.C., 1962), p. 84.

79 "Quite a moment": *We Seven*, p. 249.

79 "Well, I'm going": *Life*, March 2, 1962, p. 31.

79 "Godspeed, John Glenn": [NASA], *Results*, p. 149.

79 "Roger. The clock": *Ibid.*, pp. 150–51.

80 "A little like riding": *We Seven*, p. 236.

80 "Working just like clockwork": [NASA], *Results*, p. 151.

80 "would take the capsule": *We Seven*, p. 261.

80 "a brilliant blue": [NASA], *Results*, p. 156.

81 "a big mass": *Ibid.*, p. 161.

81 "The particles were a mystery": *We Seven*, p. 300.

81 "The idea that I was": *Ibid.*, p. 303.

81 "any banging noises": *Ibid.*, pp. 303–304.

82 "We suspect this": [NASA], *Results*, p. 186.

82 "clear, straw-colored": *We Seven*, p. 323.

82 "Roger, retros are firing": [NASA], *Results*, p. 188.

82 "We recommend that": *Ibid.*, p. 190.

82 "This was a bad": *We Seven*, pp. 315–16.

83 "Beautiful chute. Chute": [NASA], *Results*, p. 191.

83 "Some years ago": [United States Senate], *Orbital Flight of John H. Glenn, Jr.* (Washington, D.C., 1962), p. 69.

83 "This is the new": Swenson, *This New Ocean*, p. 434.

83 "Well, it's been": Pierce, *Glenn*, p. 159.

83 "Glad to be back": *New York Times*, February 24, 1962, p. 13.

83 "great professional skill": Pierce, *Glenn*, pp. 166–67.

84 "We have stressed": *Ibid.*, pp. 167–68.

84 "I still get": *Ibid.*, pp. 179, 184.

84 "Freedom, devotion to God": *New York Times*, March 2, 1962, p. 18.

85 "We have an infinite": *New York Times*, March 3, 1962, p. 8.

85 "From swimming down": *New York Times*, March 4, 1962, p. 46.

85 "This mission would": *New York Times*, April 7, 1962, p. 8.

86 "for demonstrating that patriotism": *DAR Magazine*, June-July 1962, p. 541.

86 "in space, one has": John Glenn, "Why Go?" *Newsweek*, October 8, 1962, p. 88.

86 "This was a definite": John Glenn, "Why I Know There Is a God," *Readers Digest*, July 1962, p. 38.

86 "What can you do": *New York Times*, September 23, 1963, p. 13.

JANE SEYMOUR FONDA (II)

Page
87   "I'm not a runaway": *Newsday,* February 18, 1964, p. 1C.
88   "I heard things": Tom Burke, "Conversation with Jane Fonda," *Holiday,* September 1969, p. 81.
88   "I said to myself": Martha Weinman Lear, "Whatever Happened to Mr. Fonda's Baby Jane," *Redbook,* August 1969, p. 130.
88   "All night long": Roger Vadim, *Memoirs of the Devil,* trans. Peter Beglan (New York, 1975), pp. 149–50.
88   "discreet and timid": John Springer, *The Fondas: The Films and Careers of Henry, Jane and Peter Fonda* (New York, 1970), p. 214.
88   "a great big opportunity": *New York Times,* May 16, 1965, II, p. 7.
88   "I am supposedly": Fred Lawrence Guiles, *Jane Fonda: The Actress in Her Time* (Garden City, N.Y., 1982), p. 125.
88   "For the first time": Vadim, *Memoirs,* p. 152.
89   "I fell in love": *New York Times,* May 16, 1965, II, p. 7.
89   "I left the walls": Thomas Kiernan, *Jane Fonda: Heroine for Our Time* (New York, 1982), pp. 142–43.
89   "It was wild": Burke, "Conversation," p. 81.
89   "I'd never find": Vadim, *Memoirs,* p. 167.
89   "she had a mania": *Ibid,* pp. 167, 158.
90   "Actress Fonda . . . does": quoted in Springer, *The Fondas,* p. 218.
90   "It's quite a part": *New York Times,* February 15, 1965, II, p. 7.
90   "Women want to possess": Kiernan, *Jane Fonda* [1982], p. 151.
90   "Jane thought she": Vadim, *Memoirs,* p. 165.
90   "I learned more": Burke, "Conversation," p. 80.
91   "These pills . . . turned": Jane Fonda, *Jane Fonda's Workout Book* (New York, 1981), pp. 16, 22.
91   "I remember that day": Oriana Fallaci, "Jane Fonda: I'm Coming into Focus'," *McCall's,* February 1971, p. 147.
92   "People change after": *Time,* September 9, 1966, p. 76.
92   "I know from": Martin Kasindorf, "Fonda: A person of many parts," *New York Times Magazine,* February 3, 1974, p. 24.

92 "I guess I'm": James Brough, *The Fabulous Fondas* (New York, 1973), p. 227.

92 "Used properly . . . it": Henry Erlich, "Jane Fonda: Shining in Two Roles," *Look*, May 13, 1969, p. 75.

92 "hysterically funny and brilliant": *Ibid.*

92 "humor is not": Vadim, *Memoirs*, p. 165.

92 "The identity I found": Burke, "Conversation," p. 81.

93 "There were reverberations": George Haddad-Garcia, *The Films of Jane Fonda* (Secaucus, N.J., 1981), p. 134.

93 "For all of ten": Brough, *Fabulous Fondas*, p. 216.

93 "It rocked me": *New York Times*, January 22, 1967, II, p. 11.

93 "I think it's nice": *Ibid.*

94 "I'm not a physical": Burke, "Conversation," p. 81.

94 "I was reacting": Kasindorf, "Fonda," p. 19.

94 "As Barbarella, I": Jane Fonda, *Workout*, p. 18.

94 "I'm no sex": Kiernan, *Jane Fonda* [1982], p. 179.

94 "My only thought": Jane Fonda, *Workout*, p. 18.

94 "Not that I am": Springer, *The Fondas*, pp. 262–63.

94 "I always felt": Dan Georgakas and Lenny Rubenstein, eds., *The Cinéaste Interviews: On the art and politics of the cinema* (Chicago, 1983), p. 115.

95 "Year after year": Jane Fonda, *Workout*, p. 18.

95 "I'm ferociously ambitious": Thomas Thompson, "A Place in the Sun All Her Own," *Life*, March 29, 1968, p. 72.

95 "I was very": Lear, "Whatever Happened," pp. 128, 130.

95 "I felt so vulnerable": Brough, *Fabulous Fondas*, p. 230.

95 "I was always": *Time*, October 3, 1977, pp. 90–91.

95 "the split between": Fallaci, "Jane Fonda," p. 148.

96 "The position I took": Leo Lerman, "Jane Fonda Talks About . . . ," *Mademoiselle*, August 1970, p. 329.

96 "What was important": Georgakas and Rubenstein, *Cinéaste Interviews*, pp. 117–18.

96 "It was a time": *Newsweek*, October 10, 1977, p. 81.

96 "It was like rumblings": Georgakas and Rubeinstein, *Cinéaste Interviews*, pp. 117–18.

96 "I hate those": Brough, *Fabulous Fondas*, p. 232.

97 "It's like preparing": Lear, "Whatever Happened," pp. 128, 130.

97 "For the first": Haddad-Garcia, *Films of Jane Fonda*, p. 46.

97   "I'm not afraid": Lear, "Whatever Happened," p. 135.

97   "You know what": Burke, "Conversation," p. 44.

97   "The war we're": Kiernan, *Jane Fonda* [1982], pp. 190–91.

98   "The one, ultimate": Brough, *Fabulous Fondas*, p. 243.

98   "really something worse": Georgakas and Rubenstein, *Cinéaste Interviews*, pp. 111–12.

98   "I try to know": Kasindorf, "Fonda," p. 22.

98   "I became so": *New York Times*, January 25, 1970, II, p. 22.

98   "using a lotta": Burke, "Conversation," p. 44.

98   "I discovered a black": Kiernan, *Jane Fonda* [1982], p. 192.

99   "It was the perfect": Guiles, *Jane Fonda*, p. 170.

99   "I had delivered": *New York Times*, January 25, 1970, II, p. 22.

99   "I wish I were": Burke, "Conversation," p. 81.

99   "If you start": *New York Times*, January 25, 1970, II, p. 22.

GEORGE CORLEY WALLACE (II)

Page

101   "It makes no difference": Bill Jones, *The Wallace Story* (Northport, Ala., 1966), pp. 120–21, 126.

101   "those who wanted": George C. Wallace, *Stand Up for America* (Garden City, N.Y., 1976), p. 84.

102   "If people want": Jones, *Wallace Story*, pp. 122–23.

102   "I think we are": *New York Times*, March 14, 1964, p. 10.

102   "a man who has": *New York Times*, January 30, 1964, p. 14.

102   "The people of Alabama": Jones, *Wallace Story*, p. 142.

102   "My purpose . . . is": *New York Times*, March 7, 1964, p. 8.

102–
103   "the left-wing influence": *New York Times*, March 18, 1964, p. 28.

103   "Racism is evil": Jones, *Wallace Story*, pp. 178, 200.

103   "Poles, Italians, Germans": *New York Times*, April 3, 1964, p. 67.

103   "carry on this fight": *New York Times*, April 8, 1964, p. 1.

103   "Governor Wallace got": *New York Times*, April 12, 1964, IV, p. 1.

103 "A man who owns": George C. Wallace, *"Hear Me Out"* (Anderson, S.C., 1968), p. 20.

103 "The federal government": Jones, *Wallace Story*, p. 243.

103 "We shook the eyeteeth": *New York Times*, May 6, 1964, p. 20.

104 "have been tranquilized": Jones, *Wallace Story*, pp. 296, 307.

104 "a David warring": Robert Sherrill, *Gothic Politics in the Deep South* (New York, 1968), pp. 225–26.

104 "This is a sad": *New York Times*, June 20, 1964, pp. 1, 12.

104 "I intend to give": Wayne Greenhaw, *Watch Out for George Wallace* (Englewood Cliffs, N.J., 1976), pp. 154–55.

105 "Today, we hear": Jones, *Wallace Story*, p. 337.

105 "We have no": *New York Times*, August 15, 1964, p. 47.

105 "A so-called civil": *New York Times*, August 22, 1964, p. 6.

105 "to keep the federal": *New York Times*, September 18, 1964, p. 24.

105 "We are going": *New York Times*, September 22, 1964, p. 25.

106 "Mass demonstrations in the nighttime": *New York Times*, February 21, 1965, p. 53.

106 "Such a march": Jones, *Wallace Story*, pp. 357–58.

106 "These folks in Selma": *New York Times*, March 8, 1965, p. 20.

107 "Voter registration and voting": *New York Times*, March 13, 1965, p. 10.

107 "if I endorsed": George Wallace, *Stand Up*, pp. 101–102.

107 "You know, George": Nicholas Katzenbach, quoted in Howell Raines, *My Soul Is Rested* (New York, 1977), p. 339.

107 "If I hadn't left": Charles E. Fager, *Selma, 1965* (New York, 1974), pp. 120–21.

107 "I'm against violence": *New York Times*, March 15, 1965, p. 22.

107 "A federal judge": Jones, *Wallace Story*, p. 404.

108 "to stay away": *New York Times*, March 19, 1965, p. 20.

108 "I've never been": quoted in Harris Wofford, *Of Kennedys and Kings: Making Sense of the Sixties* (New York, 1980), p. 193.

108 "I know you": Martin Luther King, Jr., quoted in Allen J.

Matusow, *The Unraveling of America: A History of Liberalism in the 1960s* (New York, 1984), p. 185.

108   "In a few years": Jones, *Wallace Story,* p. 432.

109   "Life simply should": *Ibid.,* pp. 437, 435–36.

109   "Governors . . . are getting": *New York Times,* September 14, 1965, p. 22.

109   "writers with possible": Sherrill, *Gothic Politics,* p. 269.

109   "What you're talking ": Michael Dorman, *The George Wallace Myth* (New York, 1976), p. 27.

109–10   "If you feel": *New York Times,* September 12, 1965, p. 50.

110   "The liberals say": *New York Times,* October 2, 1965, p. 1.

110   "Let the people": Marshall Frady, *Wallace* (New York, 1968), p. 182.

110   "Would you agree": George Wallace, *Stand Up,* pp. 108–109.

110   "I've been dying": *New York Times,* February 25, 1966, pp. 18, 1.

111   "Now folks . . . we": Ray Jenkins, "Mr. & Mrs. Wallace Run for Governor of Alabama," *New York Times Magazine,* April 24, 1966, p. 74.

111   "No, there ain't": *New York Times,* April 15, 1966, p. 23.

111   "I'm not fighting": Jenkins, "Mr. & Mrs.," pp. 77, 94.

112   "I ain't . . . The Club": Frady, *Wallace,* p. 37.

112   "Alabama is taking": Sherrill, *Gothic Politics,* p. 301.

112   "There's not a bit": *New York Times,* September 6, 1966, p. 42.

112   "I don't have any": *New York Times,* November 10, 1966, p. 30.

112   "There's a chance": *New York Times,* November 11, 1966, p. 26.

113   "You want to know": *New York Times,* December 17, 1966, p. 20.

113   "Schools, that'll be one": James Kilpatrick, "What Makes Wallace Run," *National Review,* April 18, 1967, pp. 402–403.

113   "I'm going over": Sherrill, *Gothic Politics,* p. 260.

113   "think they can": *New York Times,* April 29, 1967, p. 15.

113   "I've read about foreign": *New York Times,* April 28, 1967, p. 28.

114   "bureaucrats with beards": Wallace, *"Hear Me Out",* pp. 129–30.

114   "You know, there's": *New York Times,* September 24, 1967, p. 66.

114   "What we have done": George Wallace, *Stand Up,* pp. 115, 116–17.

114   "to make a major": *New York Times,* February 9, 1968, p. 21.

114   "an insult to the majority": *Washington Post,* March 4, 1968, p. A6.

114   "When we get": Ray Jenkins, "George Wallace Figures to Win Even If He Loses," *New York Times Magazine,* April 7, 1968, pp. 66–68.

115   "I don't have any": *Newsweek,* May 6, 1968, p. 31.

115   "The nights were worst": George Wallace, *Stand Up,* p. 121.

115   "a good crease": *New York Times,* July 5, 1968, p. 14.

115   "probably showed too much": *New York Times,* August 30, 1968, p. 15.

116   "for saying it": *New York Times,* September 26, 1968, p. 1.

116   "We can win": *New York Times,* October 4, 1968, p. 1.

116   "They lie when": *New York Times,* October 27, 1968, p. 71.

116   "Whoever becomes president": *New York Times,* November 2, 1968, p. 22.

116   "The movement is highly": *New York Times,* November 6, 1968, p. 23.

117   "It's a fine": *Washington Post,* November 6, 1968, p. A9.

117   "The principles and philosophy": *New York Times,* November 7, 1968, p. 23.

117   "After all . . . we've": *Montgomery Advertiser,* November 7, 1968, pp. 1–2.

117   "Our movement of millions": *Montgomery Advertiser,* December 18, 1968, p. 10.

117   "Just write . . . that": *New York/Times,* December 8, 1968, p. 48.

PHYLLIS STEWART SCHLAFLY (II)

Page

119   "Mrs. Schlafly fights": *St. Louis Globe-Democrat,* December 28, 1963.

119   "Phyllis Schlafly stands": Phyllis Schlafly, *A Choice Not an Echo* (Alton, Ill., 1964), cover.

119   "History shows that": *Ibid.*, p. 120.

120   "like gelatin, 'peace' ": *St. Louis Globe-Democrat*, March 12, 1964.

120   "Who really picks": Schlafly, *A Choice*, back cover.

120   "Just as one can": *Ibid.*, p. 82.

121   "They saw the whole": Interview, October 31, 1983; Schlafly Papers.

121   "Goldwater has the magic": Schlafly, *A Choice*, pp. 79, 81.

121   "Republican national conventions": Interview, October 31, 1983; Schlafly Papers.

121   "Putting up my": Carol Felsenthal, *The Sweetheart of the Silent Majority: The Biography of Phyllis Schlafly* (Garden City, N.Y., 1981), p. 176.

121   "Slogans have always": *St. Louis Globe-Democrat*, August 14, 1964.

122   "Why is Khrushchev": Phyllis Schlafly and Chester Ward, *The Gravediggers* (Alton, Ill., 1964), pp. 5, 6, 8, 63, 11.

122   "It looks as though": *St. Louis Globe-Democrat*, October 22, 1964.

123   "the decisive issue": Phyllis Schlafly and Chester Ward, *Strike from Space: A Megadeath Mystery* (Alton, Ill., 1965), pp. 92–93.

123   "the racial revolutionaries": Phyllis Schlafly, *Safe—Not Sorry* (Alton, Ill., 1967), p. 71.

124   "I'm thrilled to learn": *New York Times*, November 23, 1964, p. 42.

124   " 'Sixty-four was": Robert Sam Anson, "Phyllis Schlafly Knows She's Right," *Mademoiselle*, April 1983, p. 172.

124   "The only talent": Felsenthal, *Sweetheart*, p. 124.

124   "The issue is not": *St. Louis Post Dispatch*, July 25, 1965, p. 3C.

124   "A few Republicans": *Ibid.*

124   "My California following": Interview, October 31, 1983; Schlafly Papers.

124   "Mrs. Schlafly was her": *St. Louis Globe-Democrat*, September 23, 1965.

124   "An eloquent spokesman": Schlafly and Ward, *Strike from Space*, p. 218.

124   "a complete handbook": brochure; Schlafly Papers.

125   "stranger than fiction": Schlafly and Ward, *Strike from Space*, pp. 8, 16, 46, 29, 32, 50, 119–20.

126   "The result is the disgusting": *Ibid.*, pp. 148, 198, 200.

126   "I just plain": Interview, October 31, 1983; Schlafly Papers.

126   "It was the principle": Schlafly, *Safe*, pp. 148–49.

126   "to purge": *St. Louis Post Dispatch*, March 8, 1967, p. 3A.

126   "My six children": political brochure; Schlafly Papers.

127   "Obviously . . . no normal": Schlafly, *Safe*, p. 156.

127   "The men in the Republican": Felsenthal, *Sweetheart*, p. 180.

127   "Phyllis exemplifies the finest": political brochure; Schlafly Papers.

127   "I believe that our women": *Ibid.*

127   "Strictly volunteers . . . not": *New York Times*, May 7, 1967, p. 33.

128   "The political world": Phyllis Schlafly, speech to Women's National Press Club, May 2, 1967; Schlafly Papers.

128   "They all want": *St. Louis Globe-Democrat*, May 8, 1967.

128   "Dear and Loyal": *St. Louis Globe-Democrat*, May 26, 1967.

128   "My object was not": *St. Louis Globe-Democrat*, August 9, 1968.

128   "Our overriding objective": *St. Louis Globe-Democrat*, May 26, 1967.

128   "secret treaties . . . imperiled": *Phyllis Schlafly Report*, August 1967.

128   "your life is no": *Phyllis Schlafly Report*, September 1967.

128   "We have a no-win": Schlafly, *Safe*, p. 6.

129   "There are a few": *Ibid.*, pp. 40, 23–24, 35.

129   "This is not": *Phyllis Schlafly Report*, March 1968.

129   "Guilt is *not*": Phyllis Schlafly and Chester Ward, *The Betrayers* (Alton, Ill, 1968), p. 7.

129   "I'm not for third": Interview, October 31, 1983; Schlafly Papers.

129   "I believe there will": *St. Louis Globe-Democrat*, March 15, 1968.

130   "I supported Nixon": Interview, October 31, 1983; Schlafly Papers.

130   "Since four of the last": campaign flyer; Schlafly Papers.

130   "It's like being": *St. Louis Globe-Democrat*, August 9, 1968.

130   "The enemy is getting": *Alton Evening Telegraph*, August 17, 1968.

130   "There are crises": *St. Louis Globe-Democrat*, August 9, 1968.

130   "Our cities have": Schlafly and Ward, *Betrayers*, pp. 5, 14, 113.

131   "I didn't want": Interview, October 31, 1983; Schlafly Papers.

131   "This is the only": *Alton Evening Telegraph*, March 7, 1969.

131   "Richard Nixon ran": Phyllis Schlafly and Chester Ward, *Kissinger on the Couch* (New Rochelle, N.Y., 1975), p. 212.

JOHN HERSCHEL GLENN (II)

Page

133   "He seemed even more": Jhan and June Robbins, "John Glenn: Aftermath of a Bad Year," *Redbook*, January 1965, p. 69.

133   "sat back and took": Frank Van Riper, *Glenn: The Astronaut Who Would Be President* (New York, 1983), p. 56.

133   "in continuing public": John Glenn, recorded interview, June 12, 1964, Oral History Program, John F. Kennedy Library, Boston, Massachusetts.

134   "One of the fascinating": Myra MacPherson, "The Hero-as-Politician," *Potomac, Washington Post*, January 12, 1975, p. 10.

134   "I think that a man": Howard H. Martin and Don Oberdorfer, "What Made John Glenn Run?" *Saturday Evening Post*, February 22, 1964, p. 23.

134   "to sit back": Michael Kramer, "John Glenn: The Right Stuff?" *New York*, January 31, 1983, p. 20.

135   "If I don't have": Evan McLeod Wylie, "Mrs. John Glenn Talks About 'The Years Since . . .' " *Good Housekeeping*, July 1965, p. 161.

135   "not very old": *Time*, January 24, 1964, p. 13.

135   "To be the oldest": Wylie, "Mrs. John Glenn," p. 160.

136   "If there is one": Mark Goodman, "John Glenn Takes an Earth Walk Again," *New Times*, January 11, 1974, p. 27.

136   "To serve in a body": *New York Times,* January 18, 1964, p. 10.

136   "Careful consideration of the current": *Ibid.*

136   "Glenn's getting into the race": *New York Times,* January 21, 1964, p. 1.

136   "We had an amateur": Wylie, "Mrs. John Glenn," p. 161.

137   "No politician . . . can": *New York Times,* February 6, 1964, p. 31.

137   "personifying the American": *New York Times,* February 22, 1964, p. 6.

137   "Suddenly I realized": Herbert Shulinder, "Was John Glenn Injured in Space?" *Popular Science,* January 1965, p. 58.

137   "It was the toughest": *New York Times,* March 31, 1964, p. 18.

137   "I didn't pass": Shulinder, "Was John Glenn," p. 58.

137   "When I moved": MacPherson, "The Hero," pp. 16, 19.

138   "My recovery has been slower": *New York Times,* March 21, 1964, p. 21.

138   "Hello, I'm Annie": Robbins, "John Glenn," p. 70.

138   "No man has a right": *New York Times,* March 31, 1964, pp. 18–19.

139   "If I told you": Wylie, "Mrs. John Glenn," p. 112.

139   "I'd reach a new": *Ibid.,* p. 163.

139   "an important asset": John Glenn, recorded interview, June 12, 1964, Oral History Program, Kennedy Library.

139   "To keep our minds": Wylie, "Mrs. John Glenn," p. 162.

139   "Although the letter": *Newsweek,* August 3, 1964, p. 70.

139   "I owe $9,473.46": *Ibid.*

140   "If our son": MacPherson, "The Hero," pp. 16, 19.

140   "If there is a war": *Newsweek,* August 3, 1964, p. 70.

140   "because . . . I'm going": Robbins, "John Glenn," p. 70.

140   "We cannot predict": *New York Times,* July 12, 1964, p. 46.

140   "something which will": *New York Times,* July 12, 1964, p. 46.

140   "could feel at home": *Newsweek,* August 3, 1964, pp. 70–71.

141   "I hadn't been able": Wylie, "Mrs. John Glenn," p. 163.

141   "development and expansion": *New York Times,* October 20, 1964, p. 49.

141   "the one that would": Wylie, "Mrs. John Glenn," p. 163.

141   "excellent transition": *New York Times*, April 10, 1965, p. 33.

142   "the tremendously exciting": *New York Times*, February 20, 1965, p. 10.

142   "Too often religion": *New York Times*, June 2, 1965, p. 19.

142   "It's my first visit": *New York Times*, October 14, 1965, p. 39.

142   "diplomatic triumph": *New York Times*, October 22, 1965, p. 5.

143   "Up to that time": Kramer, "John Glenn," p. 22.

143   "at this time": *New York Times*, January 13, 1966, p. 69.

143   "components of real": John Glenn, "Eulogy," in Pierre Salinger et. al., eds., *"An Honorable Profession": A Tribute to Robert F. Kennedy* (Garden City, N.Y., 1968), p. 13.

143   "Man tries something": *New York Times*, February 23, 1967, p. 23.

143   "The really important": *Chicago Tribune*, February 21, 1967, IA, p. 4.

144   "We do not plan": *New York Times*, April 14, 1967, p. 79.

144   "There was cause": *Time*, January 19, 1968, p. 44.

144   "The fact is": Van Riper, *Glenn*, p. 216.

144   "a man you can": *New York Times*, May 13, 1968, p. 22.

144   "sliding into fewer": *Washington Post*, May 13, 1968, p. A4.

144   "through a very poor": Glenn, "Eulogy," pp. 11–13.

145   "It was my awful": [United States Senate Judiciary Committee], *Hearings Before Subcommittee to Investigate Juvenile Delinquency* (Washington, D.C., 1968), p. 114.

145   "I can now count": Glenn, "Eulogy," p. 13.

145   "The family of my friend": *Hearings*, pp. 114, 116.

146   "It was all marked": Betty Garrett, "Annie and John Glenn: A Love Story," *McCall's*, March 1975, p. 30.

146   "Evoking our memories": Glenn, "Eulogy," pp. 13–14, 10.

JANE SEYMOUR FONDA (III)

Page

147   "From the beginning . . . I": *New York Times*, January 25, 1970, II, p. 15.

148   "I suppose I could": Martha Weinman Lear, "Jane Fonda: A Long Way from Yesterday," *Redbook,* June 1976, p. 145.

148   "no one was surprised": Joan Didion, *The White Album* (New York, 1979), p. 42.

148   "I have always": Oriana Fallaci, "Jane Fonda: 'I'm Coming into Focus'," *McCall's,* February 1971, p. 148.

148   "I needed to go": *Ibid.*

148   "I still had": *Ibid.*

149   "I can't bear": Patricia Bosworth, "Movies: 'Astonish Me!' " *McCall's,* April 1970, p. 14.

149   "a married woman": "Playboy Interview: Jane Fonda and Tom Hayden," *Playboy,* April 1974, p. 88.

149   "I'm very optimistic": *New York Times,* January 25, 1970, II, p. 22.

149   smoking marijuana: *Ibid.*

149   "They told the press": Peter Collier, "The Red Man's Burden," *Ramparts,* February 1970, pp. 26–27.

150   "I'm here to learn": Peter Collier, "I Remember Fonda," *New West,* September 24, 1979, p. 20.

150   "It was the first": Fallaci, "Jane Fonda," p. 148.

150   "I knew the importance": Leo Lerman, "Jane Fonda Talks About . . . ," *Mademoiselle,* August 1970, p. 330.

151   "There is so much": Collier, "I Remember," p. 21.

151   "The hardest thing": Lerman, "Jane Fonda," p. 330.

151   "I could be on": Fred Lawrence Guiles, *Jane Fonda: The Actress in Her Time* (Garden City, N.Y., 1982), p. 200.

152   "People think actresses": James Brough, *The Fabulous Fondas* (New York, 1973), p. 271.

152   "You suddenly open": *Washington Post,* July 29, 1973, p. K2.

152   "Greetings, fellow bums": *New York Times,* May 10, 1970, p. 1.

152   "Who's getting rich": Thomas Kiernan, *Jane Fonda: Heroine for Our Time* (New York, 1982), p. 227.

152   "When I left": John Frook, "Nag, Nag, Nag!" *Life,* April 23, 1971, p. 52D.

152   "I realized that": Fallac., "Jane Fonda," p. 151.

153   "It was hard": *Ibid.,* p. 149.

153   "Do you know": *Ibid.*

153   "The new Jane": *Vogue*, June 1970, pp. 106–107.

153   "Jane Fonda, the doll": Fallaci, "Jane Fonda," pp. 151, 149.

153   "I suddenly felt": Lear, "Jane Fonda," p. 148.

153   "What society has": Brough, *Fabulous Fondas*, p. 273.

154   "inevitable product of a society": *Newsweek*, November 16, 1970, p. 65.

154   "hierarchy of the prostitute": Martin Kasindorf, "Fonda: A Person of Many Parts," *New York Times Magazine*, February 3, 1974, p. 24.

154   "Huey Newton is": Kiernan, *Jane Fonda* [1982], p. 232.

154   "They thought I was": Fred Robbins, "Jane Fonda, the Woman," *Vogue*, November 1977, p. 322.

154   "I'm not a cynical": Kasindorf, "Fonda," p. 26.

154   "Listen . . . your job": Fallaci, "Jane Fonda," p. 140.

155   "Here is another": *Ibid.*

155   "I was never": Kiernan, *Jane Fonda* [1982], p. 260.

155   "We will kill": *New York Times*, December 16, 1975, p. 26.

155   "America is a sinking": *Newsweek*, November 16, 1970, p. 66.

155   "Very few people": Fallaci, "Jane Fonda," p. 122.

156   "Don't ask me": *Ibid.*, p. 151.

156   "It's been very": *New York Times*, February 17, 1971, p. 20.

156   "I'd better call": *New York Times*, March 21, 1971, II, p. 1.

156   "What we are": *Ibid*, II, p. 3.

156   "When the time": Brough, *Fabulous Fondas*, p. 280.

157   "I'm not here": *San Francisco Chronicle*, March 8, 1971, p. 2.

157   "I would hope": *New York Times*, March 21, 1971, II, p. 3.

157   "a film which says": Frook, "Nag," p. 52C.

157   "I began to realize": *New York Times*, October 31, 1971, II, p. 17.

158   "We work for": "Calendar," *Los Angeles Times*, February 20, 1972, p. 22.

158   "It's a grotesque": *Los Angeles Times*, May 11, 1972, IV, p. 2.

158   "The Oscar is what": *Washington Post*, May 15, 1972, p. B7.

158   "It's very hard": *Los Angeles Times*, May 11, 1972, IV, pp. 14, 2.

159   "I was tired": Donald R. Katz, "Jane Fonda: A Hard Act to Follow," *Rolling Stone,* March 9, 1978, p. 44.

159   "In one section": Lear, "Jane Fonda," p. 150.

159   "It's going to be": Edwin Miller, "Fervent Eyes of Jane Fonda," *Seventeen,* September 1972, p. 192.

159   "more destruction to": "Playboy Interview," p. 78.

159   "I implore you": *New York Times,* July 15, 1972, p. 9.

160   "Tonight, when you": *Los Angeles Times,* August 26, 1972, I, p. 16.

160   "Can we fight": *Los Angeles Times,* September 11, 1972, I, p. 21.

160   "They fear if Nixon": *Los Angeles Times,* September 26, 1972, I, p. 5.

160   "Given the things": *Washington Post,* July 26, 1972, p. A14.

160   "The people who are": *New York Times,* July 29, 1972, p. 9.

160   "Genocide . . . is more": *Los Angeles Times,* July 31, 1972, I, p. 3.

160   "Vietnam rekindled an enormous": "Playboy Interview," p. 100.

161   "travel of people": *New York Times,* September 21, 1972, p. 55.

161   "Don't forget that": "Playboy Interview," p. 80.

161   "I discovered that": *Village Voice,* November 7, 1974, p. 95.

161   "We decided to": *Redbook,* February 1977, p. 168.

161   "We are campaigning": Kiernan, *Jane Fonda* [1982], pp. 286–87.

161   "The U.S. election . . . did": *Los Angeles Times,* December 21, 1972, I, p. 26.

162   "hypocrites and liars": Guiles, *Jane Fonda,* p. 272.

162   "I'm quite sure": *New York Times,* April 7, 1973, p. 11.

162   "We have no reason": *Los Angeles Times,* April 19, 1973, I, p. 25.

162   "not simply because": "Playboy Interview," p. 74.

162   "Possessions used to be": *Ibid.,* p. 182.

162   "Some people think": Kasindorf, "Fonda," p. 28.

163   "will not change": Jane Fonda, "A Vietnam Journal: The Birth of a Nation," *Rolling Stone,* July 4, 1974, pp. 50, 52, 56.

163   "a first step": Dan Georgakas and Lenny Rubenstein, eds.,

The Cinéaste Interviews: On the art and politics of the cinema
(Chicago, 1983), p. 116.

163 "People say to me": Lear, "Jane Fonda," p. 150.

164 "I've changed tremendously": *New York Times*, April 11,
1976, II, p. 19.

164 "I'm reaching middle": "Calendar," *Los Angeles Times*,
December 26, 1976, p. 48.

164 "It is very important": *New York Times*, October 31, 1976,
II, p. 17.

164 "The alienation that I felt": *Redbook*, February 1977, pp.
168, 170.

GEORGE CORLEY WALLACE (III)

Page

167 "If this administration": George Lardner, Jr., and Jules Loh,
"The Wonderful World of George Wallace," *Esquire*, May
1969, p. 128.

167 "represented only the tip": *New York Times*, May 27, 1969,
p. 17.

167 "We shall continue": *New York Times*, March 12, 1969, p.
45.

168 "I don't have": *Newsweek*, July 14, 1969, p. 96.

168 "Take your children": *New York Times*, September 8, 1969,
p. 20.

168 "Vietnamization . . . is not": *Washington Post*, December
1, 1969, p. A1.

169 "When I was saying": *New York Times*, December 12, 1969,
p. 59.

169 "I look under": *Washington Post*, February 27, 1970, p. A2.

169 "This ain't any": *Newsweek*, March 9, 1970, p. 20.

169 *"If the people"*: *New York Times*, March 20, 1970, p. 22.

170 "to register the bloc": *New York Times*, April 24, 1970, p.
1.

170 "If I'm out": *Washington Post*, May 4, 1970, p. A23.

170 "Goddam niggers": James Wooten, "Wallace's Last Hurrah?" *New York Times Magazine*, January 11, 1976, p. 56.

170   "It's going to be": *New York Times,* May 7, 1970, p. 1.

170   "IF YOU WANT": *New York Times,* June 7, 1970, IV, p. 1.

171   "Sure are a lot": *New York Times,* June 3, 1970, p. 31.

171   "Alabama still keeps": *New York Times,* June 3, 1970, p. 1.

171   "Because that means": *Washington Post,* June 4, 1970, p. 1.

171   "There wasn't anything": *U.S. News and World Report,* June 15, 1970, p. 25.

171   "became somewhat like": Cornelia Wallace, *C'nelia* (Philadelphia, 1976), p. 224.

171   "They's people who": Stephan Lesher, "Who Knows What Frustrations . . . ," *New York Times Magazine,* January 2, 1972, p. 32.

172   "People's wives help": *Washington Post,* May 7, 1972, p. G1.

172   "the Jacqueline Kennedy": *New York Times,* June 25, 1971, p. 36.

172   "Alabama belongs to all": *New York Times,* January 19, 1971, p. 16.

173   "There was no": *New York Times,* April 3, 1971, p. 1.

173   "They'll tell you": *New York Times,* June 25, 1971, p. 36.

173   "That banking crowd": *New York Times,* June 28, 1971, p. 35.

173   "a colossal mistake": *New York Times,* August 6, 1971, p. 35.

173   "exporting heroin [and]": *New York Times,* July 21, 1971, p. 14.

173   "the conflicts between": *Time,* August 23, 1971, p. 10.

173   "All I'm trying": *New York Times,* August 22, 1971, IV, p. 3.

174   "Too long, this party": *U.S. News and World Report,* January 24, 1972, p. 51.

174   "the president asked": Frank Trippett, " 'Lordy, Ain't It Sweet!' on the Wallace Wagon," *Life,* March 31, 1972, p. 43.

174   "I'd say, 'Look . . .' ": Lesher, "Who Knows," p. 33.

174   "I put 'em": *Washington Post,* May 7, 1972, p. G14.

174   "I never was": *New York Times,* February 26, 1972, p. 14.

175   "on a night": George C. Wallace, *Stand Up for America* (Garden City, N.Y., 1976), p. 154.

175   "It's people who like": *New York Times,* April 4, 1972, p. 36.

175   "We're going to": *New York Times,* April 8, 1972, p. 12.

175   "But what kind": *New York Times,* April 15, 1972, p. 12.

175   "I'm going to say": *New York Times,* May 7, 1972, p. 45.

175   "He was changing": James Wooten, "Wallace and Me: The End of the Road," *Esquire,* November 7, 1978, p. 101.

175   "a pretty good": *New York Times,* April 29, 1972, p. 12.

176   "Every dog has": *Washington Post,* May 7, 1972, p. G14–15.

176   "We've accepted nondiscrimination": *New York Times,* May 7, 1972, p. 45.

176   "I like the touch": George Wallace, *Stand Up,* p. 7.

177   "This must be": *Ibid.,* pp. 7–8; Cornelia Wallace, *C'nelia,* p. 31.

177   "Knock me out": Cornelia Wallace, *C'nelia,* p. 39.

177   "What am I going": *Ibid.,* pp. 72–73.

178   "The campaign is": *New York Times,* May 25, 1972, p. 31.

178   "It wasn't politics": Cornelia Wallace, *C'nelia,* p. 108.

178   "really the majority": *Washington Post,* July 11, 1972, p. A13.

178   "And all he really": Richard Nixon, *The Memoirs of Richard Nixon* (New York, 1978), Vol. 2, p. 149.

179   "If [the Democrats]": *New York Times,* November 8, 1972, p. 30.

179   "It's difficult to": *New York Times,* October 30, 1972, p. 19.

179   "and something about": George Wallace, *Stand Up,* pp. 174, 161, 173.

179   "The thought crossed": *New York Times,* May 14, 1973, p. 21.

180   "He's got this terrible": Wayne Greenhaw, *Watch Out for George Wallace* (Englewood Cliffs, N.J., 1976), p. 239.

180   "But if I could": George C. Wallace, "Introduction" in George Wallace, Jr., *The Wallaces of Alabama* (Chicago, 1975), p. ix.

180   "You know, when": *Newsweek,* February 26, 1973, p. 29.

180   "I can't exactly": *New York Times,* May 14, 1973, p. 21.

181   "This is the finest": Greenhaw, *Watch Out,* p. 247.

181   "I can't walk": *Newsweek,* July 16, 1973, p. 26.

181   "All of us": *New York Times,* November 19, 1973, p. 25.

181   "This is nothing": *New York Times,* November 30, 1973, p. 24.

181   "those federal bureaucrats": *New York Times,* April 21, 1974, p. 27.

182   "Not long before": *New York Times,* June 3, 1974, p. 22.

182   "the governor of all": *Newsweek,* May 20, 1974, p. 46.

182   "Because of his": *New York Times,* May 17, 1974, p. 35.

182   "As far as I": *New York Times,* November 8, 1974, p. 45.

182   "the symptom, not": George Wallace, *Stand Up,* p. 169.

183   "He said he": Nixon, *Memoirs* 2, pp. 638–39.

183   "Let me tell you . . . the New": *Washington Post,* September 11, 1974, p. A19.

183   "They're thinking what": *New York Times,* October 25, 1974, p. 21.

183   "The people in government": *New York Times,* January 21, 1975, p. 14.

183   "Gerald . . . why don't": Jules Witcover, *Marathon: The Pursuit of the Presidency, 1972–1976* (New York, 1977), p. 169.

184   "I'm one of the few": Greenhaw, *Watch Out,* p. 81.

184   "a lovely talk": *New York Times,* October 15, 1975, p. 34.

184   "I've seen Europe": Witcover, *Marathon,* p. 171.

184   "a political revolution": *New York Times,* November 13, 1975, p. 1.

184   "that great mass": *New York Times,* January 2, 1976, p. 20.

184   "Being a southerner": *Newsweek,* November 24, 1975, p. 39.

184   "President Wallace invited": Wooten, "Wallace's Last Hurrah," pp. 52, 54.

185   "You're not president": *New York Times,* February 13, 1976, p. 31.

185   "quit all this": *New York Times,* March 9, 1976, p. 22.

185   "phony health issue": *New York Times,* March 11, 1976, p. 72.

185   "Nothing's that tough": Elizabeth Drew, *American Journal: The Events of 1976* (New York, 1977), pp. 125–26, 124.

186   "All the other": *New York Times,* March 25, 1976, p. 30.

186   "The people I have": *Washington Post,* March 29, 1976, p. A1.

186   "I don't know": *New York Times,* May 3, 1976, p. 10.

186   "I lost. The people": Drew, *American Journal,* p. 257.

186   "They were all": *Washington Post,* July 13, 1976, p. A1.

187   "The monster bureaucracy": *New York Times,* July 16, 1976, p. 16.

187   "Every hotel has": *Chicago Tribune,* July 14, 1976, I, p. 6.

PHYLLIS STEWART SCHLAFLY (III)

Page

189   "The trouble is": Phyllis Schlafly, "The Vital Role of Conservative Women," *Human Events,* April 12, 1969, p. 6.

190   "I am the mother": [United States Senate], *Hearings Before the Committee on Armed Services.* Ninety-first Congress, first session, May 1969, pp. 1402–1405.

190   "The vote on": *Phyllis Schlafly Report,* September 1969, p. 2.

190   "America has been": *Phyllis Schlafly Report,* March 1970, p. 1.

191   "a voice for victory": *Alton Evening Telegraph,* September 2, 1969.

191   "his magnificent speeches": *Phyllis Schlafly Report,* December 1969, pp. 4, 2.

191   "Only with a responsible": *St. Louis Globe-Democrat,* December 11, 1969.

191   "Our citizens are": *Alton Evening Telegraph,* December 11, 1969.

191   "YOUR HOME NEEDS": *Alton Evening Telegraph,* March 16, 1970.

191   "The reason I like": *St. Louis Globe-Democrat,* October 26, 1970.

192   "professional agitators . . . spineless": *St. Louis Globe-Democrat,* September 21, 1970.

192   "shake all those": Phyllis Schlafly, *The Power of the Positive Woman* (New Rochelle, N.Y., 1977), p. 39.

192   "Do you know": Interview, October 31, 1983; Schlafly Papers.

192   "building roads in": *New York Times,* September 12, 1970, p. 5.

192   "The road situation": *St. Louis Globe-Democrat,* October 16, 1970.

192   "My opponent says": *St. Louis Post Dispatch,* October 25, 1970, p. 3C.

192   "Examining the demographics": Interview, October 31, 1983; Schlafly Papers.

192   "In Illinois, the fault": *Phyllis Schlafly Report,* November 1970, pp. 1, 3.

193   "died of a broken": *Phyllis Schlafly Report*, February 1971, p. 3.

193   "Will Ping-Pong": *Phyllis Schlafly Report*, May 1971, p. 1.

193   "How Do You Rate": *Phyllis Schlafly Report*, March 1971, p. 1.

193   "Republicans in increasing": *Phyllis Schlafly Report*, June 1971, pp. 2, 4.

193   "I know for a fact": Interview, October 31, 1983; Schlafly Papers.

193   "the freedom to commit": *Phyllis Schlafly Report*, July 1971, p. 1.

194   "Is there anyone": Phyllis Schlafly, "Are We 'Hell-Bent on National Suicide'?: A Speech with Supporting Documentation," October 1971, p. 39; Schlafly Papers.

194   "The new U.S.": Joseph Vecsey and Phyllis Schlafly, *Mindszenty the Man* (St. Louis, 1972), p. 201.

194   "paranoiac secrecy": *Phyllis Schlafly Report*, May 1977, p. 3.

194   "The crying need": Vecsey and Schlafly, *Mindszenty*, p. 5.

194   "We must teach": *St. Louis Globe-Democrat*, December 18, 1971.

194   "I thought it": *St. Louis Post Dispatch*, June 10, 1973.

195   "Of all the classes": *Phyllis Schlafly Report*, February 1972.

195   "I did the whole": Interview, October 31, 1983; Schlafly Papers.

195   "No more unequal": [United States Senate], *Hearings Before the Committee on Foreign Relations. Ninety-second Congress, second session, June 29, 1972*, pp. 329, 334.

196   "just sat it": Interview, October 31, 1983; Schlafly Papers.

196   "The ERA thing": *Ibid.*

196   "It took practice": *St. Louis Post Dispatch*, June 10, 1973.

196   "Girls, there is": Robert Sam Anson, "Phyllis Schlafly Knows She's Right," *Mademoiselle*, April 1983, p. 256.

196   "The psychology of winning": Interview, October 31, 1983; Schlafly Papers.

196   "Their motive is": *Phyllis Schlafly Report*, November 1972, p. 4.

197   "The women libbers": *New York Times*, January 15, 1973, p. 12.

197   "The U.S. Constitution": *Phyllis Schlafly Report*, June 1973, section 2.

197   "there are always": *Alton Evening Telegraph*, February 7, 1973.

197   "The world has": *St. Louis Globe-Democrat*, April 4, 1973.

197   "I consider you": *New York Times*, May 3, 1973, p. 49.

197   "I'm having a ball": Dale Wittner, " 'All Women's Liberationists Hate Men and Children,' " *Chicago Tribune Magazine*, May 20, 1973, p. 22.

198   "The Equal Rights": Nick Thimmesch, "The Sexual Equality Amendment," *New York Times Magazine*, June 24, 1973, p. 8.

198   "Not too bad": Lisa Cronin Wohl, "Phyllis Schlafly: 'The Sweetheart of the Silent Majority,' " *Ms.*, March 1974, p. 55.

198   "Whereas the Equal": Phyllis Schlafly, "Why Stoop to Equality," *DAR Magazine*, June-July 1973, p. 538.

198   "Now we have": Phyllis Schlafly, "What Our POWs Can Teach Us About America," *DAR Magazine*, February 1974, p. 93.

198   "The trouble with": *Phyllis Schlafly Report*, March 1974, p. 1.

198   "any great disaster": *Los Angeles Times*, March 24, 1974, I, p. 3.

198   "The conservative American": *Phyllis Schlafly Report*, March 1974.

199   "It isn't enough": *St. Louis Globe-Democrat*, June 3, 1974.

199   "We women . . . have": *Chicago Tribune*, August 19, 1974, I, p. 5.

199   "They always come": *Washington Post*, July 11, 1974, p. D1.

199   "emotional generalities or vulgar": *Chicago Tribune*, June 10, 1975, II, p. 2.

199   "It's obvious that": *Los Angeles Times*, April 13, 1975, V, p. 18.

199   "If I had": Linda Witt, "Equal Rights at the Schlaflys," *People*, March 30, 1981, p. 104.

200   "No president could": Phyllis Schlafly and Chester Ward, *Kissinger on the Couch* (New Rochelle, N.Y., 1975), p. 281.

200   "But since it": *St. Louis Post Dispatch*, January 30, 1976.

200   "I was trying": *St. Louis Globe-Democrat*, April 28, 1979.

200   "I've debated all": *New York Times*, December 15, 1975, p. 44.

200   "the voice of": *St. Louis Globe-Democrat,* October 11, 1975.

200   "I am articulating": *St. Louis Post Dispatch,* January 30, 1976.

200   "NOW is for": Carol Felsenthal, *The Sweetheart of the Silent Majority: The Biography of Phyllis Schlafly* (Garden City, N.Y., 1981), pp. 273–74.

200   "It is self-evident": Schlafly, *Positive Woman,* pp. 12–13, 16, 68, 76.

201   "For the first": *Phyllis Schlafly Report,* October 1975, section 1.

201   "Kissinger has trapped": Schlafly and Ward, *Kissinger,* p. 744.

201   "The crisis confronting": Phyllis Schlafly and Chester Ward, *Ambush at Vladivostock* (Alton, Ill., 1976), p. 152.

201   "religious and family-oriented": *New York Times,* August 17, 1976, p. 36.

201   "I felt it": Interview, October 31, 1983; Schlafly Papers.

201   "because Reagan is": *New York Times,* August 17, 1976, p. 36.

201   "we would have": *Phyllis Schlafly Report,* September 1976, section 2.

202   "one of the most": *St. Louis Globe-Democrat,* September 1, 1976.

202   "If we just": *St. Louis Globe-Democrat,* October 21, 1976.

202   "Surveying America after": Schlafly, *Positive Woman,* pp. 139, 141.

202   "I don't think": *St. Louis Globe-Democrat,* December 31, 1976.

JOHN HERSCHEL GLENN (III)

Page

203   "I'm green with": *Chicago Tribune,* July 20, 1969, I, p. 4.

203   "I'd give anything": *New York Times,* July 22, 1969, p. 26.

203   "One reason why": *Ibid.*

204   "No other pursuit": *New York Times,* December 12, 1969, p. 42.

204 "dedication to my": *Washington Post,* December 12, 1969, p. A2.

204 "guarantee excitement and": *New York Times,* January 18, 1970, p. 39.

204 "above 6 percent": *Wall Street Journal,* May 4, 1970, p. 20.

204 "cynical southern strategy": *Cleveland Plain Dealer,* April 25, 1970, p. 7C.

205 "Rightly or wrongly": Betty Garrett, "Annie and John Glenn: A Love Story," *McCall's,* March 1975, p. 32.

205 "our planet [is]": *Cleveland Plain Dealer,* April 29, 1970, p. 18.

205 "can buy an": *Washington Post,* May 4, 1970, p. 1.

205 "Everyone assumed if": Garrett, "Annie and John Glenn," p. 32.

205 "Everyone is losing": *New York Times,* May 5, 1970, p. 20.

205 "Today's young people": *Cleveland Plain Dealer,* April 16, 1970, p. 7E.

206 "I was in California": *New York Times,* May 5, 1970, p. 20.

206 "Two wars": Michael Kramer, "John Glenn: The Right Stuff?" *New York,* January 31, 1983, p. 22.

206 "The American people": *Chicago Sun Times,* February 20, 1977, p. 53.

206 "I don't think": Mark Goodman, "John Glenn Takes an Earth Walk Again," *New Times,* January 11, 1974, p. 26.

206 "unique and dubious": *New York Times,* June 27, 1971, p. 22.

206 "I had no": Garrett, "Annie and John Glenn," p. 32.

207 "really didn't have": Howard Kohn, "How John Glenn Got Rich," *Rolling Stone,* November 24, 1983, p. 76.

207 "Those inns are": Kramer, "John Glenn," p. 22.

207 "what elementary questions": *New York Times,* February 20, 1972, p. 49.

207 "Many have regarded": *Newsweek,* February 7, 1972, p. 9.

208 "people writing for": Jerry Bledsoe, "Down from Glory," *Esquire,* January 1973, p. 86.

208 "They have medical": *New York Times,* February 20, 1972, p. 49.

208 "We're doing well": Bledsoe, "Down from Glory," p. 176.

208 "I don't rule": *Newsweek,* February 7, 1972, p. 9.

208 "to sit back": *New York Times,* December 1, 1972, p. 35.

208 "I warned him": Goodman, "John Glenn Takes," p. 28.

209 "pure political blackmail": *Washington Post,* September 27, 1973, p. E2.

209 "Suddenly, inexplicably, I": *New York Times,* September, 23, 1973, p. 23.

209 "I never pulled": Myra MacPherson, "The Hero-as-Politician," *Potomac, Washington Post,* January 12, 1975, p. 8.

209 "It's quite obvious": *Washington Post,* September 27, 1973, p. E2.

209 "seldom was heard": Garrett, "Annie and John Glenn," p. 32.

209 "The bond between": Goodman, "John Glenn Takes," pp. 30, 27.

210 "The main issue": *Washington Post,* April 20, 1974, p. A2.

210 "I don't need": *New York Times,* March 11, 1974, p. 15.

210 "NIXON/METZENBAUM": *Washington Post,* May 5, 1974, p. A1.

210 "If he has": *New York Times,* April 21, 1974, p. 49.

210 "John Glenn's leadership": *New York Times,* May 4, 1974, p. 47.

210 "Howard, I can't": quoted in Frank Van Riper, *Glenn: The Astronaut Who Would Be President* (New York, 1983), pp. 265–66.

211 "People are disgruntled": *U.S. News and World Report,* May 20, 1974, p. 36.

211 "There is a": *Washington Post,* November 2, 1974, p. A3.

211 "Who would have thought": Garrett, "Annie and John Glenn," p. 32.

212 "I just want": *Washington Post,* November 2, 1974, p. A3.

212 "Honesty is a passive": Garrett, "Annie and John Glenn," p. 134.

212 "You sit in": *Chicago Tribune,* July 23, 1975, p. 4.

212 "that a few [marines]": *Congressional Record,* Ninety-fourth Congress, first session, p. 14651.

212 "I think there": Paul Healy, " 'Mr. America' in the Senate," *Saturday Evening Post,* December 1975, p. 40.

213 "I like to look": *Current Biography, 1976,* p. 159.

213 "If I'm picked": *Chicago Tribune,* July 23, 1975, p. 1.

213   "a throwback to": *Washington Post,* December 13, 1975, p. B13.

213   "I don't know": *New York Times,* July 9, 1976, p. A12.

213   "I don't have to": *Chicago Tribune,* July 15, 1976, I, p. 6.

214   "The key to": *New York Times,* July 15, 1976, p. 26.

214   "We must select": Richard Reeves, *Convention* (New York, 1977), p. 74

214   "John . . . I've called": *Ibid.,* pp. 189–90.

JANE SEYMOUR FONDA (IV)

Page

217   "One of the subliminal": *San Francisco Chronicle,* April 25, 1978, p. 48.

217   "All we wanted": George Haddad-Garcia, *The Films of Jane Fonda* (Secaucus, N.J., 1981), pp. 69, 205.

218   "We had no": Jacoba Atlas, "Will the Real Jane Fonda Please Stand Up?" *Parents Magazine,* December 1977, p. 37.

218   "All my life": *Newsweek,* October 10, 1977, p. 87.

218   "I'm still working": Margaret Ronan, "Jane Fonda—Rebel with Many Causes," *Senior Scholastic,* March 9, 1978, p. 3.

218   "The rebel has": *Time,* October 3, 1977, pp. 90–91.

218   "I am not proposing": *Los Angeles Times,* October 29, 1977, I, p. 2.

218   "I hate the": Aljean Harmetz, "Fonda at Forty," *McCall's,* January 1978, p. 127.

219   "I'm surprised to find": *New York Times,* December 13, 1977, p. 51.

219   "I saw Kimberly": *New York Times,* March 11, 1979, II, p. 19.

219   "You can't make": *San Francisco Chronicle,* April 25, 1978, p. 40.

219   "Only one of the": *New York Times,* March 11, 1979, II, p. 19.

219   "I was out": "The California Workout: An Interview with Jane Fonda," *Harper's Bazaar,* January 1980, p. 83.

219   "She's the kind": Haddad-Garcia, *Films of Jane Fonda,* p. 218.

219 "I look for things": "Calendar," *Los Angeles Times,* December 24, 1978, p. 5.

220 "I discovered that": Jane Fonda, *Jane Fonda's Workout Book* (New York, 1981), p. 23.

220 "I guess I'm": *Los Angeles Times,* January 29, 1979, IV, p. 7.

220 "I've reached the conclusion": Haddad-Garcia, *Films of Jane Fonda,* p. 68.

220 "material that could": *New York Times,* February 28, 1979, p. C22.

220 "Good evening. The world": Walter Cronkite, quoted in Mark Stephens, *Three Mile Island* (New York, 1980), p. 4.

220 "Reality has a way": Jane Fonda and Tom Hayden, "Mobilizing Against the Nukes," *New York,* April 16, 1979, p. 43.

221 "If we continue": *New York Times,* May 7, 1979, p. B13.

221 "reconsider the assertion": *San Francisco Chronicle,* July 4, 1979, p. 8.

221 "How can I": *Los Angeles Times,* July 25, 1979, II, p. 7.

222 "What is at stake": *Los Angeles Times,* August 8, 1979, I, p. 11.

222 "We can not only": *San Francisco Chronicle,* August 13, 1979, p. 3.

222 "We believe all": *New York Times,* September 24, 1979, p. B1.

222 "We do all": Cheryl McCall, "Strange Bedfellows," *People,* October 15, 1979, p. 146.

222 "Obviously there are": *Newsweek,* October 8, 1979, p. 30.

222 "I'm not a political": *San Francisco Chronicle,* October 27, 1979, p. 18.

222– "Nowadays you have": Ian Urquhart, "The Tom and Jane
23 reruns," *Macleans,* October 8, 1979, p. 29.

223 "It is *unbelievable*": Cliff Jahr, "Dolly, Lily and Jane," *Glamour,* February 1981, p. 144.

223 "I make all": Louise Farr, "Jane Fonda," *Ladies' Home Journal,* April 1980, p. 39.

223 "The business isn't": Carol Lynn Mithers, "Jane Fonda: An interview," *Mademoiselle,* February 1982, p. 34.

223 "to promote alternative": *Los Angeles Times,* September 25, 1982, I, p. 1.

223 "Discipline . . . is liberation": Blair Sabol, "Fitness," *Mademoiselle,* March 1980, p. 38.

223   "I am no longer": Jane Fonda, *Workout,* p. 24.

224   "I like to think": Sabol, "Fitness," p. 40.

224   "I don't pretend": Farr, "Jane Fonda," p. 40.

224   "I actually reexperienced": Aimée Lee Ball, "The Unofficial Jane Fonda," *Redbook,* January 1982, p. 28.

224   "like a blithering": *San Francisco Chronicle,* January 17, 1982, "Datebook," p. 23.

224   "The first day": Mithers, "Jane Fonda," p. 34.

225   "What was so great": *San Francisco Chronicle,* January 17, 1982, "Datebook," p. 23.

225   "I knew what that": [Henry Fonda], *Fonda: My Life* (New York, 1981), p. 376.

225   "I knew that for": Lois Armstrong, "For Jane Fonda," *People,* April 12, 1982, p. 30.

225   "It's the hardest": Ball, "Unofficial," pp. 28, 30.

225   "I could see": Armstrong, "For Jane Fonda," p. 30.

225   "There was an element": Ball, "Unofficial," p. 30.

225   "We took a reality": William Wolf, "Principles and Profits," *New York,* December 14, 1981, p. 91.

226   "We're trying to use": Mithers, "Jane Fonda," p. 28.

226   "I have a frantically": Jane Fonda, *Workout,* pp. 56, 228, 30.

226   "When you're a": Mithers, "Jane Fonda," p. 34.

226   "The very things": Ball, "Unofficial," p. 28.

227   "I feel very": Dorothy Ann Glasser and Stephen Decatur, "Jane Fonda," *Ladies' Home Journal,* February 1982, p. 22.

227   "to blend personal": *San Francisco Chronicle,* January 17, 1982, "Datebook," pp. 17, 22.

227   "If my father": *New York Times,* March 30, 1982, p. 1.

227   "Reconciliation is what": Michael J. Bandler, "Jane Fonda—A Heritage of Talent," *Parents Magazine,* December 1982, p. 126.

GEORGE CORLEY WALLACE (IV)

Page

230   "He exploded, it just": *Chicago Tribune,* December 4, 1977, I, p. 6.

230   "All I was": *Washington Post,* September 11, 1976, p. A1.

230   "Being in politics": *Washington Post*, September 9, 1976, p. A1.

230   "He's my friend . . . he'd have": *New York Times*, November 4, 1976, p. 24.

230   "We are not in": *New York Times*, December 2, 1976, p. 30.

231   "If I decide": *Washington Post*, May 17, 1977, p. A6.

231   "no longer endure": *New York Times*, September 7, 1977, p. C2.

231   "It's a private": *Washington Post*, September 7, 1977, p. C1.

232   "there exists such": *New York Times*, September 13, 1977, p. 24.

232   "The reason for": *New York Times*, September 16, 1977, p. B8.

232   "George wanted the divorce": Joyce Leviton, "I Didn't Want the Divorce," *People*, May 8, 1978, p. 34.

232   "private and personal": *Washington Post*, December 18, 1977, p. A23.

232   "My wife and I": *New York Times*, January 5, 1978, p. B10.

232   "Anything can be": *Washington Post*, January 5, 1978, p. A5.

232   "I'm sure the people": *Washington Post*, January 7, 1978, p. A5.

232   "whatever I want": Marguerite Michaels, "Politics and Divorce—and Another Campaign," *Parade, Washington Post*, April 2, 1978, p. 4.

233   "Crusading is for": *Ibid.*, pp. 4–5.

233   "I even got": *New York Times*, May 18, 1978, p. B11.

233   "Having thought all": *Washington Post*, May 17, 1978, p. A1.

233   "Maybe a little": *Washington Post*, May 18, 1978, p. A10.

233   "Maybe I got to": *New York Times*, May 23, 1978, p. C4.

233   "Well, I just": James Wooten, "Wallace and Me: The End of the Road," *Esquire*, November 7, 1978, p. 102.

234   "I used to think": *Washington Post*, June 4, 1978, pp. B1–2.

235   "I expect to remain": *New York Times*, June 22, 1978, p. 20.

235   "I just don't": Wooten, "Wallace and Me," pp. 90, 103.

235   "I know I will": *New York Times*, October 10, 1978, Supplementary Materials, p. 29.

236   "I was not an enemy": *New York Times*, January 7, 1979, p. 26.

236 "It's good that": *Ibid.*

236 "I do love": *New Orleans Times Picayune,* January 7, 1979, I, p. 12.

237 "splendid racial relations": *Washington Post,* January 11, 1979, p. A15.

237 "Oh, I ain't": *New York Times,* March 23, 1979, p. 29.

237 "I might be agreeable": *New York Times,* July 3, 1979, p. B4.

237 "I told you": *Los Angeles Times,* May 12, 1979, IA, p. 1.

237 "I have no political": Joyce Leviton, "The Wallace Saga Goes On," *People,* September 17, 1979, p. 38.

238 "I'm out of it": *Chicago Tribune,* March 9, 1980, II, p. 15.

238 "I'm very happy": *New York Times,* September 10, 1981, p. B4.

238 "Now, you know": *Chicago Tribune,* December 6, 1981, II, p. 14.

238 "I now realize": Will Norton, Jr., "George Wallace, Ten Years Later," *Christianity Today,* April 9, 1982, p. 53.

238 "Regardless of your color": *Washington Post,* May 23, 1982, p. A15.

239 "I promise you": *New York Times,* May 23, 1982, p. 20.

239 "We in Alabama": *Washington Post,* September 1, 1982, p. B1.

239 "No, I have": *Time,* October 11, 1982, p. 15.

239 "I was *for*": Roy Reed, "George Wallace's Bid for the New South," *New York Times Magazine,* September 5, 1982, p. 44.

239 *"I'm glad we're":* *Washington Post,* September 1, 1982, pp. B3, B1.

240 "I am very proud": *New York Times,* September 8, 1982, p. 10.

240 "I'm the only": Michael Posner, "An Old Warhorse in the New South," *Macleans,* September 20, 1982, p. 24.

240 "tax loopholes for": *New York Times,* September 26, 1982, p. 21.

240 "I'm very humbled": *Washington Post,* September 29, 1982, p. A1.

240 "Oh, no . . . they'll": *New York Times,* September 30, 1982, p. B14.

240 "When you have": *New York Times,* October 3, 1982, IV, p. 5.

241 "For God's sake": *Washington Post,* January 18, 1983, p. A3.

241 "In times like these": *New York Times,* January 18, 1983, p. 1.

241 "Some of you": Fred Bruning, "A Governor Snookers a Nation," *Macleans,* February 7, 1983, p. 9.

241 "I'm a born-again": Charles L. Sanders, "Has Gov. George Wallace Really Changed?" *Ebony,* September 1983, p. 46.

241 "I feel good": *San Francisco Examiner & Chronicle,* September 18, 1983, p. A11.

PHYLLIS STEWART SCHLAFLY (IV)

Page

243 "Rosalynn Carter is": Carol Felsenthal, *The Sweetheart of the Silent Majority: The Biography of Phyllis Schlafly* (Garden City, N.Y., 1981), pp. 245–46.

243 "The Executive branch": *St. Louis Post Dispatch,* February 5, 1977.

243 "I think the father": *Alton Evening Telegraph,* January 11, 1977.

244 "My husband lets": Joseph Lelyveld, "Should Women Be Nicer Than Men?" *New York Times Magazine,* April 17, 1977, p. 126.

244 "a victimless crime": *St. Louis Globe-Democrat,* May 20, 1977.

244 "The most dramatic": *Phyllis Schlafly Report,* January 1977, section 1.

244 "the greatest invasion": *St. Louis Globe-Democrat,* March 14, 1977.

244 "If President Carter": *Phyllis Schlafly Report,* July 1977, p. 4.

244 "Is our situation": Phyllis Schlafly, "Weapons Versus Theories and Treaties," *DAR Magazine,* October 1977, p. 811.

245 "These are the most": *Newsweek,* July 25, 1977, p. 35.

245 "God is on": Felsenthal, *Sweetheart,* p. 50.

245 "the only woman": *Chicago Tribune,* December 15, 1977, III, p. 4.

245   "Illinois is a big": Interview, October 31, 1983; Schlafly Papers.

245   "one minority vote": *Chicago Tribune*, December 8, 1977, III, p. 8.

245   "Fred kept saying": *Chicago Tribune*, December 15, 1977, III, p. 4.

245   "The football game": *Washington Post*, April 11, 1978, p. A19.

246   "Our final victory": *New York Times*, May 28, 1978, p. 44.

246   "There are no": *New York Times*, June 14, 1978, p. 18.

246   "How can you": *St. Louis Globe-Democrat*, September 23, 1978.

246   "Of course I'm": *St. Louis Globe-Democrat*, April 28, 1979.

246   "Where the ERA": Phyllis Schlafly, "The Effects of Equal Rights Amendments in State Constitutions," *Policy Review*, Summer 1979, p. 25.

247   "the greatest victory": *San Francisco Examiner and Chronicle*, October 28, 1979, "This World," p. 34.

247   "legally, morally, and": *Washington Post*, March 23, 1979, pp. C1, C3.

247   "Who's goin' to": *New York Times*, March 23, 1979, p. A18; October 14, 1979, p. 26.

247   "The news photo of Mrs.": *Phyllis Schlafly Report*, May 1979, section 1.

247   "SALT stands for": *Phyllis Schlafly Report*, August 1979, section 1.

248   "Would you be": *Phyllis Schlafly Report*, June 1979, section 1.

248   "Many people seem": *Phyllis Schlafly Report*, October 1979, section 1.

248   "With God's help": *Washington Post*, October 14, 1979, p. A10.

249   "We cannot gain": *Phyllis Schlafly Report*, December 1979, section 1.

249   "For seven years": *Chicago Tribune*, January 29, 1980, I, p. 7.

249   "President Carter did": *Phyllis Schlafly Report*, August 1981, section 1.

249   "If this administration": *New York Times*, February 9, 1980, p. 9.

249   "The purpose of our": *St. Louis Globe-Democrat,* March 14, 1980.

249   "You did promise": *Phyllis Schlafly Report,* August 1980, section 1.

249   "I've worked hard": *St. Louis Globe-Democrat,* May 14, 1980.

250   "We realized that": *New York Times,* July 30, 1980, p. B6.

250   "the finest statement": *St. Louis Globe-Democrat,* September 20, 1980.

250   "There has been": *St. Louis Globe-Democrat,* August 5, 1980.

250   "certainly blessed America": Henry Schipper, "Some Girls," *Rolling Stone,* November 26, 1981, p. 23.

250   "I'm on top": *Los Angeles Times,* November 6, 1980, V, p. 1.

250   "the idea of": Linda Witt, "Equal Rights at the Schlaflys'," *People,* March 30, 1981, p. 106.

250   "What we have": *St. Louis Post Dispatch,* February 1, 1981.

250   "let Congress know": *St. Louis Globe-Democrat,* March 4, 1981.

251   "what you have left": *St. Louis Post Dispatch,* February 1, 1981.

251   "I'm in favor": *St. Louis Globe-Democrat,* March 4, 1981.

251   "There is no excuse": *Phyllis Schlafly Report,* November 1981, section 1.

251   "By bearing and": *Phyllis Schlafly Report,* April 1981, section 1.

251   "The most cruel": [United States Senate], *Hearings Before the Committee on Labor and Human Resources.* Ninety-seventh Congress, first session, April 21, 1981, pp. 397, 400.

251   "a tremendous victory": *New York Times,* June 26, 1981, p. 12.

251   "Women were honored": Barbara Grizzuti Harrison, "The Woman Who Is Fighting the Law That Most Women Want," *McCall's,* April 1982, p. 103.

252   "As I travel": Phyllis Schlafly, "What Women Really Want," *Seventeen,* May 1982, p. 190.

252   "Thanks . . . we made": *New York Times,* July 1, 1982, p. 12.

252   "I've always been": *San Francisco Examiner & Chronicle,* December 11, 1983, "Scene," p. 2.

252 "I am into": *St. Louis Globe-Democrat,* October 27, 1982.

252 "A woman should": Harrison, "The Woman Who," p. 102.

253 "I talk on": Robert Sam Anson, "Phyllis Schlafly Knows She's Right," *Mademoiselle,* April 1983, p. 172.

JOHN HERSCHEL GLENN (IV)

Page

255 "If I can": *Chicago Sun Times,* February 20, 1977, p. 53.

256 "All his adult": *Ibid.*

256 "planning"—"I hate": *Congressional Record,* Ninety-fifth Congress, first session, p. 15292.

256 "a big, amorphous": *New York Times,* March 19, 1977, p. 25.

256 "any future combat": *Congressional Record,* Ninety-fifth Congress, second session, p. 1725.

257 "inducing even greater": *Congressional Record,* Ninety-fifth Congress, second session, p. 22792.

257 "The SALT process": *Congressional Record,* Ninety-fifth Congress, first session, p. 31908.

257 "Now is not the time": *Congressional Record,* Ninety-fifth Congress, first session, p. 38577.

257 "Perhaps this is the": *Congressional Record,* Ninety-fifth Congress, second session, p. 35547.

257 "without bombs, without": *New York Times,* February 3, 1978, p. 8.

258 "We have only": *Congressional Record,* Ninety-fifth Congress, second session, p. 17155.

258 "Let there be": *Congressional Record,* Ninety-fifth Congress, first session, p. 4089.

258 "to insure Taiwan's": *New York Times,* February 5, 1979, p. A8.

258 "You can draw": *New York Times,* February 19, 1979, p. 4.

259 "I have never": *Time,* April 23, 1979, p. 20.

259 "Verification must be": *New York Times,* April 8, 1979, p. 1.

259 "I guess the idea": Howell Raines, "John Glenn: The Hero As Candidate," *New York Times Magazine,* November 13, 1983, p. 52.

259 "When we don't": *New York Times,* September 7, 1979, p. 6.

259 "we were blind": *San Francisco Chronicle,* June 15, 1983, p. 12.

260 "The Soviet invasion": *Congressional Record,* Ninety-sixth Congress, second session, p. 5463.

260 "I'm not opposed": *Washington Post,* October 21, 1980, p. A4.

260 "The complexity and": *New York Times,* May 22, 1980, p. B8.

260 "There have been some": Elizabeth Drew, *Portrait of an Election* (New York, 1981), p. 182.

260 "who understands war": Eugene Kennedy, "John Glenn's Presidential Countdown," *New York Times Magazine,* October 11, 1981, p. 111.

260 "I'm Annie Glenn's": Frank Van Riper, *Glenn: The Astronaut Who Would Be President* (New York, 1983), p. 21.

260 "They ran as a team": *U.S. News and World Report,* December 1, 1980, pp. 31–32.

261 "Define a vision": Kennedy, "Presidential Countdown," p. 32.

261 "Right now there": *New York Times,* April 26, 1981, IV, p. 3.

262 "We have always": *New York Times,* April 14, 1981, p. C7.

262 "In the military": Kennedy, "Presidential Countdown," p. 104.

262 "Government still has": *U.S. News and World Report,* September 28, 1981, p. 34.

262 "Some things about politics": David McCullogh, "Can John Glenn Be President?" *Parade, Washington Post,* June 13, 1982, p. 6.

263 "To say that": Morton Kondracke, "John Glenn's Right Stuff," *New Republic,* May 26, 1982, p. 15.

263 "When we cut": *New York Times,* August 8, 1982, IV, p. 21.

263 "wrapping even more": John Glenn, "Is the Tarapur Agreement Any Good?" *Washington Post,* August 1, 1982, p. B7.

263 "In some ways": *New York Times,* August 8, 1982, IV, p. 3.

263 "I felt very": *New York Times,* August 13, 1982, p. A12.

264 "If Ted Kennedy": *New York Times,* October 19, 1982, p. A22.

264   "I'm glad to be": *Los Angeles Times,* November 15, 1982, I, p. 17.

264   "Small-town Ohio": *Washington Post,* October 18, 1982, p. A5.

264   "stability and a sense": *New York Times,* November 7, 1982, IV, p. 3.

264   "Whatever other problems": Van Riper, *Glenn,* pp. 314–15.

264   "That's what I did": Raines, "John Glenn," p. 66.

264   "I have a big": Kramer, "John Glenn," p. 25.

265   "Being back home": Van Riper, *Glenn,* pp. 30–31.

265   "truly the heart": *Time,* May 2, 1983, p. 16.

265   "My own life": *Newsweek,* May 2, 1983, p. 29.

265   "My ambition is": *Time,* June 20, 1983, p. 24.

Index